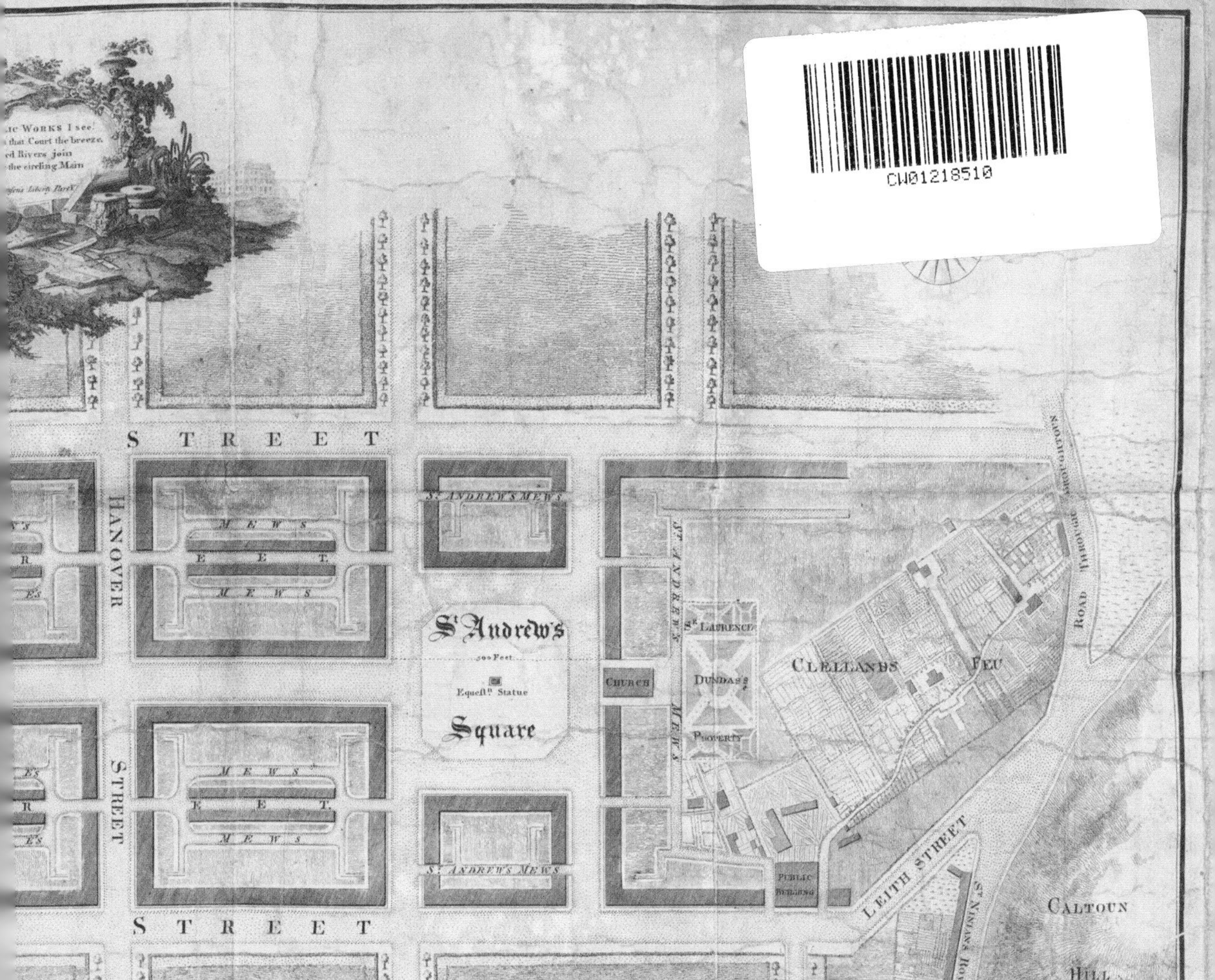

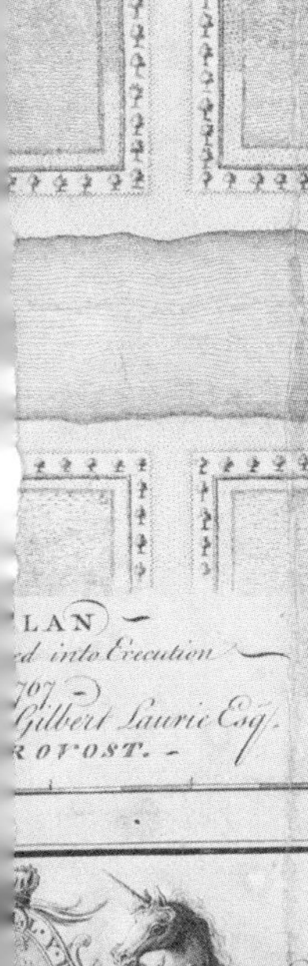

Patron of Every POLITE and LIBERAL ART
NORTH-BRITAIN; One of the happy Consequences of the Peace, Security, and
Inscribed By His Majesty's, Most devoted Servant and Subject,
JAMES CRAIG.

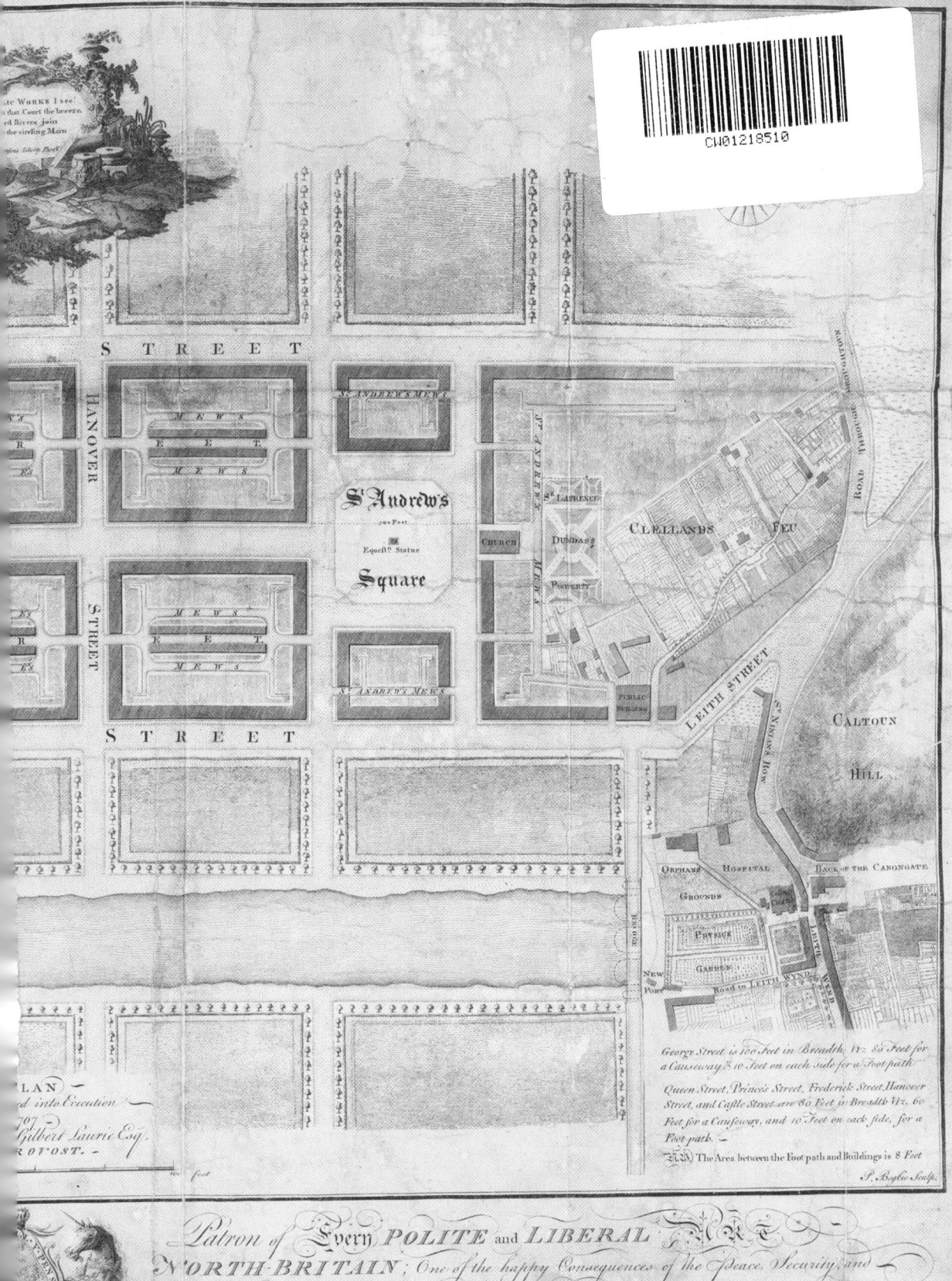

The New Town *of*
Edinburgh

The New Town *of* Edinburgh

An Architectural Celebration

Edited by
Clarisse Godard Desmarest

John Donald

ENDPAPER:
James Craig, Plan of the New Town of Edinburgh, 1768
(Courtesy of the National Library of Scotland. Available under
Creative Commons Attribution (CC-BY) 4.0 International Licence)

FRONTISPIECE:
George Walker, *Edinburgh from the South East*, 1797. The New Town was
seen from the outset as coupled with the Old Town, and Calton Hill was
quickly adopted as part of the ensemble. (City of Edinburgh Council)

First published in Great Britain in 2019 by
John Donald, an imprint of Birlinn Ltd
West Newington House
10 Newington Road
Edinburgh EH9 1QS

ISBN: 978 1 910900 35 2

Copyright © The contributing authors severally 2019

The right of the contributing authors to be identified as the
authors of this work has been asserted by them in accordance
with the Copyright, Designs and Patents Act, 1988

All rights reserved. No part of this publication may be reproduced,
stored, or transmitted in any form, or by any means, electronic,
mechanical or photocopying, recording or otherwise, without
the express written permission of the publisher.

The publishers gratefully acknowledge the support
of the University of Picardie Jules Verne,
University of Edinburgh and the Strathmartine Trust

towards the publication of this book

British Library Cataloguing-in-Publication Data
A catalogue record for this book is available
on request from the British Library

Typeset by Mark Blackadder

Printed and bound in Malta by Gutenberg Press

Contents

List of Contributors ... ix

Foreword by David M. Walker ... xiii

Acknowledgements ... xv

    Introduction ... 1
    Clarisse Godard Desmarest

1. Edinburgh: Smart City of 1700 ... 19
    Murray Pittock

Part 1: Earlier Contexts

2. Scotland's Planned Towns and Villages over the Centuries ... 41
    Aonghus MacKechnie

3. City and State in the Designs of the 6th Earl of Mar ... 64
    Margaret Stewart

4. Georgian New Towns of Glasgow and Edinburgh ... 78
    Anthony Lewis

PART 2: NEW TOWN AND OLD TOWN

5. Royal Welcomes in Edinburgh New Town: 99
Portraying Civic Identity in 1822 and 1842
Giovanna Guidicini

6. The Spatial and Social Characteristics of Craft 114
Businesses in Edinburgh's New Town c.1780–1850
Stana Nenadic

7. Mobile City: Edinburgh as a Communications 128
Hub 1775–1825
Richard Rodger

8. Commerce and Conservation: Edinburgh 147
New Town in the Early Twentieth Century
John Lowrey

PART 3: NEW TOWNS ELSEWHERE

9. The Edinburgh of the South: Seeking the New Town 165
Robin Skinner

10. The 'Enlightened' Factory: Textile Industry 182
and the 'Planned Village Movement' in
Scotland (1785–1800)
Ophélie Siméon

11. Citizenship, Community and the 193
New Towns in Post-War Scotland
Alistair Fair

Part 4: Age of Conservation

12. Un idéal médiéval dans l'Athènes du Nord: 217
    Patrick Geddes et Édimbourg
    Pierre Chabard

13. Edinburgh Old Town and New Town: 234
    A Tale of One City?
    Ranald MacInnes

Part 5: The New Town Celebrations

14. Commemorating the Founding of the   253
    New Town of Edinburgh in 1967 and 2017
    Clarisse Godard Desmarest

Notes   272

Select Bibliography   305

Index   312

Contributors

Pierre Chabard is an architect and a senior lecturer at ENSA Paris-la-Villette. His work has been focusing on Patrick Geddes and the town planning movement, and most recently on the cultural industry of architecture in the post-modern period. He has co-edited *Yours Critically* (2016), *Raisons d'écrire: Des livres, des architectes (1945–1999)* (2013) and *La Défense: Dictionnaire et Atlas* (2012).

Alistair Fair is a lecturer in architectural history and Chancellor's Fellow at the University of Edinburgh. A historian of twentieth-century architecture and planning in Scotland and the wider UK, his most recent book *Modern Playhouses: An Architectural History of Britain's New Theatres, 1945–1985* was published by Oxford University Press in 2018.

Clarisse Godard Desmarest FSA Scot is a lecturer at the University of Picardie Jules Verne and a fellow of the Institut Universitaire de France. Her recent publications include 'The Melville Monument: Shaping the character of the Scottish metropolis', *Architectural History*, vol. 61, 2018. She is a visiting research scholar in the School of History, Classics & Archaeology at the University of Edinburgh (2019).

Giovanna Guidicini is a lecturer in architectural history and urban studies at the Mackintosh School of Architecture, Glasgow School of Art. Her research considers the role of urban and palatial environments as performative spaces during festivals, ceremonies, and triumphal entries, particularly in Scotland and Italy. Her most recent publication is 'Ordering the World: Games in the Architectural Iconography of Stirling Castle, Scotland', in *Games and Game Playing in European Art and Literature, 16th–17th centuries* (2019).

Anthony Lewis is curator of Scottish history for Glasgow Life Museums. He has researched Edinburgh's first New Town for over 25 years, and is the author of *The Builders of Edinburgh New Town 1767–1795* (2014).

John Lowrey is a senior lecturer in architectural history at Edinburgh School of Architecture and Landscape Architecture (ESALA), part of Edinburgh College of Art within Edinburgh University. He has specialised in the study of classical architecture in Scotland and in the architectural history of Edinburgh. He has published widely on the New Town, the Greek Revival, Scottish landscape design and on the Scottish Parliament site.

Ranald MacInnes is Head of Place and Publishing at Historic Environment Scotland, the national heritage agency. He teaches conservation history and is a Fellow of the Institute of Art History, University of Glasgow, and a visiting lecturer in architectural history at the University of Strathclyde. He has published widely on architectural history and conservation and has written planning guidance including the founding Edinburgh World Heritage Site masterplan.

Aonghus MacKechnie is former Head of Casework, Heritage Directorate, at Historic Environment Scotland. His published work reflects his interest in the architecture and culture of the Renaissance and the Early Modern periods in Scotland, Romanticism, and the history and culture of his native Highlands. He is author of *Carragh-Chuimhne* (2004), co-author of *A History of Scottish Architecture* (1996), *Scottish Architecture* (2004), and most recently, *Scotch Baronial: Architecture and National Identity in Scotland* (2019).

CONTRIBUTORS

Stana Nenadic is Professor of Social and Cultural History at the University of Edinburgh. Her research and publications are focused on the social, cultural and economic life of artisans and business owners, the middle ranks, gentry and professionals since the eighteenth century, mainly with reference to Scotland.

Murray Pittock FRSE has been Vice-Principal and then Pro Vice-Principal of the University of Glasgow since 2010. Outside the university, Murray is Scottish history advisor to the National Trust for Scotland, and has worked closely with government. He has made around 1,600 media appearances in 55 countries in relation to his research; recent books include *Material Culture and Sedition* (2013), *Culloden* (2016), *The Scots Musical Museum* (2018) and *Enlightenment in a Smart City: Edinburgh's Civic Development, 1660–1750* (2018).

Richard Rodger is Professor of Economic and Social History at Edinburgh University. He has published widely on the economic, business and urban history of Britain since 1800. His book *The Transformation of Edinburgh: Land, Property and Trust in the Nineteenth Century* (2001) was awarded the Frank Watson Prize for works on Scottish history. Rodger was elected to the Academy of Social Sciences in 2004.

Ophélie Siméon is a graduate from the École Normale Supérieure (Lyons), and an associate professor of British history at Sorbonne Nouvelle University (Paris). She is the author of *Robert Owen's Experiment at New Lanark: from Paternalism to Socialism* (2017).

Robin Skinner is a senior lecturer in the School of Architecture at Victoria University of Wellington. He lectures and researches on the architecture of the Pacific and colonial New Zealand.

Margaret Stewart is a lecturer in architectural history, Edinburgh School of Landscape Architecture and Architecture, University of Edinburgh. She is the author of *The Architectural, Landscape and Constitutional Plans of the Earl of Mar, 1700–32* (2016). She is currently making a documentary film about the early history of large-scale formal landscape design in Scotland c.1700.

Foreword

In 1958 the American historian Henry-Russell Hitchcock wrote of Edinburgh that it was still the most extensive example of a Romantic Classical city in the world. Although we were to lose one square and most of another in the following decade, sixty-one years later that statement is still true as a result of Sir Robert Matthew's initiative in organising a great international conference on the future of the city in June 1970. It left a City Council all too well disposed to redevelopment in no doubt as to the importance of what was in their care and triggered the still ongoing programme of grant-aid which has secured its survival.

As Henry-Russell's text made clear, Edinburgh is not only the western world's most extensive Romantic Classical city but also one of its finest with classical public and commercial buildings which have long been recognised as masterpieces of their respective genres, its merits bringing UNESCO World Heritage Site status in 1995. As A.J. Youngson had set out in his magisterial *The Making of Classical Edinburgh* (1966), what made it so was the unique combination of Enlightenment thought, the well-integrated architectural ambitions of the city and the charitable and family trusts which owned the land, a feu system which encouraged long-term investment and of course a great deal of money. But perhaps the most important elements were the topography that enabled the long east–west axes to be absolutely level, the relationship of the New Town to the Old and the way that was exploited and refined over time.

This collection of essays by the leading authorities in their respective fields brings the story of the city's architecture and planning far beyond Youngson's closing date. It sets the city in a much wider context embracing subsequent and current research, the parallel developments in Glasgow and that of the history of planned towns and settlements in Scotland as a whole.

Professor David M. Walker, OBE
Former Chief Inspector of Historic
Monuments for Historic Scotland

Acknowledgements

In addition to thanking the contributors of this volume, I would also like to thank the following colleagues and friends who contributed to the success of the two conferences, or who otherwise helped in the process of peer-review for this volume: Alasdair Allan, Marion Amblard, Patricia Andrew, Christian Auer, Charlotte Barcat, Jean Berton, David Black, Iain Boyd Whyte, Ian Campbell, Pierre Carboni, Kirsten Carter McKee, Emmanuel Cocher, Jocelyn Cunliffe, Xavier Dectot, Mark Dorrian, John Gerrard, Miles Glendinning, Sally Goodsir, Iain Gordon Brown, Trevor Harris, Jennifer Hogg, Louisa Humm, Sally-Anne Huxtable, Sabrina Juillet-Garzon, Andrew Kerr, Lucinda Lax, Olivier Lazzarotti, James Legard, Jacques Leruez, Allan MacInnes, Margaret Mackay, Marie-Madeleine Martinet, Esther Mijers, Marie-Françoise Montaubin, Robert J. Morris, John C. Morrison, Helena Murteira, Philippe Nivet, Steven Robb, Joe Rock, Helen Scott, Philippe Sénéchal, James Simpson, Edward Taylor, Simon Texier, Marie-Hélène Thévenot-Totems, Ashleigh Thompson, Nicholas Uglow, Annemarie Uglow-Klein, David M. Walker, Diane Watters, and Adam Wilkinson.

I am also grateful to the following institutions for the help and support which they provided: University of Picardie Jules Verne (CORPUS), Institut Universitaire de France, University of Edinburgh, Strathmartine Trust, French Consulate in Edinburgh, Scottish Government, City of Edinburgh Council, Société Française d'Études Écossaises, Association Franco-Écossaise, Société des Anglicistes de l'Enseignement Supérieur, Edinburgh World Heritage

Trust, Simpson & Brown Architects, Taylor Architecture & Urbanism, and Scottish Historic Buildings Trust.

Thanks are also due to the staff at Birlinn for their kind assistance in this publication, as well as to my family for their constant support and love.

Clarisse Godard Desmarest

Introduction

Clarisse Godard Desmarest

This volume of essays is the outcome of two conferences: one hosted by the University of Picardie Jules Verne in Amiens on 5–6 October 2017, and a follow-up event at the Patrick Geddes Centre in Edinburgh, on 14 June 2018. The latter symposium, a prime example of European academic collaboration, was jointly organised by John Lowrey and myself of, respectively, the Universities of Edinburgh and Picardie Jules Verne. This set of two conferences was the main event marking the celebration of the 250th anniversary of the creation of the New Town of Edinburgh, a unique architectural ensemble in respect of its size, monumentality and degree of preservation.

The New Town featured at the centre of the city's rationale when an application was lodged with UNESCO for Edinburgh's recognition, and, ultimately, its greater protection – the application was successful, and the City of Edinburgh became a World Heritage Site in 1995.[1] By then, preservation more generally was fairly well accepted as a concept, and the city no longer faced the level of degradation it had witnessed in the 1960s.

The 2017–18 conferences provided the platform to reflect on the city's past, from the time of its construction – the foundation stone of the first house in the New Town of Edinburgh was laid in October 1767 – up to now, when contemporary projects in the New Town, as also in the Old Town, will undoubtedly change the face of the city for future generations. As part of the larger approach taken to the topic, a discussion was introduced on new towns in

Scotland, from the first earliest coherent (post-Roman) urban development strategy implemented by David I (r.1124–53), to post-Second World War schemes which formed part of the central government's interest in 'planning' – one element of the nascent Welfare State. Also, the eighteenth-century New Town of Edinburgh was set in a comparison with other broadly contemporary urban schemes, including Glasgow, London, Lisbon and Paris. Mid-nineteenth-century Dunedin, New Zealand, was also explored in connection with its Scottish namesake.[2]

The conferences occurred at a decisive moment in the recent history of Franco-Scottish relationships, when the Consulate had just relocated from the grand Georgian terraced houses it occupied on Randolph Crescent, in the New Town, to a more central building in West Parliament Square, in the Old Town. In his opening speech to the event in the Patrick Geddes Centre, Emmanuel Cocher, French Consul in Edinburgh, recalled the historic links that tie our two countries, and referred to the inauguration by General Charles de Gaulle of the 'Scottish Free French House' on 23 June 1942. An eastern New Town location, a house in Regent Terrace on the southern side of Calton Hill, was then chosen for the official presence of the *France Libre*. Cocher acknowledged the latest support provided by the Scottish Government to help secure the new and much more prominent location for the French Consulate and Institute, now in a building – the former Electoral Commission[3] – set close to the Royal Mile and which looks directly onto St Giles' Cathedral and Parliament Square. The centrality of Scotland's Continental ties was further alluded to by First Minister Nicola Sturgeon on a two-day visit to Paris for the official launch of the Scottish Hub, and in her speech at the British Embassy on 25 February 2019. The Scottish Government was officially represented at the event in the Patrick Geddes Centre by Alasdair Allan, Minister for International Development and Europe (2016–18). And in Amiens the city hosted a reception in the City Hall for all conference attendees.

This volume of essays – all peer-reviewed – reflects on the intellectual, economic and political contexts which provided the impetus for the city of Edinburgh to expand north of the Old Town, some sixty years after the Union with England had taken place. Although the term 'Old Town' was first noted in *Proposals for Carrying on*

INTRODUCTION

Certain Public Works in the City of Edinburgh, a pamphlet published in 1752,[4] the term 'Auld Reekie' was used earlier, when Edinburgh was already being affectionately referred to as 'old'.[5] The New Town, with its ashlar-faced buildings of the durable local Craigleith sandstone, was a sparkle of order and modernity in the extended metropolis; its plan (adopted in July 1767 by the Town Council) was rectilinear, and featured a central axis with a square at each end and an open 'single aspect' street north and south.

Public architecture and urban schemes of large scale were important expressions of national pride in this period, as was stated by Robert Adam in the introduction to his *Ruins of the Palace of the Emperor Diocletian at Spalatro*, in 1764: 'Public buildings are the most splendid monuments of a great and opulent people.' The revitalisation of a city offered great opportunities for architects and urban planners. This was certainly true in Edinburgh and Glasgow, and also in Lisbon – a city which was destroyed after a severe earthquake in 1755. Hearing of the Lisbon catastrophe while on his Grand Tour in Rome, Robert Adam, an ambitious young Scottish architect, produced a scheme to rebuild the city in the spring of 1756.[6] The symmetry and disciplined order in the design (Figs 0.1 and 0.2) had elements in common with James Craig's New Town plan for Edinburgh: notably a single grand central street terminated by a free-standing classical building, a symmetrical arrangement of parallel subordinate streets, squares and gardens, all showing the same urban language. The interest in circus or crescent was an ever-present idea in Craig's work and was used by him as a variation of the gridded plan. As was also comparable to the case of Edinburgh, Adam's proposed scheme for Lisbon included '*maisons de la noblesse*', '*maisons de la bourgeoisie*', *les 'faubourgs dans lesquels sont tous les métiers qui sont dangereux dedans une ville*' – introducing a similar spatial segregation, separating quarters for the aristocracy and gentry from those for craft workers. Two churches featured at either end of a central axis, as in Craig's plan. Although the Lisbon scheme was never carried out and is more a piece of hopeful academic study than a fully substantiated proposal (Adam had no first-hand knowledge of Lisbon), it shows how important urban projects were to architects; Adam's design also hints at the Bernini Piazza fronting Saint Peter's in Rome and carries an overall theatrical Baroque

FIGURE O.1.
Bird's-eye view of Lisbon, plan proposed by Robert Adam c.1756. (Sir John Soane Museum, London, Adam vol. 9/56)

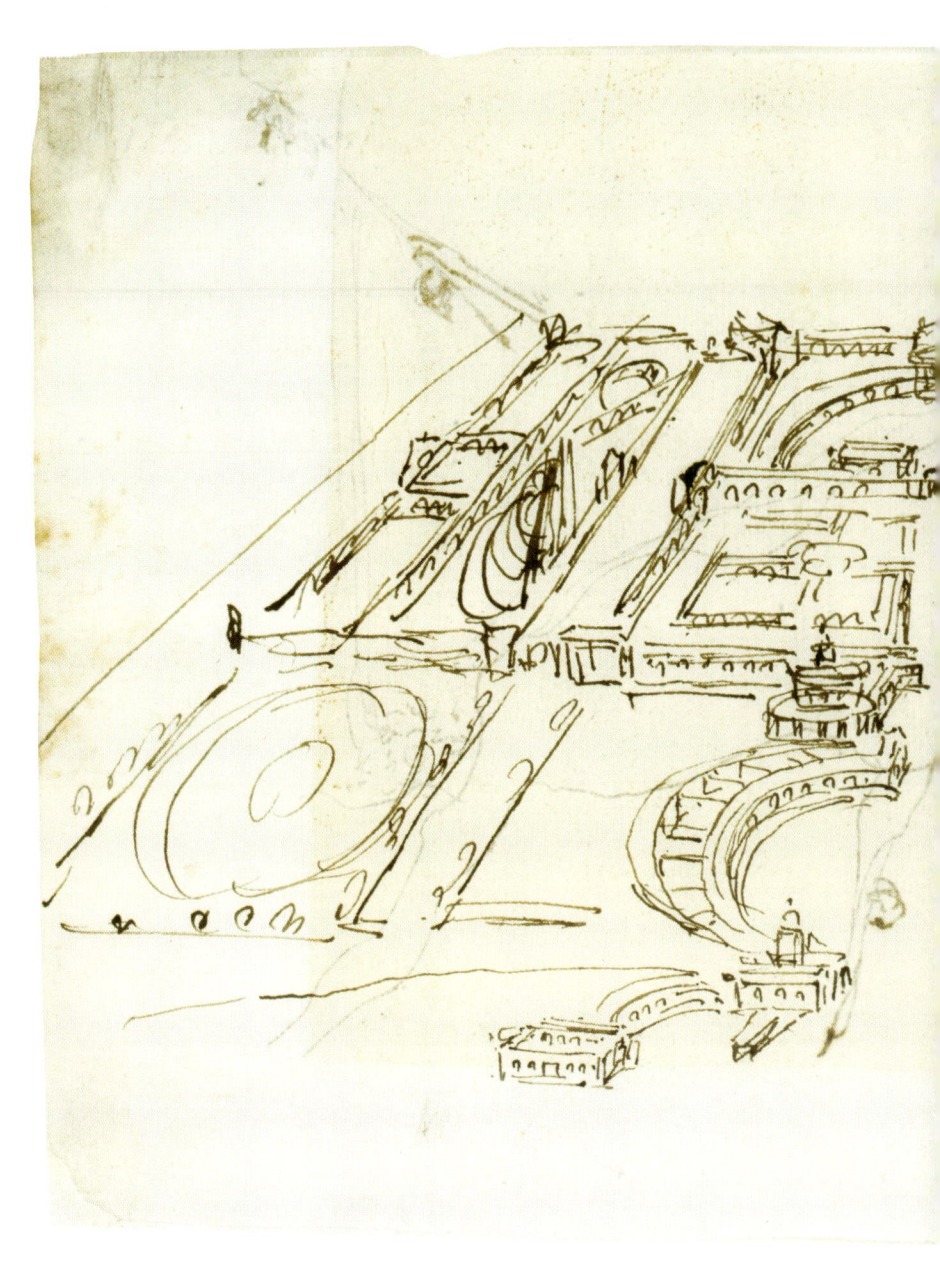

extravagance, especially the grand sequence of spaces through the centre of the plan in the form of a circular '*grand basin*' and a '*petit basin*'.

Similarly, in Edinburgh, other designs produced by Robert Adam were not carried out in the New Town; this is the case perhaps most

INTRODUCTION

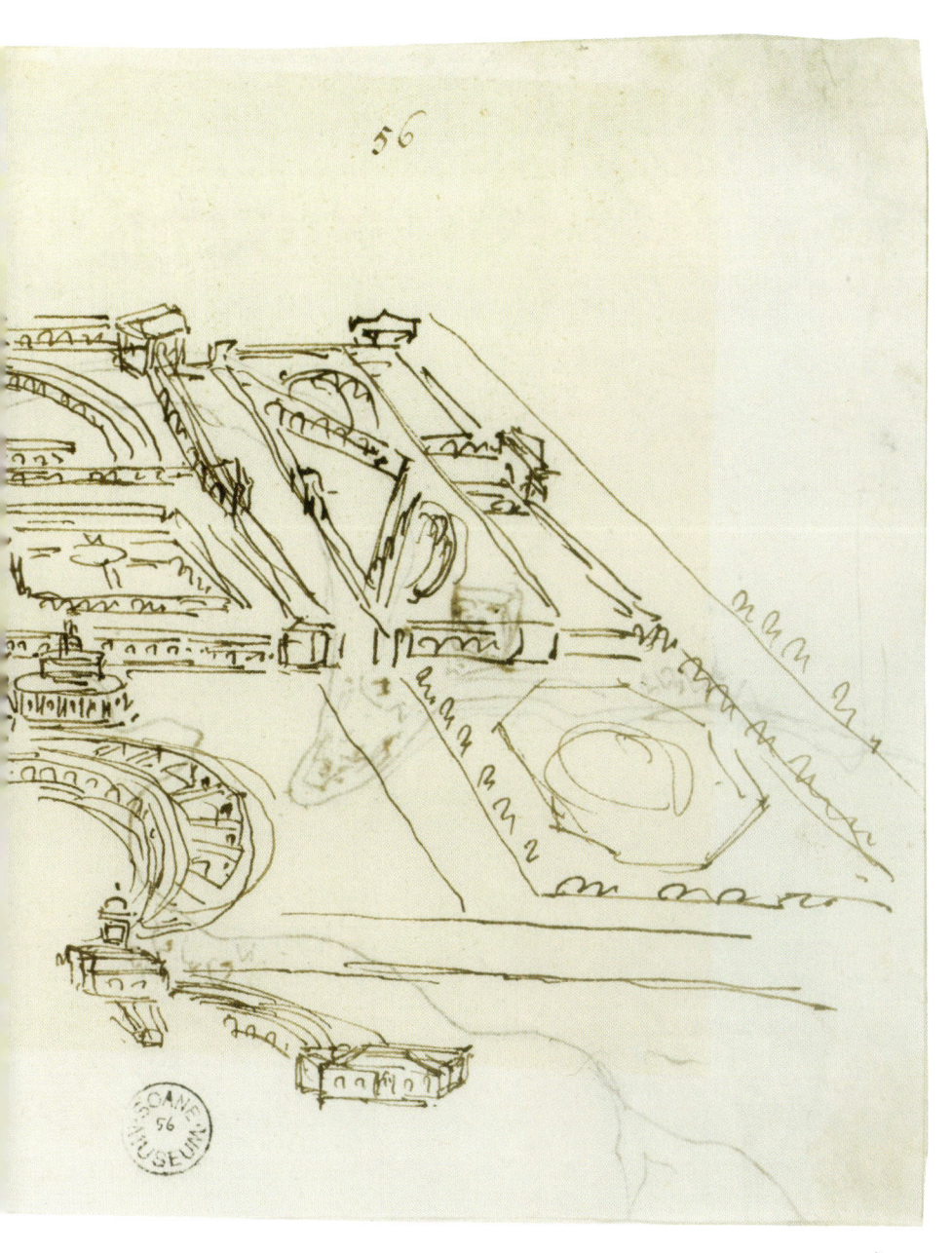

notably with St George's Parish Church (west Charlotte Square)[7] (Figs 0.3 and 0.4) – eventually built by Robert Reid (1811–14). With a cosmopolitan polish and an established office in London, Robert Adam and his brother James had an acute sense of British nationalism and its iconography, while also conscious of their

FIGURE 0.2.
Robert Adam scheme of 1756 for rebuilding central Lisbon (unexecuted), drawing in pen, undated. Inscribed in ink in contemporary hand: (on left-hand side of drawing) A. Place pour les/Maisons de la Noblesse; B. Maisons des/ Bourgeoises; C. Petit Basin à un/Coté La Bourse, à/l'autre le Marché/ publique; D. Grand Basin tout/autour des Magasins/ des Marchands; EE. Les faubourgs dans/lequels sont tous/Les Métiers qui/sont dangereux dedans/une Ville; (on right-hand side of drawing) F. Salle de Comédie; G. Salle de la Musique; H. Les Eglises; I. Douane; K. Salle des Marchands. Lettered in ink within the plan: Jardins Publiques [in two places]; Grand Basin; Lazaretto; La Mer and Fortresse. (Sir John Soane Museum, London, Adam vol. 9/60)

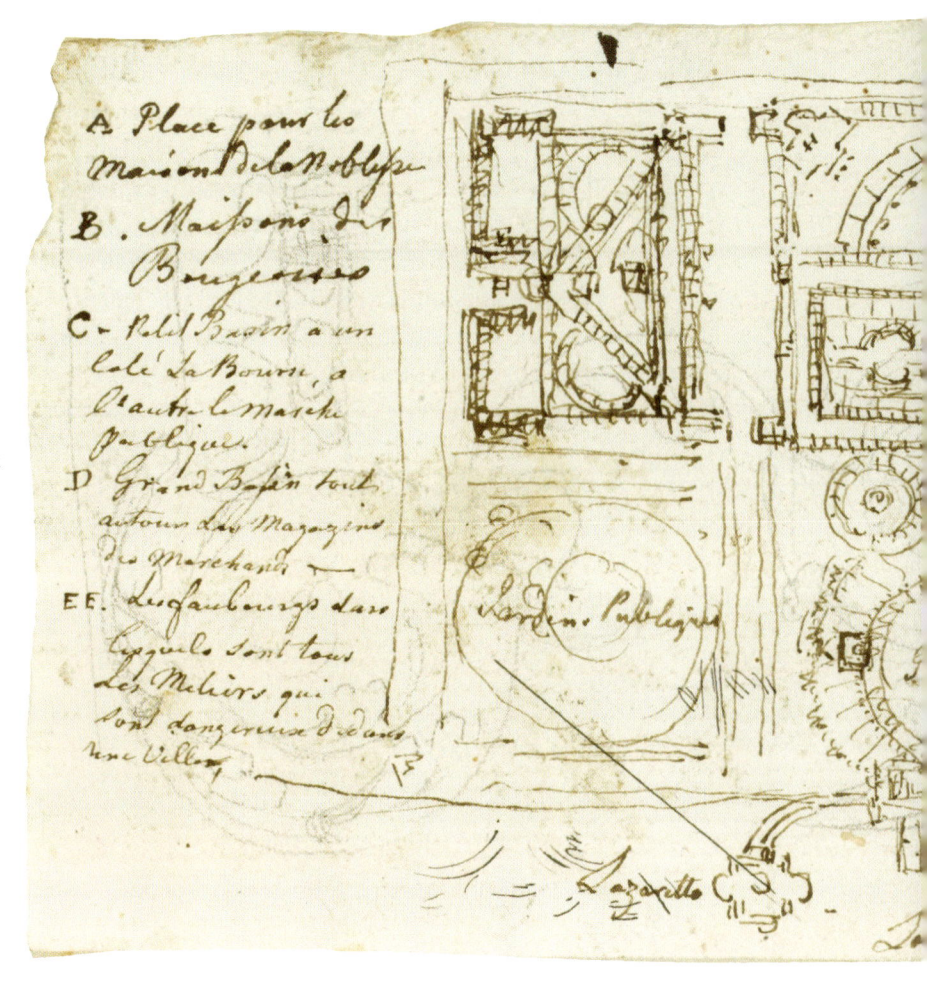

Scottish identity; James Adam invented a thistle-detailed '*châpiteau écossais*' as well as a 'Britannic order' for the new British Parliament House designed by his brother in 1762–3.[8] Even though Lisbon's Pombaline planners (the reconstruction was driven by the Marquês de Pombal) aimed for the renovation of the entire city, Lisbon, as reconstructed, became a two-faced city where the traditional patterns of urban life contrasted with the new symmetry and regularity of the grid.

Edinburgh New Town was designed as a residential suburb for the more affluent and the merchant classes, and became associated with a new political rhetoric; one of the plans for the New Town had been a Union Flag design, and the names of the streets reflected a strong sense of Britain, united under the House of Hanover. In an era which saw the consolidation of the Union after the failure of the 1745/6 Jacobite uprising, and the strengthening of the Scots' role in the Empire, the Old Town, by contrast, came to symbolise disorder and unrest, backwardness and Jacobitism, as conveyed by an ever more Anglo-centric rhetoric – mainly the result of the Scottish elite's migration to London. From neatly ordered Princes Street – designed partly as a viewing terrace – there was what was soon regarded as the comparative chaos of the ancient city's outward-facing buildings, whereas the New Town lying to the north embodied

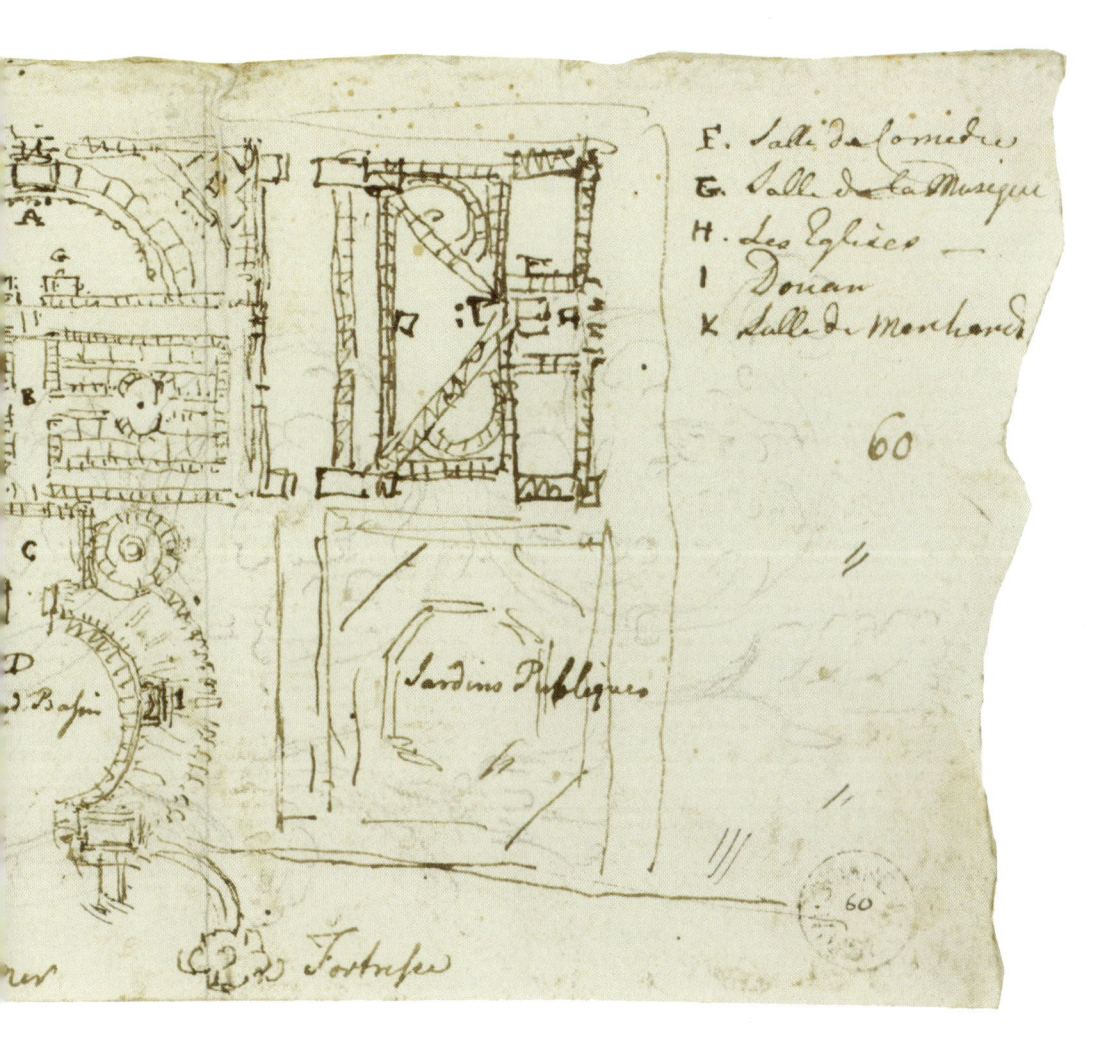

FIGURE 0.3.
Plan of Charlotte Square Edinburgh and streets adjacent, partially executed proposal by Robert Adam, 1791. (Sir John Soane Museum, London, Adam vol. 32/3)

the future of the nation within Britain. The meaning of the encounter between Old and New Towns changed, however, in the nineteenth century with urban improvement carried out in the Old Town, and a new attitude towards it shaped by Romanticism. The Mound, connecting the Old Town to the New, became a focus of attention, and for that location two of the most talented architects of their times, Thomas Hamilton and William H. Playfair, provided designs for a National Gallery and a Royal Scottish Academy (Figs

0.5 and 0.6). Both designs show the architects' response to the urban picturesque, and the necessity of preserving the views to the Castle when approaching Princes Street from the east.

In James Craig's New Town some changes also of course happened: for example, Physicians' Hall was opened on Queen Street in 1844 after a design by Thomas Hamilton.

In his chapter on 'Edinburgh: Smart City of 1700', Murray Pittock points out that, for the development of ideas in the capital, the New Town development signified the end of the very same close-knit society which had made possible the emergence of the Enlightenment from its roots in the Old Town. Pittock, therefore, nuances the view of A.J. Youngson who, notwithstanding his major contribution to the field of economic, social and architectural history, suggests in his work on the New Town, *The Making of Classical Edinburgh* (1966), that the intellectual success of Edinburgh depended on urban changes. While acknowledging the centrality of the proposals which led to the development of the New Town, Pittock considers that there was a strong focus on urban improvement even before 1700. In his analysis of the mechanics of change, he suggests that the urban transformations in Edinburgh resulted as much from basic necessity as from Sir Gilbert Elliot's and Lord Provost George Drummond's proposals (or indeed earlier projects by James VII and the Earl of Mar).

Youngson's volume was first published in 1966 in anticipation of the 200th anniversary of the New Town, a celebration which attracted a high degree of interest among Edinburgh inhabitants. The bicentenary events, analysed by Clarisse Godard Desmarest in Chapter 14, were contemporary to a revival of Scottish nationalism and marked the beginning of modern conservation in the city; an international conference on 'The Conservation of Georgian Edinburgh' was held in Edinburgh in 1970. That Franco-Scottish intellectual connection continues today, almost fifty years after François Sorlin, chief inspector of the Centre des Monuments Historiques, argued, in a presentation comparing the New Town to the Marais, that Edinburgh could learn from Paris the need for a strategic plan to avoid decay, problems of traffic, and to prepare for the growth of commercialisation.

One of the purposes of this book is to set the New Town within

FIGURE 0.4.
St George's Parish Church (west Charlotte Square), unexecuted proposal by Robert Adam, 1791. (Sir John Soane Museum, London, Adam vol. 32/4)

earlier contexts. Over centuries, Scotland had pursued innovation, improvement, commerce and contact externally with England and the Continent; and it was an urbanising land of (ideally, stone-built) planned towns. Aonghus MacKechnie's chapter shapes this context for building a new town for Edinburgh in the eighteenth century. Margaret Stewart explains that the Earl of Mar had understood what was wanted for Edinburgh well before the *Proposals*. In her discussion of Mar's schemes for London, Paris and Edinburgh, Stewart shows

INTRODUCTION

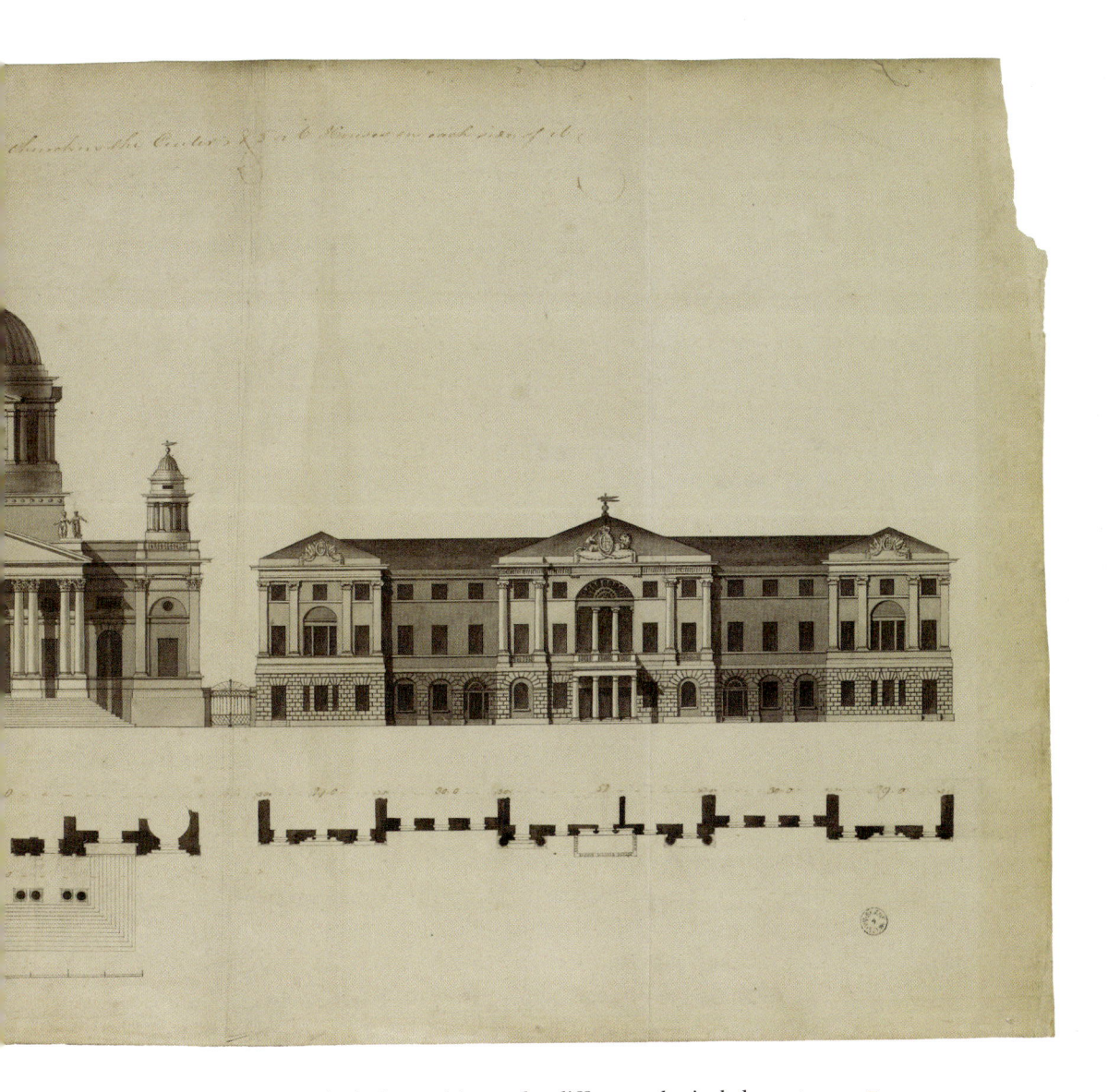

that Mar was particularly sensitive to the different physical characters of the capital cities he hoped to see remodelled, and that he stuck close to then-current planning ideals, coupling these with the local historical and cultural values of each city. In his study of Allan Dreghorn's plan for Glasgow, Anthony Lewis shows that, contrary to common understanding, Glasgow was well ahead of Edinburgh by several decades in setting out a new urban development; and his chapter serves as a reminder of Glasgow's equally notable spirit of

FIGURE 0.5.
(Overleaf) Thomas Hamilton, *Design for National Gallery and Royal Scottish Academy*, pen and ink, pencil and watercolour on paper, 74.0 × 130.0 cm, 1848. (Copyright Royal Scottish Academy)

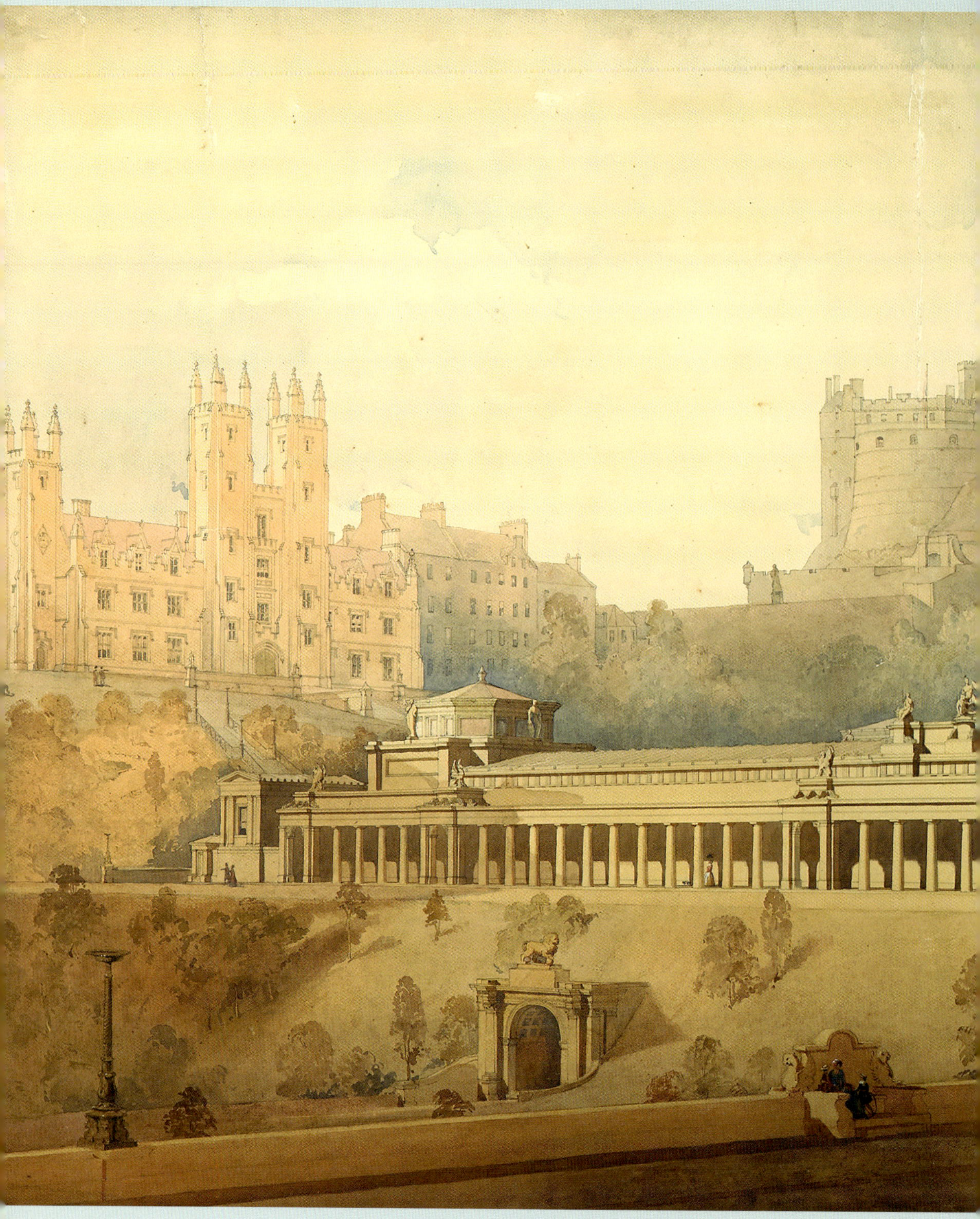

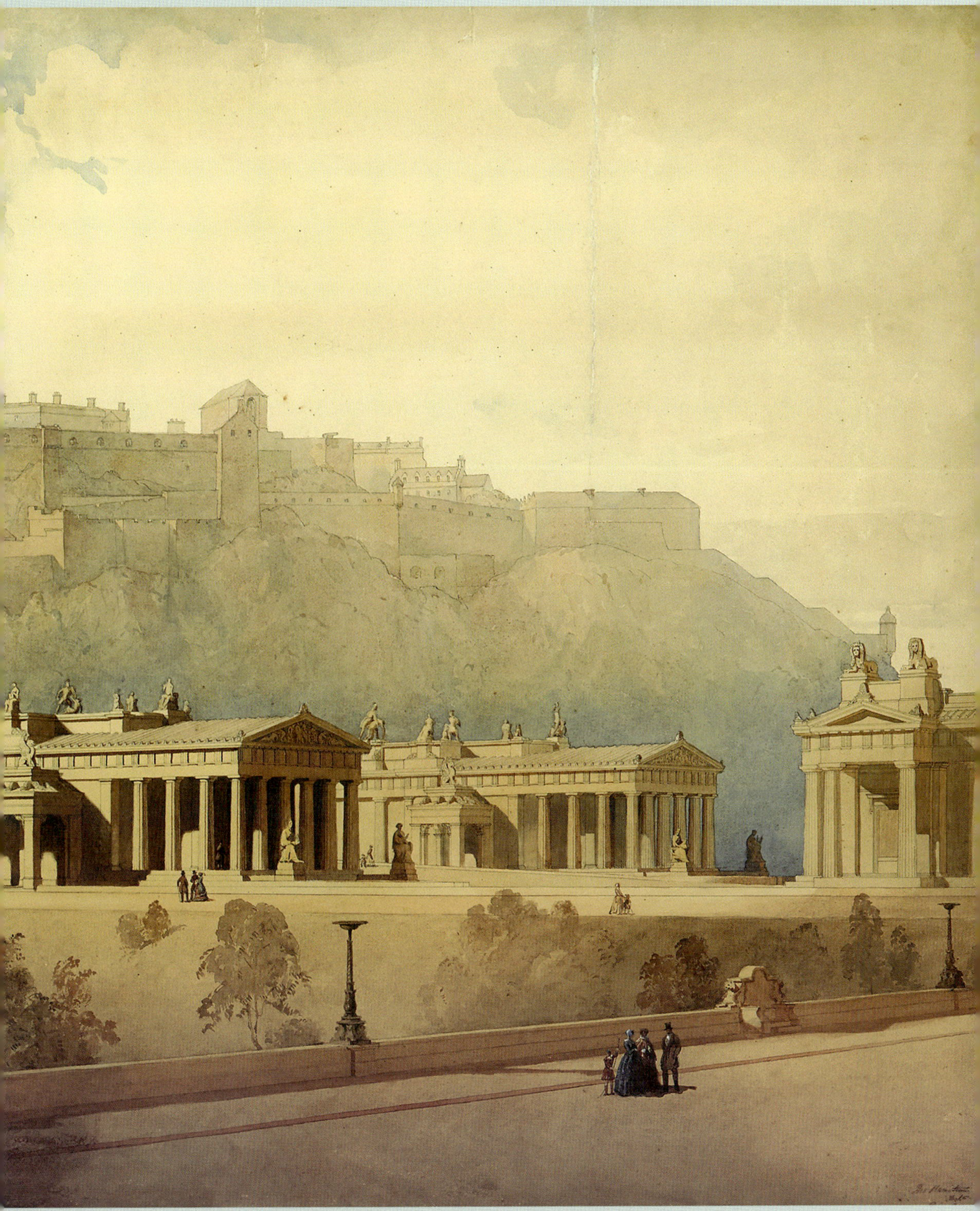

FIGURE 0.6.
William Henry Playfair, *Design for National Gallery and Royal Scottish Academy on the Mound*, east elevation, 1848. (University of Edinburgh, N/A 5028)

innovation, alongside its correspondingly early profiting from slavery – profits which, as Lewis points out, could be invested in architecture.

In her analysis of the planned routes through Edinburgh of King George IV in 1822, and of Queen Victoria and Prince Albert in 1842, Giovanna Guidicini shows that the New Town was chosen as the backdrop for officially welcoming the monarch, contrary to a previous tradition of royal entries through the Old Town. By focusing on the spatial and social characteristics of craft businesses in the New Town, Stana Nenadic sheds light on a flourishing area of craft production, of which little remains today. By looking at provisions of hotels and lodgings, as well as at postal services and journey times, Richard Rodger analyses the transformations of Edinburgh at the turn of the nineteenth century; in an age when mobility was increasingly understood as underpinning commercial success, Edinburgh functioned as a hub for communications with strategic county towns and burghs. John Lowrey's chapter focuses on a more recent period, and the growth of commercialisation in the New Town in the early twentieth century. Addressing a slightly later period, in an analysis of post-Second World War concern for planning, Alistair Fair demonstrates that ideas of sociability – built 'civility' – were very much to the fore in the New Town's twentieth-century successors.

Taking a comparative approach, Robin Skinner reconsiders Charles Kettle's 1848 plan for Dunedin (New Zealand), a city whose plan is traditionally considered as inspired by its Scottish namesake. In his chapter, the similarities and variations between the two cities

FIGURE 0.7.
(Overleaf) David Octavius Hill, *Edinburgh Old and New*, oil on panel, date unknown. (National Galleries of Scotland, purchased 1942)

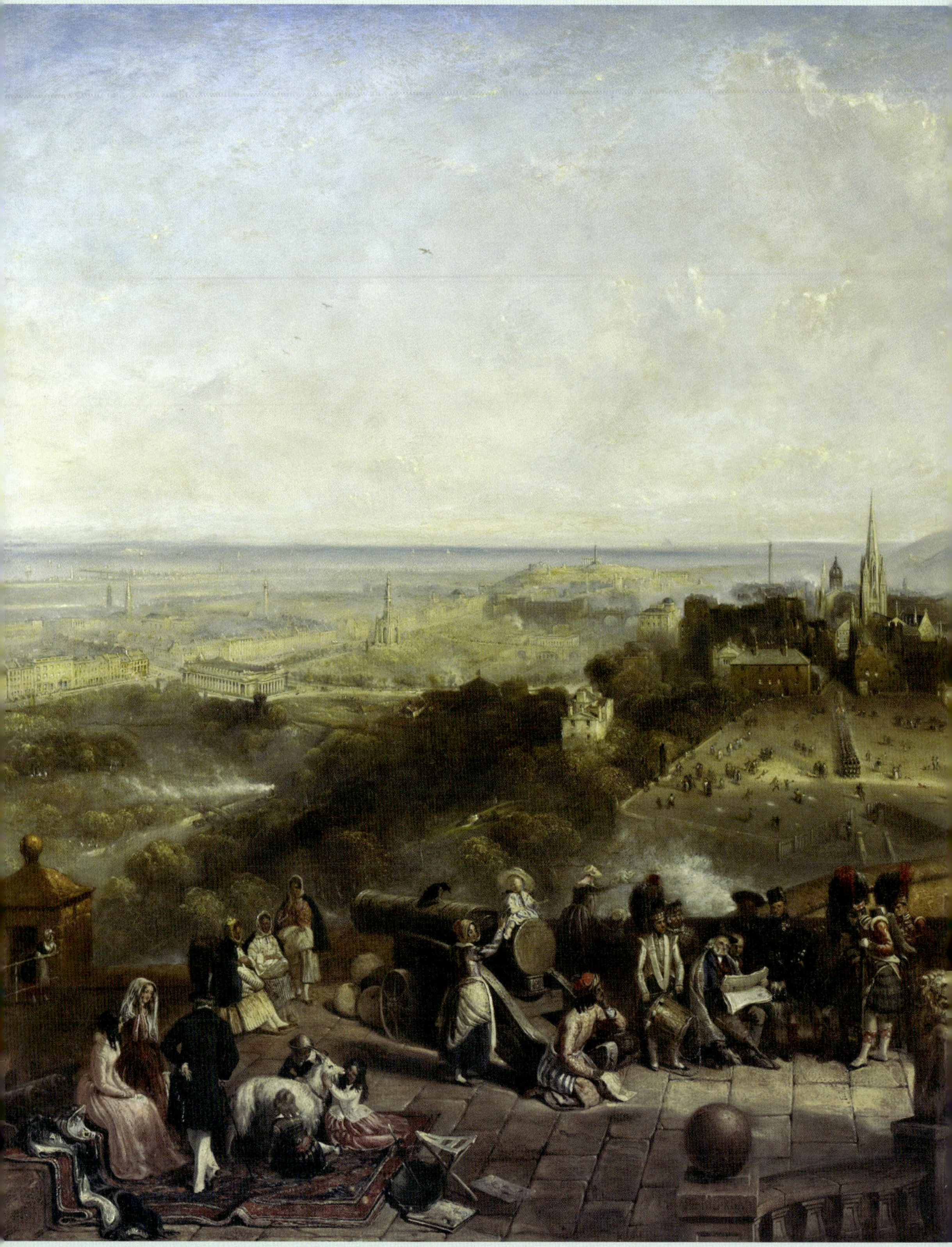

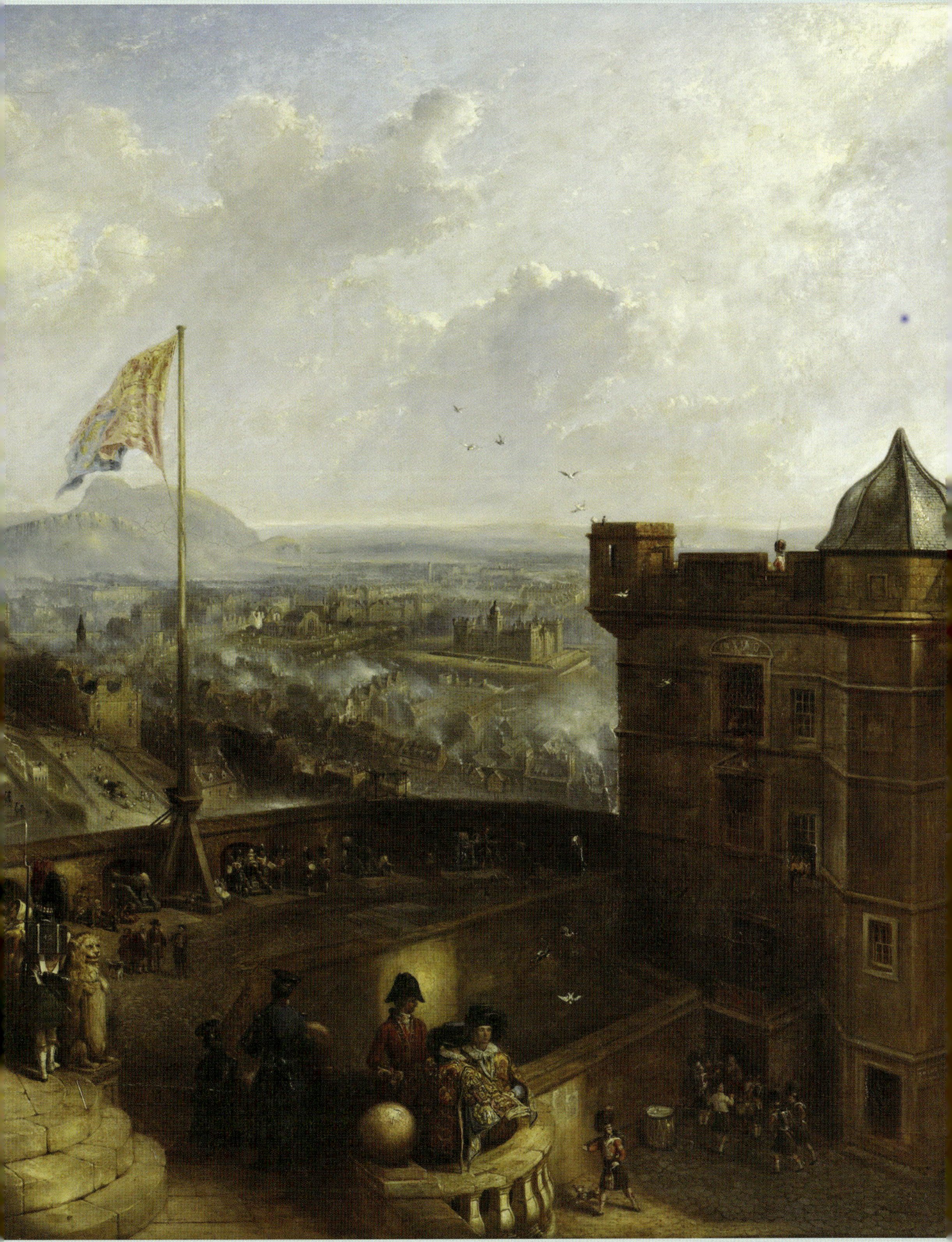

are identified, showing precisely where references to the New Town were valued and applied by Dunedin's planners and where they were not.

The age of conservation is the central theme of two of the book's chapters. Firstly, that by Pierre Chabard, who situates Patrick Geddes's initiatives in urban renewal in the Old Town within contemporary French and English theory in urban planning. And then, in an examination which focuses on more up-to-date conservation in Edinburgh, Ranald MacInnes explores some of the complex and often contradictory architectural and political impulses between 'old' and 'new'.

Ophélie Siméon's chapter rather contrasts with the others in the book because her topic steps beyond the bounds of cities, into the Scottish countryside. She highlights that Scotland in the eighteenth and nineteenth centuries was a land of planned towns, a feature rare in contemporary Europe where the energy for Improvement and large-scale reconstruction of the landscape was not, generally, the same. In doing so, Siméon shows how the Enlightenment ideals behind the Edinburgh New Town also found a powerful outlet in the wider countryside.

By drawing on multiple approaches to the new town phenomenon in Scotland, this volume pays tribute to Scotland's vibrant capital, and offers the reader insights into the most recent research on Scotland's urban and suburban development more generally.

It is hoped, also, that this publication will find its place among established publications, including Youngson's *The Making of Classical Edinburgh* (1966), Brogden's *The Neoclassical Town in Scotland* (1996), John Frew and David Jones's *The New Town Phenomenon: The Second Generation. Proceedings of a Conference held at the University of St Andrews, 20 November 1999* (St Andrews, University of St Andrews, 2000), and Charles MacKean's *Edinburgh, An Illustrated Architectural Guide* (Rutland Press and RIAS, 1992).

CHAPTER 1

Edinburgh: Smart City of 1700

Murray Pittock

This chapter focuses on social diffusion, the process whereby the distinctively Scottish features of urban space, its inhabitants and interactions, created the conditions in which particular associations, cultural practices and ideas arose out of the peculiarly Scottish architectural environment of Edinburgh. Such mechanisms created the discrete conditions for a nationally inflected Enlightenment.[1]

Why is this kind of approach needed, and what claims can be made for its validity? First, it is important to note the all too frequent absence of the mechanics of change in understanding the development of the Enlightenment. The Old Town was central in the development of such mechanics: the New Town was the product of the Enlightenment, not its catalyst. It is thus fitting to begin a study of the New Town of Edinburgh by examining the central role played by the Old not only in its development, but in the creation of the intellectual infrastructure that made the New Town possible.

The material conditions for the development of the Scottish Enlightenment in Edinburgh were similar to the conditions deemed necessary today for the growth and development of innovative ideas in cities. These include – in the classic formulation of Jane Jacobs – the intermingling of residential and commercial properties (what was once called 'efficient specialization' in segregated neighbourhoods is today seen as presaging economic decline); small and short blocks (the varied closes and wynds of old Edinburgh met this criterion admirably); buildings of different ages, types and size, and high concentrations of people. Nobel prizewinner Edmund Phelps is only one recent commentator who ascribes the rapidly rising growth rates of the modern era to 'population density'. Few early modern cities were more concentrated than eighteenth-century Edinburgh.[2]

In the contemporary policy realm, it is a commonplace that innovative cities share frequently replicated characteristics: a supportive policy environment, a geographically contiguous employment district and a diverse workforce. Vancouver and San Francisco are prime examples. Edinburgh in 1700 was another. The city and its institutions were geographically concentrated (this results in a 20–30% uplift in patents per capita in modern cities);[3] its workforce was diverse in point of foreign origin and foreign education. As Phelps puts it, 'people are better able and more apt . . . to innovation when they have been left free to venture from their homes . . . to soak up information on old and new products and new lifestyles', while 'a 2015 study by McKinsey found firms in the top quartile for racial diversity are 35 per cent more likely to make bigger profits than their industry average'.[4] Edinburgh had strong Netherlandish and French communities, as well as many Scots who had been educated or sojourned in these countries.

Moreover (at least until 1707) the Scottish government provided a steady diet of often supportive policy interventions directed at the capital. When the great and the good of the Estates, the courts and the Privy Council encountered suboptimal urban conditions in carrying out business or in their daily lives in the capital, they naturally turned to the powers they possessed to ameliorate the conditions they experienced. To some extent these conditions survived the Union of 1707 and the loss of the Privy Council the following year. Today, effective, connected leadership and engaged citizens are seen as central to 'Smart City' development: both of these factors, as will be seen, were to be found in Edinburgh between 1680 and 1750 in the shape of a nobility engaged with the professions, and a strongly associational culture with multiple overlapping memberships of clubs and societies among those professions themselves. It should be noted here that 'nobility' in Scotland was a category extending beyond the category of Lords of Parliament (those holding titles equivalent to English barons) into the Scots baronial class, commonly called lairds, chiefs of the name and of major septs, landed baronets and their relations. An estimated 2.45% of the Scottish population were 'noble' in these terms at the Union, a proportion much more in keeping with Continental than English norms. Scotland was more like France than England in the proportion who were noble by rank, title or close relationship. While in England the size of the gentry was estimated at 15,000 in the eighteenth century (0.3% of the population), with the nobility proper numbering only a few hundred, the nobility made up 1–5% of the French population and reached 50% in some pockets of Spain. As late as 1771, 'great landowners' were 'defined as owning more than £2,000 Scots' (£167), hardly a challenging level in English terms, even given that prices were only slowly converging with English norms.[5]

The wealth and power of this class presaged a strong focus on urban improvement before 1700. The entry to Parliament Close was widened to 9m after the fire of 1676, 'to admit of the passage of coaches'. Cattle drovers were required (though many ignored the requirement) to follow a set route 'up the Castle Wynd and down Bell-house brae to the flesh market or slaughter houses at the north loch', to avoid causing undue disturbances to the citizenry. Animal slaughter was moved to the Nor' Loch (though offal and excrement remained a problem), and after the introduction of a water supply (see below) and the development in 1678 of a Cleansing Committee, 'street cleaning and public lighting of streets' was made a priority, not least due to Privy Council pressure: the leaders of Scottish society did not like getting dirty.[6]

In 1675 a water supply (it was historically difficult to secure good supplies on the high ridge of the city) began to be piped to the High Street from Toddie's Well in Comiston, a development supported by the 'hydrostatic knowledge' of George Sinclair, on the staff of the University of Glasgow. A reservoir at the top of the Royal Mile held around 200,000–225,000 litres of water. This enabled the initiation of street cleaning and similar hygienic measures. 'At least eight fountains' supplied water, while the Council soon 'found it possible to allow the use of the surplus water first to such trades as brewers then very gradually to private houses'. In 1682, thirty muckmen were appointed to clean the streets before 9am (7am in summer), headed from 1684 by a 'General Scavenger';

in the same year, 'the council . . . funded two new public privies'. In 1685, the throwing of refuse from windows was banned (apparently rather ineffectively), but from 1687 'streets and closes were raked and cleaned three times a week', while in 1692 the muckmen 'were given the additional responsibility of patrolling the streets between 9pm and midnight every Saturday to report on people pouring waste from their window' to the famous Edinburgh (and Antwerp) cry of '*Gardez l'eau*'. From 1687, '20 close carts' were put in place nightly by 10pm for rubbish removal. Receptacles for ashes and sweepings were put in each close. In 1688 'the magistrates were given authority to compel the heritors of houses to make pavements before their tenements' and inhabitants were 'required . . . to keep vessels in their houses big enough to hold foul water for 48 hours'. Dirty water thrown from windows was banned – once again, together with rubbish – in 1701. By 1726 (the year after manure began to be sold commercially in the burgh), the streets were being cleaned every day except Sundays.

Following the formal introduction of lanterns outside doors in the 1660s (some lighting had been in place in the Hie Gait a century earlier), a system of public street lighting also began to take shape by the end of the seventeenth century. Amsterdam and Paris also introduced their first lighting systems in the 1660s (Paris had 'true public street lighting' with nearly 3,000 lanterns from autumn 1667). In Edinburgh, 'public lamps were furnished to illuminate the winter nights' from 1688 (there were 107 streetlamps by 1747). London introduced 'the convex lamps of the City' in 1695 and 'globular' ones in the West End in 1709. The characterisation of Edinburgh as barbaric and squalid by some English visitors was as least as much a tactic for projecting their own superiority over its alien cultural qualities as an objective assessment. Moreover, the filthiness of London was also proverbial: in 1714, 'the French envoy complained repeatedly about the effect on his breathing of the coal smoke that enveloped London', and later in the century the 'stench from corpses . . . buried in shallow graves' was remarked on. Edinburgh's 'Europeanness in behavior, dress, fodder and speech was what struck visitors most forcibly . . . English travellers could only describe the capital and its inhabitants by reference to foreign countries.'[7] What is very clear from these developments is the fact that –

as Bob Harris and Charles McKean have pointed out – 'the distinctive language of urban improvement was already very well established by the early eighteenth century'.[8]

If these public health measures (not always observed, it is true) began to promote a more hygienic city, health and safety was also important amid the closely packed 'lands' or flatted houses which were liable to both fire (such as the major conflagration of 1700) and collapse (as when the side wall of a six-storey land gave way in the High Street in September 1751). The burgh authorities responded to the intense risk of fire by introducing early examples of both fire and planning regulations, the major conflagration of 1700 being met with closely and intensively stipulated regulation of the use of naked flames. In 1701, extensive new fire regulations prevented the use of candles in shops where combustibles were present, and limited fires to hearths. Such regulations can only have encouraged more socialising out of doors and in taverns. The city was supported in such ambitions for its infrastructure by the Scottish Parliament, which legislated as early as 1621 for all new domestic roofs in Edinburgh, 'being the heid burgh of this realme', to be leaded not thatched; in 1681, this legislation was extended by the 'Act anent thecking of houses in Edinburgh and some other Burghs royall' which 'obliged all heritors of thatched houses to replace the thatch with lead, slate or tiles within a year', though 'thatch could still be found throughout the city' many years later. In 1674, the Town Council encouraged a move from timber to stone in building, and on 7 May 1678, the Privy Council backed the Town Council's intention to ensure that all future building should be in stone. Elaborate building regulations and the drive towards consistency of practice supported by the Dean of Guild's Court succeeded earlier legislative practice in the eighteenth century and helped to support 'a kind of architectural uniformity later seen in more striking form in the building lines of the New Town'. The Dean of Guild ordered 'road repairs', and support for the infrastructure continued to be a feature of Old Town life: in 1747, 'each coach' in the city was obliged to 'lay on the Easter Road to Leith ten cart fulls of gravel for every coach that has plied the streets yearly'. The engagement with the Scottish Estates in sustaining and developing this infrastructure was critical to the rapid improvement of the Edinburgh townscape planned – and to an extent achieved – in the early part of our period. Later, the burgh's relatively extensive powers helped to secure it.[9]

The Old Town (a term apparently unknown until the 1752 *Proposals* which led to the development of the New Town) was thus central in the development of this noble and professional Edinburgh: a focus on the New Town has arguably contributed to the relatively inadequate specification of the causes of Enlightenment. In A.J. Youngson's classic work on the New Town, *The Making of Classical Edinburgh*, the older city is characterised as 'a very small town, spilling out from the narrow confines of the old Flodden Wall . . . cramped and overcrowded'. This may be technically correct, but Youngson's rhetoric supports his subject by also implying that Edinburgh's success as an intellectual capital depended on the major urban changes that followed the 1752 *Proposals*, and would have been impossible without them. The *Proposals* themselves sought to diminish the Old Town in order to stress the necessity of '*Certain Public Works*' to change the city for the better: thus they bring home the point that Edinburgh 'admits but of one good street', and that the New Town would provide the capital's elite with an incentive to live in 'splendour and influence . . . at home', rather than have 'an obscure life in LONDON'. Interestingly, however, the New Town did not retain the nobility in Edinburgh in residence. It was the century before it was built which was the sweet spot for the intersection of a native nobility's defence of its declining status and the professional defence of threatened institutions, both taking place in a confined geographical space with a workforce of exceptional diversity for the time, with unusually good transport links by land and sea, which gave in Edward Glaeser's words, 'a huge edge' to the success of early modern cities. If, as Peter Burke has argued, 'the group identity of the clerisy' was becoming stronger in the early modern period, the political and indeed to an extent existential threat posed by the Union to Edinburgh's capital status could only serve to intensify this process: crystallising and developing centres of professional power were faced with the dissolution of the state in which they were located at a critical point in their own rise to prominence. Nor would one have to be an opponent of Union to participate in the growing solidarity that resulted from these critical circumstances: by no means all supporters of the Union were enthusiasts for its consequences, a fact easily forgotten by posterity.[10]

The Scottish capital (although physically indeed a 'very small town' in Youngson's phrase) was Great Britain's second largest city throughout the 1680–1750 period, with a population of some 47,000–54,000 in 1691 and (despite the initially economically dampening effects of Union) some 53,000–57,000 in 1755. Scotland was 'one of the least urbanised' European countries in the seventeenth century, but its capital was still substantial in Continental terms, if not in the first rank of cities. Like all Scottish burghs, the heart of Edinburgh was the Hie Gait or High Street, from which 'the principal streets led'. Its 'ports' were also normative as was the 'secondary space for service activities lying towards the edge of the burgh', for example the Grassmarket. The 'mercat cross' provided the 'key site of authority' here as in other burghs until its removal in 1756, the avatar for a major relocation of urban power across the Nor' Loch. Just as 'spatial intentions are ... the basis of all architectural decisions', so the nature and power of that space and its use are determining factors in human behaviour and circulation. As Manuel de Landa puts it, 'the urban infrastructure may be said to perform ... the same function of motion control that our bones do in relation to our fleshy parts', while Phelps argues that 'population density' creates the best environment for being open to 'change, challenge, and lifelong quest for originality, discovery, and making a difference'. This circulation – traceable although not stable, because of the immateriality of the social – produces communication. Edinburgh was densely populated, and as we shall see, the population was not only closely clustered together, but quite diverse, with many more intersections which were professional or associational (clubs and societies) than those based solely on kin and family. Such associations in their turn eased the friction in daily transactions, whether social or economic, and helped to circulate innovation more rapidly.[11] Early modern Edinburgh was a place of instant communication by virtue of its dense living, rapid building, closely packed tenements (it was not unknown for one to be able to shake hands with a neighbour opposite, and the High Street itself was less than 5m wide at the Luckenbooths) and above all narrow space. The city proper measured only 900m × 500m from the Castle to the Netherbow, the West Port to the backs above the Nor' Loch.

The capital's cityscape was largely a series of intimate spaces, miniaturised public environments, accessed through close stairs and courts, some closed off for privacy. Each 'land' or high flatted dwelling had a separate address, with tenants or owners usually on different floors, sometimes sharing a floor (though this became more unusual as time went on). Property in tofts or strips ran down the closes, while the more public street front faced the main Hie Gait or Canongate. There were some 300 closes or wynds off what would come to be known as the Royal (Scots) Mile in a configuration of ancient date (the Scots mile is roughly 1,800m rather than 1,600m). Despite much new building, the infrastructure of the past remained. As Richard Rodger notes, 'Reincarnated, medieval merchants would have been able easily to find their way around eighteenth-century Edinburgh.'[12]

In 1751, there were 6,845 houses in Edinburgh proper (some of huge size and occupied by many families), with a further 2,219 in the Canongate.[13] This eastern burgh, which ran down to Holyrood Palace, was also traditionally the residence of the nobility and of some of the foreign embassies. Nobility with seats in the provinces might also retain a townhouse in the Canongate or elsewhere in or near Edinburgh. Following the Union, Canongate declined, and 'growing poverty' was being recorded in the burgh in the 1720s. However, in that decade a number of the lesser nobility began to drift back to the Canongate, which thereafter retained a strong upper-class enclave until at least the end of the 1760s.[14]

In Edinburgh proper, tall flats or 'lands' stretched up far from the ground: the '"great tenement" between Parliament Square and the Cowgate, burnt in 1700' was fourteen storeys high.[15] Although these were socially stratified, with the wealthier residents on the lower or middle floors above the ground and the poorer folk in attics, ground floors or basements, and although there were certain areas of the capital with townhouses or smaller lands which were sought by the well-to-do, it remained the case that the nobility, professionals and poor of the city lived next to each other. With much of daily life carried on out of doors, poor and rich inevitably mixed. The cityscape's manifold different kinds of space helped to promote the intensely networked life for which it was later to be known. As Adam Smith remarked in a more general context 'market-extent, and thus intensity of specialisation, is a function of population density'. In few places was the population so dense or the human institutions and associations which were its infrastructure so specialised and complex as in Edinburgh. But the Scottish capital was also much more of a capital city in its development and facilities than anywhere else in Great Britain outside London: in Edinburgh eyes, if the English city was 'capital City of the Southern Part of *Britain*', then Edinburgh was 'the Chief City in the Northern Part . . . and second Town in this Island'.[16]

Edinburgh was certainly by far the wealthiest city in Scotland, paying in the range of 32–40% of the country's taxes in the years between 1649 and 1705 while having only 5% of Scotland's population in its greater urban area. Leith alone was responsible for 63% of French wine imports, and Edinburgh wine importers dominated the Scottish market, while 80% 'of the vessels in the Dutch trade sailed to and from the Firth of Forth'. By 1660, the Edinburgh goldsmiths 'were making loans and dealing in foreign exchange from their booths round St Giles and were commonly issuing bills of exchange'. These goldsmith-bankers also developed an 'arbitrage and futures business' whereby they gained a margin on exchange rates and interest rates in purchasing assets for delivery from the Highlands; later they acted as brokers for 'lost property offices'.[17]

The Scottish Exchange on London was important to the country's trading prosperity within the British Isles, for 'on the eve of the . . . Union . . . around one half of the total export trade of Scotland was already directed towards England' (this figure was 64% in 2014, not that much of an increase for 300 years of Union). The Scottish Exchange (which persisted after the Union) was a sign of Scotland's 'own commercial law and separate economy', giving the country 'some of the elements of a foreign exchange as well as an inland exchange', even after 1707. Scotland's long history of an insufficiency of native bullion leading to multiple currencies circulating within its borders also had a legacy in innovations like the overdraft and the early adoption of paper currency, with Royal Bank and Bank of Scotland £1 notes beginning 'to displace silver and gold in smaller transactions' by the 1740s.[18]

Many of these innovations had their roots in small offices in Edinburgh, such as the 'little wooden shop, high and low [on two storeys], on the South of the old Kirk' let to the goldsmith John Law on 24 June 1681 for 68s 4d per annum. In October 1683, Law moved to the east side of Parliament Close; two years later a 'piazza or open-air Exchange' was constructed for merchants in Parliament Square. Law's nephew, also John (1671–1732), later Controller General of the Finances of France, was to be a controversial pioneer of paper currency, originator of the scarcity theory of value and French central banking.[19]

Scotland itself had increasingly developed internal markets. In the city of Edinburgh, almost 10% of households 'had stock valued at 10,000 Scots merks or above': about €170,000 at 2018 prices. At the heart of the city, a high proportion of the population belonged to the social elite, with 6% belonging to the gentry/nobility, 12% merchant and 14–15% professional by background at the close of the seventeenth century. Scotland's foreign trade was 'still largely . . . in the hands of Edinburgh merchants'. At the same time, the professional groups that Edinburgh boasted were proportionately significantly more influential than those in London. Although the English capital was ten times the size of its Scottish counterpart (c. 550,000 in 1700), the professional classes – even in inner London – did not exceed 6–7% of the population. Edinburgh's professionals reached this figure across the greater urban area (population up to 55,000) as whole, and were significantly higher in the core city of 45 hectares. As Helen Dingwall notes, 'Compressed by geographical constraints into a tiny area, the burgh had nonetheless a surprisingly complex social and economic composition.'[20]

Edinburgh's close vertical environment of stacked living – like that of Paris – complemented its horizontal one of urban propinquity to create 'a city bustling with creative energy . . . an incubation of the kind of ideas that could revolutionize urban life'. To English visitors, it came as a considerable surprise that 'every Family, of the best rank, generally have but one Floor, some only half a Floor' in which to live. The Countess of Balcarres shared a close with milliners and tailors, and this was by no means unusual. Sometimes the merchants' booths themselves were stacked, as with the Luckenbooths near St Giles which reached six floors in height, or the 'krames' or smaller booths in the Dutch fashion, which clustered there and round the High Kirk. The grandest public architecture reflected the heritage of French influence: the Netherbow Port or gate which marked the division between Edinburgh proper and Canongate was modelled on the Porte Saint-Honoré in Paris when it was built in 1606. Other reminders of France – and the Netherlands – were found throughout early modern Edinburgh, such as Mary of Guise's palace at the top of the Lawnmarket, with its 'garden grounds sloping to the Nor' Loch behind', or the French Ambassador's chapel at 'the foot of Libberton's Wynd', as well as more mundane examples of relatively regular streetfronts. At the Restoration, large numbers of nobles and professionals who had been exiled in France or the Netherlands returned to Scotland, and the pace of both cosmopolitan contact and innovation grew, with 'Scottish intellectual discourse . . . rendered cosmopolitan by frequent foreign travel'. As the Marquis of Argyll put it in the late 1660s, 'he that hath lived lock'd up in one Kingdome' was 'but a degree beyond a Country-man, who was never out of the bounds of his parish'.[21]

Cosmopolitanism in this era contained the implications of being open-minded and impartial, not subject to cultural prejudices, urbane and nowhere a stranger. The degree to which professional and noble Scots enjoyed educational, cultural, political and mercantile connections abroad, quite different from the quasi-colonial *de haut en bas* ethos of the Grand Tour, with its acquisition of objects abroad for British consumption and enjoyment, was one of the key denominators of difference in the social outlook of the Scottish capital. In the latest age of independent Scottish nationhood, the country had a global footprint, where 'intellectual, political, religious and commercial associations combined . . . to promote regular contact between Restoration Scots and an extensive overseas diaspora', which during the seventeenth century had begun to radiate into the nascent British Empire, though its European dimensions were to remain important into the nineteenth century.[22]

Edinburgh also had the inbuilt and later inherited advantages of housing the infrastructure of government and its national institutions. These included – among many others – the 'Cunzie House' or Scottish Mint; the townhouses of the Archbishops before 1689; Parliament House, completed in 1639, whither up to 1,200 men on horseback and 40 coaches processed at the Riding of Parliament and the role of the High Commissioner, whose 'procession and the posting of royal proclamations were retained' after the 1707 Union. The Place Royale in Parliament Close had an equestrian sculpture of Charles II which was a lead replica of that at Windsor, 'the first depiction of a British monarch . . . as a Roman Emperor'; towards Holyrood there was the Canongate Kirk, built by James Smith in 1688–9 for James VII and still used by the Crown. From 1700, Old Bank Close was home to the Bank of Scotland, founded five years earlier, while private bankers such as John Coutts had begun to appear by the 1730s: in succession to the goldsmiths, private banks proliferated in eighteenth-century Scotland. The Company of Scotland, developed as a 'global trading vehicle', with a broader shareholder base than either the English East India Company or the Bank of England, was based in 'Milne's Square on the High Street'. Edinburgh's Post Office may have come late to the fray in the wake of Italian developments in the sixteenth century, but its 8d Edinburgh–London service in 1633 anticipated the Paris postal system by twenty years, though the three collections a day from Paris postboxes were to render the French capital's the first truly modern system in Europe. Edinburgh developed a sixpenny delivery service to Ireland in 1662 and within Scotland seven years later.[23]

At the mercat cross by St Giles' and Parliament Square where 'proclamations and public acts are read and published by sound of trumpet', the city had its core locale of power and administration. It was hardly surprising that such a densely populated, cosmopolitan and strongly associational city, which conducted so much business out of doors, should have become one of the centres for innovation and diffusion of ideas in eighteenth-century Europe. The removal of the mercat cross in 1756 (the same year of the last celebration of the old feast of Beltane, 1 May), four years after the *Proposals* for the New Town were published, was to mark the opening of a new era in the social circulation of Edinburgh.[24] The cross's removal was seen by some as the final end of Stuart Scotland, and the ascent of Great Britain:

We heels o'er head are tumbled down,
The modern taste is London town.

Whether this was the case or not, its disappearance was part of a wider movement whereby 'Town crosses, the pre-eminent and usually the most readily visible civic symbol . . . , disappeared from many burghs in the second half of the eighteenth century.'[25]

But it is at least arguable that the transformations heralded and aspired to by Sir Gilbert Elliot's *Proposals* began much earlier, not least during the residences of James, Duke of Albany, at Holyrood in 1679–82. James was a supporter of 'internal freedom of trade for the three kingdoms and the colonies, an imperial trading system'. Scottish participation in this system on its own terms had 'priority over institutional convergence or . . . full economic union', and James was able to convince the English Privy Council to allow Scots to share from the 1670s in the activities of the Royal African Company and Hudson's Bay Company and to trade freely in New York. Following a 1681 report from the Committee for Trade, which noted 'growing dependence on English markets' in Scotland, James 'duly authorized Scottish ventures in South Carolina in 1682 and East New Jersey from 1685'. Scots Law was initially practised in the South Carolina jurisdiction. The stage was set for the development of the Company of Scotland.[26] During his time at Holyrood and as king he would oversee the development of the Advocates' Library, the Royal College of Physicians, printing and a number of other innovations, including 'the royal charter of the Edinburgh Merchant Company', granted on 28 November 1681, the day before the College of Physicians.[27] James also instituted the offices of Historiographer-Royal (1681) and Geographer-Royal for Scotland (1682), which remain live to the present day. The Duke was likewise the force behind the commissioning of the de Wet portraits of the Stuart royal line at Holyrood (themselves part of a major influx of Dutch art and artists at this period). His understanding of the need to extend the burgh (James supported the bridging of the Nor' Loch) arguably underpinned the later development of the New Town, which was certainly enabled by the king's Charter to Edinburgh of 25 September 1688, 'to extend its bounds on all sides, to make streets, acquire grounds and houses compulsorily and to levy taxes for the same'.[28]

James was building on developments which – influenced by the international disruptions of the Thirty Years' War and the Wars of the Three Kingdoms, which displaced intellectuals and nobles alike

– had begun to see innovative practice gathering apace in the Scottish capital. By 1656 there was a botanic garden in Black Friars Wynd, succeeded by the 1676 gardens at Holyrood and Halkerston's Wynd, which covered 2 hectares by the last quarter of the eighteenth century with a 42-metre conservatory front and several thousand species of plants. Dr Andrew Balfour (1630–1694) and Sir Robert Sibbald (1641–1722) founded the Hortus Medicus in 1670, a medicinal plant garden possibly inspired by its Amsterdam predecessor, begun in 1638, or by those of Leiden (1590) or Padua (1545). Holyrood had also had a garden since the 1640s, while 'Heriot's yeards' by the school on Lauriston Place, had a garden with '*physical, medicinal,* and other *herbs*' in 1661, which has been claimed as the 'first Botanic Garden in Scotland'. By 1683, a *Gard'ners Kalendar* was being issued in Edinburgh.[29]

Sibbald and Balfour decided to create a physic garden. Initially no more than 12 metres square, by 1675 the garden was 90m × 58m and the following year James Sutherland was made 'Intendant of the Physic Garden'. By 1695, the cost of bringing in 'forraigne plants and seeds' was a notable one for the burgh, but the Physic Garden in turn brought in income through sales: in 1691 alone Sutherland 'supplied 45 varieties of trees and shrubs' to one customer, the Earl of Morton at Aberdour Castle. The Garden was also used for teaching the 'rudiments of botany', instruction in the medical use of plants and 'to provide pharmacists with fresh plants': a multiple role which embodied the 'useful learning' core to the Scottish Enlightenment. Sutherland compiled a catalogue of the then 2,000 plants in 1683, while in 1700 (the year after it received the royal warrant) the Garden's stock formed the basis for the College of Physicians' pharmacopoeia, which remained the standard text through many revisions up till 1864. The integration of the physic garden with medical education was an innovative alignment foreshadowing the Temple of Science developments initiated by Johann Christian Senckenberg (1707–1772) in Frankfurt two generations later.[30]

Transport grew increasingly sophisticated. There were twenty hackney coaches in Edinburgh by 1673, with a cost of a shilling from the High Street to the Cowgate or Grassmarket and 2s to Leith. Coachmaking began in Edinburgh in 1696, and Robert Gibb had a good deal of the business, buying Gibb's Close at 250 Canongate; Alexander Forsyth, another coachmaker, acquired property at 57 Canongate (Forsyth's Close from 1719). A sedan chair service was also introduced in 1687. Paris had been the first with a 'rental service' of this kind in 1639, and had also introduced public transport by carriage by the beginning of the 1660s; in London at the beginning of the eighteenth century there were 200 sedan chairs for hire, '300 from 1713'; Edinburgh had 90 in 1738, which was a higher coverage per head of population. Sedan chairs were numbered from 1738; coaches from 1747. In Edinburgh the sedan chair service cost 7 shillings Scots (about 6½d at the then current exchange rate) for a journey from the Castle to the Abbey. Alexander Hay had the monopoly for eleven years, and kept chairs at six 'convenient stances' on what is now the Royal Mile, each with two men in attendance. Sedan chairs did not make an appearance in Bath and Bristol (at 30,000, the second largest English city) until the middle of the eighteenth century (priced at 6d for 500 yards and a shilling for a mile). In the late 1730s, the Edinburgh chairs were priced at 6d for trips in the city and suburbs, 2s 6d for half a day, 4s a day and £1 for a week's use: rather cheaper than Bath or Bristol. There were easily enough sedan chairs to clutter up the streets, with petitions against their being placed 'before . . . houses and shops' in 1747 and 1749. Although Edinburgh was not leading innovation here, it nonetheless was again an early adopter, possibly through awareness of its 'capital' status. Amsterdam, for example, was more resistant to coaches because of noise issues. The transport arrangements of the Scottish capital also bore witness to the degree of circulation within it, and the strength of its internal and external communication channels.[31]

People of title were spread throughout the city. In 1694–8, 28% of persons with title were reported in Old Kirk parish (bordering on the Canongate on the south of the Hie Gait), 22.5% in New Kirk (round St Giles' on both sides of the street), 18% in Tron (south of what is now South Bridge), 14% in College, 10% in Tolbooth (Lawnmarket north), 6% in Greyfriars (south towards Grassmarket, Greyfriars and Heriot's), and 1% in Lady Yester's (south of Cowgate), and this of course excludes the nobility in the Canongate burgh. Many even from modest professions were relatively well to do. In

1698, in Lady Yester's Parish, Sir Robert Cheisly was assessed for 40,000 merks, William Steen the Master of the High School, at 10,000, and Alexander Herriott, a teacher of book-keeping, at 5,000 merks.[32]

After the Union, the nobility continued to live not only in the Canongate, but in the heart of Edinburgh proper. Despite allegations as early as 1718 concerning 'a great decay of the inhabitants of this city', the recrudescence of upper-class occupation in the 1720s means that Gilhooley's 1752 Street Directory lists many names of the landed and lawyerly gentry: Lord Minto in Paton's Land, the Earl of Dalkeith in Kennedy's Land (next to Allan Ramsay the bookseller), Lady Balmerino and Lord Dun in Milne's Square (both Jacobites); Dundas of Arniston in Carrubber's Close; the Marquess of Tweeddale in Tweeddale Court; Lord Milton, the Lord Justice Clerk, in Hyndford Close; Lady Lovat among six nobles in Blackfriars Wynd; the Countess of Balcarres in Dickson's Close; Lockhart of Carnwath in Niddry's Wynd/Carnwath's Court; Lord John Drummond in Parliament Close; Lord Belhaven in Libberton's Wynd; Murray of Broughton's wife at Baillie's Land in the Grassmarket, and many more. The Scottish nobility permeated the capital throughout, and it was impossible to mix socially in its tight spaces without interacting with them. Small wonder these mobile, highly educated and often patriotic people remained influential in the city. They were also highly visible in an age when clothing possessed an unequivocal social register: for example the use of 'red-heeled shoes' as a marker of status, which derived from French practice.[33]

After the Union the remaining – and relics of the former – institutions of an independent state were overwhelmingly based in its capital: packed into a tight space, highly educated, underemployed and with a need to assert their importance to each other and the world, what Nicholas Phillipson terms 'a local aristocracy and a dependent literati' trying 'to find a way of asserting their importance in a kingdom becoming a province' were ripe agents and audiences for innovation and new intellectual approaches.[34] As the recent ex-capital of a recent ex-state which already had – and to a significant extent retained – an advanced and complex set of cultural, financial, educational, legal, political and social systems and capital, Edinburgh was also an exceptional case. Like Amsterdam, Edinburgh enjoyed

– and this is a relatively neglected element in histories of the city – a cosmopolitan social structure. In such circumstances, the benefits of compactness are enhanced. Not only does 'the geographical concentration of information' make it 'easier to obtain', but when it is 'concentrated in a small space, it . . . became much easier to estimate its value by face-to-face contact with the sources'. The more cosmopolitan their background, the more difficult it is to channel or repel this process, as 'new information becomes easier to absorb and apply when it reaches potential users from various directions and is continually renewed'. Information in short becomes more rapidly socialised in diverse societies, because their heterogenous groupings are more accustomed to circulation and find a commonality in its language and the language of innovation that more homogenous groupings find in family or social ties. Such a flow of information accelerates in a small space, as 'spatial concentration' underpins the 'localization advantages' of information flows, and gives them more strength to resist 'legal prohibitions or active opposition from forces that consider their vested interests under threat from . . . change'. This opposition happened in Edinburgh, just as it happened in Amsterdam.[35]

Individual institutions and the associations that supported and intersected with them were important contributors to the application of reason to knowledge in a context of material improvement which marked the Scottish Enlightenment from its beginnings. Edinburgh's botanic garden was supplied by seeds from the continent, while concerts began by 1693, and a school of music taught by Matthew McGibbon was licensed in April 1696. In 1702, the pertinacious Sir Robert Sibbald sought to found a Royal Society of Scotland in the capital, in which literacy rates were around 65% at a minimum. The city's newspapers, beginning with the 1661 *Caledonian Mercury* and the 1699 *Edinburgh Gazette*, and progressing through the *Edinburgh Courant* (1705), *Paris Gazette* (1706), *Scots Courant* (1710), *Scots Postman* (1708), the *Edinburgh Gazette* and the *Thistle* (an attempt 'to produce a London-style news-magazine like *Fog's Weekly Journal*'), provided a dynamic if insecure public sphere, many years ahead of the pattern of the periodical press elsewhere in Scotland. Edinburgh papers began to make their way to London: the *Edinburgh Evening Courant* (1718) seems to have been the first available in London coffee houses, reversing the normal expectations of the subsidiarity of the 'provincial press', and stressing Edinburgh's dominant role in cross-border exchange. Accounts of controversial practices from the colonies, such as suttee, were printed in the Edinburgh papers. By 1740, 'bookselling and printing' provided 3% of the Edinburgh labour market, while by 1748, 510 book imprints were produced; speciality books in areas like cookery were available from the 1730s, while the production of professional and official documentation (most of the publishing business) underlined Edinburgh's capital status.

There were libraries at the University (11,000 volumes in 1710) and the Faculty of Advocates (5,000 at the same date following its 1680 foundation); in the 1720s, the Writers to the Signet opened a library. In 1725, Allan Ramsay (1684–1758) opened the first circulating library in the country with a subscription of 10s annually, which was followed by libraries at Bath (1728) and Philadelphia (1731). Ramsay's library survived for over a century, passing to John Yair in 1740 and to his widow in 1758, the year of Ramsay's death. In 1770, it reached 30,000 volumes. Ramsay's library was an act of cultural innovation: but it was clear that the environment that sustained it contained – given the presence of at least three major libraries in the capital and others outside – a plethora of potential early adopters, to whom the free availability of books on a commercial basis beyond the libraries established in the legacy institutions of the former Scottish state offered an additional benefit.

Edinburgh also had a very strong charitable ethos, in contrast to tendentious claims that the Foundling Hospital *Messiah* charity concert in London in 1749 was a pioneering occasion. Such assemblies were by then already frequent in Edinburgh: in February 1740 alone there was both an Assembly for the benefit of '*Indigent Families*', priced at a handsome 10s 6d a ticket, and one by the Governor and Directors of the Musical Society for the benefit of the Royal Infirmary, more economically priced at 2s 6d a ticket. On 13 June 1733, there was a special benefit performance of *The Beggar's Opera* in its June run for the Royal Infirmary. The presence of Scottish gentry and the highly educated in the capital in disproportionate numbers provided the basis for charitable giving, their social capital being complemented by financial capital: in 1739, for example, the Jacobite nobleman Laurence Oliphant of Gask gave £5 for the 'Orphan-School and Hospital' of Edinburgh. Such 'celebrity' gifts were infused with the status of the giver and helped – as they would today in the wake of A-list gifters – to multiply more modest donations. In addition, the gift of a man like Oliphant would be an example to those of his political persuasion that charitable giving for the infrastructure of the capital and the care of its disadvantaged was a good Jacobite habit. Charity was by no means politically restricted, however: both the College of Physicians and the Faculty of Advocates offered free consultations at certain times, while the burgh itself made many pension and hardship payments.

At the same time, the arts grew in importance at a rapid rate: almost a declaration of cultural independence to replace its lost political equivalent. Allan Ramsay was central here, not only in founding the circulating/subscription library system, but also in his role (together with his friend the Englishman Richard Cooper) in developing the Academy of St Luke art school, his innovative practices in auction sales, his development of early bird and season ticket options and his responsibility for Edinburgh's first dedicated theatre. His shop and flat above in the Luckenbooths, bought for a not insubstantial £570 in 1725, became a centre for Edinburgh cultural and intellectual life. With respect to his theatre of 1736, Ramsay argued that

> the City of Edinburgh will Reap the Benefits in Particular since it will not only engadge our own Gentlemen and Ladys to water within our walls but also bring many of a Polite Tast from the Northern Countys of England who will Rather Chuse to come 50 or 100 miles North to Edinburgh as to travel 200 miles South to London where all the needful Supports & comforts of Life are not a whit Better or more abundant but much more expensive.

'The metropolis of a Nation', Ramsay concludes, 'should be encouraged in every thing that is Improving & Pleasing'. It is very telling that when Elliot's *Proposals* for the New Town were written less than twenty years later, at the core of the metropolitan qualities to be emulated lay 'the pleasures of the theatre, and other public entertainments' suitable to maintain the interest and 'splendour and influence' of 'people of rank'. Ramsay's formulation of a northern cultural metropolis clearly foreshadows the vision of Sir Gilbert Elliot and Lord Provost Drummond with respect to the New Town.

Ramsay's theatre was only one of the aspects of the development of a distinctive cultural infrastructure in Edinburgh, which fed both the creative and intellectual economies of the capital in the years before the New Town. A close examination of the city in the latter years of the seventeenth century strongly indicates that many of the key areas of infrastructure and distinctive urban and patronage networks associated with the Enlightenment were already coming into being. Edinburgh was a place which could – despite much opposition and frustration – develop and commercialise new artistic and cultural ventures in a context of densely concentrated multiple weak ties operating in close propinquity. Edinburgh's city and social structures were the twin engines of its Enlightenment.[36]

Part 1

Earlier Contexts

CHAPTER 2

Scotland's Planned Towns and Villages over the Centuries

Aonghus MacKechnie

The Planned Towns Movement of 1720s–1860s Scotland was when landowners created hundreds of new towns and villages as commercial and social enterprises, a topic assessed first by Houston in 1948, and then, most extensively, by Lockhart.[1] Edinburgh's New Town is sometimes regarded as exemplifying that movement. This chapter, however, argues for a separate, and wider, context for Edinburgh: namely, the context of Scotland as a land of new planned towns and villages over the past near-millennium, since the time of King David I's creation of Scotland's early burghs in the twelfth century. Its narrative continues up to the First World War (1914–18), and so omits interwar housing and post-war new towns – whose study is the preserve of modernists.

BACKGROUND CONTEXT

Long before Scotland was a political entity, an urbanising of sorts existed. This is seen for example at clustered Neolithic developments such as Skara Brae (c.3100–2500 BCE), or the Iron Age 'Broch villages'. Such sites display no formalised 'grand plan', but they do indicate planning in the sense of selecting locations for building, deciding what to build and deciding who the neighbours would be: a society with structured decision-taking and hierarchy of authority; some people had the right to build at such sites where others perhaps had not. And of course control and hierarchy are fundamental to seeing through adherence to any coherent urban plan. Scotland's Roman period was so episodic that, while numerous forts or settlements were constructed, rather unusually no newly made Roman settlements appear to have become towns – a contrast to the norm elsewhere in the 'European' Empire, as shown by the legion of legacy towns such as Chester or Köln, where even the Roman-period place-names survive.[2]

St Andrews has been an important centre since at least the mid eighth century, one of only two shrines outside Italy to claim an apostle's relics.[3] It was therefore a place of pilgrimage, and so was to some extent necessarily urbanised to meet pilgrim needs. Its town plan was most likely decided or affirmed in the twelfth century, when it was made a burgh. Campbell has argued that it was consciously modelled on the ninth-century Vatican Borgo, meaning that here was a Rome of the North long before Edinburgh became an Athens of the North.[4] All this constitutes a serious political claim from embryonic Scotland for international recognition, status and distinction: membership of the elite 'club' of Christendom's kingdoms. Also, in Fife, royal Dunfermline was a major centre from the mid eleventh century at least, and while yet to become a burgh, it was inevitably urbanised to some extent to service royal, governmental or courtier and visitor needs.

King David I's Burghs

So, although urban or urbanising centres pre-existed, Scotland's earliest coherent (post-Roman) urban development strategy was implemented by David I (r.1124–53). David's vision was to mainstream his consolidating Scotland within a modernising and commercial north European community: by generating a powerful economy, developing trade, introducing coinage,[5] founding religious houses and inaugurating a programme of creating burghs.[6] Burghs were urbanising places with commercial/trading privileges and the right to levy tolls/customs on merchandise. Nearly 500 burghs or reconstituted burghs existed by 1814. Here we look briefly at some of the earlier examples.

The place-name 'Old Melrose', distinct from its non-adjectival

David I-period namesake of Melrose, evidences medieval new-town planning on a new site. After all, it was vital that chosen locations for new burghs optimised the potential to generate wealth; this could mean rejecting established centres for new ones, and perhaps deciding to retain an established name (rather than found a 'New Melrose') indicates a 'brand' value too important to lose.

David's burgh of Peebles illustrates the continuing fondness for a specific choice of settlement site type: a place where waterways and valley bottoms meet, that is, a communications hub. At Peebles – a half-millennium before Edinburgh – a new town was developed beside, or bridging to, an old town.[7]

Peebles illustrates another standard urban planning feature or commonality – a wide main street lined by houses, each fronting a narrow, carefully measured 'lotted', or allotted, land.[8] Dumbarton's planners wanted this same formula, having been granted burgh status by King Alexander II in 1222; but geography dictated that the new burgh's plan, unusually, was necessarily curved around its shoreline to optimise the main street's length along its peninsular site.

Burghs often had a building of authority near one or both ends of the main street: perhaps a church (religious authority) or a secular authority – at Peebles, a royal castle. And from at least the thirteenth century, burghs had tolbooths (Berwick's is the earliest documented),[9] denoting civic authority, sometimes closing a main street, or simply on one side of the main street, as at Dunbar (where the tolbooth's crow-stepped detailing indicates a building or reconstruction date of c.1500). Tolbooths would typically have, at minimum, a ground-floor prison, with a hall above for meetings, official tasks and ceremony, plus a safe storage for the tolls from which they derived their name; and (like a church) a steeple or tower to signal their importance.

Street plans were sometimes contrived to swell outwards somewhere along their length, for markets, or sometimes (at Elgin and Edinburgh, for example) also for important buildings. Sometimes market places were splayed outwards on plan towards T-junctions creating triangular 'squares', as at Selkirk (made a royal burgh 1328, but a more ancient major settlement), or Stirling. Some burghs had architectural 'island' sites; these are sometimes said to be infills of unusually wide streets, but evidence to demonstrate that as a developmental process or fact seems unclear. Haddington exemplifies this feature, and Kelso too, except that at Kelso one end of the 'island' is an enormous open space, or square, terminated by the town's 'T-junction'. The reason for that square's scale is a puzzle, but it may relate to a legacy abbey boundary or enclosure, or perhaps to a reconstruction after the English invasion of 1545 when the abbey was 'owaier trowe' (overthrown), its towers undermined and the town burnt.[10]

David's Principal Burghs

By the time of David's death in 1153, seventeen communities had been granted burgh status, either by the king (royal burghs) or other elites, ecclesiastical or secular. David's four principal burghs were Edinburgh, Stirling, Berwick and Roxburgh, each having a royal castle on a naturally defensive site overlooking a suitable site for building a town. At the sister burgh of Canongate (absorbed by Edinburgh 1856) plus Edinburgh itself, one street connected the royal castle and the religious centre (soon also a royal residence), stressing the religious and secular powers enfolding the place, with the Castle having visual primacy, and the whole a metaphor for the bipartite power over the nation. A comparable arrangement, though minus the direct axial connection, was created for Elgin, whose high street extends towards the southern bounds of the Castle to the west, and the cathedral to the east. Like Inverness, Forres, or – later in the century, Inverurie – Elgin's creation was due to David's and his successors' plan of securing Moray within the consolidating kingdom.

Roxburgh and Berwick

Roxburgh and Berwick, at the other end of the country from Moray, were conceived for a different, non-military, peacetime strategy. It is possible that both were created by David when he was Prince of Cumbria (which then included southeast Scotland), before he became king in 1124, and each was given a carefully chosen site. They would be complementary wealth generators, connected (as was Peebles) by the transport route of the River Tweed: Roxburgh, the internal regional market,[11] would partner outward-facing maritime Berwick.

Roxburgh's medieval burgh seal displays impressive architecture, possibly a vast town gate (Roxburgh was walled), but clearly signalling architectural ambition.[12] Berwick, with its excellent natural harbour, quickly became Scotland's pre-eminent international maritime commercial centre, with an established cosmopolitan merchant community, and thus it was part of the north European maritime trading network. Berwick (or 'South Berwick' as it was sometimes then known) was Scotland's commercial 'capital' and the leading burgh in the twelfth and thirteenth centuries.[13]

The location chosen for both burghs was a site surrounded and protected on three sides by water, and at the entrance of each a protective royal castle was built, beside which (possibly from the outset) a fosse or ditch secured the town's fourth side. Roxburgh's (vast) castle stood at the narrow isthmus of the town's peninsular site (Fig. 2.1), but Berwick's promontory site had no isthmus, meaning that its fosse (partly surviving today and known as 'Spade's Mire'), was necessarily more extensive. At each, the area thus cordoned off included both a defined or walled town plus agricultural land – including 40 acres for common grazing in the case of thirteenth-century Berwick.[14]

Berwick's plan is said to have been set out during the time of David I by Mainard the Fleming, a king's burgess in the town, who thereafter set out the plan for St Andrews – each of these centres having had a pre-existing settlement, modernised and much-enhanced in the twelfth century.[15] At St Andrews, a trinity of three roads converge towards the religious/pilgrimage centre, while at commercial Berwick things seem reversed, as incoming roads passed satellite religious sites before converging at the river, the commercial hub.

At Roxburgh, the dramatically scaled and multi-towered Kelso Abbey was afterwards (1128) set on the riverbank opposite, to the east, on a lower site, distant but visible from both castle and town; a similar castle-to-abbey relationship or formula was seen at

FIGURE 2.1.
Roxburgh: lidar image, 2017, showing the peninsular site formed by the confluence of the rivers Teviot and Tweed. The castle (bottom) guarded the site's only landward approach, and beyond that the gridded street layout of the long-gone twelfth-century burgh is seen, bounded by the burgh ditch. (Copyright HES: https://canmore.org.uk/collection/1550233)

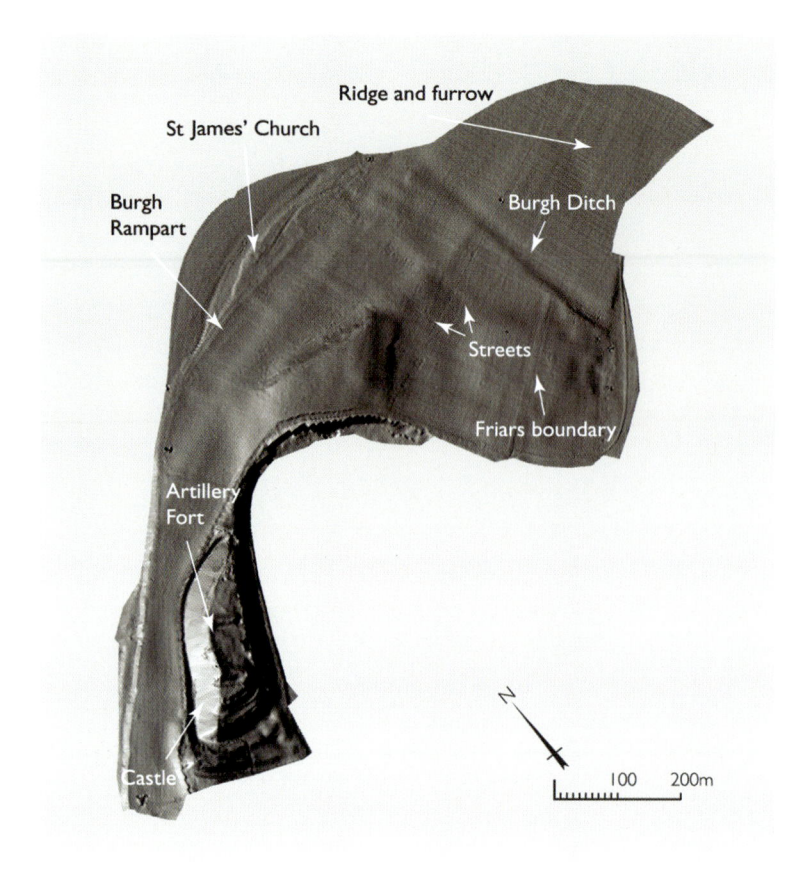

Stirling–Cambuskenneth (where a river also divided the view) and, as we saw, Edinburgh–Holyrood. This was a clear royal planning strategy – spreading these supreme architectural signals of royal power over the wide landscape underlined the 'universalism' of a royal authority that was confirmed (from less impressive locations) by the Church. Evidently Berwick – the only one of the four principal burghs not to receive the same treatment – was regarded differently. This was possibly because its role was different, being more a sort of 'capital', as noted above, or possibly because the geographical contours would have made the hierarchical arrangement difficult had an abbey been set east of the Castle. Otherwise, twelfth-century abbeys in that region were built at 'lesser' locations such as Melrose, Jedburgh and Dryburgh.

The story of medieval Berwick's town planning, though poorly documented, is more complicated than can be represented by the work of Mainard alone. The town plan comprises several discrete sequential elements, as was the case at medieval Perth.[16] Similarly, medieval Edinburgh's Royal Mile, however superficially resolute in its compliance with the 'masterplan', comprised discrete planning episodes.[17]

Berwick's 'main street', Marygate, seems almost like a burgh layout in its own right – being (like Dunbar and Peebles) approximately 20–25m wide and fairly straight, although slightly flared outwards at either end (perhaps initially to accommodate markets), and its houses front long rectangular plots. Marygate is punctuated at both ends, with the Town Hall at one end, where its tolbooth predecessor had stood since at least the thirteenth century, occupying the sort of prime axial position that 'planners' allotted major structures in burghs elsewhere, such as Peebles. It is possible that the old Marygate (rather like Church Street, to be discussed later) had narrowed as it approached the town centre, and that later its narrowest part was widened dramatically to become the burgh's premier street.

The proposition here is that Marygate's northeast side was rebuilt behind the backs of the former streetfront buildings, which had to be demolished to facilitate this development, and that its widening continued at least as far as the area opposite Golden Square where today the widening is abruptly interrupted. In contrast, Marygate's pre-existing southwest building line seems to have been retained in this putative replanning, given that its precise building line continues towards Woolmarket (previously, Crossgate, the road to the market cross),[18] which retains both that same alignment plus the old, narrow road-width. If this analysis is correct, and specific elements of Berwick's earlier medieval town plan can be distinguished from other phases, then when might Marygate's widening have been done?

There are three immediate suggestions. Most probably, it accompanied Berwick's designation as a burgh, meaning it was implemented in or around the 1120s for David (by Mainard?) in accord with both his town-planning ideals and his vision for a commerce-driven European Scotland. Alternatively, the widening could have been done at some point afterwards simply in response to Berwick's growing commercial success and consequential urban pressures – demanding, for example, an improved market area to match those in northern Europe, or the inevitable civic need for a tolbooth, which required a town centre location. Thirdly, a replanning might have accompanied a phase of necessary reconstruction such as that which followed the 1216 English attack and burning when the town's walls were extended and Berwick refortified (although this might rule out a role for Mainard).[19]

Church Street (formerly Suttergate),[20] as we saw, continues northwards from that same Marygate/Woolmarket junction. It widens towards Wallace Green and terminates abruptly, having been blocked as a cul-de-sac by the sixteenth-century town wall. Until then, Suttergate had probably been the main coastal road north (broadly, today's A1), traversing the pass at Pease.[21] However, the fact it was Marygate and not Suttergate which became the Tudor-period north gateway suggests it was already pre-eminent; much earlier, in 1301, when soldiers 'rode up the great street' towards the 'palys' (presumably within the Castle),[22] it seems unlikely this was other than the already much-widened Marygate.

Marygate continues northwards, and again widens, to become Castlegate, at the head of which is a road junction and triangular 'square': perhaps another market place. The main road continued beyond the medieval town boundary or wall[23] to the satellite settlement of Bondington (where Castle Terrace is now) where it divided into routes towards Duns/Melrose/Edinburgh or Kelso/Roxburgh. The junction beside the Castle provided a connection (via the modern High Green) to the coast road north. At this 'square', Berwick Castle had a town-plan relationship analogous to that of Melrose Abbey to Melrose's similarly triangular 'square' and intersecting road network, suggesting a further set of common principles concerning the planning of new towns. Stirling's market place was similarly placed as close to the Castle as could be, and likewise with a slope, helpful for drainage.

The street name 'Briggate' is recorded from the twelfth century, and by at least the 1160s a bridge spanned the Tweed.[24] Bridge Street seems a more obviously discrete planned element, being a straight connection with Hide Hill along the line of a former town wall (and possibly on reclaimed former shoreline), but continuing at its other end beyond the present bridge to the site of a predecessor bridge at Love Walk.[25]

A now mysterious circular place ('placea rotunda') at the western end of Hidegate was owned by the abbot of Jedburgh in 1296 within which was a property called 'la Roundele'.[26] Its intriguing structure seems unique within medieval Scotland. But it is unlikely that la Roundele had simply an ecclesiastical purpose, given that it had numerous rooms and cellars. This means we should probably resist

FIGURE 2.2.
(Opposite) Berwick-upon-Tweed: aerial view from the northwest, 1999, showing Elizabethan defences (centre), beyond which is Marygate, the former burgh's premier street, which may owe its broadened form to a twelfth-century replanning for David I. (Copyright HES: https://canmore.org.uk/collection/1761871)

the temptation to suggest it was a Crusader's version of Jerusalem's Holy Sepulchre (such as the circular version built by Simon of Senlis at Northampton, which David would have known).

1296, Warfare and a Collapsed Relationship

This story about crown-led modernisation, sophistication, urbanisation, commercialism and progress was the story of Scotland's 'Golden Age' of the twelfth to thirteenth centuries. Since 1266 (under King Alexander III whose queen, Margaret, was sister to the future Edward I) Scotland had been at peace with its neighbours, generating wealth, and creating innovative and expensive buildings; and Scots (according to the *Melrose Chronicle*) considered Edward of England 'the flower of the chivalry of the whole world', 'that true treasure of Christ'.[27]

That story needs to be counter-balanced by the bad news story, however. Relations between Scotland and England had always been broadly cordial, with no warfare between the two since 1217. All this soured from 1291, and in 1296 Edward, now King Edward I of England, annexed Berwick, massacred its people, and invaded Scotland with the intention of absorbing it within England. There ended Scotland's Golden Age.

As for the lucrative Roxburgh–Berwick axis: Roxburgh returned to the plough and today is an archaeological site; and Berwick became a provincial frontier stronghold, 'neither accepted as English nor able to be Scottish',[28] but permanently English from 1482. Maps help to evidence the two burghs' decline: both are present on Matthew Paris's mid-thirteenth-century map, and both are absent from Thomaso Porcacchi's map of 1572 where instead Duns is highlighted.[29]

Edward's initial idea to replan Berwick was unfulfilled[30] because, to England, Berwick's possession was less commercial than symbolic and strategic, valuable as anti-Scottish economic warfare and as a military base. So (as argued above) the street plan of Scotland's greatest burgh of the twelfth to thirteenth centuries largely survives.

From 1296, centuries of intermittent invasion and war damage followed. Roxburgh Castle was held by the English almost continuously from 1296 to 1460 (albeit recaptured in 1318 and 1342 when held briefly by the Scots). It was dismantled by the Scots in 1460 and again fortified by the English in the 1540s and 1650s. Its military attributes and the symbolism of its possession gave it a psychological value to the English almost comparable with that provided by Berwick; and perhaps partly because of this the town was abandoned, to be replaced by an enlarged Kelso. Without a town to dominate, the symbolism of possessing Roxburgh Castle diminished.

The Scots tried repeatedly to win back Berwick because of its vital importance to them, but England had a stronger army. The ongoing warfare impacted on north Europe's trade, of course, but was economically, socially and architecturally devastating to Scotland. After another English invasion in 1385, for example, Melrose Abbey was rebuilt by Paris mason John Morow, only to be wrecked again in the 1540s invasions (the 'Rough Wooings'), when the region was again devastated.

Reflecting on that age of warfare, Donnelly opined 'The years up to 1296 in Scotland . . . had witnessed population growth and economic output never seen again before the eighteenth century.'[31] Merriman considered that the impact of the 1540s war damage was measured by the fact Haddington's kirk was not reroofed until 1978;[32] yet the kirk still lacks its Imperial crown spire (one of several such Renaissance spires, the best-known being that of St Giles', Edinburgh). The symbolic crown was presumably dismantled as a hazard to artillerymen when the tower became a gun platform in the 1540s.[33]

The consequences of this incessant warfare raise a question rarely asked. How is the obvious handicap to Scotland's economic and architectural development, and the corresponding demand to rebuild, reflected in its towns and buildings? Have we looked beyond the ruins of abbeys and castles? Of course, Robert I rebuilt or repaired Dunfermline Palace and Abbey, and in 1318 he attended the consecration of St Andrews Cathedral (which may still have been partly incomplete). But what else was reconstructed?

As shown by their late Renaissance ornament and rebuilding dates, some tower-houses were made habitable again and aggrandised after the 1540s (notably from the 1570s onwards – for instance, Cowdenknowes, 1574). But did anything positive in terms

FIGURE 2.3.
(Opposite) Duns: sketch illustrating the medieval town with extensions along the main roads in/out of the town and the wider Newtown Street, plus the slip road created when this street was blocked by estate consolidation. It is possible that Duns's new town dates from the later 1480s, after Berwick was permanently lost to England, or was possibly part of the sixteenth-century post-war reconstruction of the region. (Cartography: Helen Stirling; map based on 1824 map of Duns by John Wood, National Library of Scotland)

of urban planning/replanning happen, as was the case with twentieth-century Europe's post-war reconstructions (and as hinted above in respect of Berwick)? Here we are not simply considering what was not, or could not be, built, because of wars. With little or nothing reaching the scale of the thirteenth-century's paradigms for two or three centuries, reconstructions so frequently necessary, and opportunities for some burghs to fill commercial vacuums left by others, what developments, if any, are seen in urban planning of the late medieval/Renaissance age? Did pre-existing tenures mean everything was simply, inexpensively and uninventively rebuilt along the old plans? There was an entire reconstruction programme necessary for the eastern Borders after the 1540s invasions alone. What is the legacy of that programme?

Duns

Tradition claims that, after destruction by an English army in 1545, Duns was rebuilt on a new site.[34] There is no documentation to support that, but the contemporary military report, which names 287 places in the area 'brent [burnt], raced [rased], and cast doune', itemises 'the towre of Dunce raced, Dounce Lawe . . . the towne of Dounce'.[35] It is in fact the formerly discrete settlement of Duns Law which no longer exists, having perhaps never been rebuilt after that attack.

Duns' plan shows the 'island' formula noticed above, a logical road network and a coherent medieval-type plan (Fig. 2.3). At its north is Newtown Street, a wide street called 'Dunse new Town' in 1744,[36] and planned so as to relate exactly to the pre-existing town plan. As it lacked buildings denoting authority, it cannot be the equivalent to 'New Town' Peebles, or even Berwick's Marygate, each of which, on plan, it superficially resembles. Newtown's west end (formerly a road that would have led northwest, over the Lammermuirs, to Edinburgh) was blocked by estate consolidation, meaning Newtown was not prized by the landowner as an estate adornment. Therefore, it was an urban expansion – town planning – made between the ages of the earliest burghs and the 'Planned Town Movement'.

TOWN OF DUNSE
1824

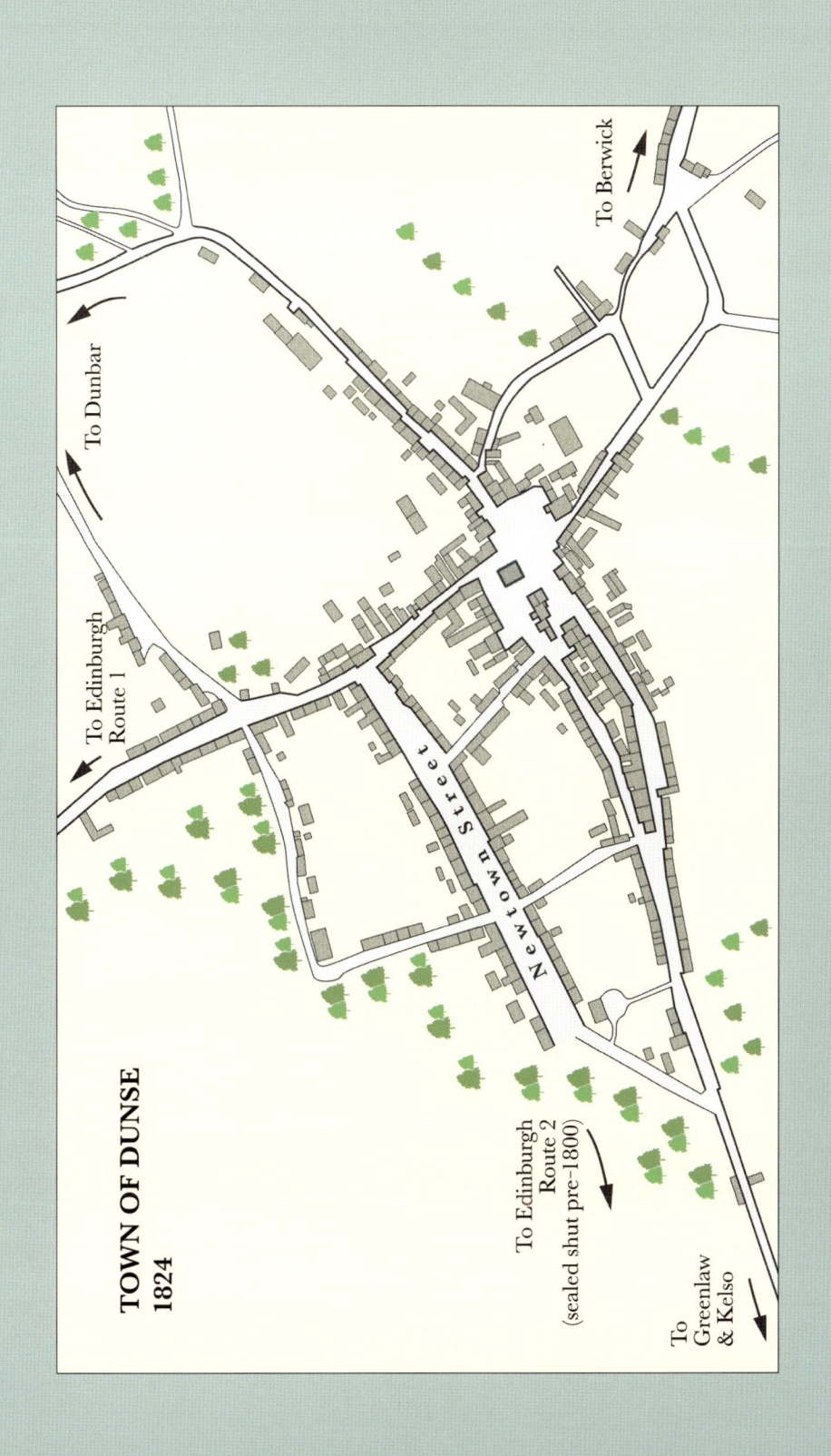

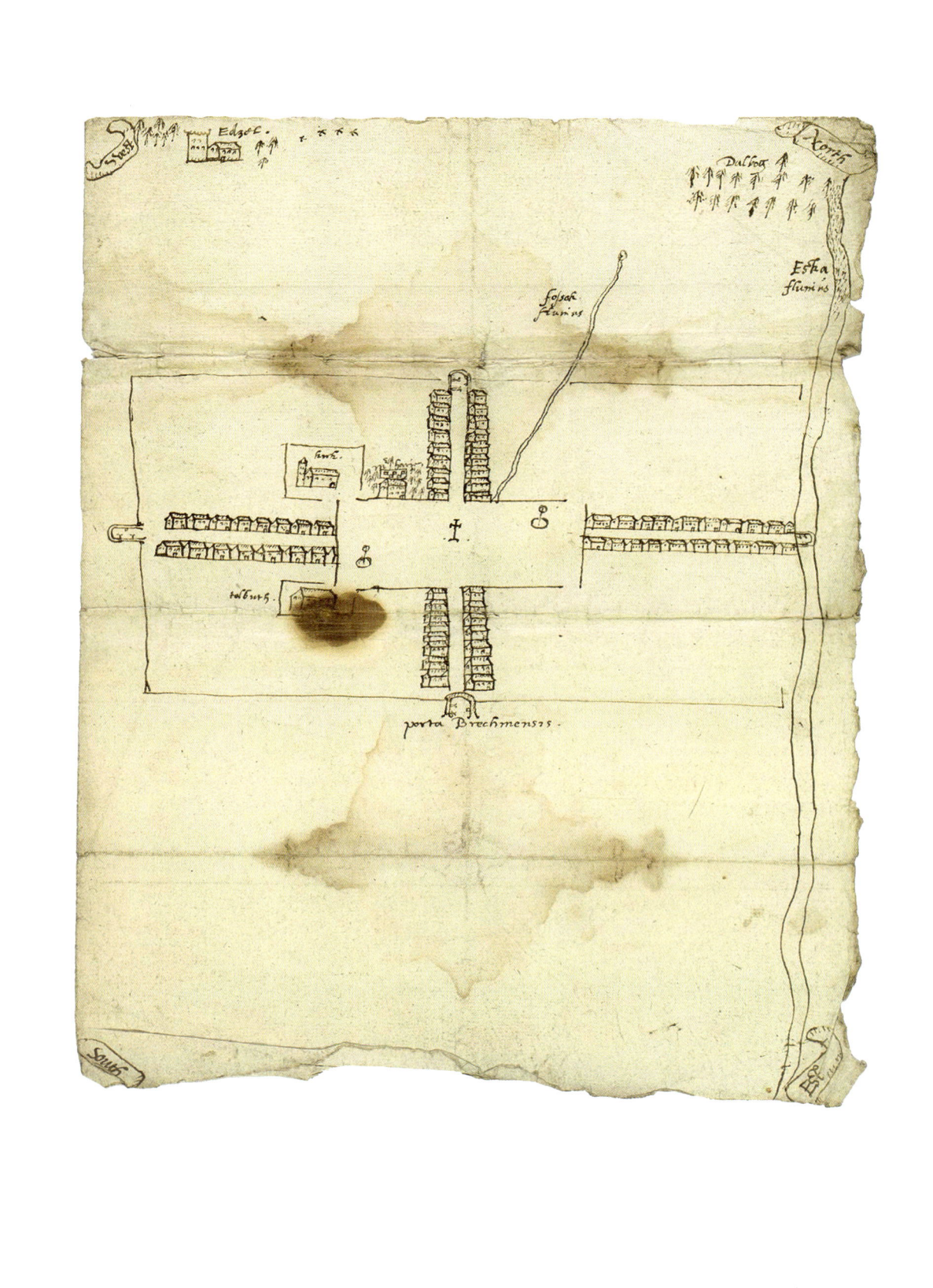

West Edzel Dulbog North
  Esha flumis
  fossah flumis
  kirk
  tolbuth
  porta Brechmensis
South East

But is a more precise date to be found? Does this expansion represent Duns new burgh taking on some former commercial duties of Roxburgh–Berwick, as Porcacchi's map may indicate? Did it follow Duns becoming a burgh of barony 1489–90, directly after Berwick's final loss? Or following Duns becoming the regional administrative centre in 1661? Or should we reconsider tradition, and ask if Newtown (and not Duns itself) is a Renaissance-age post-war reconstruction and plan, perhaps a response to a need to accommodate the community from Duns Law? Such questions need to be asked, of both Duns and elsewhere, because their answers will increase understanding of Renaissance Scotland's new town planning.

FIGURE 2.4.
(Opposite) Edzell: projected 'new Citie of Edzel' as intended by Sir David Lindsay, Lord Edzell, 1592. (Copyright Lord Balneil and the Balcarres Heritage Trust)

THE LATE RENAISSANCE

Around 1600, new towns – effectively, colonial plantations – were built in the Highlands: Stornoway, a burgh in 1607, and Campbeltown, established 1609. Campbeltown has a traditional-type main street connecting the harbour to the onetime Earl of Argyll's castle (where Castlehill Church is now), and a tolbooth. Stromness, in Orkney, was developed from the 1620s, where instead of shoreside houses having lotted lands they have piers and slipways, because wealth was from the sea.[37]

These new towns aligned with James VI's aims to underline his authority and modernise 'remoter' areas, especially after the monarchy's emigration to England in 1603. But these were not the first planned towns of James's reign.

In 1592, a new town – 'citie' – of Edzell was planned for Sir David Lindsay, who is best-known today for Edzell Castle's rhetorical Renaissance garden.[38] Lindsay had engaged German expertise to exploit his mineral resources. Housing would follow, and the Edzell plan was a consequence of that anticipated need. The intention was to have four streets in a cross-plan, each leading from a rectangular central *place* – like some of medieval France's bastide towns – church and laird's house in one quadrant, tolbooth opposite. Edzell's houses would presumably be 'normal' and two-storeyed – suggesting stone? This throws up another issue.

Scotland's architectural historians have generally disliked suggesting that buildings other than castles or public structures might pre-date the eighteenth century. But Edzell makes us ask what masons built when they weren't building elite structures. Does burgh housing contain ancient stone walling, disguised by modernisation to appear of later date? Is there any, or little, ancient walling? Or lots?

Changing Hierarchies

Hierarchies, change and continuity – and a variable primacy between religious or secular authority – are clearer to assess. Again, at Peebles, by the later eighteenth century, when the Hanoverian monarchy was secured and royal absence from Scotland was normalised, the royal castle was long obsolete. But the psychological and townscape values of the site continued, and an establishment church (built 1784) and a jail (c.1780) invaded the former castle site.[39] (A similar process is noted above, at Campbeltown, where the church was rebuilt on the premier site after the ducal family no longer required it.)

Inveraray

Edinburgh shares with Inveraray a premier ranking among planned towns. Both church and castle were located within Inveraray's medieval town, but for the 3rd Duke of Argyll's post-1743 reconstructions, the castle site was supreme. The church and town were exiled to a shared new site, the new church having primacy only within the relocated town. The new castle and new town faced each other in perpetual display of hierarchy, precisely as Edinburgh's castle overlooked both the Old and New Towns, where it still today articulates martial and royal control. Inveraray Castle's Gothic design signalled the absentee laird's continuing ancient entitlements, while its fosse was a practical defence, such protection being thought necessary until the defeat of Jacobitism in 1746, when the militarised challenge to the Hanoverian establishment was permanently extinguished. Shortly afterwards, New Town Edinburgh further emphasised establishment hierarchy by celebrating establishment power in street names (George Street, Queen Street, and so on) – contrasting with the old utilitarian street names such as 'West Port'.

Continuing Recovery

Meanwhile, early-modern Scotland was growing wealthy again – especially Edinburgh, Berwick's successor as powerhouse – through commerce, mortgaging, property, manufacture and trade, while Leith adopted Berwick's old but ended maritime duties. The 'Edinburgh–Leith' relationship slightly resembled the old Roxburgh–Berwick axis, and was a direct consequence of the latter partnership's having been forcibly terminated.[40]

All this brings us to the period after direct English economic hostility, and to the age of planned towns, which, as already stated, is well published elsewhere, and so outwith the scope of this chapter. Yet new urbanising continued afterwards, with diverse industry-driven motivators, such as distilling, developed in 'remoter' places. In the 1760s Bowmore was the first island 'planned town' (Stornoway, as argued above, having been more of a colonial venture), but Islay's distillery villages continued being built up till Bunnahabhain in 1881, each planted in 'remote', Romantic, but navigable places.

A rare UK government work was the new town of Gretna, built from 1916 to serve a munitions factory; it was accessible by rail and, being on the west, 'safer' from potential air assault. An exemplar English Garden City town, resembling Letchworth, Gretna was built by English architects including Raymond Unwin.

Urban planning by Scots outwith Scotland would constitute a separate study. A possible example from the 1690s may have been the trading and colonising venture that – denied access to its initial target territories in Africa and India – foundered at Darien (modern Panama), and to which architects Sir William Bruce (c.1625–1710) and Master James Smith (c.1645–1731) subscribed. The Darien House in Edinburgh was a handsome classical structure, and it seems likely that some form of housing was planned for the intended colony. Afterwards, British Empire settlements frequently referenced the homeland – seldom more explicitly than Dunedin (discussed elsewhere in this volume).

Back to Edinburgh

Now we return to Edinburgh to highlight, firstly, four non-New Town episodes in its planning history, and then to notice a shift in New Town builders' political signalling.

James VII's Charter, 1688

Firstly, in 1688, King James VII granted Edinburgh a charter providing for civic improvement and expansion north and south: anticipating bridges, 'buildings, spaces, houses and streets', compulsory purchase, stone pavements and street lighting.[41] King James's forfeiture in 1689 and 'the alteration of the government'[42] stalled that energy until the 1760s – and instead, urban planning from 1689 included the anti-Jacobite fort and linear satellite town at Fort William, plus reconstruction of war-tattered Dunkeld and the fortification of Inverness. Scotland had plunged into what would be over a half-century's intermittent civil warfare, which the new monarchy and its British army would win. Establishment hostility from 1689 was directed towards the more evidently pro-Stuart/Jacobite Highlands, where fortifications and counter-fortifications were built. Fort William, and the new town alongside, initially called Maryburgh, were named in honour of the new monarchs. The fort was a reconstruction of a 1650s English one, and the reason for selecting that location was indicated in 1691 by the fort's governor, Colonel John Hill: 'this being the center off the Highlands, and neer to which all the men of actione are';[43] it was from there that soldiers were sent to implement the royal order to massacre the people of Glencoe, in 1692, the new regime's idea of an 'Example of justice & severity'.[44]

James Smith's Counter-Reformation Canongate Kirk (1688–9) is the clearest executed example of King James's ideas impacting on Edinburgh's town planning. (His Thistle Chapel within the Abbey, destroyed by anti-Catholic rioters in 1688, hardly impacted on urban planning.) Unbuilt Smith projects, including domed churches, might have been intended for a baroque Stuart New Town rather than the sober Hanoverian one we have.[45]

Picardy

Secondly, in 1730, Alexander McGill designed Edinburgh's – or Scotland's – first symmetrical neo-classical terrace: a planned village comprising thirteen houses (replaced in the 1800s by Picardy Place) and named Picardy because it was constructed for weavers imported from Saint-Quentin (Picardie region of northeast France), whose duties were to develop the linen industry.[46] A taller centre house was for the enterprise's main French figure, Nicolas D'Assaville.

Old Town

Thirdly, to return to the Old Town: Parliament Close, created in the 1630s as a prestigious and possibly stone-flagged area, was made a French-type *place royale* in 1685 by installing a statue of the king. The statue was of Charles II, who died while the project was in hand, but whether the impetus came from Charles, from the future King James, the Town Council, or from elsewhere, remains unclear.

Connecting to the New Town necessitated replanning the affected parts of the Old Town. For example, the creation of South Bridge was accompanied by the creation of Hunter Square: a 1780s space bounded by neo-classical buildings. One of the buildings was the 1630s Tron Kirk, which was much rebuilt, converted from streetscape to a standalone building faced entirely (expensively) in dressed ashlar, with an entirely new classical façade to the new square.[47]

Dean Village

Fourthly, Well Court (1883–6) within Dean Village was an innovative, utopian workers' development with housing and social spaces; it was the creation of philanthropist John Ritchie Findlay, the style a revived Scots, the whole a little planned village in its own right. The buildings all sported Scots Renaissance detailing; there was a Stirling Tolbooth-type steeple, Earl's Palace oriels, and the houses were lofty, traditional tenements. Well Court's pretty architecture was due to the talent of its designer, the architect A.G. Sydney Mitchell (1856–1930), but driven by the fact that Findlay's own house overlooked

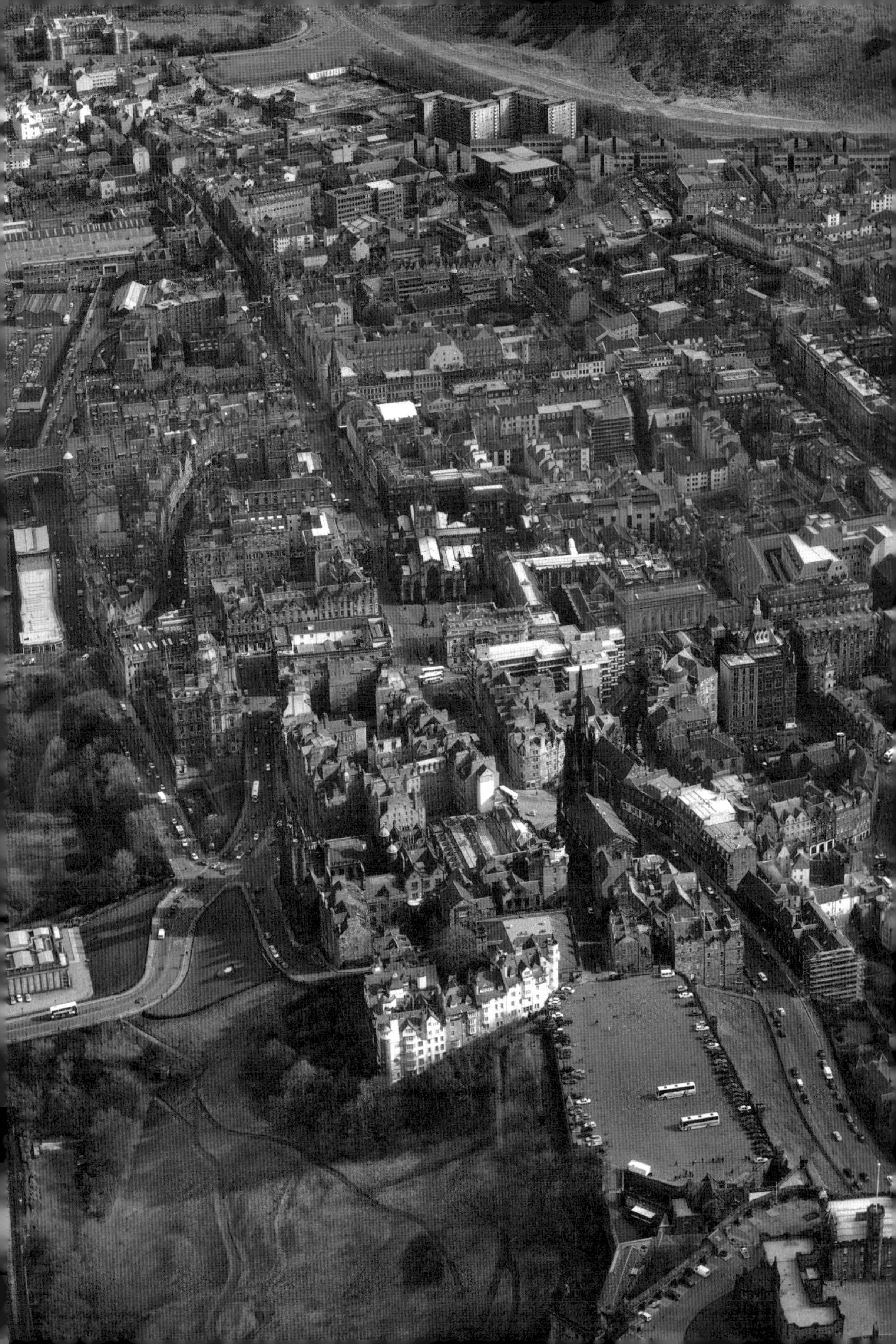

the place meaning that its appearance, and use of a clearly 'national' style, were the priority.[48]

Scottish National Portrait Gallery

This chapter closes with a return to the New Town and to John Ritchie Findlay. Findlay's initiatives included the Old Town's *Scotsman* building, complete with a mammoth masthead inscription blaring towards the New Town, and creation of the Scottish National Portrait Gallery in York Place, designed by Robert Rowand Anderson (1834–1921). This was an 1880s Gothic building, within, and wholly contrasting with, the stripped classicism of the New Town.

The New Town stood apart: neither a wholly new Edinburgh, nor a replacement or extension, but instead a supplement to its Old Town. In dressed ashlar it visualised a substitute for lost status – once a capital, now a provincial northern city. It celebrated establishment triumph in its very streetscape through insistent reference to Hanoverian monarchy and British union in its street names, sneering perhaps at crushed Jacobitism, because establishment contempt for Jacobitism was still strong in 1770s Edinburgh. This was before what our generation can regard as the rational counter-politics of Jacobitism had fully mutated into harmless Romanticism and Highlandism.

Now, for the first time, New Town norms were challenged ideologically by a counter-style and by a building which celebrated Scotland's past, including its centuries-long age of independence, with a 'hall of heroes'. The main doorway was framed by statues of Sir William Wallace, Guardian of Scotland, and King Robert Bruce: heroes not of establishment orthodoxy, New Town street names and union with England, but of Scotland's Wars of Independence against England, when Berwick was lost.

FIGURE 2.5.
(Opposite) Edinburgh Old Town: aerial view from the west, 1994, showing the Royal Mile, which since the twelfth century has connected the Castle (bottom) to Holyrood Abbey and the Palace of Holyroodhouse (top), the Castle and Abbey being visible from each other. The Castle was within the burgh of Edinburgh, Holyrood within the sister burgh of Canongate.
(Copyright HES: https://canmore.org.uk/collection/1060107)

CONCLUSION

As stated above, this chapter intentionally avoids both the New Towns Movement and the post-war new towns such as the internationally acclaimed Cumbernauld. But it does highlight that, before the end of the thirteenth century, Scotland contained numerous well-established 'new town' burghs which generated an increasingly powerful economy, and in turn an ambitious and accomplished architecture on a scale and quality comparable with that of England or France. That architectural ambition was exemplified by St Andrews Cathedral – almost as lengthy as some French cathedrals such as Notre Dame, albeit lacking their loftiness. This was a 'Golden Age' which ended with the destruction of Berwick's central role in delivering the means of Scotland's conspicuous wealth, followed by centuries of economically crippling neighbour action.

Initially, architecture after 1296 was significantly more modest than before, though wealth returned in the Early Modern era. Arguably, not until Union-age Scotland after 1707 – with England in controlling possession of, and therefore with a stake in, the country – was English economic hostility modified, a new economic management of the country implemented and the New Towns Movement dramatically unleashed.

The Scottish phase of England's Berwick has been highlighted as a rather neglected topic deserving consideration by the archaeologist and historian; and two further, connected, areas have been suggested for more in-depth study: is there evidence of Renaissance-period post-war urban planning/replanning to match the post-war castle and abbey reconstructions? We know reconstructions took place, as in, say, post-war Germany. If we look, might we identify lesser structures surviving from that wider period?

It is argued too that hierarchies in town planning applied in David I's time as much as in that of 1740s Inveraray (or today), with an interplay between ecclesiastical and secular authority, as social elites (kings, lairds) commanded greater sites than the Church. Peebles illustrates the shift from royal to ecclesiastical and parliamentary control paradigms on the burgh's pre-eminent site. Scottish royal presence was clearly long over by the eighteenth century, an age when Jacobite sympathies had not been extinguished after attempts to reclaim the throne for the Stuarts, with Scotland still in disgrace, as it were. Therefore the Church – which safeguarded establishment interests and prayed for Hanoverian monarchs – and the justice system which likewise served, or protected, the establishment – could move in to dominate the street scene and display their authority.

And back to New Town Edinburgh: a symbol of progress supposedly possible only through erasing both Jacobitism and a political Scotland. The orthodoxy promulgated by Walter Scott, of Scotland as a Romantic but rather expunged place of the past, was now challenged head-on by the National Portrait Gallery. This new building instead signalled the concept of Scotland as an accomplished ancient nation, with its own ancient monarchy and a continuous flow of heroes – resurrecting, above all, the pre-union cult of martial heroes. It was an early signal of the reassertion of a viable political Scotland that is debated today.

Had it not been for the loss of Berwick, and the stifling of Roxburgh, there would have been less of an Edinburgh. This book to celebrate Scotland's greatest urban initiative since David I – the New Town of Scotland's capital – might have been a book about Berwick, not Edinburgh.

This chapter has highlighted that Edinburgh is 'Edinburgh as we know it' only because of Berwick's exit from 1296. But the main point is that Scotland, over centuries, pursued innovation, improvement, commerce, European/neighbour contact, wealth generation, and was an urbanising land of (ideally, stone-built) planned towns. The still-undead clichéd Romantic stereotype of a land of hills and Highland cattle must be set beside an anti-Romantic reality of a wealth-generating urban dynamic which can be evidenced to have existed, overcome stern challenges and driven the country for a near-millennium. And it takes nothing from the importance of Edinburgh's New Town to say so.

Acknowledgements

I am grateful to Linda Bankier for advice concerning the history of medieval Berwick, and to Lord Balneil and the Balcarres Heritage Trust for access to the Crawford family's archive and for permission to reproduce the image of Edzell.

CHAPTER 3

City and State in the Designs of the 6th Earl of Mar

Margaret Stewart

Following his leadership of the failed 1715 Jacobite Rising, John Erskine, the 6th and 11th Earl of Mar (1675–1732), lived the remainder of his life in exile on the Continent. Between 1722 and 1726 he wrote a constitutional plan based on the idea of a federation of Scotland, England, Ireland and France. Its principal aims were to dissipate the risk of intercontinental warfare and competition for trade between the UK and France. His plan included the dissolution of the 1707 Treaty of Union between Scotland and England, and 'to strengthen Ireland [and Scotland] against its jealous neighbours [England]'. The four new states were to be consolidated by the establishment of their own free parliaments, judiciaries, national banks, religious toleration and infrastructure projects.[1] This short chapter and the accompanying maps illustrate the city plans for London (Fig. 3.1), Paris (Fig. 3.2) and Edinburgh (Fig. 3.3). Mar employed his considerable skills as a landscapist to complement his constitutional plan and included city proposals as articles in his constitutional plan. The schemes illustrated here are digital reconstructions based on Mar's own surviving written descriptions held in archives in the UK.

London

For Mar 'the happy situation of London has been the principal cause of the glory and riches of England'. His primary aim was, in anticipation of King James VIII and III's restoration to his ancient kingdom, to construct a magnificent new palace on the site of Buckingham House, and a new royal villa in Hyde Park, both, of course, to be designed by Mar himself (Fig. 3.1).[2] Mar would also have known the plans by Christopher Wren, Nicholas Hawksmoor, William Talman and John Evelyn, who had all drawn up schemes following the great fire of 1660, and there are visible similarities between Wren's and Mar's plans, although as we shall see regarding his Edinburgh plan there were precedents nearer his own time that he would, as a well-travelled European, have consulted. According to Mar, the citizens would have new wide streets, fresh air, public gardens, theatres and academies to boost their pride in England's and their monarch's achievements. To improve amenity the low-lying ground between the Thames and Hyde Park was to be laid out as gardens and parks intersected by canals so that the king's barge could take him from his front door to the River Thames and then upriver to Hampton Court Palace. The Hyde Park villa was to have gardens with fountains fed by reservoirs to the north. There was to be another residential district towards Arlington Street, and the land between it and St James's Park was for aristocratic houses with extensive gardens. The road network was to be improved, new streets cut through Westminster to St Paul's Cathedral, a new main thoroughfare to extend southwest to Richmond, and another on the northeast side to Greenwich. Southwark's industrial-trading function was to be improved by constructing a network of canals to link its two river frontages and increase the number of quays for warehouses. The river bank opposite Whitehall was to become public gardens serving Southwark's growing industrial population. The scheme was well adapted to London's role as a rising mercantile centre in the 1720s, and the potential for water transportation was fully exploited.

FIGURE 3.1.
(Overleaf) London: the (unexecuted) scheme anticipates a villa and a palace for King James VIII and III returning from his long exile. It also addresses London's current problem of controlling new developments, the separation of residential and industrial areas and its communication networks. (Digital reconstruction on facsimile of John Rocque's *Map of London*, 1741–5. Copyright Margaret Stewart and Leah Hanks, 2013)

Paris

Like London, the Paris plan (Fig. 3.2) was primarily concerned with the site of the royal palace but London, Mar said, was a low-lying city that could develop canal systems, whereas Paris would

Proposal by the 6th Earl of Mar for the improvement of London, 1722–27

- Canal/reservoir
- Lock
- Street
- Residential
- Building
- Bridge
- Plantation
- Embankment

Old Mother Red Caps
PANCRAS
TOTTENHAM COURT
LAMBS CONDUIT FIELDS
White Conduit House
Frog Hall
ST JAMES'S PARK
TOTTHILL FIELDS
NEWINGTON
LOCK FIELDS
KENNINGTON
Walworth
Camberwell Mill
Lamastre Lane
NORTH FIELD
LOUGHBOROUGH HOUSE
Lambeth Bridge

Legend:
- Canal/reservoir
- Lock
- Street
- Residential
- Building
- Bridge
- Plantation

FIGURE 3.2.
Paris: by including schemes already underway or already on the drawing board during his stay near Paris in the 1720s, Mar discloses his intimate knowledge of current planning in Louis XV's royal works. (Digital reconstruction on Roussel's map, 1730–39. Copyright Margaret Stewart and Leah Hanks, 2013)

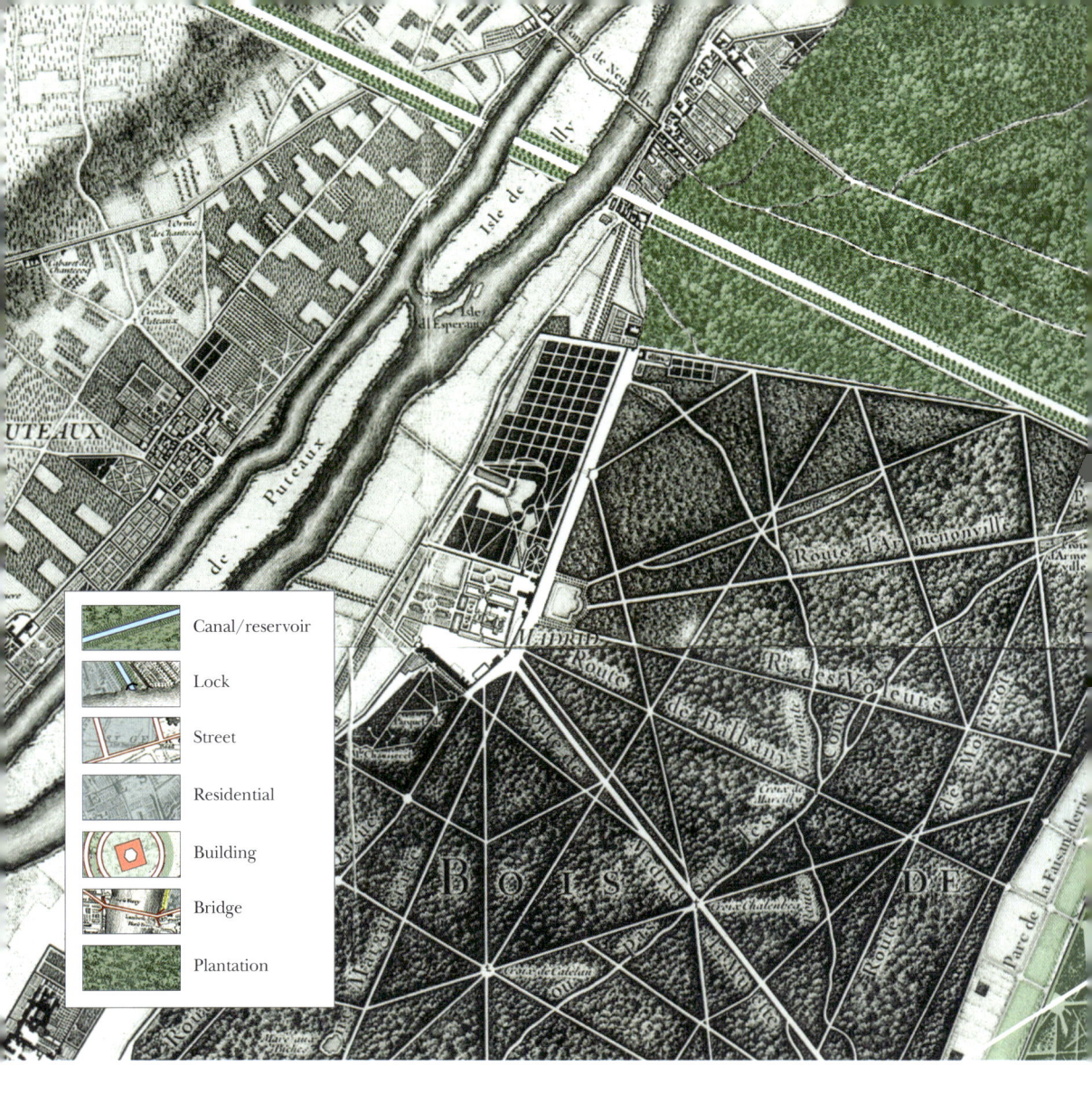

benefit from building a new palace on the Hill of Chaillot, where 'the observation of so fine a situation for their principal pallace' had 'escaped' the king's architects.[3]

France had been the forcing bed for the development of European urbanism since the mid seventeenth century, and the earliest modern civic panorama terrace was the Cours-la-Reine, created along the banks of the Seine in 1616. Cartesian geometry enabled the creation of axial planning, circuses, terraces and the new urban *places* devised by André le Nôtre (1613–1700) for Louis XIV. Further unexecuted plans to connect the royal town of Saint-Germain-en-Laye with the Tuileries Palace, and the palace of Versailles with the

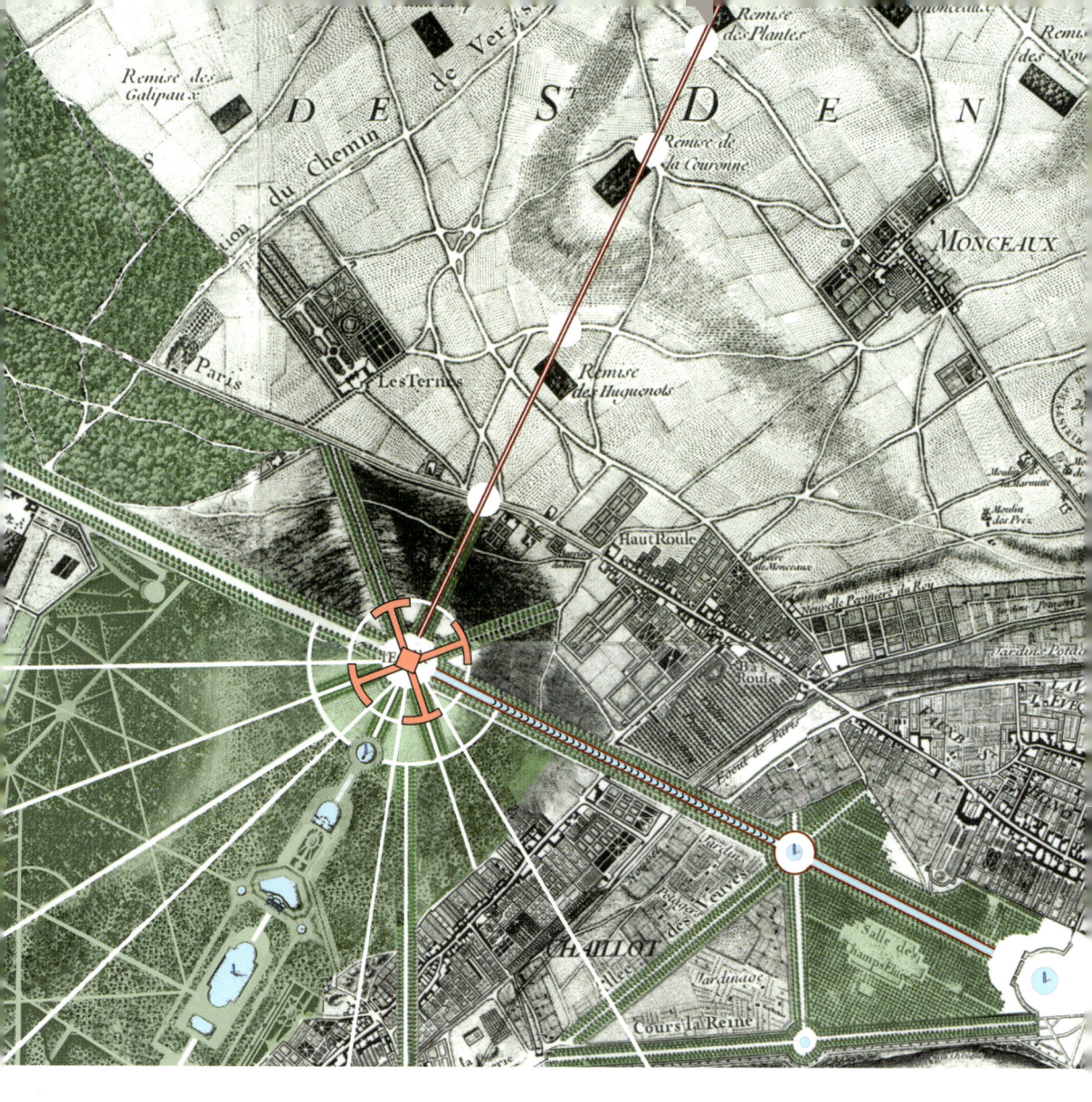

Louvre in the heart of Paris were proposed. Le Nôtre had even imagined sea-going vessels docking in the Grand Canal at Versailles.[4] However, Mar's proposal provided a new dimension – the importance of the king's outlook over Paris and the Île-de-France, as well as the view towards the king's palace.

Mar said in his manuscript that he drew out his plans for London and Paris on Guillaume Delisle's maps and that Delisle submitted these to a meeting of the Académie Royale des Sciences in Paris.[5] Though the original plans are lost, the records of the Académie corroborate Mar's claim. In 1725 Delisle was the most distinguished cartographer in France. His maps of Paris and London were largely concerned with showing his calculation of the meridian and with exact comparative measurements of the dimensions of the two cities. Mar's name was not acknowledged in his presentation but that these were the same plans on which they had collaborated is evident from the description: Delisle had obtained precise survey details from a friend in London for the districts of Southwark and Westminster, and he describes the plans as including '*les nouvelles augmentations de cette ville*'.[6] In 1730 Delisle's meridian plans came up for discussion again in the Académie and here the reference is more explicit – the commentator, M. Davall, mentions that both plans showed certain new buildings for the cities.[7] Davall adds that the plans were not deposited in the archives but belonged to a M. Bauch, a pupil of M. Delisle.[8] There is no mention in the Académie records of Delisle drawing out the Edinburgh plan for Mar.

Paris and London were to be mutually symbolic and formal and, like Mar's landscape schemes, they were conceived on a grandiloquent scale. Mar's model was French *aménagement* which Louis XIV had hoped in vain might reinvent France as a modern commercial state.[9] By the later eighteenth century, transportation, health and the prominent positioning of educational and public buildings began to overtake monarchical display as the primary aim of civic design. This was the sort of city the Scots patriot and polemicist Andrew Fletcher of Saltoun had envisaged in the first decade of the eighteenth century. Fletcher compared London favourably with Edinburgh, in the context of his engagement in, and deep hostility to, the proposed treaty of Union between the two parliaments.[10] Mar's constitutional plan is an adaptation of some of Fletcher's ideas about federal union and the economic potential of cities, but in terms of layout and planning Mar was in the vanguard of the new urbanism that was just emerging in the European capitals in the early decades of the eighteenth century. He proposed what we regard nowadays as mandatory in civic design – controlled decentralised expansion, transport networks and compulsory purchase for the public good. His urbanism was strongly French in its dynamic geometry, and as far back as 1709 he had imitated Versailles's 'zoning' for the design he made for his 'New Town' at Alloa, at his Lowland estate in Scotland.[11] He further developed this in the plans for London and Edinburgh by segregating the residential, bureaucratic, trading and industrial quarters and, most innovatively, in providing public parks for the cities' populaces.

Mar wrote his plan in 1725 at about the time when the Avenue des Champs-Élysées was created but before the avenue was extended to Neuilly. He included this extension and suggested an even further lengthening across the river to the hill at Chantecoq. He also suggested that all the land to the north and east of the Bois de Boulogne as far as Passy and the Château of Meudon should be made part of the royal parks. Essentially, the scheme provided an intersection between the Avenue des Champs-Élysées and the Avenue de Neuilly with a new avenue connecting Saint-Ouen and Meudon. He also proposed new gardens for the palace and a long cascade down the centre of the Avenue des Champs-Élysées. The Louvre, he said, could now be used for 'accademies, Coleges, Theaters and [for] other public uses . . . and the Gardens of the Thuileries might still continue to serve for the public walk for that end of the Town.' He proposed two kinds of panorama terrace – one encircling the Palace, and two straight ones running along the long east and west sides of the hill of Chaillot.[12] These would allow the king to see in every direction, along the windings of the Seine with its bridges, and out across the Île-de-France. This was a scheme of beautification, and its only practical function, apart from the improved road network, was to provide reservoirs along the apex of the Hill of Chaillot to feed the king's fountains and supply water to the city.

Edinburgh

King James VII and II, when he was still Duke of Albany and York and was resident at Holyrood House as Royal Commissioner to the Scottish Parliament between 1679 and 1682, proposed several city improvements. He advocated the construction of a new town on the Bearford's Park, the site which later became Craig's New Town. In order to link the site with the Old Town, a bridge was essential, and it would undoubtedly have been constructed at that time had the Scottish Parliament not decided that James had forfeited his crown and was no longer king in 1689.[13]

Edinburgh comprises a series of plateaus and hills running east to west that inhibit movement between the north and south sides of the city. Taking up and enlarging James's proposal, Mar proposed levelling the topography by constructing not one but two high-arched bridges over the Cowgate and the Nor' Loch. This would facilitate transport of heavy building materials to the new site. He suggested a grid plan (Fig. 3.3) with panorama terraces – one on the north taking in views of the Firth of Forth and Fife, and one on the south towards St Giles' crown steeple, the Castle and the Old Town. Cross-streets in the new grid would emphasise directional views and the two towns would become a single spectacle. To preserve the outlook he suggested that building along the outward faces of the terraces, on the bridges and on the slopes of Arthur's Seat should be forbidden. Calton Hill and Holyrood Park were to be commercial woodland plantations divided by avenues and circuses in all directions. A new southern suburb for family villas with gardens was to be built roughly where the Grange district is now. These southern districts were essential to preserve the Old Town as the mercantile and civic heart of Edinburgh.[14] Looking at Mar's plan it is easy to see that aspects of it were incorporated into the final plan of 1767. Craig and his advisers omitted the southern districts but they were eventually begun in the last decade of the eighteenth century.

For Edinburgh Mar looked to the Scottish Historical Landscape, a style of landscaping that acknowledged the historic sense of place by highlighting natural features and historic monuments using formal avenues. Directed vistas and panorama terraces had been used as the organisational principle for rural landscapes in Scotland since the later seventeenth century, and Mar had further developed this style at Alloa between 1702 and 1715. The next we know of a further proposal following the Duke of Albany and York's of 1688 is in 1715, when Sir George Drummond, the city's enterprising provost, described in a letter to King George I

> [the] sad ruin and desolation come upon this city by the union in its ceasing to be the metropolis of our nation, the meeting place of the house of parliament, Privy Council, resort of our peers, gentry and others.[15]

The Town Council even threatened to take measures for the dissolution of the Treaty of Union of 1707 if the situation was not rectified.[16] Drummond was nothing if not persistent and he eventually secured an act of parliament on 24 June 1723 to provide funds for introducing a supply of fresh running water to flush through the Nor' Loch, for the formation of a street to access the city's property on the north side of the town, and for purchasing the Calton estate. All of these measures are included in Mar's proposal and shown in Fig. 3.3. The purchase of the Calton Crags suggests direct knowledge of Mar's proposal because he was the only planner to date to include this in his design. The purchase was not part of the later *Proposal* of 1752. Very little happened, and the advent of the Jacobite war of 1745 meant yet another postponement. In 1752 Lord Minto published a pamphlet entitled *Proposals for Carrying on Certain Public Works in . . . Edinburgh*.[17] It mentions Andrew Fletcher of Saltoun's ambition for Edinburgh but makes no direct reference to Mar's plan, which is hardly surprising given the latter's official status as a Jacobite traitor. Nevertheless, Mar's suggestions for a regular grid bounded by streets with open outlooks to the north and south sides of the site, and the canalisation of the Nor' Loch with walks and terraces along its sides, as well as his emphasising economic benefits and the importance of modernisation, were all included in the *Proposals*. The high-arched bridges were not included in the *Proposals* but the South Bridge was underway two years before the design competition was launched in 1766.

Edinburgh is often described as picturesque. To be picturesque it would have to have been composed of sinuous lines and inspired by a vision of contrived ruins carefully distributed to give a sense of irregularity analogous with a poetic and pictorial love of wild nature. Post-1745 Scotland's anxious desire to meekly align itself with English cultural values, and in landscaping this meant adopting English picturesque values, has played a part in this misinterpretation. In addition the impact of the English style on landscape theory and popular consciousness has been overwhelming, and this has prejudiced other possible interpretations, particularly the traditional Scottish formal style present in Mar's and all the proposals leading up to and including Craig's plan. The *Proposals* give no suggestions about what style the new town should be but it does cite two cities

FIGURE 3.3.
(Overleaf) Edinburgh: Mar's vision of long axial boulevards, circuses and new districts was entirely in keeping with Continental urbanism of the period. However, the utilisation of natural topography is unprecedented in city plans of the early 1700s although widely used for designing Scottish rural landscapes. (Digital reconstruction on Edgar's plan of Edinburgh, 1754. Copyright Margaret Stewart and Pete Mullin, 2004)

Proposal by the 6th Earl of Mar for the improvement of Edinburgh, 1722–27

— Aquaduct
— Streets
— Residential
— Bridges
— Plantation

Parliament House and Statue of K. Cha: 2.d
Tolbooth Kirks. Picardy

Calton Hill

Bridge

Salisbury Craigs

St Anth.y
Chapel

Arthur

Croft an way

PARK

Gibbet Toun   Gibbet

as models.[18] These were Turin, with its new additions designed by Filippo Juvarra for the construction of a new palace and military quarter between 1716 and 1728, and Berlin developed from the late seventeenth to the early eighteenth century with broad avenues and city squares. These are particularly sophisticated choices, indicative of an appreciation of current advances in European urbanism. Back in the 1710s and 1720s Lord Mar and his architectural ally, James Gibbs, were familiar with the works of the great Baroque architect Filippo Juvarra.[19]

It is certainly true that between 1752 and the competition of 1766 the English picturesque style had nudged European formal planning off the drawing board. However, this aesthetic is absent from Craig's rigorous orthogonal, and from the criteria outlined in the *Proposals* of 1752. Edinburgh's New Town is not simplistically picturesque but a merging of European formality with the principles of the by now established criteria of the Scottish Historical Landscape. The street lines of the New Town are directed on views of historic and natural features and the entire ensemble is conceived as a visualisation of authentic historical commemoration and future prosperity: from its ancient origins within a real wilderness to its remodelling into a city embodying national aims of survival, renewal and modernity.

Conclusion

We can see that Mar was only one of several people involved in working out the elements of the New Town scheme, but he was certainly the first to give the proposal firm, clear and detailed parameters and to articulate its impact. Parts of his plan were incorporated into the reductive scheme set out in the *Proposals* and Craig's winning design. The winning design was far from being innovative or original but it was a direct response to certain clear assumptions that had been understood since the seventeenth century about what was wanted for Edinburgh.

Visibly similar in style and scale, Mar's city plans successfully created a sense of political unity and equality between the partner states of his hoped-for federation – a political ambition that was entirely redundant by the later eighteenth century. Mar was particularly sensitive to the different physical characters of the capital cities he hoped to see remodelled, and though he was ambitious and imaginative he was never impractical. In addition, he stuck close to current planning ideals coupling these with the local historical and cultural values of each city.

Edinburgh's simple orthogonal grid set the pattern for the next 150 years, a pattern of outlooks providing unique and alluring harmonisations of mountainscape, sea, ancient and modern structures – a manifestation indebted to the design criteria of the Scottish Historical Landscape. Its durability as a style and a concept was demonstrated by the ease with which civic monuments were introduced in the early nineteenth century to form Edinburgh into the great Romantic Classical city we now know.

CHAPTER 4
Georgian New Towns of Glasgow and Edinburgh

Anthony Lewis

This chapter focuses on two Scottish Georgian-period architects: Allan Dreghorn (1706–1765), from Glasgow, and James Craig (1739–1795), from Edinburgh. Dreghorn's architecture had a significant impact on Glasgow, a city whose dramatic expansion began in the seventeenth century with the erection of buildings devoted to education, administration and business: notably the Tolbooth, College, Merchant House and Sugar House. For the English diarist and spy Daniel Defoe, writing in 1707 (but published in 1724–5), Glasgow was 'the cleanest and beautifullest, and best built city in *Britain, London* excepted'.[1] He was impressed, in particular, by the old bridge, the uniform stone façades, wide streets and arcades (known as 'piazzas'), as well as by the Tolbooth, College, Cathedral and the Duke of Montrose's house. He noted 'Glasgow is a city of business', which was doing well thanks to commerce, and to its merchants' 'addiction to trade' with America, London and Europe. Defoe reported on the transformation of Port Glasgow, and alluded to the production of Glaswegian tartans, muslins, cloths and gloves for Scottish, English and plantation markets. The tobacco and sugar trades with the West Indies were not mentioned at length, although the revenues of slavery provided Glasgow with the necessary income for its expansion. Could Dreghorn supply architecture to match the city's reputation for beauty and modernity?

The narrative of Glasgow's architectural development for the early eighteenth century begins with Daniel Campbell's Shawfield townhouse of 1711–12. Campbell, a Member of Parliament for Glasgow, chose Colen Campbell (1676–1729), a Scottish architect who had settled in the metropolis, to build a townhouse and possibly also a country house. Shawfield was situated to the north of Glasgow's then centre, and his estate of Woodhall to the east. The design for Shawfield was published in the architect's own book, *Vitruvius Britannicus*. Shawfield's architecture was not widely different from other small houses built by Scotland's essentially Edinburgh-based architects such as James Smith and Alexander McGill. Although Shawfield was damaged during the 1725 Malt Tax riot and is long gone, some photographs of a ruined Woodhall survive.[2] Woodhall was developed in the 1740s by Edinburgh architect John Douglas, and is usually not referred to in standard histories on Glasgow's architecture.

The Duke of Montrose's house, to which Defoe referred, was built from 1717 to 1718 in an attempt to emulate Shawfield mansion. The Duke consulted James Smith and Alexander McGill for new foundations, vaults, coach-houses and entrances. But because of delay in construction, the Duke, who resided mostly in London, turned to the London-based Scottish architect James Gibbs. However, Gibbs's estimated cost – ten thousand pounds[3] – meant that the old house was instead repaired, with new floors and plastering.

Defoe also praised Glasgow's uniform street architecture. The Town Council proposed improvements for new domestic architecture, replacing the older thatch-roofed and timber-built tenements – to prevent fire hazards in the meandering wynds and closes running off the High Street and Saltmarket. In April 1722 magistrates prescribed building conditions for King Street, and the new cross-street for Trongate (Fig. 4.1). Glasgow would be beautified in a 'decent and uniform manner' with properties following the 'same model' on a 30-foot-wide straight street. The regulations gave uniform dimensions and materials.[4] By 1725 Princes Street followed King Street. Merchants and tradesmen purchased plots and built properties, including carpenter John Craig senior and mason Gavin Lawson, who presumably took on contracting for building properties. Although not envisaged in 1722, a sugar house was built in King Street. Resident merchants purchased shares in it and lived beside it. The combination of industry and housing was a hallmark

FIGURE 4.1. *A View of the Trongate of Glasgow from the East*, lithograph by Robert Paul, engraved by Gul. Buchanan, 1750. (Copyright Glasgow Museums, 1912.34.k)

of Glasgow's New Town architecture. Meanwhile, the improvement of ports, jetties and quays to improve commerce at Port Glasgow and Broomielaw, closer to the city, progressed while the city expanded.

Despite the 1725 riots, urban improvement continued into the 1730s and beyond; new stone, slate-roofed buildings were built. William Adam designed a library for Glasgow College in 1732. In September 1737 he was paid £12 12s for his plans for a prestigious 'intended square' at Glasgow cross.[5] By then, Adam was also working on Dundee's Town House, having already completed Aberdeen's. However, the Town Council turned to their own men, Craig and Dreghorn. The magistrates and the two architects planned a new city centre; a uniform street architecture, a new cross, a square, a commercial quay for the harbour, a new town hall with a new matching church and a new assembly room. Unlike Edinburgh, there was no proposed relocation to nearby fields.

Allan Dreghorn was the architect chosen to deliver the plans of the hall, church and assembly room. He belonged to a family of builders. His father Robert Dreghorn had established a carpentry business in which he was joined by Allan and his brother Robert, and soon after Allan became its figurehead. He was elected a trade councillor and Deacon, or leader, of the incorporation of wrights; his business talent must have been appreciated because he succeeded fellow wright John Craig as the city's Treasurer. Tradesmen and architects were then given central roles in Glasgow's Town Council; the three most important posts in a Town Council were those of Lord Provost, Treasurer and Dean of Guild. Although such positions were held elsewhere by merchants rather than by tradesmen, Craig and Dreghorn – both wrights – became treasurers in the 1730s: Craig from 1733 to 1735, and Dreghorn from 1739 to 1740. They could provide advice and knowledge on the costs of architecture, and help with the planning of new Glasgow. In 1741, Dreghorn was succeeded by another wright, James Nesbitt; these men worked together from time to time afterwards, including for the new church, and the quay at Broomielaw.

In March 1734 Craig and Dreghorn applied to build a new wharf for themselves at Broomielaw, beside the Town Hospital and ropery, to enable them to move incoming cargoes of timber to their own nearby wood-yard.[6] In the same petition, Dreghorn also applied for ground to build himself a house beside that same site. Over time, Craig and Dreghorn became neighbours with riverside houses, a wood-yard and properties. Four years later, Craig and Dreghorn, and their new partner, Robert Luke, a goldsmith and investor in Glasgow's soap and candle factories and easter sugar house, set up a slit mill (later called the Smithfield Company) on the banks of the River Kelvin, to the west of the city, in Partick. The mill made nails, screws and other metal tools such as spades, picks and barrows – all of which were needed for construction. Dreghorn could, therefore, control the costs for his buildings by supplying timber and metal goods on his own terms.

Planning for his retirement, Dreghorn purchased land in 1749 situated near his Smithfield mill at Garrioch and Ruchill, also by the River Kelvin. The city's architect, carpenter, timber merchant and former treasurer also now joined prestigious businessmen as one of the founding partners of Glasgow's Ship Bank: a group that also included William McDowall of Castle Semple, Andrew Buchanan of Drumpellier, Colin and Robert Dunlop of Garnkirk and Alexander Houston, each of whom had commercial interests in tobacco, sugar and slavery, all of which helped finance the expansion of Glasgow. Like them, Dreghorn also became a landowner in America; he owned plots in Fredericksburg, Virginia. It was not unknown for tradesmen and architects to be entrepreneurial. Both William Adam and John Douglas had multiple business interests, owning estates at Blair Adam, Kinross-shire, and Pinkerton, respectively. Allan Dreghorn, however, was *the* Glaswegian architect with an estate and stakes in a bank. Glasgow's only other tradesman of the time to be called an architect was his old business partner, John Craig senior, and that was only in retrospect, after his death in 1754, when his son, John Craig junior, took over his business.

In 1739, Dreghorn was the architect in charge of repairing Glasgow's medieval cathedral, a symbol of Glasgow's past. The title 'architect' denoted his rise in status. Magistrates turned to him again in 1740 to build the city's new church – the building today known as St Andrews in the Square. He was instructed to follow James Gibbs's St Martin-in-the-Fields, and Dreghorn clearly drew inspiration from that building. This church, the town hall and other public works in Glasgow, such as the wash house on Glasgow Green, dominated Dreghorn's career. Glaswegians such as Dreghorn and his business partners, and lord provosts, wished to present themselves as men of taste and quality. Gibbs's work in London appealed to them, and possibly some of the new houses that Glasgow's tobacco and sugar merchants built for themselves were also inspired by James Gibbs's *Book of Architecture* (1728).

At the same time as he bought Ruchill House, Dreghorn secured the acquisition of a site for building his own townhouse, by the banks of the Clyde. The Town Council recorded his willingness to build on it in 1751–52. Meanwhile he also oversaw the design and construction of the new town hall's piazza, and possibly also other new urban properties such as the Virginia Mansion for Lord Provost George Buchanan, the Saracen's Head in 1754, and Lord Provost

John Murdoch's house in 1757. These houses, like Shawfield House, had vistas towards the River Clyde, from where the city's fortunes were made. By the late 1750s, Dreghorn had both acquired another estate in north Glasgow, Hogganfield, and planned another public building in the New Town – an assembly room, on the third floor of a new tenement to the west of the town hall.

As the city's architect and treasurer, Dreghorn controlled the cost of building Glasgow's New Town. As a timber and metal merchant, as well as a banker, he could agree on contracts and accounts, and could manage the costs of ground, material and wages. The team he worked with mostly derived from Glasgow's trade incorporations, together with others working for the Adam practice at Hamilton Palace. Dreghorn's abilities to present architecture that his patrons wanted at an affordable price, and to develop a network of business contacts, made Dreghorn's career successful. Only St Andrews Church in the Square, fragments of the town hall and of his own home, have survived to this day.

Archives on Dreghorn are scarce, unlike what survives concerning James Craig, the architect of Edinburgh's New Town plan. Also, central Edinburgh has far more surviving Georgian architecture than Glasgow, and the New Town's gridded pattern remains essentially intact. The façades and interiors of some houses and tenements on George Street, Queen Street, and the more minor streets, best represent the builders' intentions. Glasgow planned a uniform urban architecture between 1720 and 1750, but Edinburgh's lord provosts did comparatively little in that period. Site visits on Multrees Hill were undertaken between 1719 and 1720, and proposals for adding 'convenient dwellings to a number of persons of note and character'[7] were discussed, but nothing happened for another thirty years.

By the time *Proposals for Carrying on Certain Public Works in the City of Edinburgh* was published in 1752, New Glasgow was well established. And yet that document made no reference to Glasgow. Instead, New Edinburgh was to equal, or better, London, Berlin and Turin. In 1753, Edinburgh Town Council obtained an Act of Parliament 'For erecting several Public Buildings in the City of Edinburgh; and to empower the Trustees therein to be mentioned to purchase Lands for that purpose and also for Widening and

Enlarging the streets of the said city, and certain avenues leading thereto'. It resulted in the building of the Merchants' Exchange in the High Street, as well as shops, coffee houses, offices and flats. John Adam was the architect of the Exchange, a building erected by the mason and deacon Patrick Jamieson, and wrights Alexander Peter and Peter Fergus, and their teams of journeymen.

A bill in favour of the building of the New Town, and of a bridge across the Nor' Loch, was presented by Lord Provost George Drummond to the Town Council in 1759. Architects and garden designers Robert Robinson and John Fergus surveyed the land surrounding Edinburgh and made a vast map in preparation for the bill to pass. Burgess-ship was offered for a pound to be able to settle and work in the New Town, thereby contravening the regulations of the incorporations, which stated that the New Town was to be a free trade zone.[8] The incorporations objected to this scheme for fear of losing on property sale and rental incomes. When 'Jacobites'[9] informed Drummond that the tradesmen had defeated his plan, the New Town was still very much a 'castle in the air'.

1759 was also the year when James Craig, then a young man, began his apprenticeship as a mason under Deacon Patrick Jamieson; Craig's father, William, had enrolled his son in 1755 when James Craig was still a student at George Watson's College.[10] Unlike the Dreghorns of Glasgow, Craig had not been born into a family of tradesmen. Nor were the Craig family ever wealthy. They lived in a rented first floor flat in a tenement at the foot of West Bow, facing onto the Corn Market and Grassmarket. William Craig's family were merchants in haberdashery, ironmongery, sugar and tobacco. Grandfather Robert Craig had been a magistrate, and Dean of Guild of Edinburgh, but went bankrupt. William Craig was the Council's sword and mace bearer in 1745, and also went bankrupt. On James's mother's side was the Thomson family. Mary Thomson was the sister of the poet James Thomson (1700–1748). James Craig illustrated his designs with edited quotations from Thomson's poems, such as *Liberty* for the New Town plans. The quotations complemented his designs as poetry and architecture offered a harmony of expressive arts; *Liberty* endorsed free trade, a value important to Drummond's proposed New Town, and to Craig's own family. Compared with Dreghorn, James Craig possessed no estate in or out of the city, or property in Virginia, no banking partners and no high office within the Town Council. Nevertheless, Craig had aspirations to be known as an architect.

As an apprentice, James Craig worked under mason Patrick Jamieson from 1759 to 1762,[11] and it is likely that Craig knew the Exchange building, and the team of tradesmen and architect John Adam. Craig's early years as an apprentice, and further as an architect – which began soon after 1762, after his father died and he had to look after his mother and aunt – are poorly recorded.

Two of his earliest known works predate the New Town's commencement – he was involved in the 1763 plan for the Nor' Loch Bridge, published in the *Scots Magazine,* and in the 1765 plan for the Middle Road District, in the Canongate.[12] But, in reality, to be able to support his family financially, he presumably carried out much more work than just this. Instead of submitting his essay piece to become a freeman mason of the incorporation, he submitted a plan for the proposed New Town of Edinburgh, in 1766, to the judgement of John Adam and other experts who all probably knew Craig – such as the Reverend John Erskine, Minister at Greyfriars, the Craig family's church. Craig's plan was chosen.

Craig proposed different versions of his plan in 1766–7, and worked on those with William Mylne, a mason he would have known through the incorporation. By 1766, William Mylne, the brother of architect Robert Mylne, was Deacon of masons and architect of the bridge over the Nor' Loch.

Without the Minutes of the New Town Planning Committee, it is hard to know what the adjustments made to Craig's first plan were. The Bridge Committee Minutes indicate that Mylne and Craig completed alterations from October to December 1766. What Mylne's 'rectified plan of the improvements', or Craig's 'two plans in different views' and 'plan of the common sewers', looked like remains unknown.[13] But some clues may be found in legal papers. In March 1773, during the legal dispute between the Town Council and the New Town's feuars, which ran from 1771 to 1776, the role Craig had in planning the New Town was debated. The arguments detail the changes made to the plan by Craig and Mylne. The Town Council argued that Craig's prize-winning plan followed much of what was finally accepted. The plan had streets and squares and, to the south of what became Princes Street, grounds were decorated with trees – which later made way for public pleasure grounds.[14]

The feuars replied a month later, probably after reading the Bridge Committee Minutes and other evidence now lost. They argued that Craig's first prize-winning plan had been replaced by William Mylne's plan, which was the basis of the adopted plan, and that it was Mylne who had removed the trees from the ground south of Princes Street. Craig was then asked to alter Mylne's plan to make the principal middle street run along the summit of the ground instead of nearer just one side.[15]

Whatever the facts may have been, Craig was still perceived as the plan's architect. Just before it was finally completed, the plan provided by Craig was described in a newspaper in June 1767.[16] It described several timber pedestrian bridges, built after the Chinese taste, crossing over the proposed canal running where the Nor' Loch previously was. The banks of the canal and the sides of the New Town were to be planted with trees; and the allotments were to be for half an acre, and to allow for one or two new houses, offices and a garden. Between June and 29 July, the committee and Craig had these Chinese bridges over the canal removed from the plan. The pleasure grounds, main street alignment and Chinese bridges thus represent three changes of intention that can be clearly identified.

Both Craig and Mylne were under the instructions of the various committees. The only professional architect on them was John Adam, although there was also Sir James Clerk of Penicuik, an amateur gentleman–architect. Decisions about the plan were made, for the most part, by Edinburgh Town Council magistrates, church ministers (including Dr Alexander Webster and Dr John Erskine), and judges in the Court of Session such as Lords Kames and Alemore. Their mission would have included the financial matters of calculating income from feuing and duties, plus the expenditure on more practical matters, such as sewers, pavements, roads, walls and railings, and the legal aspects of establishing how feuing and building were to be administered.

For Craig, working with William Mylne was no different from working with the surveyor John Laurie, with whom Craig made the feuing plans of the New Town to match the building plan. Laurie had been involved with the New Town since the competition began in 1766, surveying the site plan. That same year, he then had two alternative plans of possible New Towns of Edinburgh published which were entitled 'A plan of Edinburgh and places adjacent...' On 29 July 1767, Lord Provost Gilbert Laurie signed the last version designed and drawn by James Craig which became the Town Council's official New Town plan. There is, therefore, no doubt that Craig was deeply involved in planning the New Town and providing designs and reports for it (Fig. 4.2).

As well as planning for the New Town's building and feuing in 1766, Craig also planned for its sanitation; he went to London for this purpose in the winter 1767.[17] Craig was 'willing to do everything in his power for the Town's advantage' and would obtain a plan of sewers that the New Town needed for its houses.[18] The report and plans are now lost, but John Adam's letter to the magistrates dated 22 October 1768 and concerning the New Town sewers alluded to London, and so possibly also to Craig's work. Adam wrote that London used a circular brick-built drain – a scheme harder to copy in stone. On grounds of cost, he favoured David Henderson's design, a drain 3 feet wide and 6 feet high with upright sides and brick arch, sufficient to enable a man to walk upright with his barrow.

The earliest official published New Town plan carrying James Craig's name was printed in 1768. More followed between then and 1769. Copies went on sale in London and Edinburgh bookshops, and from the architect himself at his own home. Craig marketed himself as the architect of the New Town plan throughout his entire subsequent career. Whatever may have been the alterations instructed by the committee to Mylne or Craig, they did not prevent James Craig from being awarded the gold medal, silver box and freedom of the city (Fig. 4.3). More importantly, no one challenged his right to sign and publish the final plan – '*inven. et delin.*', meaning that he both made (invented) and drew (delineated) the plan. Craig was the architect who designed the New Town plan.[19] But, when the project's reputation faltered from 1769 to 1776, in light of the North Bridge collapse, Ayr Bank crash and a dispute between the Town Council and the New Town's feuars, the architect faced problems. He feared being famous for planning a failing project, and had no easy way to gain control of its architecture other than by offering new street plans and buildings – which he chose to do.

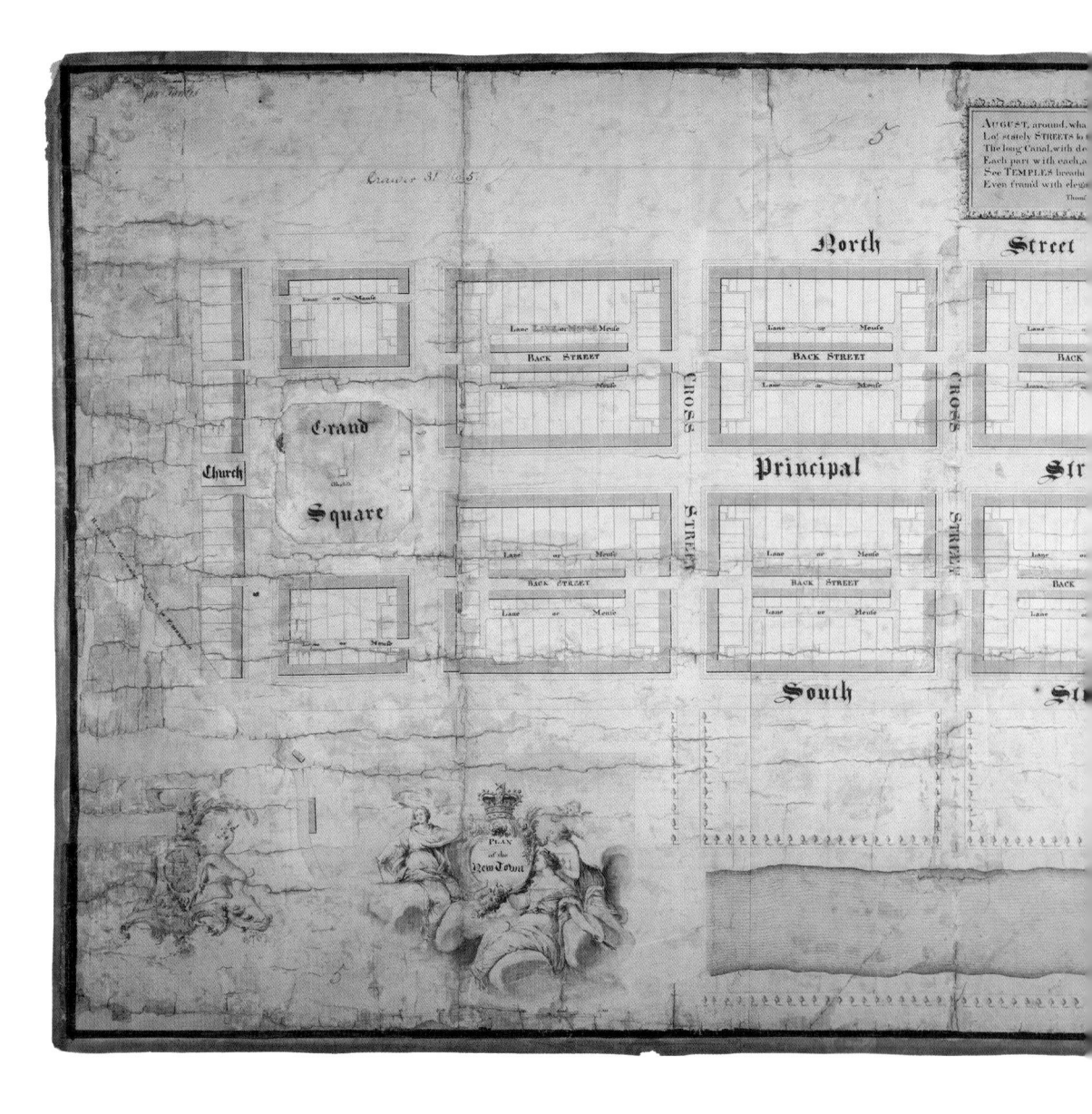

FIGURE 4.2.
James Craig's New Town Plan for Edinburgh, 1767. (Edinburgh City Museums, 1978/37)

What he did was to design brand new plans to regain public and political confidence in the New Town, and his abilities as a town planning architect. These plans were made in 1770, 1774 and 1781 for the Town Council, and Royal Court in London. They all featured a great central circus which was on plan offering a garden 152.4 metres wide (500 feet in Craig's measurements), with a statue of King George III in the centre. On his visit to London in 1767–8, when he sketched buildings, studied sewers and presented his New Town plan to King George III for royal assent, Craig met Sir John Pringle, the King's Physician. The kind doctor even treated the architect for illness. The two men kept in touch and, between 1770 and January 1771, corresponded about the first of Craig's circus plans. Craig sent Pringle a design and letter about his circus plan. Although this letter and plan do not appear to be in an archive now, the letter Pringle sent in reply to Craig is. The doctor told the architect how much he enjoyed Bath's circus, and the concept of a central circus or octagon, such as he may have known or been told of in Paris. He did not, however, approve of a segmented circus or series of crescents with a central obelisk, which Craig had shown. Pringle preferred either a statue, ideally of the monarch, or basin

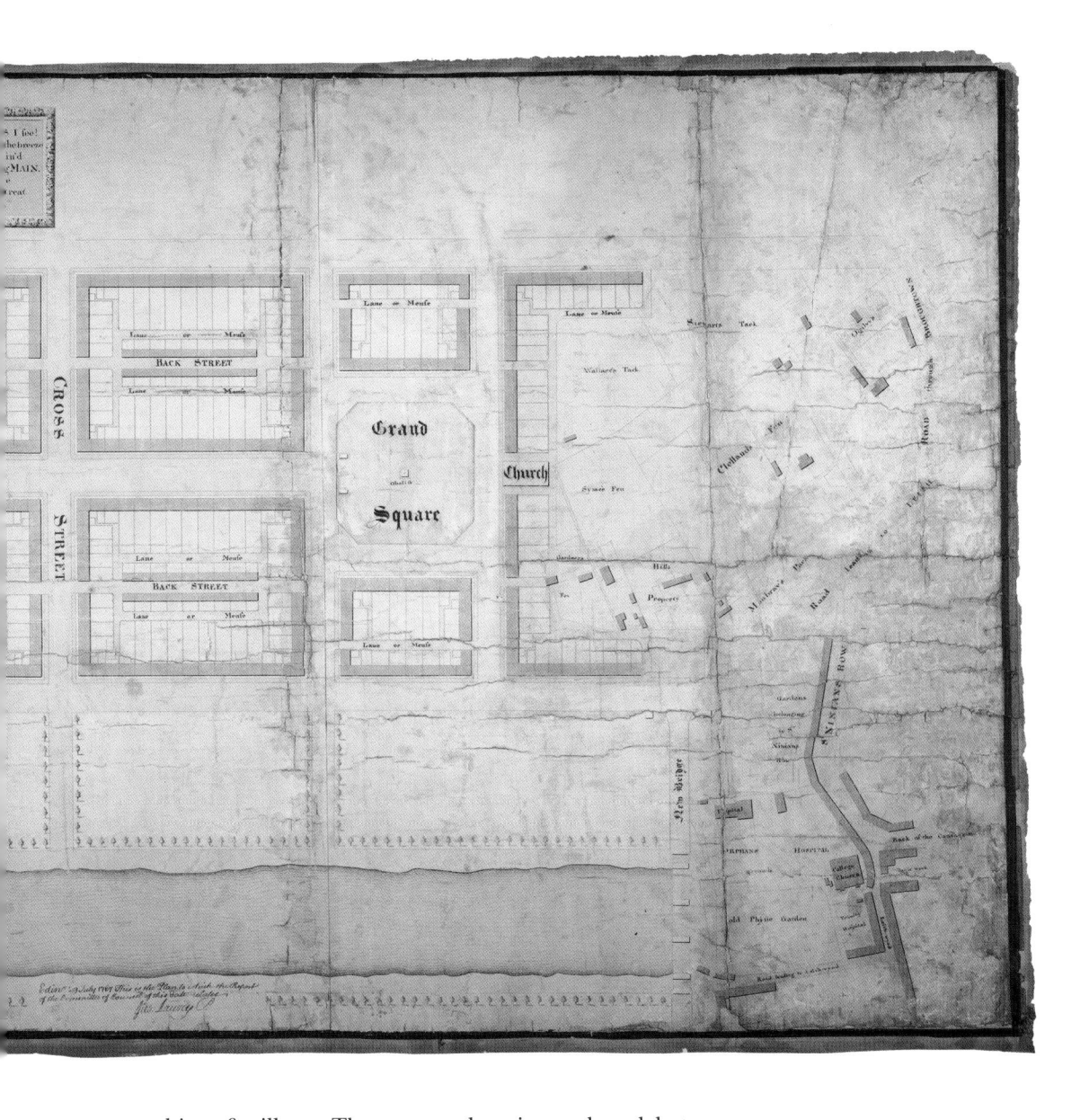

FIGURE 4.3.
Copy of the gold medal (both sides) awarded to James Craig in 1766 for his New Town plan. This copy was made for the foundation of the Royal College of Physicians of Edinburgh, in 1775. (Copyright Royal College of Physicians of Edinburgh)

of water to be used in the event of a fire or for keeping dust down in summer.[20] In response, in 1773, Craig planned a square to the east of Register House for the lawyer Walter Ferguson. This square became St James Square, and the architect planned a central basin of water in the middle of it.[21] He also introduced the idea of a central statue of King George into the circus.

Craig's circus plans would have increased the monumentality of the New Town; the concept of a concentric double circus plan was unusual, but not completely unheard of. In 1766, the Shooters' Hill New Town (New Plumstead), in Kent, was promoted.[22] It had a double circus for 1,500 houses with an assembly room in the middle.[23] By January 1767 a subscription of £150,000 was launched to have that project built by an 'Eminent Master Builder at the West End'.[24] By March, more detailed descriptions were given, and a published plan promised. It was to be at the top of a hill linked by a new main road, with a double circus: external for people of 'inferior rank', and internal for fifty houses for 'persons of fashion'. There was also a central octagonal assembly room surrounded by a water pond, 30 feet wide. Access to the rooms was by four Chinese bridges. The town would have had a spa, as well as four great arches for the four avenues of that concentric circus plan. The surrounding area was to be landscaped with flowering shrubs, evergreens, Chinese temples and statues on pedestals, to enhance the vistas. Everyone could perceive Shooters' Hill as Nature and Art blended together to render it 'the most capital in Great Britain, but, without the least exaggeration, even in Europe'.[25] The *London Evening Post* reported that the royal children, the Dukes of Cumberland and Gloucester, had all inspected both the plan and the site, and had approved everything of it all.[26]

The circus plans Craig promoted may have reflected the popularity and fashions for circuses in London, Bath and Shooters' Hill. He also proposed four segmented crescents for four streets. Craig had no octagonal assembly room, but offered a large central garden and royal statue.[27] Like Wood, or John Gwynn, the author of *London and Westminster Improved* (1766), Craig looked for a reputation as a good city planner, and for patronage. Also like Gwynn, Craig had a preference for professional architects over speculative developers whom Gwynn called 'ignorant and capricious persons'; Craig kept a copy of Gwynn's pamphlet in his library.

The failure to complete the Royal College of Physicians Hall (1776–8) in George Street to his plans was a blow to Craig. Despite this, he persisted in promoting himself as *the* architect who really cared the most about New Town architecture.[28] Although Edinburgh Town Council's politics were turbulent between 1774 and 1781, Craig still presented himself as the New Town's architect. In 1774 he submitted another circus plan to the Town Council, which it refused to adopt. He persisted with the idea of a New Town circus and tried a third time in 1781, having won the support of the new party in power at the Town Council. Both Craig and Lord Provost David Steuart were looking for support from New Town feuars. The Lord Provost organised an extraordinary meeting for these feuars to encourage planning a New Town circus which would then promote much needed new house building, and revenues.[29] The feuars supported the proposal. In June 1781 the annual general meeting of feuars considered the circus plans in more detail. They would have seen Craig's circus plan, sections and elevations. A design competition took place,[30] with a five guineas reward for the winner.[31] For Craig, the winner of the competition, the reward meant even more than just money; it seemed the wheel of fortune was turning his way and he would have control over New Town plan and buildings.

It was, perhaps, no coincidence that at the same time as Craig's circus plan proposal of 1781 was accepted by Lord Provost Steuart, and the feuars, the architect had his portrait painted for his own home by David Allan (Fig. 4.4.).[32] For the painter, the commission provided an introduction to other potential patrons. The architect was portrayed holding his compass in the process of preparing a circus plan, similar to the design of 1774. We know that Craig owned a set of mathematical instruments, and surveying equipment, moulding profiles, drills and rulers – all were necessary tools to design, and make sample pieces and mouldings. Of his collection, only a compass and a pair of divided scales remain. The scales were for protracting angles and setting out dimensions for plans and maps to different scales. His compass was placed in a box inscribed 'James Craig, Architect, Edinburgh, 1781'. The case, and scales, came into the possession of Edinburgh's city architect in 1943, and became part of the city museum's collection in 1952 through the city architect Ebenezer MacRae, a supporter of conservation in Edinburgh. In the portrait, the architect is also represented with the full plan of the Royal College of Physicians Hall; the architect therefore appeared as the significant visionary author of Edinburgh's New Town.

Craig's career and architecture remains understudied. Despite the lack of material evidence about the creation and administration of his New Town plans between 1770 and 1781, some archival documents allow us to better understand the ideas and processes he used to produce his work. Craig owned books about Paris's Academies of Arts, published in the 1680s, by authors Leclerc, Le Brun and Lamotte. Charles Lamotte's book on poetry and painting proposed a harmony of sensations where the sister arts of painting and poetry worked together. There is no doubt that Craig valued such qualities for a design; perspective, proportion, regularity and symmetry. The illustrations on his New Town plans are further evidence of this.

These mathematical qualities of architecture and design can also be associated with Newton's science and belief in God's universe. Circles of light moving in harmony in God's universe, theorised by Newton, also appealed to James Thomson, author of *The Seasons*. In turn, Thomson was celebrated by James Craig in his architecture. In this context, as well as in contemporary town planning fashion, such as at New Plumstead, the double circus plans may also reflect

FIGURE 4.4.
(Opposite) David Allan, portrait of James Craig (1739–1795), architect, 1781. (Copyright National Galleries of Scotland. Given by the Royal Academy 1910. Photographer: Antonia Reeve)

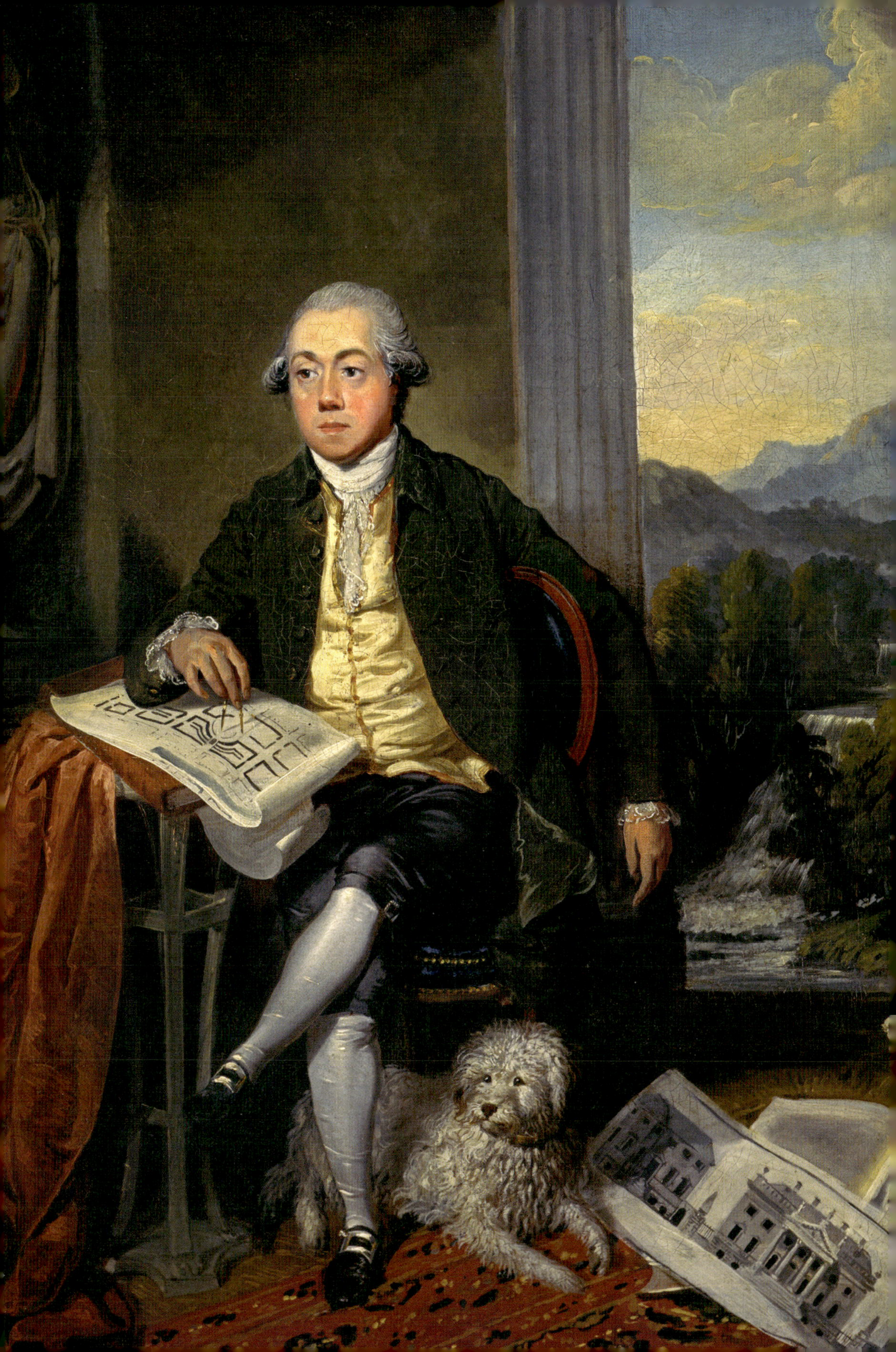

on universal mathematical and scientific principles, the harmonies of the arts and an aesthetic of the divine city.

Leclerc, Lamotte, Newton and Thomson might have approved of other books in Craig's library, such as Robert Morris's *Essay in Defence of Ancient Architecture* (1728) and John Wood the Elder's *The Origin of Building* (1741). Circus plans were also used by these architects as representations of divine order and harmony. Craig's double circus plan intended to show New Edinburgh as the home of good governance, as epitomised by the statue of King George III and the surrounding churches; this is no surprise, given Craig's own family background and connections with the Church of Scotland. A study of Craig's library allows us to understand his mathematical discipline, and his appreciation of a well-organised plan for the city, as a means to good social order and government. Other examples of Craig's rigorous mathematical approach can be seen in squares and street plans for Robert Hope in Edinburgh, and for Glasgow Town Council and Colonel Blythswood in Glasgow.

Other books in Craig's library further illuminate the Scottish qualities of his New Town plans. Books on mathematics by Colin McLaurin and David Gregory, and on aesthetics by Alexander Gerard, had academic lineages with the universities of Glasgow, Edinburgh and Aberdeen. So too did books by his friend and judge Lord Kames, author of *Elements of Criticism* (1762). Gerard wrote on the sublime, beauty and harmony, praising grandeur and simplicity. In architecture, Gerard sought out its ability to match these qualities with strength and durability to honour the patron's wealth and magnificence. He believed that beauty was easier to conceive when uniformity and variety were contrasted with one another. These were all qualities of Craig's architecture. Lord Kames's views were similar; in *Elements of Criticism* he argued that a circle was more beautiful than a square because its simplicity and beauty were seen more quickly. He went on to discuss squares and parallelograms. On plan, a parallelogram could represent the windows and doors of a house, but to be beautiful it needed to be drawn with proportion. The analogy of a parallelogram representing house building was appropriate to the aim of the New Town too. Like Gerard, Kames praised simplicity as a means to perceive beauty. The mathematical principles of Craig's apparently simple plans gave his architecture strength and beauty. Also, like Gerard, Kames argued that to establish a perception of beauty, uniformity had to be contrasted with variety. The only members on the New Town committees that Craig was in contact with after the New Town plan was set were John Adam and Lord Kames. Kames was an expert in feuing,[33] and interested in architecture and Scottish New Towns.[34] In 1782, Boswell reported finding Craig and Kames discussing the New Town plan.

Almost as if he was following classical Vitruvian instruction on the education of an architect, Craig studied mathematics, perspective, geometry, moral philosophy, music, medicine, art, law, history and the principles of good taste. The mathematical and geometric shapes Craig used for all his Edinburgh town plans include circles, crescents, octagons, parallelograms and squares. Although noted for a sometimes sketchy style of drawing, the finished plans were clean and precise, and often coloured with watercolours, inks, poetry, figures and monuments. If Craig's town plans were linked together in an overall plan of Edinburgh then his preference for a city made of a variety of shapes would be obvious.

Given his record of illustrating plans with quotations from Thomson, Craig presented himself as an architect of poetry, or at least as one able to translate literature into plans for cities, harbours and churches; he read about iconology and was aware of the relationship between architecture, sculpture and painting. In this context, Craig's collection of works by Thomson, as well as by Joseph Addison, gave additional ways to interpret his architecture.

Craig's work instruments are rare examples of surviving architects' tools in this period in Scotland. The analysis of Craig's library has shown that Craig wanted to establish his credentials as a professional architect who had studied and adopted academic practices established in Paris, as well as the aesthetics presented by Scottish professors and ministers. As individuals, tradesmen were not as famous as Craig, Robert Adam or Sir William Chambers, but collectively they had a significant part to play in the design and construction of houses, offices and public buildings in the New Town and elsewhere in the city and in neighbouring Leith. Craig provided the overall design, which was ultimately stifled by the plans made by tradesmen in the New Town – because of their activities, building a circus or enlarging Physicians' Hall became impractical.

The comparison of Allan Dreghorn's and James Craig's architecture has allowed us to suggest that the two architects worked in very different circumstances: Dreghorn could control the costs of his architecture, thanks to his political role, whereas Craig could not. Secondly, Dreghorn enjoyed the status of being Glasgow Town Council's preferred architect, which Craig did not – but he still wanted to be seen as *the* architect of Edinburgh's New Town. Lastly, as the analyses of the two architects' interests have shown, Dreghorn and Craig equally looked at the architecture and academies of Georgian London and Bourbon Paris. Both wanted to be seen as not merely tradesmen, but as professional architects and town planners who had the knowledge and skills to improve their native cities. Demonstrations of their learning and aesthetic sensibilities were important to gather support from patrons in the Town Council, and from residents, as they shaped perceptions of the positive changes architects could make to urban life, and the prospects of living in Scottish New Towns.

Part 2

New Town and Old Town

CHAPTER 5

Royal Welcomes in Edinburgh New Town: Portraying Civic Identity in 1822 and 1842

Giovanna Guidicini

The visits to Edinburgh by King George IV in 1822, and by Queen Victoria and Prince Albert in 1842, were part of carefully planned tours of Scotland to make themselves known to – and to familiarise themselves with – the northern part of their dominion and its inhabitants. Royal welcomes of this kind were common occurrences in the early modern period, and led the ruler through the main public spaces of the royal burgh – now known as the Old Town. However, during the nineteenth century it was the New Town that was chosen as the setting for the ceremonies welcoming the monarch, with the Old Town marginalised to a side role. I argue that the choice of this new spatial setting celebrated a changing perception of Edinburgh's identity and role within a pan-British and post-Enlightenment context. The urban spaces selected for and involved in this celebration of renovated civic pride were not bland and interchangeable containers for rituals, but rather essential performers themselves, reinforcing and expressing three-dimensionally the political narrative supporting the event.

The entries organised for King George in 1822 and for Queen Victoria and Prince Albert in 1842 have been recorded in detail, making it possible to quickly sketch both monarchs' welcoming routes between their ports of arrival and the Palace of Dalkeith, where in both cases they sojourned during their stay.[1] King George IV arrived at Leith on 14 August 1822; his Scottish trip was part of a series of official visits which included Ireland and Hanover, and

FIGURE 5.1.
(Opposite) Base image: *City of Edinburgh Drawn and Engraved for Gray's Annual Directory*, by W. & A.K. Johnston, Edinburgh, 1837. In blue, King George IV's route on 15 August 1822. In orange, Queen Victoria and Prince Albert's route on 1 September 1842 (the Queen's landing location at Granton Pier does not appear on this map). The paired squares mark the location of the barrier on each occasion. (Base map copyright National Library of Scotland)

which were meant to raise the king's popularity and public profile. On the day following his arrival, the king and his entourage proceeded in a carriage via Bernard Street and Constitution Street up Leith Walk (Fig. 5.1). They met Edinburgh's civic leaders in the Picardy Place–Union Street area, where a temporary gate was ceremonially opened to allow His Majesty to enter, and where the keys of the city were presented to him. The procession continued towards St Andrew Square, along Regent Road, and down Abbey Hill to the royal Palace of Holyroodhouse, which the king briefly visited, before proceeding to Dalkeith Palace. The procession for Queen Victoria was similar in principle, if not in precise route (Fig. 5.1): on 1 September 1842 Queen Victoria and Prince Albert arrived at Granton Harbour from England, and proceeded in a carriage up Granton Pier, Inverleith Row and Brandon Street. Here a barrier gate had been erected for performing the ceremonial delivery of the keys, an event which was, however, postponed at the last minute. The carriage proceeded through Pitt Street, Dundas Street and Hanover Street to Princes Street, then past General Register House to Waterloo Place, Calton Hill road and Norton Place, after which the procession passed Comely Green and Piershill on the way to Portobello, from where it headed to the queen's temporary residence at Dalkeith Palace.

Edinburgh had a longstanding tradition as the civic location for celebrating a monarch's arrival: from new royal brides – Margaret Tudor in 1503, Mary of Guise in 1538 and Anne of Denmark in 1590 – to monarchs taking on their duties – young James IV in 1579, and the widowed Mary Queen of Scots returning from France in 1561; as well as to absentee kings of Scotland fleetingly visiting the country – James VI and I in 1617 and Charles I in 1633.[2] Triumphal entries were commonly celebrated all around Europe to welcome monarchs within a civic precinct, often a capital city; they were inspired by the ancient Roman celebrations honouring a general or an emperor's military successes, with an added dimension of Christian morality.[3] Also, these public glorifications of dynastical continuity strengthened the bond between the celebrated guest and the capital's urban community, representing in these instances the nation at large. Triumphal welcomes gave the hosting city a chance to covertly present the ruler with sensitive issues for

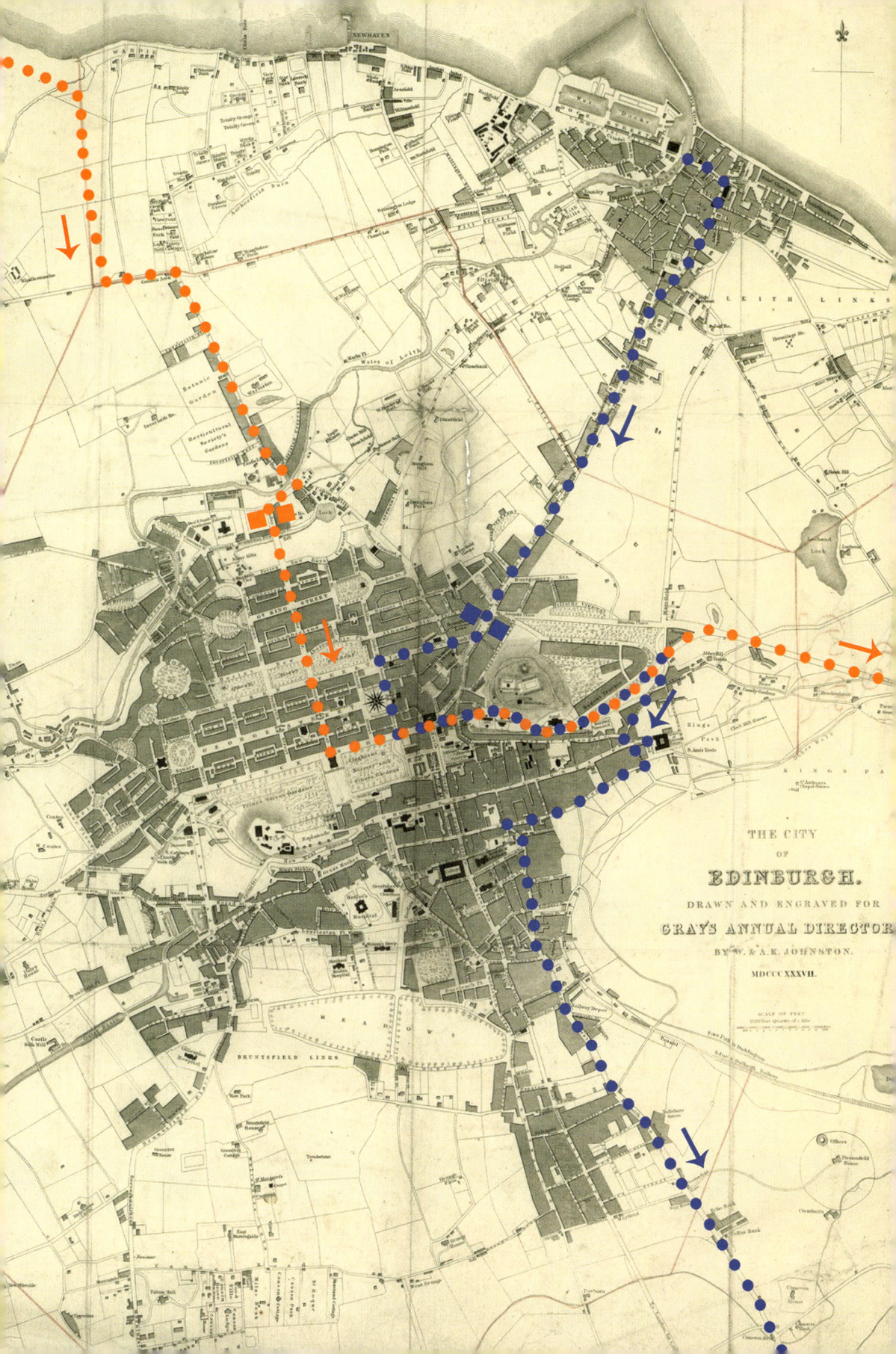

THE CITY
OF
EDINBURGH.
DRAWN AND ENGRAVED FOR
GRAY'S ANNUAL DIRECTORY
BY W. & A.K. JOHNSTON.
MDCCCXXXVII.

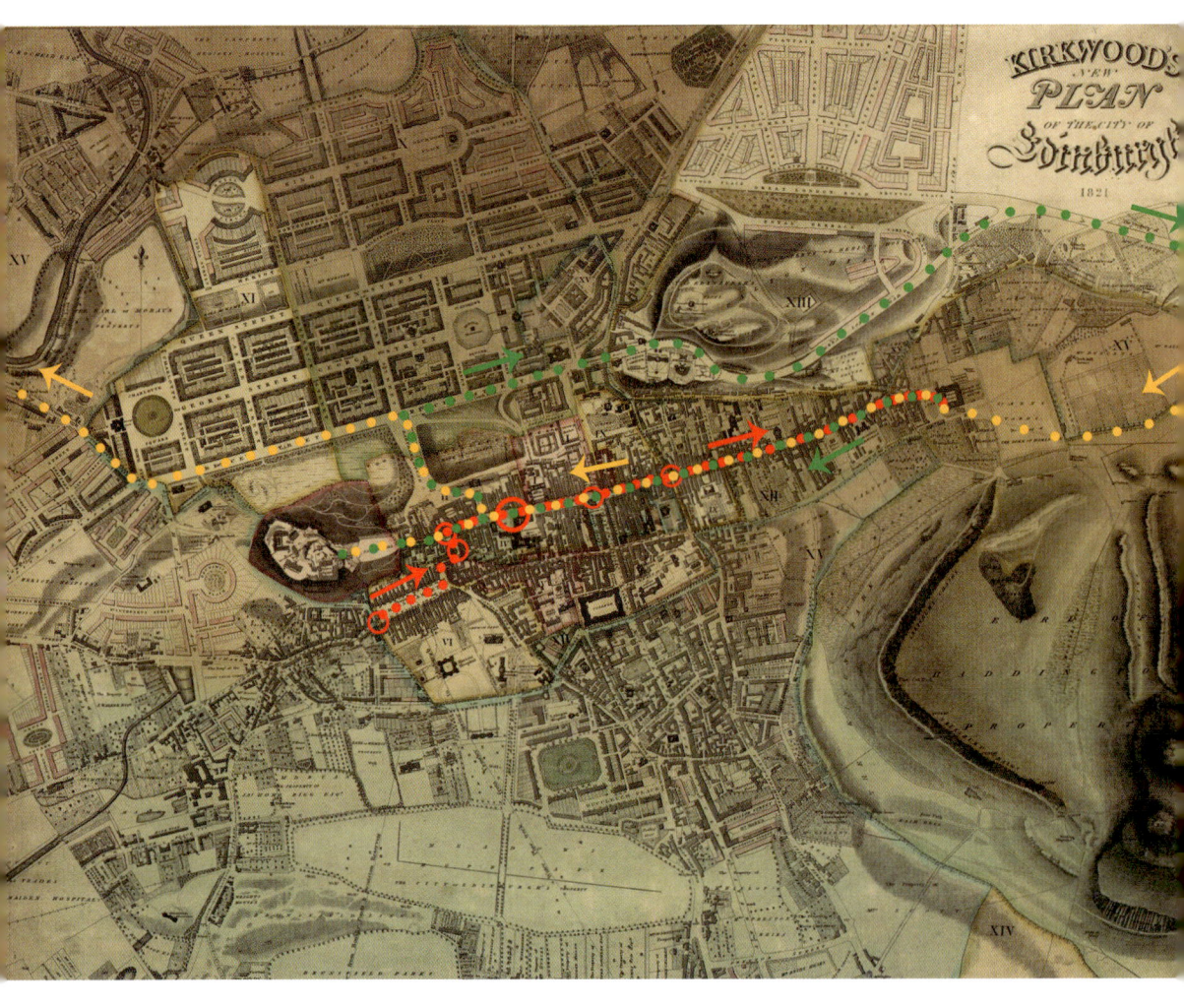

consideration, to express expectations and even complaints, and to respectfully make recommendations.

The civic stage for these performances was what is now known as the historic Old Town, but which then represented the totality of the royal burgh of Edinburgh. The burgh was bound by its walled defences, by geographical frontiers – the Nor' Loch to the north and the Castle rock to the west – and by the neighbouring community of Canongate to the east.[4] The triumphal route, with minimal alterations, was a repetitive one, centred on public structures and landmarks. Generally, the ruler was admitted into town at the urban city gate of the West Port, then the procession promenaded through the Grassmarket up the Over Bow to the Butter Tron – a public weighing station – and then went down the High Street between two densely built-up frontages of tall, adjoining tenement buildings. The procession passed next to the Tolbooth – a multi-purpose public building used as meeting space, court room and jail – by the Market Cross and St Giles' Cathedral. It then reached a second weighing station at the Salt Tron, at the site of the current Tron Kirk, and exited the city at the Netherbow gateway (Fig. 5.2). The stations coincided with gateways, commercial structures, administrative buildings and religious landmarks. All these buildings symbolically represented and physically hosted the activities upon which Edinburgh's prosperity and very identity were then based, reiterating the burgh's established position as a highly sought-after place to live, and its undisputed role as mercantile and political backbone of the Stewarts' reign.[5]

Even from this cursory comparison between the routes of the two nineteenth-century celebrations and their early modern counterparts, it is evident that the focus of royal welcomes moved, from what is now called the Old Town to a New Town that was still under construction on the other side of the drained Nor' Loch. However, while the urban setting changed – and the implications of this change will be introduced and discussed shortly – the monarchs' responses to the events as recorded in contemporary chronicles are surprisingly comparable. In both early modern and nineteenth-century ceremonies, monarchs recognised the importance of building visual and emotional bonds with the spectators gathered for the event. In 1617 King James VI and I arrived at the West Port in Edinburgh, 'where he made his entrie on horseback, that he might the better be seene by the people; wheras before, he rode in the coach all the way'.[6] In 1842 Queen Victoria also decided – abandoning her initial hopes of privacy and informality during her 'little trip' to Scotland[7] – to engage visually with the crowd, deliberately ordering the procession to proceed slowly, refusing to have the hood of the carriage drawn up in the drizzling weather, and frequently smiling and waving to the cheering crowd.[8] King George IV, a controversial character much in need of displays of goodwill and support, also 'expressed himself most anxiously to gratify his subjects by presenting himself fully to their view',[9] and willingly braved a chilly Scottish

FIGURE 5.2.
(Opposite) Base image: *Kirkwood's New Plan of the City of Edinburgh*, Edinburgh, 1821. In green, close-up of George IV's route through the Old Town on 22 September 1822. In yellow, close-up of Queen Victoria and Prince Albert's route through the Old Town on 3 September 1842. In red, for comparison, the traditional early modern route through the Old Town: the burgh's key public buildings are circled. (Base map copyright National Library of Scotland)

drizzle. In taking action to personally engage with the masses of subjects lining the streets, and to enact an image of royal benevolence and goodwill, Queen Victoria and King George IV showed their understanding of public civic spectacle to work as bonding exercises with their as-yet-unknown Scottish people, promoting lasting affection and a sense of personal familiarity.

These spectacles obviously worked both ways as displays of goodwill; the rulers' arrival and parade through the city was also an opportunity for Edinburgh's inhabitants and civic authorities to present themselves to them, and to the national and international audience who were part of the event, under the best possible light. Scotland still partly enjoyed a reputation for rough manners, inadequate housing and harsh climate,[10] and triumphal entries had traditionally played a part in staging a more refined image of the country with which to impress royal guests. On her arrival in 1538, James V's new wife Mary of Guise had declared herself pleasantly surprised to find Scotland not at all as barbarous and devoid of commodities as it had been described to her back in France.[11] Nineteenth-century entries also became occasions for the citizens and spectators to display politeness and civil manners in both attire and behaviour. An enthusiastic, grand but also orderly and uneventful welcome would dispel any murmur of disloyalty towards the House of Hanover, possibly still lingering after the last Jacobite Risings.[12] During the 1822 celebrations, it was noted with gratified relief that 'There was not one whose behaviour would have been offensive in a private drawing-room; and but few, comparatively, whose appearance might not have entitled them to admission into one.'[13]

In both the early modern celebrations and the nineteenth-century welcomes, the issue of demonstrating that Scotland's potential ruggedness had been restrained and contained was addressed in a similar manner, through the appearance of Scotland's most northern inhabitants – performers costumed as 'hielandmen' during the former,[14] and theatrically clad, tartan-wearing clan men for the latter. In Sir Walter Scott's vision for George IV's entry in 1822 in particular, visual demonstrations of Scottishness – the wearing of the tartan, for example, which Scott redesigned and reintroduced as quirky but socially acceptable attire – became components of a politically bland Celtic extravaganza, superseding their earlier status as identifiers of political support to the Jacobean cause and, implicitly, demonstrations of ideological backwardness and cultural un-refinement.[15] In *Hints Addressed to the Inhabitants of Edinburgh and Others, in Prospect of His Majesty's Visit*, King George IV was pointedly referred to as the descendant of a long line of Scottish kings, in whose veins ran Bruce's blood: 'in short, we are THE CLAN, and our king is THE CHIEF',[16] smoothly integrating Scotland's traditional social structure within a Hanoverian-friendly narrative. This change was made possible not only by the political stability granted by the victorious Hanoverians – King George himself is depicted wearing a kilt in David Wilkie's famous painting of the monarch, eager to claim visual connections to distant Scottish ancestry – but by the staging of such potentially loaded spectacles in the wide, safe streets of a New Town reminiscent of Bath and London. Both in the early modern period and in the nineteenth century, by being summoned within the orderly civic space, highlanders and northerners were to leave behind their rustic excesses and unreasonable views, and become the model subjects modern society expected them to be, influenced and instructed by the values inscribed in and embodied by the urban setting.

In their time, the Old Town and its buildings had themselves represented innovative values, such as mercantile entrepreneurship, non-feudal allegiances, openness to international influences, and willing observance of communal regulations embodied by elected bodies; but both the physical environment and the values it represented now fell short of modern expectations. In the mid eighteenth century, Edinburgh's reputation as an internationally renowned place of learning and scientific advancement consolidated, strongly influenced by the spread of the Enlightenment's modernising ideas, but the city's physical form had only recently begun to align with its progressive reputation. Until the mid eighteenth century, the burgh of Edinburgh had developed very little outside the boundaries of the walled Old Town, and its attempts to establish itself as Britain's northern capital were – it was perceived by the local intelligentsia – hampered by what was now perceived to be an old-fashioned urban layout. The Edinburgh New Town was built as a response to these needs for modernity and renovation: the construction of the New Town was not meant to merely increase the size of the burgh, but to dramatically mark a change in character and identity, as a physical embodiment of Edinburgh's intellectual revival.[17]

The change of focus in the procession from the traditional landmarks of the Old Town – the ancient gateways of the West Port and Netherbow, the Tolbooth, the densely built-up High Street and the steep Overbow – to the dynamic, forward-thinking New Town as the stage for the welcoming ceremonies was meant to make this new identity physically present to the royal visitors. In both cases, a narrative was created for the ruler to explore by a sequence of civic spaces, working with decorations, speeches, tableaux vivants and theatrical performances, to create a multi-layered event.[18] The New Town civic spaces and monuments – in a variety of architectural languages, such as the neo-classical, Greek revival and Baronial styles – represented Enlightened values and offered the actual facilities where intellectual advancement would take place: an observatory, classical monuments to great and valorous Scottish figures, a prestigious high school, theatres and academies, and other shrines to the arts, in an urban setting speaking of progressive thinking, social engagement and civilised, ordered decorum.[19] Formal facade design grouped tenement buildings together, creating the illusion of palatial respectability; large gardens provided space for genteel exercise, and wide streets favouring commodious means of transportation were cleared of menial traffic, which was now confined to separate, lesser service alleyways. Indoors, the real or perceived issues of overcrowding and lack of cleanliness attributed to the Old Town were tackled by a new attention to privacy and separation from neighbours, decorum, but also visibility and external display through architectural language.[20] The needs for entertainment, civic participation and self-improvement were addressed by new purpose-built structures; foundation stones for the National Monument of Scotland, the Victoria Hall and the General Assembly building were meaningfully laid down during the 1822 visit (the first) and the 1842 visit (the last two), inviting the monarchs to witness the ongoing civic renovation.[21] By being guided through the new urban landscape, the monarchs were shown the built evidence of the city's intellectual progress and civility that they must have been hearing about – or at very least its aspirational promise, as many buildings were not yet completed.

The chronicles describe what the monarchs saw, and their reaction to the display. George IV admired 'the magnitude of the buildings' and 'the splendour of the windows'[22] while moving up Picardy Place, and 'the Melville Monument, standing in the centre in solitary grandeur; the magnificent vista on the right, formed by George Street, and terminated by the lofty dome of St George's Church'.[23] The involvement of Queen Victoria with the various buildings encountered en route is even more marked. The royal party would have enjoyed the view from George Street east to St Andrew Square and the Melville Monument (the square was established in 1772), and west to Charlotte Square and the dome of St George's Church (established in 1814). The queen made positive remarks regarding St Andrew's Church (completed 1784), and questioned her companions about Chantrey's statue of George IV (1831) and about 'that great and imposing Grecian building, the Royal Institution',[24] the name and purpose of which she was immediately informed of. The queen also showed great interest and asked many questions about the as yet unfinished monument to Sir Walter Scott, on Princes Street.[25] The procession passed the Royal Hotel, Adam's General Register House (1774–89) and the Theatre Royal. Queen Victoria was greatly impressed by Calton Hill, and in her own personal account she noted down an interestingly eclectic list of the buildings which had caught her eye: the National Monument, Nelson's Monument, the Gaol, the National School.[26]

The public buildings and institutions, the wide streets, ordered layout and regular facades both reflected and encouraged positive social effects such as civility and politeness, promoting compliance and diligence in the population, and represented – according to a slightly paternalistic Anglo-centred narrative – the newly found order and structure of Scottish society after the political chaos of the Jacobite years. In 1752 Sir Gilbert Elliot of Minto's *Proposals for Carrying on Certain Public Works in the City of Edinburgh* was published. It unfavourably compared old-fashioned, peripheral Edinburgh (and by extension, Scotland) to modern and established London and England, suggesting improvements to turn Edinburgh into a worthy capital of northern Britain, both companion and competitor to London in the south, and an 'Athens of the North'.[27] The Scottish people – genteel-looking, well behaved and suitably attired – were then every bit as restrained, orderly and civilised as the New Town itself, worthy inhabitants of that genteel urban landscape.

Some of the inhabitants were more directly and personally involved with the celebrations, not only as onlookers but as organisers of the temporary apparatus decorating the streets of the city. The exceedingly long list of those involved in the urban decorations in 1822 mentions several types of organisation – administrative bodies like the Royal Exchange and the North British Fire Office; insurance companies such as the Caledonian Insurance Office and the Scottish Life Insurance Company's Office; offices for newspapers such as the *Advertiser* and the *Scotsman*; banks and other large enterprises including the Commercial Bank, the Post Office, the Waterloo Hotel and the Albyn Club; and companies such as the British Linen Company. Private individuals, both of high rank such as the Duke of Atholl and Lady Duncan, and those belonging to the middle classes such as 'Messers Gow & Son, music sellers . . . Mr. Paterson, saddler . . . [and] Mr Gianetti, profumer'[28] also took charge of a large part of the decorations – although information on what exactly was created is not very specific, nor did it show particular originality.

In 1822, two arches were erected, one on Bernard Street and one on Constitution Street: 'both were adorned with flowers and evergreens, and a variety of flags, among which the British Union Jack was the most conspicuous'.[29] General themes of the decorations were the Scottish crown and sceptre, the royal initials and joyful welcoming mottos. An elegant crown bearing the words 'Descendant of the immortal Bruce, thrice welcome'[30] placed King George in 1822 in his rightful position alongside his Scottish ancestors, making him a familiar and agreeable figure to his local subjects. Similarly in 1842 Edinburgh, public buildings and bodies, such as the Royal Exchange, the Royal College of Surgeons, the Scotsman Office and the Bank of Scotland, all organised illuminations and ornamentations. The Scottish Widows' insurance company funds erected an arch supported by thistles and a crown. The great bulk of decorations were put up by private houses, hotels and shops – such as the hotels run by the Mackays and the Barrys, the painter Mr Hay, the wine merchant Mr Hewat, and the confectioner Mr Mackie. Mr Stewart, painter, produced a decoration representing an arch in Nicolson

Square, while Gordon's on the Mound made an arch of evergreens with medallion portraits and decorations.[31]

The impressive list of societies, business and enterprising individuals that were involved in the construction of ceremonial structures and decorations both in 1822 and in 1842 represents a clear change from earlier times. During the sixteenth century, decorations and welcoming pageants were generally in the hands of the civic authorities as representatives of the burgh acting in the interest of the community. In August 1561 it was up to the City Council – the Provost, the Bailies, the Dean of Guild and the Treasurer, together with the influential craft deacons – to deliberate how the money for Mary Queen of Scots' entry was to be raised and allocated, from ordering construction timber and cloth for uniforms, to purchasing silver plates to give to the queen as a present.[32] The local authority's understanding of the events and ability to coordinate them – or the citizens' willingness to take them on board – seem to have dramatically diminished over time. Some of their proposals – for example, that all fellow citizens were to wear identical outfits for the 1822 visit – were criticised as both impractical and interfering.[33] This worked to the advantage of active entrepreneurs with ideas and means who, much to the magistrates' irritation, built cheap, insecure stands on their own initiative on the pavements of Edinburgh, providing extra space for paying visitors.[34] In 1822, the organisation of the welcome for King George IV fell to Walter Scott as 'the local magistrates, bewildered and perplexed with the rush of novelty, threw themselves on him for advice and direction about the merest trifles; and he had to arrange everything, from the ordering of a procession to the cut of a button and the embroidering of a cross'.[35]

The civic authorities seemed hardly more in control in 1842 when, unaware of Queen Victoria's landing in Leith in the early hours of the morning and possibly intentionally misled because of political squabbles with Prime Minister Sir Robert Peel, they were 'struck at once with surprise and dismay . . . started up to a man, and . . . rushed to their carriages, *sauve qui peut* . . . [and] pursued their break-neck way down the steep and narrow Canongate'.[36] The magistrates' rushed departure caused commotion in those assembled in the High Street, and 'the confusion became quite like that of a routed army'.[37]

A more modern understanding of self-promotion and advertisement took the place of traditional organisational structures in setting up the event, but the former side-lined and overlapped the latter rather than entirely eliminating it. Similarly, the spaces of the New Town took the leading role in hosting the ceremonial welcomes, but the Old Town was marginalised rather than entirely erased from the narrative of the event. For one, in its dominating position over the volcanic ridge leading to Edinburgh Castle, the Old Town was never too far away, both geographically and in the eyes and minds of the visiting monarchs. George IV marvelled at the fascinating contrast between his surroundings and 'the smoky piles of the Old Town, towering in irregular majesty' in the background.[38] While riding with Prince Albert on Queensferry Road on 3 September, the queen remarked that 'the view of Edinburgh from the road before you enter Leith is quite enchanting . . . fairy-like, and what you would only imagine as a thing to dream of, or to see in a picture'.[39]

Both King George and Queen Victoria did visit the Old Town a few days after their official welcomes, but this was simply a tourists' visit of their two residences, the Palace of Holyroodhouse and the Castle, with the burgh being an in-between space to be passed through, devoid of the politicised messages – speeches, triumphal arches, delivery of gifts – that had created the complex dialogue between royal and civic authority (see Fig. 5.2). During their ascent – as the traditionally downward route onto the High Street had been reversed – both George and Victoria were struck by the overall quaint appearance of the burgh much more than by the significance of its various buildings and locations, about which they did not ask questions and which were not explained to them. While in her carriage on the way to the Castle in 1842 Queen Victoria found nothing else to enquire about but a group of Newhaven fisherwomen, declaring herself 'much pleased with their picturesque appearance'.[40] Not only side-lined or ignored, some of the traditional buildings had actually been removed as obstacles to traffic, their prominent position in the middle of the High Street not now justified by an equally prominent role in the civic life – or by a popular interest in the values they stood for. In 1822, in preparation for George IV's arrival, 'The Magistrates determined upon the removal of every obstruction or deformity along the route of the procession. The Weigh-house, at the head of the West Bow, a massive but unshapely building, which had stood for upwards of five hundred years, was accordingly removed.'[41] The Netherbow – a civic gate also pivotal for the early modern triumphal route – had already been taken down in August 1764 'having been considered as an impediment to the street'.[42] During the New Town-based welcome celebrations, the cumbersome presence of the Old Town could have been politically loaded, as a permanent reminder of a not-so-distant time when Edinburgh was the capital of an independent kingdom. However, its potentially threatening characters were blurred over, and its picturesque aspects were decontextualised and reframed as harmless, diplomatically neutral tourist attractions, as had happened under Sir Walter Scott with the potentially Jacobite associations of northern Scottish culture.

The Scottish past and the built environment it referred to was intended for entertainment rather than educational purposes.[43] Besides, Scottish history – Scott's own renegotiated version of it – could offer a new basis to a community challenged by modern issues of social mobility, self-interest and commercial individualism.[44] As such, some elements were purposefully taken out of context and reinserted in the New Town environment as entertaining and familiarly reassuring, if rather hollow, public rituals. One of them was the ceremony of welcome at the gate and delivery of the keys, performed – or in the latter case at least attempted – in the New Town in both 1822 and 1842.

Traditionally in Edinburgh, the delivery of the keys and associated ceremonies took place at or in the immediate vicinities of the West Port. This, for example, had been the case for James VI in 1579, for Anne of Denmark in 1590 and for Charles I in 1633, while James VI and I in 1617 had been presented at the gate with 'the scepter off the citie', probably with a similar meaning of homage and submission.[45] This ceremony reminded the rulers of the burgh's right to regulate admittance into the urban precinct, and to reassure them of the burgh's loyalty and goodwill. The West Port represented an actual civic border marking the extent of the city's right to regulate taxation, imports and exports, access, and even citizenship and personal freedoms. With the construction of the New Town, the city's Regality had expanded well beyond the West Port and the Old Town's walled boundary, and the old protectionist notions these civic borders embodied had been left behind; Pilrig Street – about half way down Leith Walk – was the new imaginary line between Edinburgh and the nearby community of Leith.[46] However, in both 1822 and 1842 the temporary bastions where the ceremony was set were, as we saw, built elsewhere: near Union Street in 1822, and at the head of Brandon Street in 1842. After all, this was not a *real* welcome into a civic precinct, but just the imaginary depiction of one for entertainment. In 1822, spectacle and pomp were liberally and imaginatively added by Scott, with elaborate approaching, ceremonial knocking and answering, after which the timber gateway built for the occasion was opened and the king and his entourage proceeded through, before receiving the keys of the city from the provost.[47]

In 1842, the barrier erected at Brandon Street ended up not being used at all, as the arrival of the queen's party unexpectedly early meant the magistrates and city representatives were not in place to play their part and the procession simply went through the unmanned structure. The barriers were subsequently removed and rebuilt at the Market Cross in the Old Town, and the welcoming ceremony was performed there when Queen Victoria passed on the High Street a few days later on the way to the Castle. The mismatch between the symbolic meaning of accessing a space and the awkward positioning of the gate within such space was not lost on the chroniclers; as remarked by Lauder, 'the spot selected was certainly good for the production of spectacle and picturesque effect – considerations which were enough to outweigh the apparent, though very unimportant absurdity of placing the gate of a city in the very middle of it'.[48]

The idea of the civilising potential of the urban space – carrying in their very names echoes of the Latin ideas of *urbanitas* and *civitas* – connects orderly behaviour with the acceptance of the physical and social limitations inherent to living in the urban environment. Nineteenth-century ceremonies shared with their early modern counterparts the setting of higher expectations of behaviour, address, and attire for those participating in the civic event, and separating the city dwellers from the potentially threatening or disappointingly 'backward' outer people. The centrality of the New Town, its buildings, spaces, inhabitants, and the modern way of thinking it represented in the ceremonial welcomes for George IV and for Queen Victoria and Prince Albert, marks a changed awareness of what Edinburgh – and, through its capital, Scotland at large – was, and stood for, in Enlightened post-1707 Union-age Britain. The spaces and architecture of the New Town were loaded with the responsibility of informing and inspiring the behaviour of people living in it; welcoming routes were selected to provide evidence of gentility and improvement; and evidence of spatial renovation was shown to the monarch as sure proof of moral and cultural regeneration.

The choice of parading the ruler through the regularised spaces of the New Town, through spaces heavily influenced by London's examples of rational, modern city planning, also served a clear political agenda. An initial plan in the form of a Union Jack devised by James Craig and drawn by John Laurie in 1766 had been abandoned as impractical, but the ideology of infusing a Unionist agenda on the new development had remained, colouring Edinburgh civic improvement in a veneer of Anglicisation. Historical elements belonging to the early modern tradition were not, however, entirely erased, as carefully handpicked ceremonies such as the delivery of the keys were translated and maintained to provide the Hanoverian sovereigns with the staged sense of continuity between past and present they needed to validate their rule. Scott understood not only the continuing role of triumphal entries in legitimising and reconciling with a monarch whose position could otherwise be questionable or problematic, but also the necessity to display through the urban route an image of Edinburgh and of Scotland appropriate for the ruler's dignified and dignifying political counterpart. However, the choice to marginalise the Old Town during the nineteenth-century ceremonies – its traditional, site-specific architecture being blamed for the perceived poverty and moral debasement of its inhabitants, and the now-superseded historic evidence it represented being conveniently limited to its entertaining, picturesque potential – shows a remarkably refined understanding of the relationship between spatial, political and behavioural considerations.

CHAPTER 6

The Spatial and Social Characteristics of Craft Businesses in Edinburgh's New Town c.1780–1850

Stana Nenadic

INTRODUCTION: BUILDING THE NEW TOWN

Edinburgh's first New Town was designed to stimulate national prosperity through investment in the commercial infrastructure and housing of the capital city and thereby bring about a 'spirit of industry and improvement'. The model was London and the context was decades of economic decline and physical deterioration.

> The meanness of Edinburgh has been too long an obstruction to our improvement, and a reproach to Scotland. The increase of our people, the extension of our commerce, and the honour of the nation, are all concerned in the success of this project.[1]

Housing provision and workshop space for the 'better class of artisan', mainly in the secondary streets and lanes, were integral to the plan.[2]

Building the New Town gave unprecedented opportunities for expansion and skills development in the different branches of the building crafts, ranging from stone masons to joiners, house decorators, glaziers and fancy metal smiths. When buildings were completed, the cabinetmakers were in demand for furnishings, along with artists and print engravers for the room decoration. Ceramic and crystal glassmakers and domestic textile designers and weavers similarly saw demand increase as wealthy elites concentrated in Edinburgh for their residence and for consumption. Even industrial and high technology firms developed lines of fine hand-crafted production for Edinburgh's New Town, such as the Carron Iron Works near Falkirk, which in addition to its output of cannon balls and iron girders, also made fine domestic ironwork for decorative railings, rainwater goods and especially its registered fire grates and stoves, elegantly designed, with matching fenders and fire irons.[3]

Locating in the New Town

The attractions of the New Town for Edinburgh's craftsmen and women, though complex and varied, were rooted in the pressures that were generated by the expansion of people and workshops in the crumbling Old Town. Edinburgh's Dean of Guild Court records are full of complaints over the inappropriate use of tenement flats for workshop uses, with noisy machinery and polluting materials that inconvenienced domestic users and threatened buildings due to vibration and weight of materials on ageing floorboards and joists.[4] Dangerous stoves and illegal chimneys were a particular cause for concern, as demonstrated in January 1809 when several residents of a Mylnes Court tenement lodged complaints against Alexander Martin, plasterer, who 'about two years ago, placed a stove for preparing stucco in his premises, situated below all three of the petitioners. The stove stands on the floor but has a pipe to conduct the smoke to a chimney'.[5] He was ordered to remove the stove. Printers in particular were subject to much concern, seen in complaints against Grant & Moire in Paterson's Court in 1792 because of the large vats of oil and open fires that were used in the business. Or, more alarming still, a complaint of 1770 against Mr Esplin, wallpaper printer, in Bell's Wynd whose equipment in a building described as 'weak and frail' was threatening to bring the tenement crashing down.[6] Such concerns were well founded, as hundreds of residents and dozens of business owners found on the night of 15 November 1824 when a great fire broke out in a large tenement in Old Assembly Close, near Parliament Square. It started in the printing office of the engravers James Kirkwood & Sons when an unattended pot of linseed oil, being heated in preparation for making copperplate printing ink, burst into flames and quickly spread into adjoining buildings.[7] On finding themselves burned out of their premises, James Kirkwood & Sons relocated to South St Andrew Street in the New Town, as did several of their neighbours. One of those affected was Charles Thomson, engraver, who provided an account of the impact of the fire when he advertised in the *Scotsman* a month later.

> Charles Thomson, engraver, regrets that, in consequence of the late calamitous Fires, he has had occasion twice to remove his Work Shops: and begs to mention, that he is now to be found at No. 19 SHAKESPEARE SQUARE, immediately behind the Theatre Royal [junction of North Bridge with Princes Street]. C.T. desires to apologise to his employers for the disappointment they have met with, and now respectfully informs them, that he is ready to receive their further orders, which he will endeavour to execute with promptitude and accuracy.[8]

Destructive fires were not the only reason for moving to the New Town. For most, it was proximity to elite customers and opportunities to advance an enterprise begun elsewhere that prompted relocation, as illustrated by John Steell (c.1779–1849), carver, gilder and print seller. Steell arrived in Edinburgh in 1806 having run a successful business in Aberdeen, advertising his removal in the press and announcing that he was commencing in business in Leith offering 'house and ship carving, gilding and print selling in all their various branches'; he also sold paper, articles for ladies' fancywork and artist materials.[9] Within a couple of years, Steell had relocated to the foot of Calton Hill, where he also had a house, and at the height of his business success c.1815 he occupied premises at 34 Princes Street. Two years later, his business was in crisis, which he attributed to losses made on portrait prints and low estimates for carving commissions. Taken into a bankruptcy (sequestration) process, Steell moved again to cheaper premises on the edge of the New Town in 1820, comprising a shop and workshop in Leith Street employing a shop man, three workmen and eight apprentices.[10] He survived the sequestration and remained active as a 'carver and gilder', moving back into the New Town at Hanover Street and then North St David Street by the early 1830s. In 1838, when he was retired from business, he was living again at Calton Hill and gave evening classes in 'ornamental modelling' at the Edinburgh School of Arts for the Instruction of Mechanics, which was in the Old Town.[11] Steell's son, who trained as a carver and gilder alongside his father, was the sculptor Sir John Steell, famous for public art such as the 1846 statue of Walter Scott in the Scott Memorial on Princes Street.[12]

Rose Street and Thistle Street

Areas close to the New Town were densely settled with craft businesses, particularly to the east around Calton Hill, Greenside and Leith Street. But it was in the secondary streets of the New Town itself – particularly Rose Street – where the New Town plan made specific provision for artisans. Rose Street was designed for mixed commercial and residential use where artisans and shopkeepers could live in modest homes alongside or above their workshops or retail premises. This was apparent by 1833–4, as revealed in the *Post Office Directory* in the first year to include a separate street listing. It was a densely occupied street, dominated by food and drink retail and with numerous lodging houses. There were services for the wealthy living nearby, such as hairdressers and florists, nurses and midwives, coach hirers, stablers and veterinary surgeons. Rose Street in 1833 also provided accommodation for over one hundred and fifty craft-based small businesses, dominated by the clothing trades and boot and shoemakers in particular, but also with large numbers of smiths and brass founders, cabinet makers and jewellers, as detailed in Table 6.1. An advertisement for the sale of property in Rose Street in 1827 reveals the close proximity of domestic and commercial space, as well as the rentals charged. It described:

> Premises, no. 86 Rose Street consisting of – 1st, Shop, two rooms etc possessed by Mr Steele, tinsmith, rent £26. House below, possessed by Mr Horsburgh, shoemaker, rent £5 10s; workshop below, possessed by Mr Roxburgh, cooper, rent £4 10s.[13]

Next door, at 88 Rose Street, was a shop, two rooms, plus a bakehouse and cellar rented for £25 with a house behind, along with a bakehouse, entered via 90 Rose Street, with a rent of £12. The purchase price was £460 for the first building, and £500 for the second. Like similarly overcrowded buildings in the Old Town, with a mix of workshops and houses, fires in Rose Street were commonplace, though less damaging owing to newer building materials and easier access for fire engines.

> Early yesterday morning [12 May 1826] a fire broke out in a back lane in Rose Street, in the tenement occupied as workshops by Mr Sommerville, painter, and Mr Hislop, dyer. The engines were soon on the spot and the fire was got out without doing much damage.[14]

Table 6.1 Craft businesses in Rose Street, 1833–4

Clothing trades	66	Furniture trades	17
Boot & shoemakers	29	Cabinetmakers and upholsterers	15
Tailors	14	Picture frame makers	2
Dressmakers	9		
Milliners	6	Precious materials trades	8
Staymakers	4	Jewellers	6
Breeches makers	2	Lapidary	1
Hosier	1	Ivory turner	1
Trimmings maker	1		
House building trades	27	Others	10
Wrights	11	Printers	3
Painters	6	Coach makers	2
Glaziers	4	Saddler	1
Masons	2	Cork manufacturer	1
Plasterers	2	Ink manufacturer	1
Slaters	2	Dyer	1
		Brush maker	1
Metalworking trades	26		
Smiths and brassfounder	18		
Farriers	3		
Bell hangers/smiths	2		
Cooper	1		
Plumber	1		
Gunsmith	1		

Source: *Edinburgh Directory for 1833–4.*

Thistle Street c.1830, with its continuation into Hill Street and Young Street at the west end, was less densely settled than Rose Street. It housed professionals and gentry along with such genteel trades as miniaturist, dressing case maker or bookseller.[15] Just a few minutes from Rose Street, it had a different spatial character and social tone, though property sales literature often stressed the potential for future changes to building uses. In 1833, for instance, a tenement in North Frederick Street at the corner with Thistle Street, given over to quality domestic flats and with an extensive streetfront and basement, was advertised for sale with change of use in mind since, 'having a considerable extent of back ground attached, which may be built on, this tenement might be advantageously converted into shops and warehouses'.[16] But conversion of premises was not always welcome to those living nearby, and complaints against craft businesses operating improperly were not confined to the Old Town. In March 1807, for instance, a Mrs Elder of Blair Street tried to build a wrights' shop in the mews lane behind the middle section of Rose Street and there were multiple objections to the noise 'night and day within three feet of valuable property' owned and occupied by the complainants.[17] A decade later, the proprietor of a townhouse at 6 Queen Street, Louis Henry Ferrier of Bellside, one of His Majesty's Commissioners of the Board of Customs, was dismayed on returning to town from his country estate to find that the stable and coach-house in Thistle Street Lane immediately behind his house, which he had sold to another landed gentleman, 'under the express condition that they should not be converted to another use' had been altered during his absence, with chimneys and a forge added, and was now being used as a blacksmiths and farriers business, producing much noise and smoke pollution. The court ordered that the building be restored to its former condition and awarded expenses to Mr Ferrier.[18] Worse still for the noise and numerous workmen was the illegal extension in 1824 to the rear of a property at 78 Rose Street by Robert Bryden & Son, bell founders and hangers, involving the construction of a large furnace and 'a great deal of hammering'. The complaint came from nearby proprietors including shopkeepers.[19]

High-density settlement of craft businesses in the New Town only began in the 1820s. A decade earlier, Rose Street accommodated a handful of boot and shoemakers towards the east end and there were many craftsmen involved in the building trades, a group whose presence was in decline by the early 1830s and had almost vanished by 1850 as building firms moved further out of the city in tandem with suburban expansion. There were numerous 'furnished lodgings' in Rose Street in 1810 and a couple of ladies' boarding schools and their teachers – the latter long gone by 1830 – along with lawyers and merchants. Most of the boot and shoemakers were gone by 1850 as they moved to cheaper premises nearby in Broughton Street to the east or Jamaica Street to the west, though Rose Street remained a focus for tailoring and dressmaking along with cabinet-makers and jewellers.

Maintaining close proximity to elite customers was part of the rationale for settling a craft-based business in the New Town, even though some of the processes involved were noxious. This is evident in an 1824 advertisement by John Kilpatrick, tinsmith, lamp manufacturer and oilman of 202 Rose Street, who advised his customers that in addition to numerous types of lamp oil for sale, he also repaired old lamps and 'cleaned, bronzed, or lacquered and made as good as new'. He fitted gas and oil supplies to domestic premises – something that only the wealthy could afford – and offered 'tinsmith work carried on in all its branches.'[20] Moreover, when a business moved out of the New Town for good commercial reasons, the proprietors were keen to keep their customers, as revealed in a *Scotsman* announcement of 1823 from long-established Rose Street fleshers, John and Thomas McGill.

> [J. & T. McGill] take this method of offering their sincere and grateful thanks to their friends and the public, for that long continued share of patronage which they have received for more than twenty years. They still hope for future countenance and support and beg leave to intimate that on Saturday first, the 19 instant, they will have removed their shop from 63 Rose Street to no. 1 New Flesh Market, where orders will be received and the meat sent to customers as usual. They trust this will not be considered inconvenient by New Town customers, when the situation is noticed, being immediately adjacent to Fish, Vegetable and Poultry Markets . . .[21]

Princes Street and George Street

The most prestigious New Town commercial streets were Princes Street and George Street and, though retail premises dominated the streetfronts, many firms also maintained workshops for their craftsmen with obvious economic benefits to be had when these were close to the wareroom. An example is illustrated in an advertisement of 1827 for 'a large front double shop or wareroom, with a large workshop behind' which was available to rent. The workshop, which was 75 feet long, was described as being 'well lighted, both from side and sky-lights' and deemed suitable for 'a cabinetmaker, upholsterer [or] printing office etc . . . such premises are not always to be found, having both workshop and warehouse connected'.[22] Such proximity was clearly desirable for management reasons and also because many proprietors were also practising master craftsmen. Moreover, craftsmen were occasionally required in the shop for customer advice, and customers sometimes visited the workshop to see commissions in progress. But having the two together could create problems relating to the exposure of genteel customers to noxious manufacturing processes along with the artisans who undertook them, whose numbers could be considerable. For instance, John Taylor & Co., sometimes styled 'Cabinetmakers to the Queen', with retail and workshop premises in West Thistle Street in the mid 1820s, moving to 109 Princes Street by the 1840s, employed 90 men and four apprentices at the Census of 1851.[23] The problem was resolved through the use of entrances on separate streets as is detailed in an account of a theft of 1830 from a jeweller at 11 George Street. The theft, of goods to the value of £600, took place overnight in the premises of David Hodges, a high-quality jeweller and silversmith specialising in tableware. The business occupied a front shop with a basement below 'which he uses as a workshop', with the latter entered from a lane behind George Street, via a door onto a common stair 'through which the tradesmen enter to their work', thus avoiding the elegant wareroom. Complex security was maintained between the shop and workshop, but a suspect customer had asked to see the workshop and in the process of being shown round was thought to have devised a way of undertaking the theft via the back door in the lane.[24]

The extent of some craft-based businesses in the New Town's principal streets can be seen through insurance records as well as employee numbers. At the east end of Princes Street, on the corner with North Bridge, was a notable building comprising the warerooms, workshop and wood-yard of William Trotter, a famous cabinetmaker, who was also a leading figure in the Town Council and Lord Provost during the 1820s.[25] The premises of the firm, then known as Young, Trotter and Hamilton, were insured through the London-based Sun Alliance Company and in 1792 the business comprised utensils and stock in the warehouse on Princes Street valued at £900; a stock of mirrors valued at £100; utensils and stock in the workshop adjoining, valued at £1,000 and timber in the yard adjoining, valued at £100 – making a total valuation for moveables of £2,100. This was a considerable sum and on a par with major textile manufacturing concerns of the day.[26] The business was so extensive that it became a tourist attraction and was detailed as a place to visit when in Edinburgh in Thomas Dibdin's *Tour in the North Counties of England and in Scotland* (1838).[27]

CABINETMAKING

Cabinetmaking firms, large and small, were found throughout the New Town and, since they were not especially noisy and made limited use of noxious materials, they rarely generated complaints. So in April 1824 William Cockburn, residing in Hanover Street, petitioned for permission to extend to the rear for a workshop on a site on Rose Street Mews Lane, behind Hanover Street. This site already had a temporary structure on it that was occupied by Alexander Dundas, cabinetmaker, which would be removed to make way for the permanent building. The request was granted.[28] At the same time and close by, was the workshop occupied by James Dowell, whose business was sequestered for bankruptcy 1829–31, giving insights into how it was run. James Dowell (1793–1857), born in Caithness, was active in Edinburgh as a cabinetmaker and upholsterer in the 1820s.[29] He operated from premises built as a coach-house in Thistle Street, behind St Andrews Church at the east end of George Street, where he also had his home, and before that from a nearby tenement at 41

Hanover Street.[30] He paid an annual rent of £27 5s for the house and workshop, and his only employee was an apprentice.[31] His bankruptcy was precipitated by a serious fire, reported in the press in May 1828, which led to the 'greater part of the furniture in progress' being lost.[32] The sequestration reveals a small and modestly furnished domestic part of the building – two rooms and a kitchen – with the contents of this and the workshop valued at just £68 4s. There was a simple working space comprising a wood-yard, a 'workshop above the dwelling house', a loft for storage above that and an 'engine house' containing a turning lathe and tools. The value of the wood was £31 4s. Though he continued in his original business and premises in Thistle Street for a short while after the bankruptcy process, Dowell shifted his activity towards furniture valuation for second-hand sales, called 'roups', which was a common secondary activity among cabinetmakers, and then worked full-time as an auctioneer, mainly selling household furniture, pictures and antiques. His later firm, known as Dowell & Co., with showrooms in George Street, was highly successful and survived into the mid twentieth century. James Dowell became a wealthy man; he was Town Councillor for the St Andrew's ward for many years and by the time of his death his home was in fashionable Royal Circus. His *Scotsman* obituary made no mention of his earlier life as a craftsman, or his bankruptcy.[33]

James Dowell's cabinetmaking and upholstery business, a fairly modest concern, represents a typical New Town cabinetmaker of the period. He had solid middle-class clients and made fashionable wares, but, though carrying relative few and small debts, was vulnerable to setbacks and eventual failure when an unanticipated crisis beset his business. That he flourished thereafter as an auctioneer is testament to his enterprise and possibly also down to simple luck, for he was in the right place at the right time, with premises in central Edinburgh at a time when the market for quality second-hand furniture was rising.[34] As a small-scale cabinetmaker with his own workshop and an apprentice, but limited stock and no retail premises, Dowell probably worked as a subcontractor for others from time to time. Bigger undertakings relied on an ability to increase their skilled workforce or subcontract according to the flow of business, hence the importance of businesses being clustered together geographically.

Another example of a New Town cabinetmaker's sequestration, when viewed through the wage book, gives an insight to how such complex relationships could operate.[35] James Watson (d. 1851) was a cabinetmaker and upholsterer with a substantial business, known as Watson & Co., that operated from warerooms and workshops in various premises in George Street from c.1830 to 1853.[36] His *Post Office Directory* listing frequently also included mention of an undertaking business run in conjunction with the cabinetmaking concern – a common combination of interests. In his early commercial life, Watson lived in a house at 3 Young Street, though later he occupied a flat above his business at 121 George Street.[37] The reasons for the sequestration are unclear, though it is possible that ill health leading to his death in 1851 was a contributory factor. The wages book for Watson & Co. covers the period c.1844–52, including a year or so after Watson had died.[38] It includes details of payment for individual cabinetmakers, upholsterers, polishers, turners, apprentices and sewing-room women. The index lists sixty-five individuals termed 'cabinetmakers' and nineteen 'upholsterers', all coming and going from the New Town workshop, though most of these were only employed for short periods. One of them, a cabinetmaker called James McCallam, was employed throughout the years covered by the wages book, he had the highest wages listed and was probably the foreman. The sewing-room women, who were not indexed, were a shifting group, but one – Ann Boak – was listed every year and monthly, and appears to have been a permanent employee who, given her higher wages, was probably the sewing-room forewoman.

The wages for most of the workers were fixed for a 60-hour, six-day week ranging from 25s for the foreman; 16s or 19s, varied according to skill and seniority, for the cabinetmakers; 15s for the upholsterers and polishers; to 5s or 6s for the apprentices, who worked a shorter week of 48–54 hours. Many of these skilled workers were also paid at piece-rates, including those who in some periods were on weekly contracts. The weekly employed men occasionally worked for longer hours and were paid overtime pro-rata. The sewing-room women, whose hours were unspecified, ranged in payments from 8s per week for the forewoman to 5s to 6s for the others. With a shifting population of employees, many short-term and on piece-rates, it is hard to gauge how many were in the workshop at any given time but a rough estimate is ten men, two apprentices and two female sewers. With short hours the norm, it is assumed that many also worked for other cabinetmaking firms or supplemented their earnings with other forms of work.

In addition to the wages paid and the hierarchies of workers involved in such a firm of cabinetmakers, the wages book offers insights to what was being made by Watson & Co., and some of the customers are also listed. For example, John Brown, cabinetmaker on 16s per week, was in regular weekly employment throughout August 1848. In September he was employed in piecework with weekly hours ranging from 34 for the week at the start of the month and just 3.5 hours in the last week of the month. In early October he was paid for making specified objects, as follows:

A birch 4ft tent bed (for stock)	9s 6d
6 folding trunk stands (for Mr Burnett)	10s 6d
A birch French bed (for stock)	15s
A mahogany four post bed (for stock)	£2 15s
A rosewood pillar and claw for marquetery tabletop (for L.B. Hare Esq.)	9s 6d
2 ditto (for stock)	19s
A Grecian ottoman on rosewood mouldings and ball, lifting top (for Sir Robert Houston)	6s
A rosewood Elizabethan cross leg stool 21×30 inches (for Alexander Haig Esq.)[39]	12s

Payment for these items together, all undertaken between 6 and 13 October, came to almost £6, which is a larger sum than John Brown commonly earned in a week, but he was acting on a subcontracting basis, possibly from a workshop of his own and employing lesser workers or apprentices to help him. From 13 October onwards and for many months thereafter he returned to hourly paid work, with another burst of subcontracting for specified items, including a mahogany dressing table and chest of drawers, in mid June 1849. Subcontracting such as this gives an insight into the labour flexibility that prevailed in the cabinetmaking trade, with skilled men sometimes working for themselves and sometimes for other firms, which underlines the advantages incurred through geographical concentration in the New Town. The records also show the range of items commonly carried in stock by a fashionable George Street firm like Watson & Co., and the identities of elite customers who included Lord Cockburn, the famous Edinburgh lawyer and antiquarian, and Mr Scott of Ettrick Bank in the Scottish Borders, who is frequently listed. There was a Lady Ross who purchased a 'Spanish mahogany half back couch'; and a James Robertson Esq. of 11 Heriot Row, who ordered a 'rosewood armchair with circular seat'. Items made for specified customers were commonly reproduced for stock and retail sale.[40]

Conclusion

The New Town made extensive provision for craft firms to operate successfully, with a relentless creation of commercial premises to accommodate them, many converted from residential use. Of course, not all commercial undertaking operated from commercial premises – indeed, one source of commonly recorded grievance was over the use of domestic property for business purposes. In 1800, for instance, a petition of complaint was submitted to the Dean of Guild Court with reference to a tenement building at 6 South St David Street by Miss J. McFarlane, Miss Margaret Campbell and Lieut. Col. John Cochrane. The object of their ire was fellow tenement occupant John Bonar, who had painted a large sign above the doorway to the common stair stating 'John Bonar Painter'. He was ordered to remove this.[41] John Bonar, of a long-established family firm, was described in the *Directory* as 'painter, house and paper ware room of 6 South St David's Street' and he also ran a 'colour shop' for selling paint at the 'head of North Bridge'.[42] He, and his father before him, had a large country house practice and doubtless his wallpaper wareroom in the New Town, which was a room in a domestic apartment that he occupied with his family, was convenient for genteel customers. That he chose to live in the New Town also suggests aspirations, though his business activity clearly annoyed the neighbours.

Although the New Town supported large numbers of craft workers as well as retail premises, the highest concentrations were skewed towards the east, in close proximity to the main road to the Old Town via North Bridge and linking into Leith Street and the route to the port of Leith. Areas on the periphery of the New Town were also a focus for certain types of elite-serving craft firms, seen at the top of Leith Street and Greenside Street, clustered around Calton Hill and down Broughton Street, where property rentals were cheaper than in the New Town. Another cluster was at the northwest end of the New Town, along the route into Stockbridge, with India Street Lane and Jamaica Street, which were part of the second New Town, built from 1802 as tenement housing for artisans. Indeed, as the second New Town was developed, craft firms followed into the secondary streets and lanes or on the periphery.

There was much fluidity in the profile of craft firms in Edinburgh's New Town, with movement in and out according to individual circumstances and the changing fortunes of particular trades. Most firms were small, though there were also some remarkably large employers of craft workers, who kept workshops behind their extensive retail premises, at least through to the mid nineteenth century. By the second half of the century, the big retail firms that maintained their own craft workshops had largely moved the latter to the industrial suburbs, particularly to the west of the city in areas like Roseburn, while maintaining their shops in George Street or Princes Street.[43]

Little remains in central Edinburgh today to remind us of this once flourishing site of craft production. A rare survival, founded in 1866, is the fine jewellers and silversmiths Hamilton & Inches at 87 George Street, which still maintains a small workshop attached to the shop with master craftsmen and apprentices in premises that have been occupied by a succession of jewellery firms since the 1830s. Though tastes have changed, much of the work undertaken by Hamilton & Inches remains the same as it was in the early years of the New Town, with original jewellery made to order and prestige commissions for tableware or presentation pieces alongside a steady flow of dented antique silver teapots or cream jugs in need of repair.[44]

CHAPTER 7

Mobile City: Edinburgh as a Communications Hub 1775–1825

Richard Rodger

When the *Old Statistical Account of Scotland*[1] was published in 1799 the country was dominated by rural parishes and regional networks of small burghs. As if to stress the point the *Edinburgh Post Office Directory* identified over 700 annual fairs scheduled that year to take place in towns throughout Scotland.[2] With few navigable rivers, slow and seasonally constrained maritime connections and a tardy uptake in canal construction – there were fifty canals in England by 1799 and three in Scotland – road connections were vital to local economies north of the border. Within this road transport system, and long before a railway network existed, Edinburgh functioned as a communications hub for county towns and a number of strategically placed burghs (Fig. 7.1).

One indication of the integrated connections operating from Edinburgh was a postal service. Over 160 places in Scotland were designated as 'postal towns', and a published timetable and frequency existed from the late eighteenth century.[3] In 1799, for example, mail coaches left every day at 8am for fifty destinations; an hour later mail coaches departed for another thirty towns. Daily afternoon and evening services departed at 4pm and 8pm to bring the total number of burghs with a daily mail service to over 100. Elsewhere towns were connected with a reduced frequency, usually three deliveries each week, though Hebridean and some north of Scotland destinations enjoyed only a weekly mail service (Fig. 7.2).

Not only did the mail service specify departures, delivery times were given too. For example, mail to 'the North and all depending

FIGURE 7.1.
Scheduled sail and steam ship routes from Leith, 1825. (Based on information from *The Post Office Annual Directory for 1825–26*, Edinburgh 1825)

on it, departs every day at Eight in the Morning, and arrives generally about 12 Noon'. The London mail 'is dispatched every day . . . at four afternoon. Arrives every morning', and was proudly hailed as the first delivery of the day in Edinburgh. The second delivery in the city was of letters from Aberdeen and Inverness via Dundee and Perth; it was 'an hour after arrival' at 12.45. Deliveries from Glasgow, Dumfries and Ireland that arrived in Edinburgh by 2pm were delivered by 5pm as the third mail delivery service of the day to Edinburgh businesses and residents. The sense of a dependable, organised service with an important contribution to business efficiency and personal contact filtered through the dry details of mail times.

Moving mail was only part of a communications network in the

FIGURE 7.2.
Postal services from Edinburgh, 1799. Note: blue signifies daily postal delivery; red indicates three or fewer deliveries per week. (Based on information from *The Edinburgh and Leith Directory, 1799–1800*, Edinburgh 1800)

city. Another was moving people. In 1774 the four-horse 'True Britain Coach' from Edinburgh to Glasgow left McKay's in the Grassmarket at 8am; a day return ticket cost £0.75 (about £90 in 2018 prices).[4] The wide Grassmarket was the long-established 'hub' for carriers to all over Scotland, and 44% of all carriers in 1774 left from there, with a further 17% departing from premises in the adjacent streets of Candlemaker Row and Cowgatehead.[5] In the next quarter century, even though the number of arrivals and departures increased by over 70%, the Grassmarket operators and firms in adjacent streets retained their dominance, totalling 62% of all coaching business in 1799.

Fodder for horses, as well as food and lodgings for passengers, were both at their greatest concentration in the intersecting Grassmarket–Cowgatehead–Candlemaker streets. Predictably, given its infancy, only a very limited number of New Town coach services existed in the early 1770s, though these included a departure point in mid Rose Street bound for Kirkcudbright, and a mail coach service at 4pm on weekdays from Drysdale's Turf coffee-house in St Andrew Street destined for London.[6] By 1825, however, the overall number of mail and coach departures from Edinburgh had more than tripled compared with the 1790s, and though there had been some consolidation in the number of operators, the Grassmarket area still retained its predominance. In the first two decades of the nineteenth century a consolidation of carriers reflected a logistical sophistication regarding routes, horsepower and manpower, and the firms' ability to meet timetables for departures and arrivals. These four firms had significantly advanced their businesses by the 1820s: Wilkinson's (14 Bristo Street) with a 14% market share; Cameron's (16 Lothian Street) and the George Inn (Bristo Street) each with a 7% market share; and Muir's (152 High Street) with 6% market share. Together these four firms operated almost 200 or 34% of all carrier 'inter-city', or more appropriately inter-burgh, routes.

Local services, naturally, were most frequent and numerous; coach stances eventually developed at the North Bridge–Princes Street intersection. An hourly coach service operated to Leith between 9am and 11pm from the Black Bull in Catherine Street (now Leith Street); three companies operated nine daily services to Musselburgh, including Waldie's 'slow-coach' service from the North Bridge with a single horse and a differentiated fare structure – it cost a third more for two horses and a third less for two-wheeled carriages. Such social stratification was explicit in the passenger transport business, and this applied equally to longer-distance routes. By naming the service 'commercial', as in the 'Commercial Traveller' 6am service of J. Scott and Co. on Tuesdays, Thursdays and Saturdays from Edinburgh to Carlisle via Biggar, Thornhill and Dumfries,

FIGURE 7.3. (Overleaf) Principal departure points for coaches from Edinburgh, 1825. (Based on information from *The Post Office Annual Directory for 1825–26*, Edinburgh 1825; base map Robert Kirkwood, *Plan of the City of Edinburgh*, 1817, reproduced by permission of the National Library of Scotland)

N. Bank Street
BANK STREET
Bank of Scotland
James Court
LAWN MARKET
County Hall
CASTLE HILL
WEST BOW
GRASS MARKET
Merchant Str.
CANDLEMAKER ROW
CHURCH YARD
Greyfriars Churches
Brown Square
Heriots Hospital
Poor House for Adults
Reservoir
MOUND

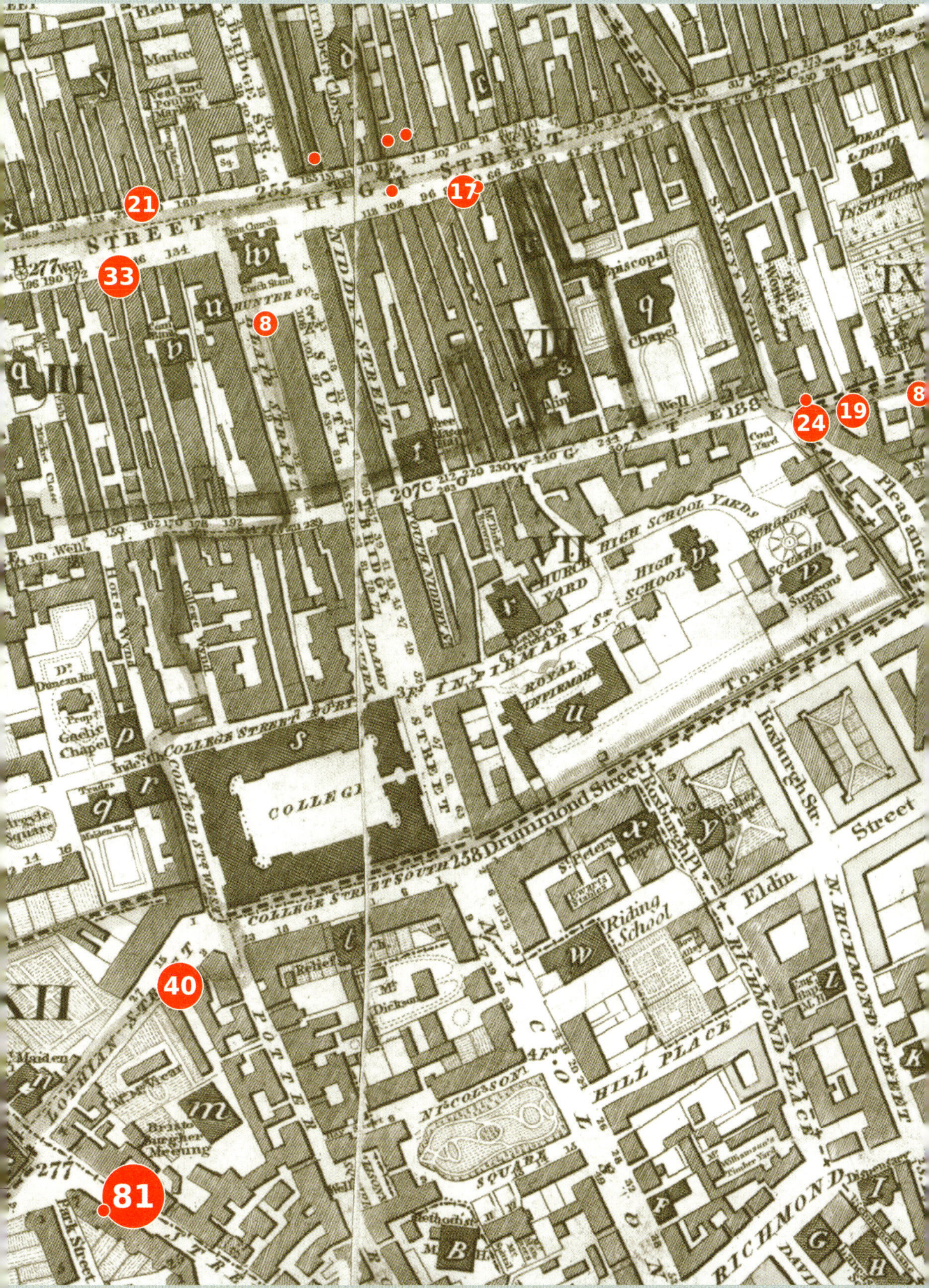
21
33
8
17
24
19
40
81
HIGH STREET
Tron Church
Hunter Sq.
SOUTH BRIDGE STREET
Market
Veal and Poultry Market
Episcopal Chapel
Well
Coal Yard
Pleasance
HIGH SCHOOL YARDS
High School
Church Yard
Surgeons Square
Surgeons Hall
INFIRMARY ST.
Royal Infirmary
Town Wall
COLLEGE STREET
COLLEGE
COLLEGE STREET SOUTH
Drummond Street
Roxburgh Str.
Roxburgh Pl.
St. Peters Chapel
Riding School
Eldin Street
N. RICHMOND STREET
RICHMOND PLACE
HILL PLACE
NICOLSON SQUARE
NICOLSON STREET
Relief
Mr. Dickson
POTTER ROW
LOTHIAN STREET
Burgher Meeting
Methodist
Horse Wynd
Dr. Duncan Jun.
Gaelic Chapel
Argyle Square
Trades
Mint
Kirk Street
RICHMOND

operators signalled that the coach was intended for travellers and 'trade'. Naming a route gave it a personality. The destination of another route, Waldie's Royal Eagle, was to Duns; Campbell's 'Thane of Fife' service was bound for Dundee and connected the Fife burghs of Burntisland, Kirkcaldy and Cupar with the capital.[7]

The routes were thus 'branded' and associated with companies, as were their particular locations on specific streets. As a result, operators' stances were established elements in the Edinburgh streetscape and formed part of the mental maps both of citizens themselves and those who journeyed to and from the capital. Travel timetables provided a rhythm to the day, for stablers, 'room setters' and boarding houses so that 'time-discipline' related not just to factory and workshop in the age of industry but to horse-drawn transport too, and so directly influenced thousands of livelihoods such as those of coach hirers, coachbuilders, saddlers, grooms, smiths and farriers.[8] Time itself was commodified as a result of the formalising of so many routes and the logistics that it implied in terms of fodder and stabling for the principal motive power – horses. Such 'horse sense' – looking after the major assets of the coaching firms – was a central element of business success before the age of steam, and indeed into the twentieth century.[9] No doubt the horse manure produced was also an accepted part of the city's 'smell scape' and certainly contributed to the cash crop available to the City's Cleansing Department since it had monopoly rights over all manure and night soil produced in Edinburgh.[10]

'Time was money', therefore, and business efficiency in terms of sending purchase orders, legal documents, goods and passengers to transact business was vital. Timetables were part of that time-keeping discipline, and routes, stabling, coach drivers, accommodation and, no less important, the quality of the roads themselves were essential elements in what might now be called a modern 'communications strategy' for the nineteenth century. Locally, roads were the responsibility of the Edinburgh Middle District which raised finance from tolls and local parish taxes to repair and maintain the principal thoroughfares into the city. Long-distance routes, however, depended on significantly improved toll roads ('turnpikes') which were an early form of a 'pay as you go' infrastructural investment and particularly important to the connections Edinburgh had

EDINBURGH AS A COMMUNICATIONS HUB

ROUTES OF THE PRINCIPAL MAILS FROM EDINBURGH.

From Edinburgh to London at A.M.		From London to Edinburgh, at P.M.
7 45	Edinburgh,	3 40
9 31	Haddington,	2 0
10 40	Dunbar,	12 54
12 18	Houndwood Inn,	11 20
1 46	Berwick,	9 56
3 21	Belford, (half an hour allowed)	7 51
5 26	Alnwick,	6 16
6 26	Felton,	5 18
7 32	Morpeth,	4 13
9 7	Newcastle, (15 minutes allowed)	2 39
10 3	Durham,	1 9
12 8	Darlington,	11 14
1 52	Northallerton,	9 36
2 50	Thirsk,	8 42
4 0	Easingwold,	7 35
5 24	York, (40 minutes allowed,)	5 33
7 9	Tadcaster,	4 35
8 29	Ferrybridge,	3 23
10 65	Doncaster, (10 minutes allowed,)	1 51
11 41	Rossington Bridge,	1 26
12 42	Barnby Moor,	12 28 P.M.
2 1	Scarthing Moor,	11 13
3 8	Newark,	10 9
3 45	Long Bennington,	9 32
4 37	Grantham, (40 minutes allowed,)	8 2
6 48	Stretton,	6 37
7 37	Stamford, (10 minutes allowed,)	5 45
9 25	Stilton,	4 9
10 12	Alconbury Hill,	3 21
10 50	Huntingdon,	2 46
12 30	Arrington,	1 6
1 39	Buckland,	11 50
3 7	Ware,	10 28
4 9	Waltham Cross,	9 25
5 46	General Post Office, London,	8 0 P.M.

FIGURE 7.4.
Journey times Edinburgh to London, 1799. (From *The Edinburgh and Leith Directory, 1799–1800*, Edinburgh 1800, p. 20)

with London. Distinct 'east' and 'west' coast rail routes to London are a well-known feature of modern Scotland, but to a considerable extent these routes were anticipated by long-distance stagecoach routes in the early nineteenth century (Fig. 7.4). Averaging a fraction under 20 miles per hour, the Edinburgh–London east-coast road journey arrived at the London Post Office after 22 hours on the road, including almost two and a half hours for five stops on the 387 mile journey, which included three slick 'pit stops' for a change of the team of horses and during which time passengers might eat, though not necessarily enjoy, a very quick meal![11]

In addition to mail and stagecoach services, more than 200 firms in the 1820s operated goods routes at least once a week to 570 destinations.[12] Together the 'big four' – Cameron, Howey and Co., David Ritchie and Hargreaves – accounted for 25% of these routes. Cameron's operated from Lothian Street, and had a central and north of Scotland business focus, as did David Ritchie. Howey and Co. operated daily goods services to thirty-nine locations, and departed from its George Inn base in Bristo Street bound for distant Campbeltown (184 miles), Fort William (146 miles), Stranraer (132 miles) and many points in between.[13] Howey and Co. advertised daily waggons to 'Birmingham, Leeds, London, Manchester, Newcastle, Nottingham, Sheffield, York, etc.' and Hargreaves' goods traffic was even more heavily concentrated on English routes 'every Monday, Wednesday and Friday starting from Wilkinson's Wool Pack Inn, 14 Bristo Street'. Further evidence of competition for the long-distance trade to the south was provided by Welsh's Waggons, which headed for many of the same English destinations as Hargreaves, also on Mondays, Wednesdays and Fridays, from their base at 3 Candlemaker Row. The multiplicity of English routes indicates how closely the Scottish economy generally, and that of Edinburgh specifically, was intertwined with that of the north of England.

The waggon trade to England required complex organisational arrangements and greater capital to sustain the thrice weekly frequency of long-distance haulage. At the other end of the business spectrum, almost 60% of goods waggon routes functioned just once a week, though some towns benefited from having two or three firms. In Fife, Auchtermuchty, for example, enjoyed the competing services of J. Goodwilly (Tuesdays), and W. Sharp and D. Fowler (both on Wednesdays). Their waggons returned on the following day to their Edinburgh bases at, respectively, Muir's, Stewart's and Cowan's premises at numbers 152, 147 and 209 High Street. Three different carriers with addresses nearby (14 Bristo Street, 153 High Street and 16 Lothian Street) competed for the waggon trade to Aberdeen. Focusing on burghs beginning with the letter 'A' gives an impression of the competition for goods traffic. Though there was only a single weekly service to and from Aberdour (19 miles, with ferry), Abernethy (43 miles, ferry), and Athelstaneford (19), there were two separate operators weekly, and normally on different days, to and from Aberfeldy (75, ferry), Aberlady (18), Airth (30), Alloa (36), Annan (80), Anstruther (49, ferry), Appin (133), and Auchterarder (55, ferry); three services each week to Alyth (66, ferry), Arbroath (79, ferry) and Auchtermuchty (38, ferry); and four to and from Ayr (83 miles).

Edinburgh was hardwired into a complex local, regional and national transport network in the late eighteenth century. Knowledge about how that network functioned was essential commercial information to business users not only in Edinburgh but in the destinations served from Edinburgh. Transport schedules imposed a discipline beyond Edinburgh, and encouraged a focus on time and work discipline. The stables, commercial depots and accommodation nearby, therefore, provided and to an extent imposed a structure on Edinburgh and its trading partners through transport networks and were in stark contrast to the livery businesses in New Town lanes intended mainly for private carriage users.

Local Traffic

Within Edinburgh the operational framework for local passenger traffic was clarified in 1805 and subsequent Local (or Private Acts) of Parliament.[14] The 'Act for regulating the Police of the City of *Edinburgh*' referred not to criminal activity but to a civic code of byelaws that developed progressively to regulate the lighting and cleaning of streets, identify and curtail pavement encroachments and obstructions to thoroughfares, fence off dangerous properties, and most importantly, to assign a revenue stream in order to monitor and, if appropriate, prosecute infractions of the byelaws.[15] After 1812, in what must be one of the earliest attempts to manage street parking, a further Local Act stated that it was an offence to park and load a cart more than 30 yards from the address.[16] In short, there was a political will to recognise that the nature of the street – gas lit, cleansed, and freed from obstructions – was a legitimate sphere of intervention in the name of urban management and commercial development. Though in 1800 Glasgow Corporation was first to engage with some of these issues,[17] Edinburgh Town Council quickly developed a form of urban management which recognised that public and private interests were not always aligned and that intervention was warranted to facilitate commerce. Administrative support, judicial process and a system of fines and imprisonment took on greater significance though enforcement was often lax.

Gradually the rules of the road were expanded in a series of Local Acts. Charges for sedan chairs were specified, and, more importantly, so were fare schedules for Hackney carriages, explicitly linked to agreed distances as defined by officially measured street lengths (Fig. 7.5) and only superseded in the 1890s when taxi meters were introduced. By 1825 three stances – the Tron Church, Princes Street and George Street – functioned as termini, and fares were charged on a graduated scale according to distance travelled. Carters, too, operated under licence, though their scale of charges combined distance with a sliding scale of additional costs according to the type and weight of loads carried, and whether goods were delivered to, or collected from, the ground or upper floors. Each carter, the regulations stated, 'shall have a sufficient horse and cart, with his name distinctly painted or fixed on the side of the cart; and particularly shall be provided with a tarpaulin or covering . . . at least twelve feet square'.[18] Clearly, the Town Council was concerned to control the activities of carters who constituted a crucial workforce in the movement of goods around the city.[19] By 1848 'not driving on the left' and 'not passing on the right' were breaches of regulations and fines could be imposed, as was 'furiously driving a horse or carriage' – equivalent to the modern offence of 'reckless' driving without due care and attention.

Stray dogs, untended animals and inconsiderate parking contributed to traffic congestion, but it was the expansion of the city and its commerce that caused problems for traffic flow and circulation, particularly in the Old Town. These circulatory issues were explicitly addressed in a series of expensive civil engineering projects funded by Edinburgh Corporation that contributed to the precarious financial position that the city experienced in the 1820s and which ultimately led to its bankruptcy in the 1830s.[20] The construction of the North Bridge (1763) and then the South Bridge (1785) demonstrated how traffic flow could be improved, specifically by by-passing the natural steep gradients to access the spinal ridge

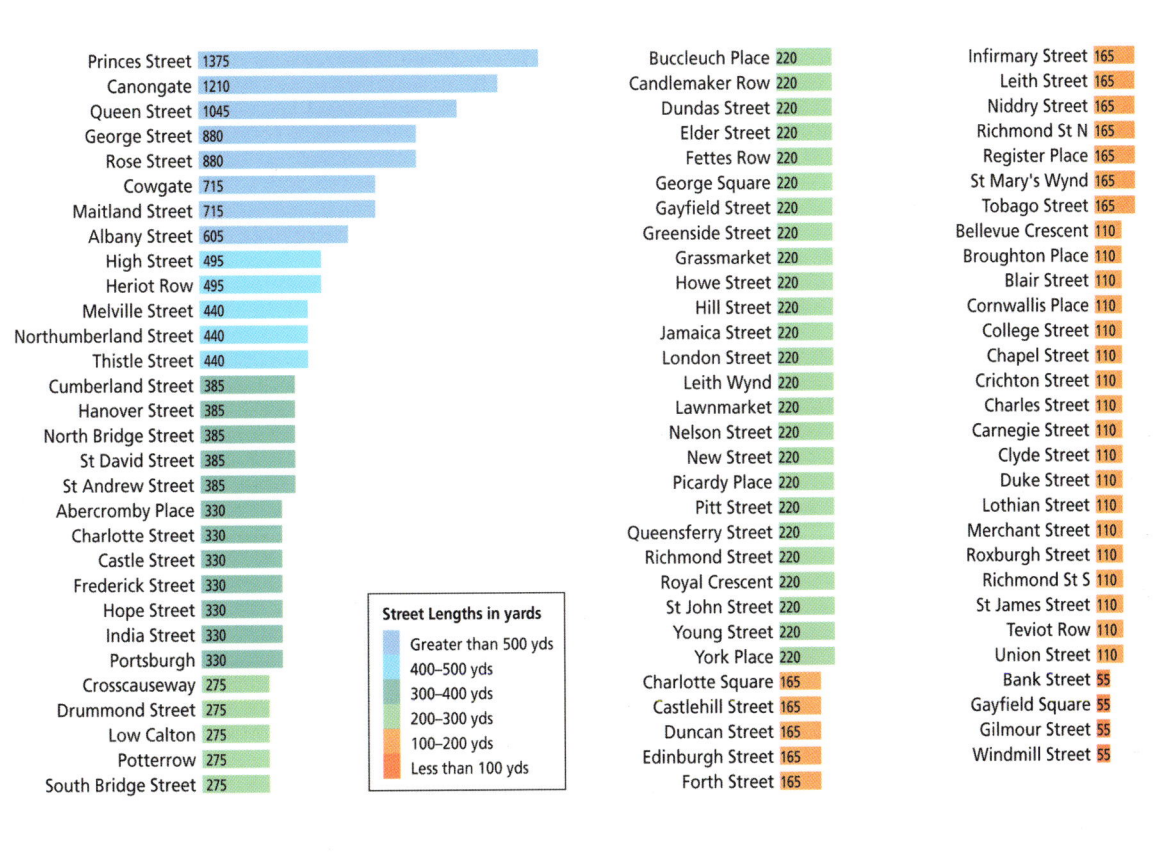

EDINBURGH AS A COMMUNICATIONS HUB

Street	Length
Princes Street	1375
Canongate	1210
Queen Street	1045
George Street	880
Rose Street	880
Cowgate	715
Maitland Street	715
Albany Street	605
High Street	495
Heriot Row	495
Melville Street	440
Northumberland Street	440
Thistle Street	440
Cumberland Street	385
Hanover Street	385
North Bridge Street	385
St David Street	385
St Andrew Street	385
Abercromby Place	330
Charlotte Street	330
Castle Street	330
Frederick Street	330
Hope Street	330
India Street	330
Portsburgh	330
Crosscauseway	275
Drummond Street	275
Low Calton	275
Potterrow	275
South Bridge Street	275
Buccleuch Place	220
Candlemaker Row	220
Dundas Street	220
Elder Street	220
Fettes Row	220
George Square	220
Gayfield Street	220
Greenside Street	220
Grassmarket	220
Howe Street	220
Hill Street	220
Jamaica Street	220
London Street	220
Leith Wynd	220
Lawnmarket	220
Nelson Street	220
New Street	220
Picardy Place	220
Pitt Street	220
Queensferry Street	220
Richmond Street	220
Royal Crescent	220
St John Street	220
Young Street	220
York Place	220
Charlotte Square	165
Castlehill Street	165
Duncan Street	165
Edinburgh Street	165
Forth Street	165
Infirmary Street	165
Leith Street	165
Niddry Street	165
Richmond St N	165
Register Place	165
St Mary's Wynd	165
Tobago Street	165
Bellevue Crescent	110
Broughton Place	110
Blair Street	110
Cornwallis Place	110
College Street	110
Chapel Street	110
Crichton Street	110
Charles Street	110
Carnegie Street	110
Clyde Street	110
Duke Street	110
Lothian Street	110
Merchant Street	110
Roxburgh Street	110
Richmond St S	110
St James Street	110
Teviot Row	110
Union Street	110
Bank Street	55
Gayfield Square	55
Gilmour Street	55
Windmill Street	55

Street Lengths in yards
- Greater than 500 yds
- 400–500 yds
- 300–400 yds
- 200–300 yds
- 100–200 yds
- Less than 100 yds

FIGURE 7.5.
Official Edinburgh street lengths, 1825. (Based on information from *The Post Office Annual Directory for 1825–26*, Edinburgh 1825, pp. xiv–xv)

of the High Street from north and south. The high-level Regent Bridge (completed in 1819) and, later, the George IV Bridge (1834) facilitated eastward and southern access to the city, respectively, and increased the development potential of land on the urban fringes. Two other planned major road projects aided traffic circulation in the city. Firstly, the Edinburgh Improvement Act (1827) not only provided for the creation of Victoria Street to facilitate easier access between the busy transport hub of the Grassmarket and the High Street, but also, by creating Johnston Terrace and the King's Bridge above an extended Kings Stables Road, facilitated access northwards and westwards and so relieved some of the congestion created at the West Port by the opening of the Union Canal in 1821. The second road project, the improvement of the Mound, was another saga of false starts but when completed eventually in 1834 gave much improved connections between Old and New Towns with a more gradual S-shape to assist horse- and human-drawn traffic on the steep gradient later to be repeated in the construction of Cockburn Street.

Nineteenth-century 'horsepower' was vitally important to the commercial lifeblood of the city and so maintaining the physical condition of the horses was no minor matter. In the 1770s, with the New Town in its infancy, Old Town 'stablers' – over 40 businesses – were highly concentrated; the Cowgate area might reasonably have been renamed 'Horsegate' given that daily activity was dominated by horse-drawn traffic. No wonder, then, that an alteration to the gradient of the West Bow and improved access to the western end of the Grassmarket were under serious consideration in the late eighteenth century, and put into effect in the 1820s. The priority was to open up access to the High Street and thus by the Mound to a New Town about to expand significantly in the wake of legal decisions in the House of Lords (1818) that reassured owners of the future value of their property.[21]

Lodgings

For horses, the working day began and ended in or near the Grassmarket. For visitors to the city, accommodation nearby, though not too near, was advantageous since the Tron, High Street and, increasingly, North Bridge and the East End of Princes Street provided the terminus for many coaching routes. Accommodation was available from 'room setters' or 'boarders' – 93% of whom in 1774 were married women – located in over sixty different closes or wynds, and therefore exclusively in the Old Town (Fig. 7.6). The expansion of the Edinburgh economy and the transport networks associated with it was reflected in the increasing numbers of these lodgings: from 100 in 1774 to almost 200 in 1800, rising to well over 500 in 1825.[22] But with the eighteenth-century Old Town increasingly congested, visitors to Edinburgh rapidly revised their preferences. Early feu charters in the eastern New Town did not require much more than sewer connections and solid cellar supports, so it was hardly surprising that many enterprising New Town residents adapted their residential properties into boarding houses. Whereas all lodgings were understandably located in the Old Town in 1774, by 1800 lodgings were divided 50:50 between Old and New Town addresses, and by 1825 it was New Town lodgings that were more numerous with 56% of the Edinburgh total. With this transition came two other consequences: firstly, the locus of Old Town lodgings drifted south, away from the High Street, and towards newly built streets around Nicolson Square; and secondly, the overwhelming predominance of married women as lodging housekeepers was shattered, falling by more than half from 90% in the 1770s to 40% in 1800.

The colonisation of early New Town streets by lodgings was impressive. Though Rose Street (20 addresses), Thistle Street (13), St James Square and Street (10), and Shakespeare Square (8) were most numerous, clusters of lodgings also existed around Register Street (7), St Andrew Square and the adjacent St David and St Andrew Streets (9). Significantly, too, the main New Town thoroughfares were also attractive locations for lodging houses on Princes Street (4), George Street (3) and Frederick Street (5). Far from a genteel residential development the New Town from its inception was a busy building site coupled with a transport hub and over ninety lodging houses and a handful of hotels. There was a degree of impermanence, perhaps even of transience, and the numerous lodging houses added to that. By 1800 the New Town had advanced westwards, although only as far as Castle Street; by 1825 Charlotte Square had been completed, and a northward expansion was underway. The locations of lodging and boarding houses moved westwards and northwards with the times, reaching Cumberland and India Streets in the 1820s. Almost every property in Rose Street seemed to offer accommodation, and Thistle Street, too, dominated the preference for lodgings (see Table 7.1).

Table 7.1 Expansion of New Town lodging houses, 1800–25

Address in	1800	1825	Address in	1800	1825
Rose Street	22	77	Frederick Street	3	11
Thistle Street	13	30	St David, St Andrew Streets	9	11
James Square, Place, Street	10	26	Broughton Place, Street	0	10
Jamaica Street	0	23	Howe Street	0	9
George Street	4	16	Castle Street	0	8
Hanover Street	2	14	Princes Street	4	5

Source: *Edinburgh and Leith Directories*, 1800, 1825.

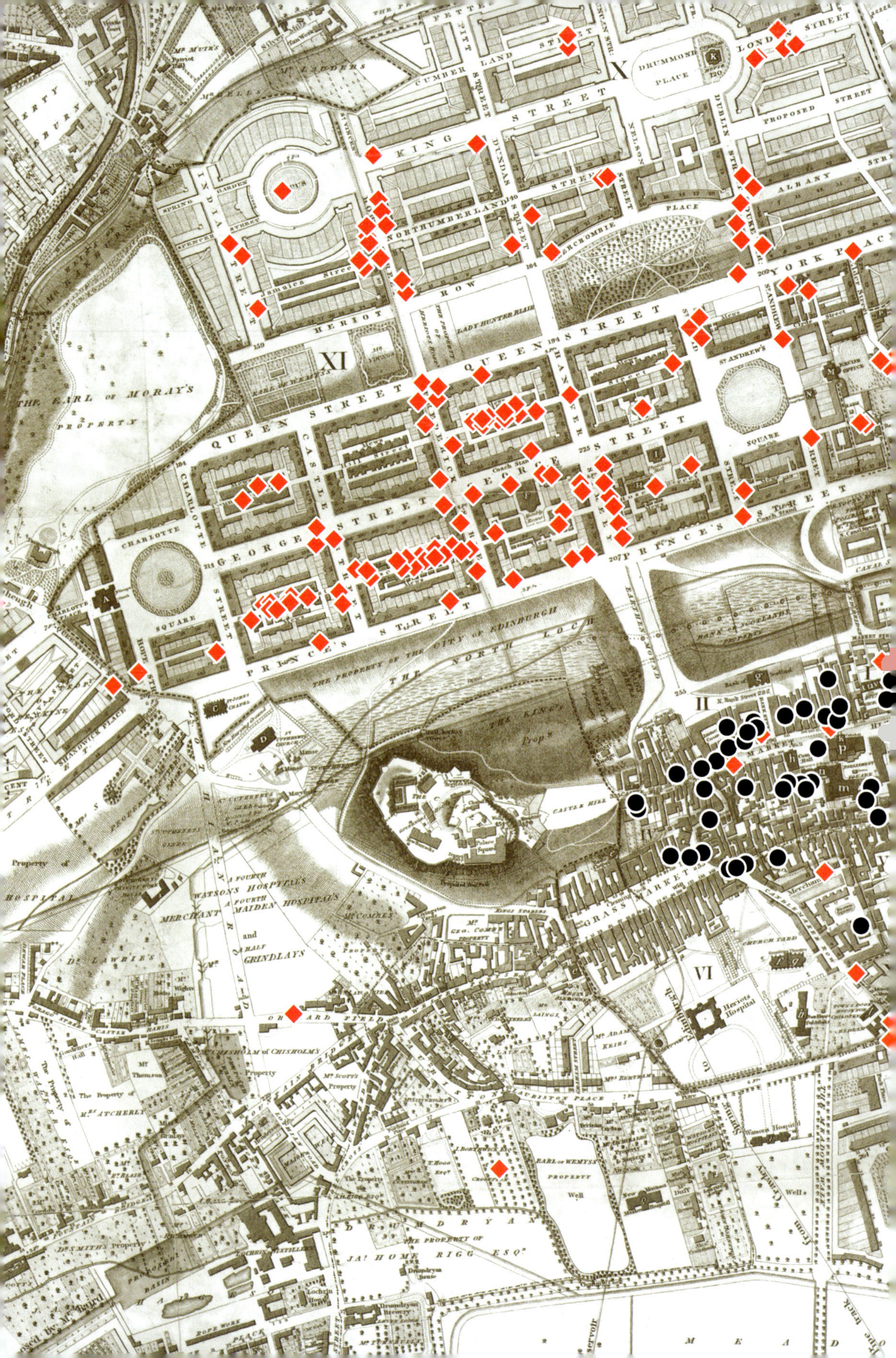

QUEEN STREET
GEORGE STREET
PRINCE'S STREET
CHARLOTTE SQUARE
KING STREET
NORTHUMBERLAND STREET
HERIOT ROW
ABERCROMBIE PLACE
DRUMMOND PLACE
CUMBERLAND STREET
DUNDAS STREET
ALBANY STREET
YORK PLACE
ST. ANDREW'S SQUARE
THE NORTH LOCH
GRASS MARKET
Heriots Hospital
THE EARL OF MORAY'S PROPERTY
XI
X
VI
II

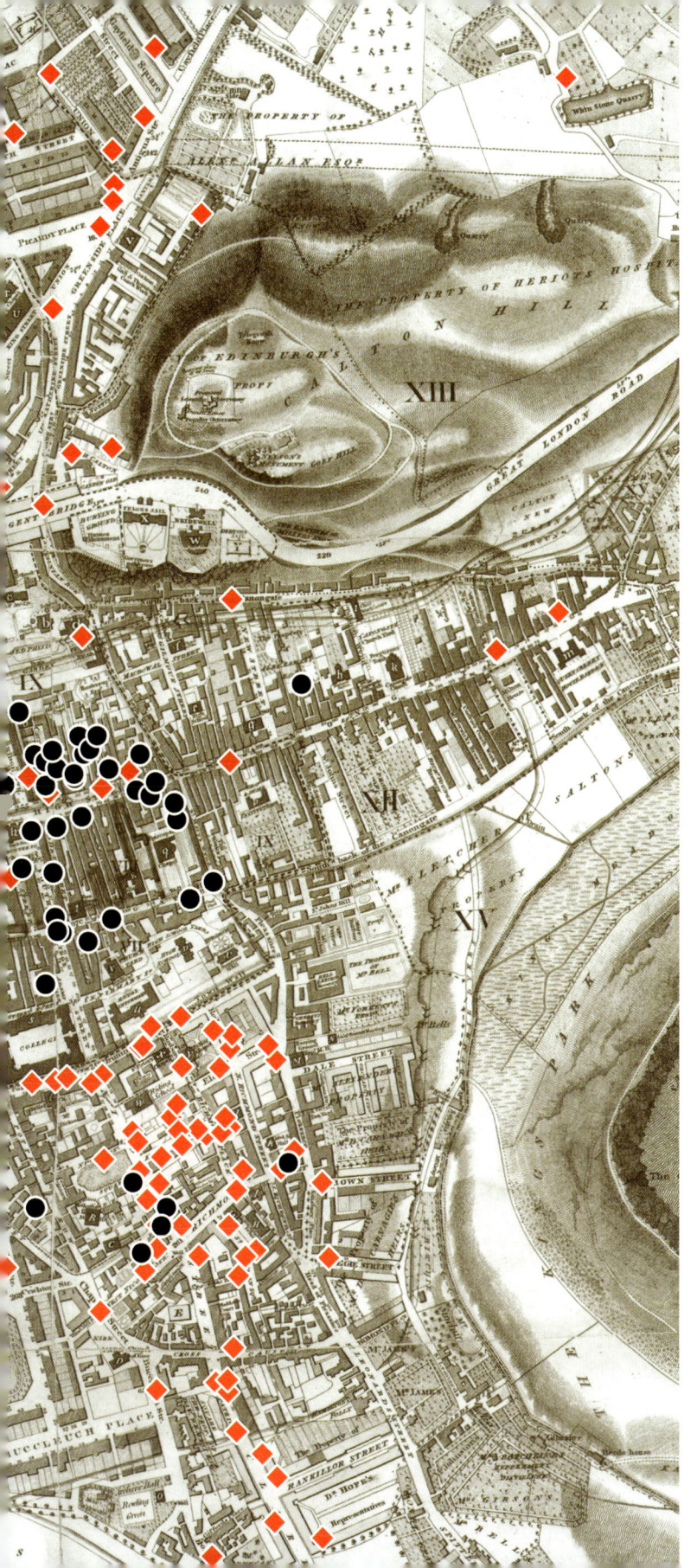

FIGURE 7.6.
Room setters and boarders, 1774 and 1825. Black circles denote rooms for rent in boarding houses in 1774; red diamonds denote rooms for rent in 1825. The impact of the development of New Town streets was evident in a dramatic decline in boarding houses in the Old Town. (Based on information from *Williamson's Directory for the City of Edinburgh, Canongate, Leith and Suburbs 1773–74*, Edinburgh 1889 edn; *The Post Office Annual Directory for 1824–25*, Edinburgh 1824; base map Robert Kirkwood, *Plan of the City of Edinburgh*, 1817, reproduced by permission of the National Library of Scotland)

With over 330 New Town lodging houses, 260 in the Old Town and a further 75 in Leith in 1825, visitors, commercial travellers, students and those on official business had a range of accommodation according to location, price and amenity from which to choose. On the verge of a railway building mania, and on the back of international interest in science, medicine and the Scottish Enlightenment, lured by the romanticism associated with Walter Scott's novels and stimulated by the royal visit of King George IV in 1822, Edinburgh was well placed to accommodate those whose varied interests brought them to the city.

There were rarely more than half a dozen hotels in late eighteenth-century Edinburgh, and all were concentrated on Princes Street and St Andrew Street around the coach stances that developed at the East End. These hotels were owned by private individuals, sometimes vintners, stablers or tavern owners who attempted a type of vertical integration by extending their existing businesses into hotels. The most durable were associated with the names of individuals – notably Alexander Walker, William Dumbreck, John Cameron and Matthew Pool – but when ownership changed, as was often the case, hotels lost their identity and market recognition. By the late 1830s, however, most hotels had acquired dedicated and durable names – Union, Albion, British, Royal, Crown, Star, Turf, York and Waterloo – in a process of place-making or branding that provided them with a commercial identity within and beyond the city.

By 1838, when the Edinburgh and Glasgow Railway issued shares for its proposed line between the two cities, the number of hotels had doubled since 1815 (Fig. 7.7). That trend continued. The 1840s was a decade of unprecedented expansion in hotel building and conversions. The number of hotels tripled. The expansion continued more steadily until a peak of just over 100 hotels was reached in 1881 when a degree of consolidation took place and the numbers returned to those of the 1850s.[23] Whereas even in 1838 only a single hotel, the York at 19 Nicolson Square, existed in the Old Town, there were seven in Princes Street alone and another seven concentrated in the New Town, on the Regent Bridge, Queen Street, and St James Square and St Andrew Square. Just over a decade later, in 1851 the ratio of New Town to Old Town hotels

EDINBURGH AS A COMMUNICATIONS HUB

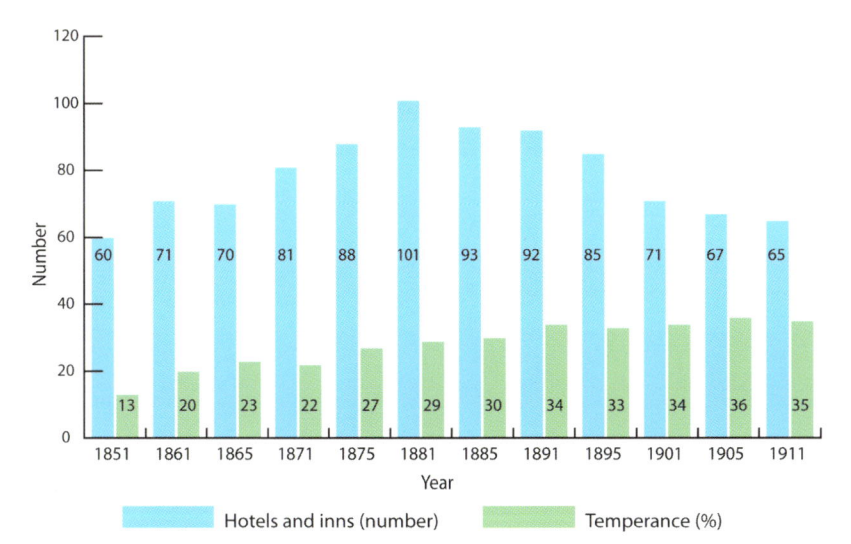

FIGURE 7.7.
Hotels and temperance hotels, 1851–1911. (Based on information in *The Post Office Annual Directory*, various years)

Year	Hotels and inns (number)	Temperance (%)
1851	60	13
1861	71	20
1865	70	23
1871	81	22
1875	88	27
1881	101	29
1885	93	30
1891	92	34
1895	85	33
1901	71	34
1905	67	36
1911	65	35

was 3:1 in favour of the New Town; by 1891 this had changed to 2:1 – twice as many hotels in the New as in the Old Town – and this remained the balance of hotel provision through to the First World War.

Within this symmetrical rise and fall in the number of hotels, the percentage of temperance hotels was highly significant, rising steadily in the third quarter of the nineteenth century and constituting a third of all hotels between the 1880s and the First World War (see Fig. 7.7). Again, New Town locations were initially preferred in mid century by temperance hotel owners – specifically South and North St Andrew Street, South St David Street and Princes Street in 1851. These remained favoured locations a decade later, but by then five temperance hotels – Aitken's, Buchanan's, Burden's, Mrs May's and Adair's – had been established in the Old Town at numbers 104, 114, 129, 170 and 219 High Street. By 1891, there were seventeen temperance hotels in the Old Town and thirteen in the New Town, a proliferation that reflected both an increasing opposition to a drink culture in the city generally, and a preference on the part of some travellers for a degree of gentility. The hotel sector experienced a considerable degree of instability. Of those hotels in business in 1851, only 55% were in existence ten years later. A quarter of the hotels trading in 1861 were defunct by 1865.

Despite the attrition, one in five hotels (21%) enjoyed a business lifespan of at least half-century between 1861 and 1911.

The legacy of the age of horse-drawn traffic had an enduring effect on the internal structure of Edinburgh. Frequent, timetabled local and long-distance services required support facilities and infrastructure. The stances for arrivals and departures, boarding houses for passengers, stables for horses, coaches and waggons, and storehouses for goods, each contributed to Old Town congestion. As the New Town became established from the 1770s, lodgings increasingly absorbed much of the passenger pressure with, first, substantial numbers of boarding houses and later with hotels. As a result, when rail passenger traffic assumed sizeable proportions in the 1850s there already existed a large number of accommodation options. Princes Street and the eastern streets and squares of the New Town were from their initial construction commercialised in terms of short lets and boarding for visitors.

The imperative of pace as a condition of modernity initiated a period of rapid change within Edinburgh in the last quarter of the eighteenth century. Mobility between and especially within towns and cities was essential – and increasingly understood as underpinning commercial success. Public authorities, by virtue of bridge-building, construction of new streets and tighter traffic regulations, aided circulation. The efficiency gains to the transport sector were considerable and the impact on Edinburgh as an expanding urban settlement with extreme topographical constraints is difficult to under-estimate.

CHAPTER 8

Commerce and Conservation: Edinburgh New Town in the Early Twentieth Century

John Lowrey

This chapter considers what has happened to James Craig's plan for the New Town of Edinburgh since the time of its commencement in 1767. It is concerned with the changes from domestic and public use to mainly commercial – how that happened, why, and what the various attitudes to these changes have been over the years, at least up to 1967 – when the celebrations for the 200th anniversary took place.

What we see in Craig's original plan of 1767 is a city without commerce – or, rather, a New Town without commerce, because the decision to make this area domestic and, to a small extent, public, was deliberate. Commerce was dealt with elsewhere – it was to be left behind in the Old Town, and basic functions, like markets, were exactly the kind of noisome activities of the city the new residents were trying to escape from. But that started to change quite quickly.

Princes Street has traditionally been the core of that commercialisation – at least as far as shopping is concerned – and, for the purposes of this chapter, we will focus on developments there to a large extent.

Princes Street is one of three principal latitudinal streets of Craig's New Town plan, but, unlike the others, it was developed with quite a large number of tenements, as distinct from the individual houses set on the other two main streets. Arguably, this already represented a commercial development because these apartment blocks were what we would now call investment properties, with proprietors who rented them to the occupants. However, the monotony of Princes Street had been a marked characteristic, as described in 1880 by James Grant in *Cassell's Old and New Edinburgh*:

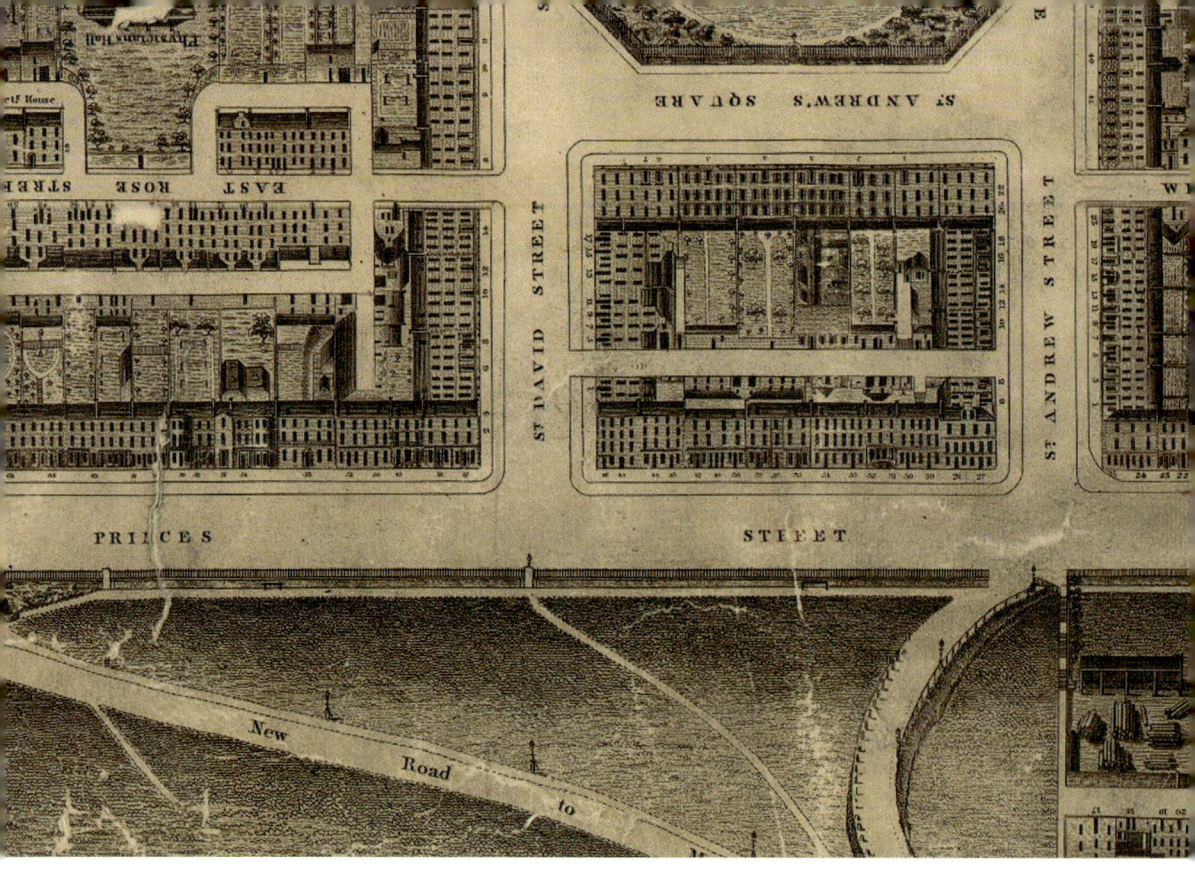

> Originally the houses of Craig's new city were one plain and intensely monotonous plan and elevation – three storeys in height, with a sunk area in front, enclosed by iron railings, with link extinguishers; and they only differed by the stone being more finely polished, as the streets crept westwards.[1]

Already on Robert Kirkwood's 1819 *Plan and Elevation of the New Town*[2] an apartment block (possibly 'Main Door tenement') at Nos 54–59 Princes Street seems to have been developed in the backlands/back garden – almost certainly a commercial development.

Broadly, we can distinguish between those buildings that were erected under the first building Act of 1769 – which did little more than enforce the building line – and those built under the 1782 (re-enacted 1785) Act, which imposed a stricter regime, much closer to that described by Grant in the foregoing quotation.[3]

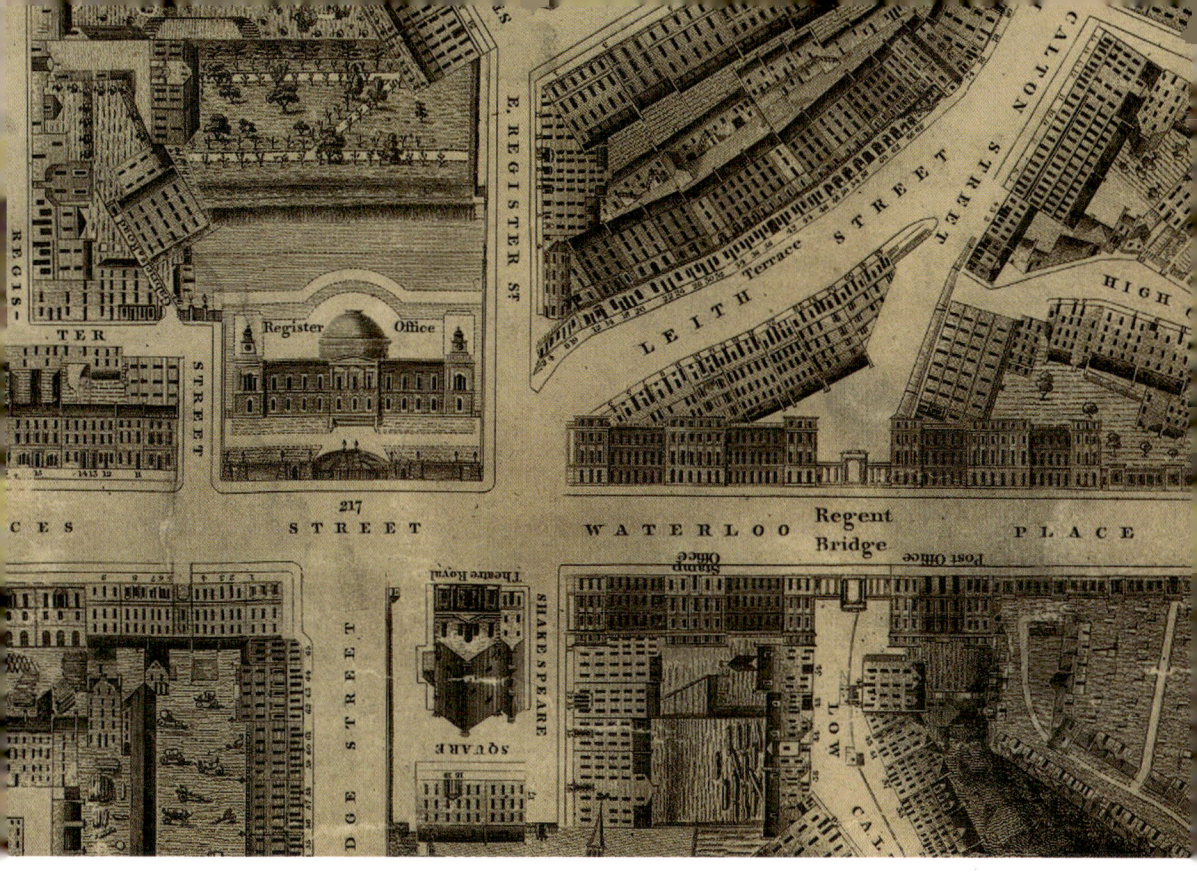

FIGURE 8.1.
Detail of the east end of Princes Street. Robert Kirkwood, *Plan & Elevation of the New Town of Edinburgh*, Edinburgh: Kirkwood & Son, 1819. (Copyright National Library of Scotland)

The elevations of the buildings show a lot of variety in the first three blocks, followed by very plain houses between Hanover Street and Frederick Street, and to the west of that some clearly rather grand buildings with rusticated basements and ashlar elevations, and the occasional flowering of detail – like, for instance, an elaborate balcony on 104 Princes Street, or the linking of numbers 129–131 by means of pilasters.

Towards the east end (Fig. 8.1), there is perhaps more variety, but there is also more of a vernacular feel – especially in the very old-fashioned house on the corner of St Andrew Street and Princes Street – part of the site afterwards occupied by J.J. Burnett's department store for R.W. Forsyth, now (2019) Top Shop. The Kirkwood elevations indicate, firstly, buildings of up to five bays wide and, secondly, a large number of single-bay elements that suggest the entrance to a common close – indicating a surprisingly large number of tenements. A possible reason for this might have been the desirability of Princes Street as a commercial prospect, the individual feus having been taken by builders who then sold on to proprietors. It may well be that the attractions of the site made it more profitable for the builders and proprietors to go for multi-occupancy rather than single owner-occupiers. This would have suited the Town Council, which would have collected feu duties from a number of householders rather than just one.

Given this commercial aspect to the Princes Street development, it would have been easy for the proprietors at a later stage to remove their tenants and develop their buildings as shops or hotels. Given the freedom of the early developments and the combination of lower-quality buildings and tenements at the east end, there may well be a connection between this and the subsequent total redevelopment of almost all of the properties at that end of Princes Street, compared with the rather smaller-scale developments in most of the rest of the street.

A variety of commercial activities had taken place by the 1880s, as described by James Grant. No. 10 changed from Poole's coffee house (1783) to Archibald Constable, publisher (1822–6); No. 3, to Walker's Hotel (1811), No. 14, to Poole's Hotel (1811), No. 16 to Weir's Museum of stuffed animals (1794), No. 53 to the Royal Hotel.[4]

By the 1820s, the insertion of a shop at both basement and ground level, which involved building out over the basement area, had become very popular, as had the development backwards into backlands. In 1836 William Forbes, the owner of a tenement on No. 80 Princes Street, proposed to erect a building on the ground behind his tenement and to adjoin it; he sought authority of the Lord Dean of Guild and Council to do this. His petition, to be served on neighbouring proprietors, was described as the second tenement west from the corner tenement on the west side of South Hanover Street and Princes Street and ground below the same.[5]

At 82 Princes Street there was an 1844 estimate made for a new roof on the cellar 'at the back of Mr Grant's shop', a water closet and back building for a library.[6] The commercialisation of ground-floor levels is shown in Alexander Nasmyth's 1825 view (Fig. 8.2).

The expansion of premises over several feus – extending sideways but keeping the existing buildings and their facades, thus creating the possibility of much larger commercial premises – was a common approach by the 1850s. Around the 1890s–1900s, those composite sites were demolished and replaced with custom-built premises.

Another form of development involved the upper floors, as shown by the 1823 petition for an attic proposal by Thomas Arrol, merchant, 92 Princes Street. The warrant, granted 1 May 1823, is an application to build storm windows (dormers) and to raise the back wall of the house – creating main rooms as opposed to garrets.[7] It runs directly counter to the 1781 Act – but this type of development was becoming increasingly common at this time.

This warrant was only part of a bigger development by Arrol and Miss Margaret Fowler (91–92 Princes Street), which involved the insertion of shops into the ground floor and the conversion of upper floors into flats. The warrant granted 10 April 1823 (Fig. 8.3) was for three shops at ground level and common close leading to flats on the right.[8] In June the same year, Arrol returned to the Dean of Guild, with a different design for the attic storey – this time a proper, architectural attic; the drawing refers to the building as a tenement.[9] The petition dated 12 February 1824 was to erect a back building.[10] The general purpose was to build up the backlands to extend shops.

A petition of Alex Macreadie, 75 Princes Street, warrant dated 27 October 1825, was for basically the same thing; a proper attic is proposed, again in direct contravention of the original building Act. The drawing indicates a distinct change in the pattern of ownership of the properties. Houses are now investments and are owned by businesses rather than individuals. Another proposal comes from the Incorporation of Cordiners and to achieve their aim they need the cooperation of their neighbours, the North British Insurance Company.

In the case of the petition of Sir James Gibson Craig, Alexander Douglas and John McKean, 15 Princes Street, warrant dated 27 April 1834, it was a classic development of a tenement. The shop front is very neatly inserted into ground level, and the whole thing is pushed out over the basement area. The shop front does not project all the way to the pavement and, instead, there is a continuous raised platform in front of the shop from which to view the goods. The flats are entered via a central doorway.

Some developments involved substantial rebuild of the whole facade, raising the height and involving the redesign of the roof. John Inglis, a builder, produced an estimate, which was followed

FIGURE 8.2. (Overleaf) Alexander Nasmyth, *Princes Street with the Commencement of the Building of the Royal Institution*, 1825. (Copyright National Galleries of Scotland)

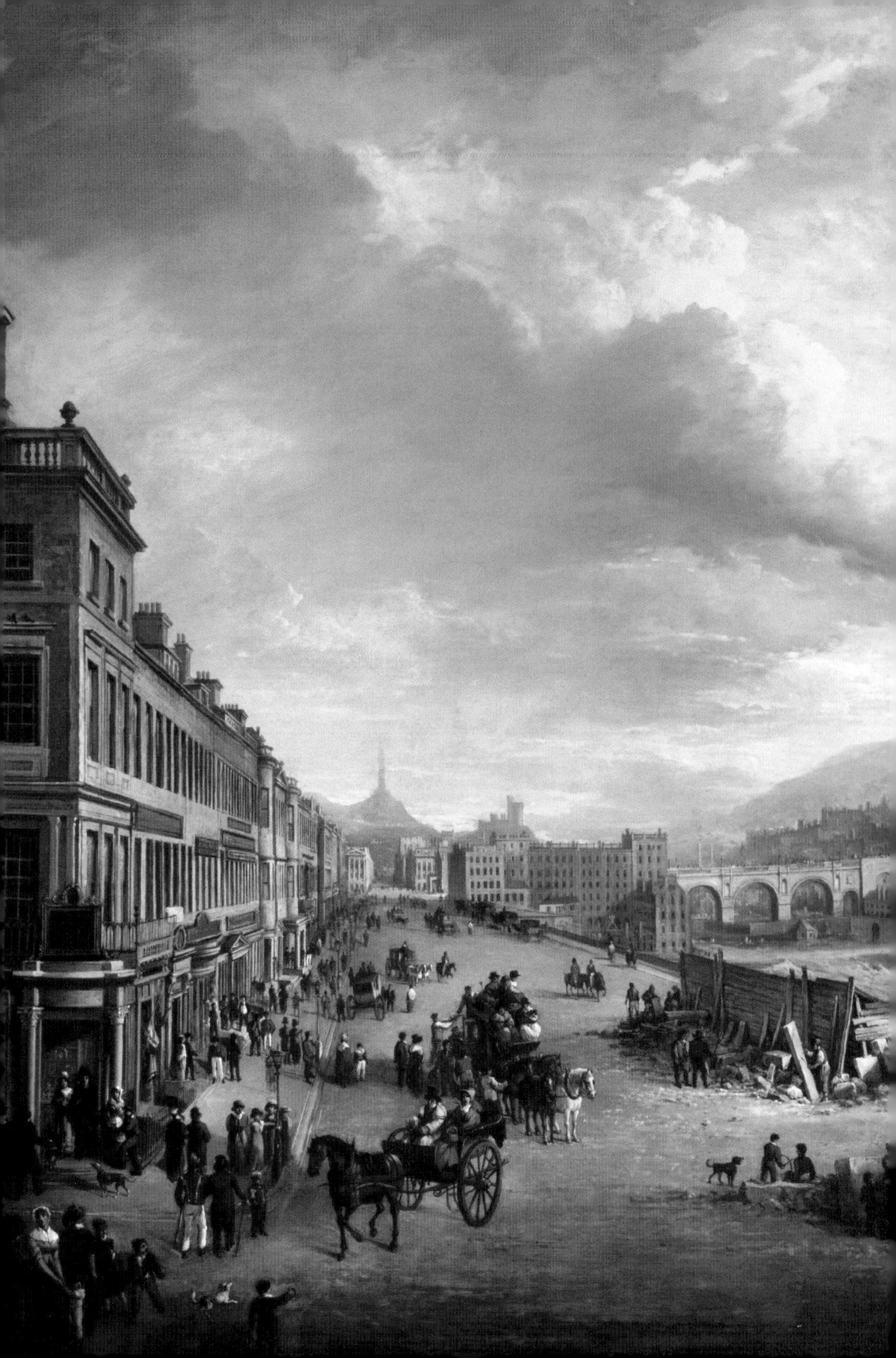

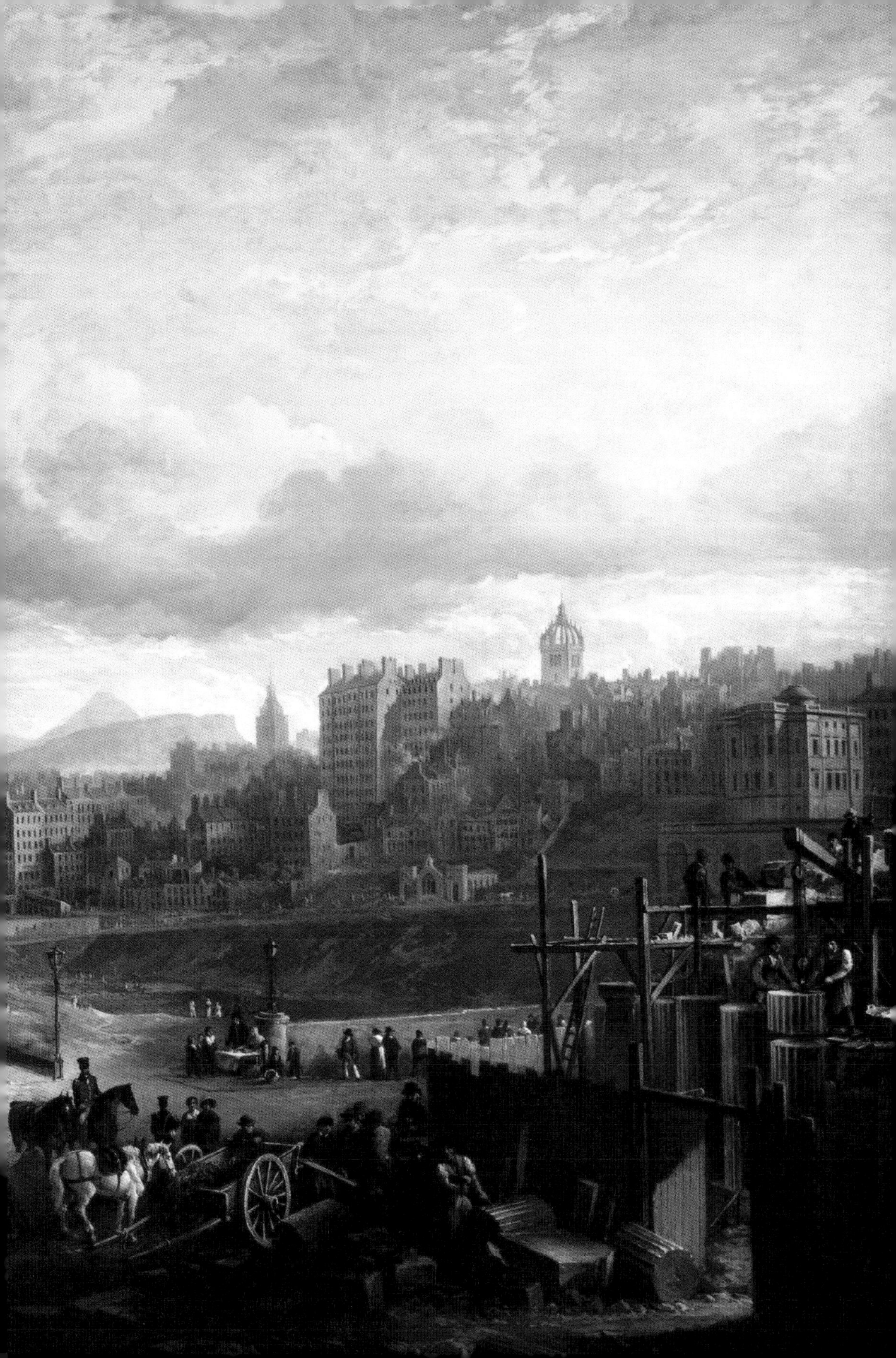

ELEVATION.

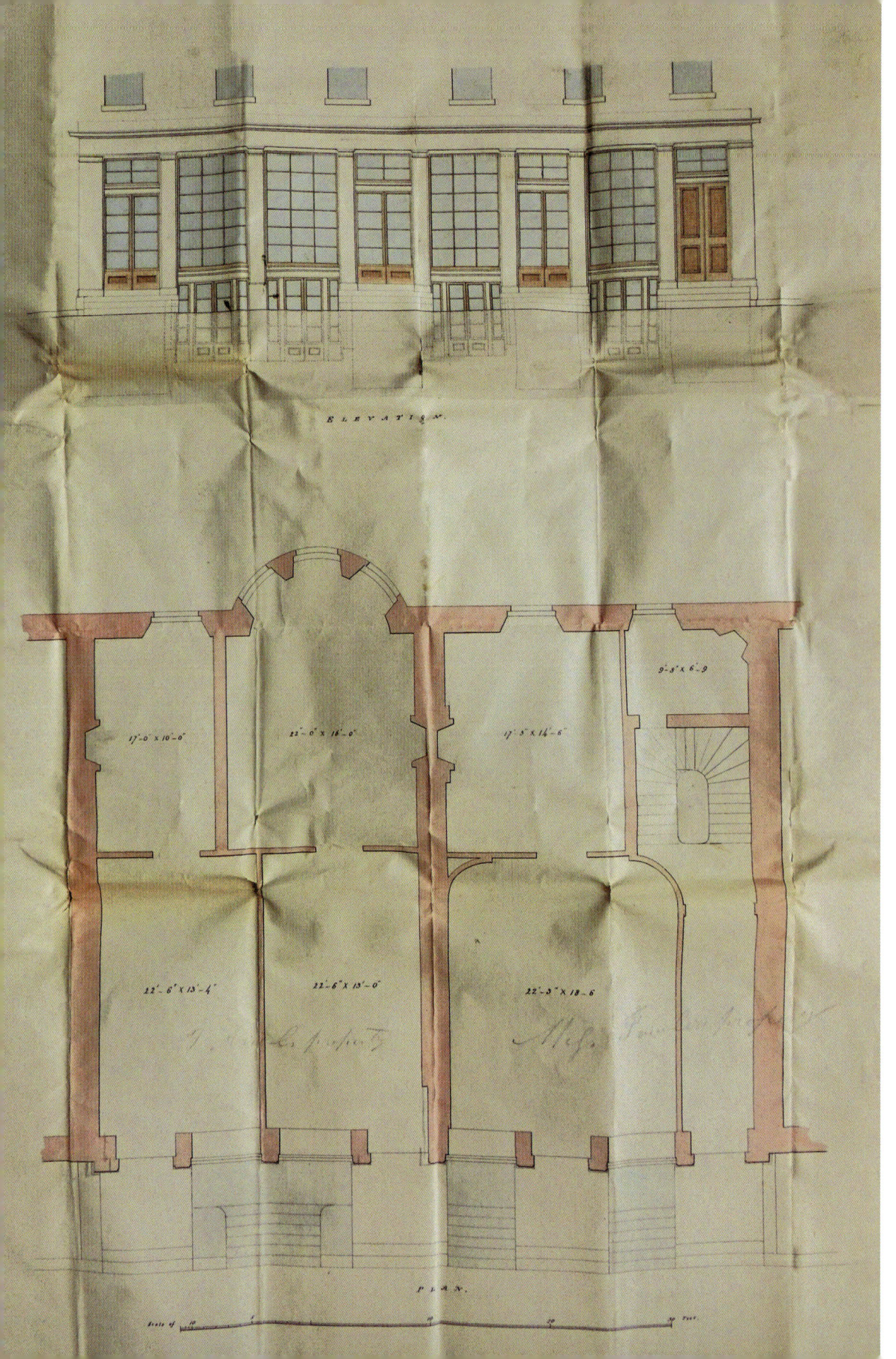

17'-0" x 10'-6"   22'-0" x 16'-0"   17'-5" x 14'-6"   9'-5" x 6'-9"

22'-6" x 13'-4"   22'-6" x 13'-0"   22'-3" x 18'-6"

PLAN.

by a receipt for payment, for putting in two storm windows in Mr Bruce's house in Princes Street for £55.[11]

David McGibbon's Royal Hotel Design (1867), and David Rhind's Life Association Building (1855–7) are examples of later larger developments, comprising a number of feus and involving total rebuilds. By the 1900s, Princes Street was a place of tremendous variety in terms of building type and architectural style.

Concerns over the commercialisation of Princes Street were highlighted by Sir Alexander Trotter of Dreghorn, who was Lord Provost of Edinburgh 1825–7. Trotter proposed a shopping arcade for the Mound (the site where the Scottish National Gallery is today, beyond the then-new Royal Scottish Academy building). Project drawings for this survive, including schemes by William H. Playfair and Archibald Elliot. Playfair proposed a surprisingly modern-looking classical shopping mall (Fig. 8.4).

The starting point for Trotter's project was a sense that the unity and domesticity of the New Town was being lost to commercialisation. What happened in the rest of the nineteenth and early twentieth centuries was a huge acceleration of that, while in the two squares and George Street (much less in Queen Street) a slightly different form of commercialisation was taking place.

The coming of the railways along the line of Princes Street played a crucial role in that respect; after failing in their first attempt to bring their line in through Princes Street Gardens in 1836, the Edinburgh and Glasgow Railway returned with another – successful – proposal for extension to North Bridge in 1844.[12]

Hugely controversial, but good for business, commercialisation ultimately brought a benefit to the public because it was through the businesses that the Gardens were eventually opened to the public in mid century. In fact, from the 1850s onwards, the Committee of Princes Street Proprietors, which first met in 1811, no longer comprised individual householders but, increasingly, the representatives of large companies, who had less personal interest in the Gardens, and presumably less objection to public access.

Around 1866, John Dick Peddie made two paintings of an 'idealised' Edinburgh. That vision was not realised, but it does point to a period of great confidence in the High Victorian age. We also find at this time, probably for the only time, a huge pride in Princes

FIGURE 8.3.
(Opposite) Elevation and plan of the ground floor: petition of Thomas Arrol and Miss Margaret Fowler, 91 Princes Street, 10 April 1823. (Edinburgh City Archives Box: 1823/35)

Figure 8.4.
William Henry Playfair, *Royal Scottish Academy on the Mound*, design for a shopping mall, 1820. (University of Edinburgh, N/A 5013)

Street as the commercial heart of the city – the fears of Trotter in the 1820s were not shared by a writer named Robert Grieve in the 1870s in an extraordinary and apparently prize-winning essay on Princes Street. According to Grieve:

> In some of the noblest continental streets there are some drawbacks, some weak points, some mean and shabby elements marring their splendour; hovels nestle in the lee of palaces, filth sullies the gorgeous basements, but in Princes Street everything is in such keeping that defects are softened into beauty. Concerning the countless changes in its buildings, the street may be described as truly British, and not Medo-Persianic, for like the constitution of our own beloved country, its perfection seems to consist in its continued possibility of alteration, and as the years roll on, the resources of art are more and more taxed, and the wealth of the nation seems to return to the heart of her metropolis.[13]

Apart from the amazing analogy he draws between Princes Street and the British constitution, this is interesting because of the connection between the street and the wealth of the nation and empire –

Princes Street was a kind of barometer of wealth. If Grieve and others are to be believed, the street was one of the most important, and certainly the grandest, anywhere; quoting someone else, Grieve wrote: 'it forms one of the grandest and noblest streets, not only in Scotland, but in the whole world'.[14] This sentiment is similar to that expressed by James Craig in quoting from James Thomson's poem 'Liberty' on the cartouche of the 1767 plan of the New Town:

> august, around, what public works I see!
> Lo! stately Streets, lo! Squares that Court the breeze,
> See! long Canals, and deepened Rivers join
> Each part with each, and with the circling Main
> The whole enlivened Isle.[15]

This place of commerce was also 'a thoroughfare where few have not to pass at least once in the day'.[16] Princes Street was built as a place of promenade, especially in the evening. Moreover, what was attractive to Grieve was precisely that the original Georgian Street could be so easily altered. Certainly, it hugely changed in this period, up to the early twentieth century. And, by the mid twentieth century, the very adaptability and 'countless changes' that he praised became the source of opposition from planners and architects.

So, by the 1930s, the scale of Princes Street in particular had grown beyond the original Georgian vision, although, in most of the New Town and even in parts of Princes Street (especially towards the west), its buildings more or less survived intact. The question from then, and more especially after the Second World War, was what was to be preserved? Original buildings? Broad lines? Was unity more in keeping with the original design? And, if so, was demolition of later accretions therefore justified?

From the 1930s to the 1980s the key themes were harmonisation and unification. The variety and eclecticism that had developed from the 1850s to the 1920s was now seen as detrimental to the street and out of sympathy with its original Georgian form. From the 1930s, we begin to see specific ideas about how to improve it. It attracted a huge amount of attention from planners, developers, architects and heritage bodies – notably among the latter the Cockburn Association, founded in 1875.

In 1937, the Pilkington Glass Company set up the Glass Age Town Planning Committee (later the Glass Development Committee), with a number of architects on it advocating glass-skinned Modernism: Maxwell Fry, R. Furneaux Jordan, Raymond McGrath, Howard Robertson, G. Grey Wornum and F.R.S. Yorke were all on the committee, and each was given a historic city site – London, Edinburgh, and other cities – the object being to bring modernity to each place.

Proposals were published in the *Architectural Review* and formed part of an exhibition that travelled around the country on the most modern train of the age. The exhibition was to extoll the virtues and modernity of glass – 600 items were on the train, and everything was made of glass – even the fabrics were of a glass fibre material. Finally, in 1938, the company sponsored a much more ambitious exhibition of the capabilities of glass by commissioning architects to redesign the central areas of a number of streets – New Bond Street and Liverpool and Broad Street stations in London, part of Portsmouth, and Princes Street in Edinburgh.

The principles and features of Robert Jordan's plans for Princes Street (Fig. 8.5) included a unified approach towards each building, an elevated walkway on the north side, a path for pedestrian access to the south side (mainly to a hugely expanded railway station rather than to the gardens), a shopping arcade in the gardens, and a completely new bridge at Frederick Street, connecting with the gardens.

The grid of the New Town plan was to be disrupted in some way that is not entirely clear because we can see that there are more than three cross-streets and – more noticeably – none of the major buildings on Princes Street were intended to survive – neither Georgian, Victorian nor Edwardian. The New Town behind would have been less affected, not being part of the project. This plan might be seen simply as a publicity stunt but its importance is greater than that because some of these ideas were to crop up again, notably the raised walkway which became policy; others, like shopping accessed from the gardens, have also been suggested in the 1990s.

More generally, this captures an attitude of the time that the street and ultimately the New Town was to be modernised and tidied up, and that is clear in other sources from the same period. Robert

Hurd and Alan Reiach's 1941 book *Building Scotland* was already looking forward to post-war reconstruction: seeing an opportunity to sweep away the old and disordered cities and replace them with cleaner, more rational, more modern design. The two young architects (recalling A.W.N. Pugin's book entitled *Contrasts* (1836), which opposed an idealised urban past with a decayed present) contrasted Princes Street with Rue de Rivoli in Paris, arguing:

> Streets for commerce should have dignified unity without dullness. Bickering shop fronts do not sell goods any more quickly. Princes Street bickers from end to end, an unseemly commercial brawl.
>
> The Rue de Rivoli quietly draws the passer-by to the shops that lie within its graceful arcade. Which makes for better business?[17]

Again there are elements here that recur – unity and harmony, and even the detail of the arcade. But the major publication that drew a radically different future for Edinburgh was the report published by Patrick Abercrombie and Derek Plumstead, *Civic Survey and Plan for Edinburgh*, in 1949.[18] The Abercrombie Report (as it became known) is one of a great many reports produced after the war for the reconstruction of Britain's cities.[19] Edinburgh's city fabric, of course, came through the war almost entirely unscathed.

For the New Town and Princes Street, the report used Kirkwood's plan as the starting point and contrast for the current situation. It stressed how the situation in 1819 was 'infinitely more pleasing'.[20] It also stressed the original municipal control of the project and then echoed writers like Reiach and Hurd: 'Without an amended architectural scheme, these changes become uncoordinated and untidy.'[21]

The proposed solution in the plan was to retain the layout, and establish basic design principles which future developers would have to adhere to. Abercrombie argued that the choice was between controlled variety and anarchy. Almost nothing was, in his view, worth retaining – except for the three clubs – New Club, Conservative Club and University Club.

Edinburghers still execrate the name of Abercrombie. The story

FIGURE 8.5.
(Overleaf) A suggestion for the redesign of Princes Street, Edinburgh, taking full advantage of modern methods of glass manufacture and glazing technique. Design by Robert Jordan, FRIBA; drawing by Norman Howard. (Reproduced from John Gloag, *Industrial Art Explained* (London: George Allen and Unwin, 1946 [1934]), plate 41)

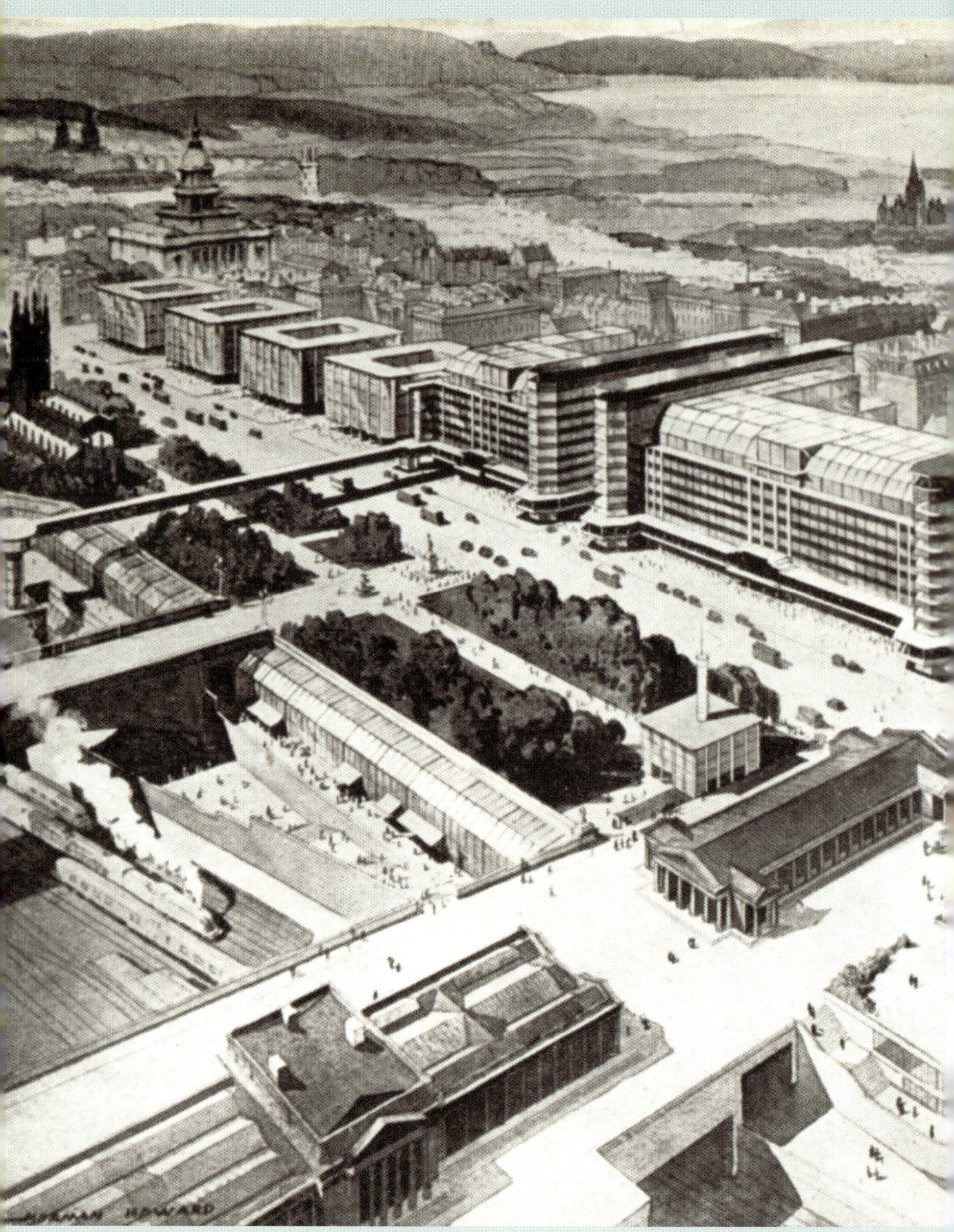
HOWARD

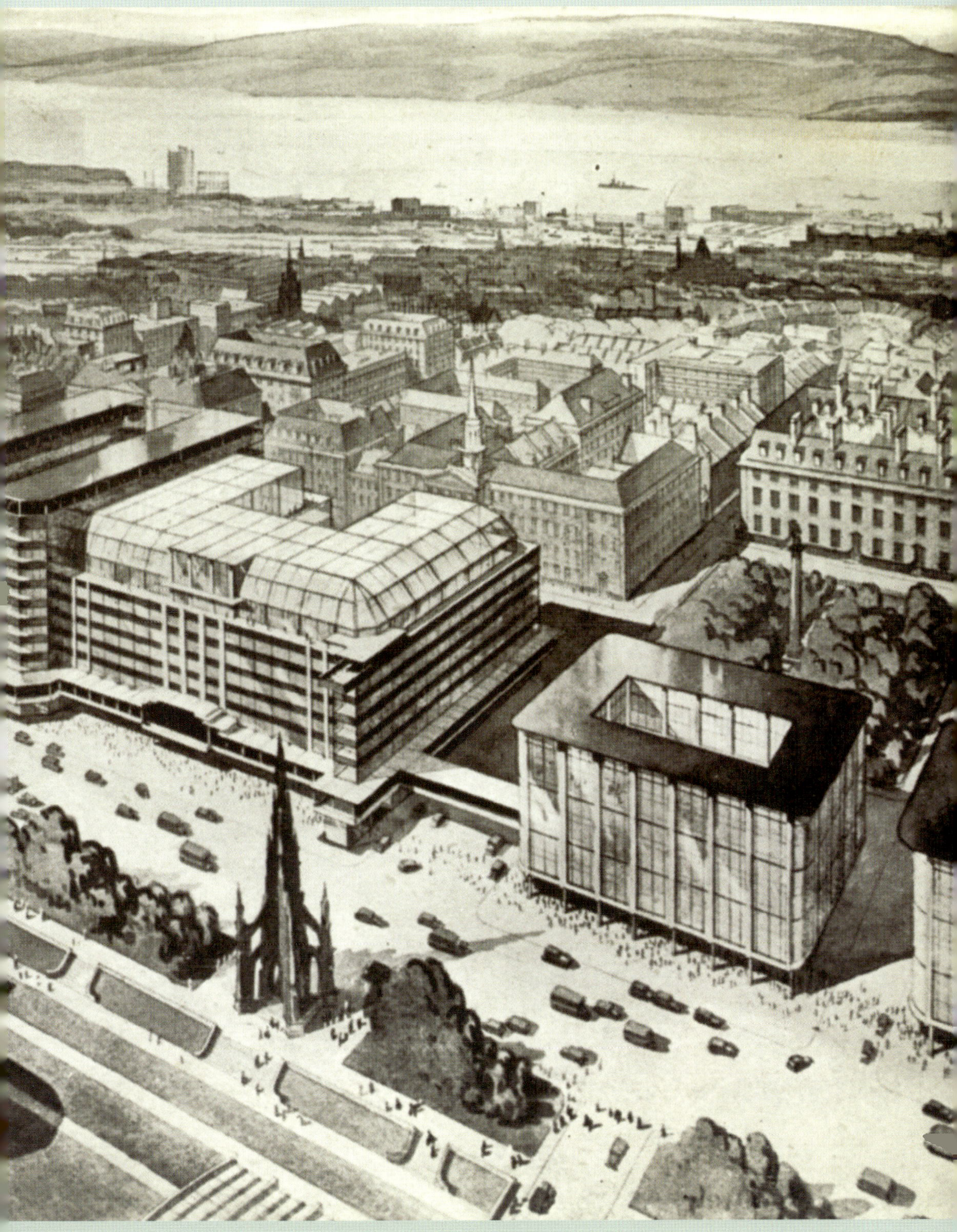

goes that, if Edinburgh carried out what he proposed, the city would have ended up like Glasgow – a city dominated by the car and the urban motorway which slashes through its centre. Abercrombie did have road proposals, notably a triple-deck roadway for Princes Street. But Abercrombie did not propose demolition of the New Town – just the buildings of Princes Street. It should be pointed out, however, that Abercrombie was not working without local input. The Clyde Report (1943) called for changes to Princes Street. Ebenezer Macrae, former City Architect, who provided the historical chapter for the Abercrombie Report, had made his opinion clear in a number of his reports for the city that much could be demolished.[22]

Abercrombie, despite the sketch designs, did not produce detailed proposals for Princes Street, even for the principles of design. That was left to a new body that was set up in the wake of the report, the Princes Street Panel (1954). Chaired at first by William Kininmonth, and from 1955 to 1965 by Kininmonth and J.L. Gleave, and then by Alan Reiach and D.S. Wishart, it sat until 1968, but some of the design principles they established lasted until the mid 1980s. Their remit extended to the whole of Craig's New Town, and their position was, first, that the Georgian New Town had disintegrated and nothing south of George Street, including George Street itself, was worth saving; second, that commercial pressures couldn't be resisted; and lastly, that the basic New Town plan had survived and should be retained. Probably the most notable, surviving impact of their influence was in one of the design principles they seem to have picked up from the Pilkington Glass exhibition of 1938, namely the raised pedestrian walkway, to give two levels of shopping.

However, a balance was to be struck between retention of the best of the old architecture and the new architecture required. But this would have involved quite drastic remodelling of the New Town, and their report, in 1967, coincided with the 200th anniversary – it was undoubtedly one of the sources of impetus for the conservation groups and the heritage lobby to fight harder and to organise to preserve the New Town. By about 1980, listed building legislation was more powerful and lobby groups were more influential, making it very unlikely that buildings such as Jenners or R.W. Forsyth would be demolished. In 1982, there was a general relisting going on, and now almost every historic building on Princes Street is listed.

PART 3

New Towns Elsewhere

CHAPTER 9
The Edinburgh of the South: Seeking the New Town

Robin Skinner

Since the 1860s Dunedin, New Zealand, has been called the 'Edinburgh of the South'.[1] This is not surprising, as the name 'Dunedin' or 'Dun Eideann' is the Gaelic form for that northern capital.[2] Emigration brought many Scottish resonances in the south of New Zealand. Towns with names such as Glencoe, Bannockburn, Stirling and Caberfeidh are scattered through the region, and Presbyterian churches abound. Dunedin's civic crest is supported on either side by a Māori and a tartan-clad Scotsman, while the region's professional rugby team is called 'the Highlanders'. There are many links between the design of Dunedin and that of its northern namesake. Dunedin's suburbs and streets are named after those of Edinburgh, and some claim that the town evidences other characteristics of Edinburgh New Town. Some writers have stated that Dunedin's design was blindly undertaken in Britain, or that its plan is a literal copy of that of Edinburgh.[3] This chapter considers the design of Dunedin in light of the Edinburgh town plan in order to assess the validity of these claims.

After the European discovery of New Zealand in the seventeenth century, British colonisation of the country was enthusiastically debated in the late 1830s. Relations with Māori, who had been in these islands since the thirteenth century, were improving. A flax trade, timber-milling, whaling and sealing were underway, and missionaries were at work. Edward Gibbon Wakefield's scheme for systematic colonisation which would create a stratified community of all classes except those at the top and bottom of society was gaining support. Led by Wakefield, the New Zealand Company proposed to apply his principles based on a sufficient price for land. Landowners, whether in the colony or remaining at home, would receive a combination of town, suburban and rural sections. Workers who arrived without funds could work in order to earn money to buy land eventually. New Zealand Company settlements were established at Wellington (1840), Wanganui (1840), Nelson (1841) and New Plymouth (1841).

The Otago Scheme

The establishment of a Scottish settlement in New Zealand was discussed too. In 1842 the East Lothian-born sculptor and politician George Rennie proposed a Scottish settlement on New Zealand's South Island under the name 'New Edinburgh'.[4] Former army officer Captain William Cargill quickly joined the project and a base office was established in Edinburgh. Talks were given, speaking tours were programmed, magazines were distributed and letters were answered. The Disruption of 1843 within the Church of Scotland further strengthened the project. This dispute, which centred on the relationship between the Church and the State, in particular the right of congregations to appoint ministers, prompted the establishment of the Free Church of Scotland. The New Edinburgh scheme became a joint undertaking between the New Zealand Company and the Lay Association of the Free Church of Scotland. The Company would provide land, transport settlers and survey the site, while the Lay Association would sell the properties and select emigrants. In 1844 the Company surveyor, Frederick Tuckett, determined that the principal settlement of New Edinburgh should be at the head of a 20 km long harbour in the lower part of the east coast of the South Island.[5] The southern climate was considered similar to that of the north of Britain.

Opinions differed within the leadership regarding the composition of the settlement. Rennie, who favoured a more religiously diverse community rather than a settlement that was solely Free Church (as preferred by the other officials), was ousted. Perhaps to reinforce that the project now had new direction, the principal settlement was renamed 'Dunedin'. In order to attract prospective settlers from the west Lowlands of Scotland, the river then known as the Molyneux or the Matau was renamed the Clutha, which was an early name for the River Clyde. Taking its name from the Māori settlement near the harbour entrance, the greater area became known as 'Otakou'. In order to reduce the possibility that this name would alienate prospective emigrants, the officials of the New Edinburgh scheme adopted the spelling 'Otago' (which closely maintains the Māori pronunciation), with the project then becoming known as 'the Otago Scheme'.[6]

The name 'Dunedin' held several familiar resonances. Appearing in poems, including works by Walter Scott, James Hogg and David Macbeth Moir, it was embedded within the Scottish Romanticism of the first decades of the nineteenth century.[7] Sometimes 'Dunedin' or 'Dun-Eidin' was listed as the place of origin for Edinburgh-published books written in Gaelic.[8] There was a small Dunedin Theatre in Nicolson Street, Edinburgh, within the site of the present-day Edinburgh Festival Theatre. In addition, between 1843 and 1844 there had been a novel proposal: the Dunedin Bank. This initiative, which offered the small investor advantageous borrowing and lending rates, would accept smaller deposits than those of the established banks. It attracted a great deal of attention in Scotland and England.[9] Although the venture soon folded, in the mid 1840s the word 'Dunedin' was associated with the lot of the common people. Giving the proposed settlement a name that held these resonances was a strategic move to tap Scottish consciousness in order to build support for the project and attract potential emigrants.

Design of Dunedin

In the early 1840s, the English surveyor Charles Kettle surveyed large tracts of land in the colony's lower North Island for the New Zealand Company. When his employment ceased in 1843 he returned to Britain, gaining work with the New Edinburgh scheme.[10] Between 26 September 1843 and 13 January 1844 he worked alongside the project leaders, attending meetings in various parts of Scotland and speaking on the colony's resources and its advantages as an emigrant destination.[11] With first-hand knowledge, he produced an up-to-date map of the colony for the New Zealand Company. While in Scotland he became acquainted with the plans of Edinburgh's Old and New Towns and the drainage of the Nor' Loch, in addition to the layouts of other Scottish settlements or planned towns. Later in September 1845 Kettle was appointed to survey the Otago settlement, taking up his position in New Zealand in February the following year.[12]

Frederick Tuckett had recommended that the principal settlement be sited on a coastal strip of flat land bounded by hilly terrain. Each landowner was to be allocated a town allotment of a quarter acre (0.10 ha), a suburban lot of 10 acres (4.05 ha) and a rural lot of 50 acres (20.23 ha). After undertaking an assessment of the area, Kettle had to produce plans delineating these sections. Up to 2,400 combined properties were to be allocated in the first five years of the scheme. The job was complicated as the low-lying flat land in the north-east was swampy and a prominent spur separated it from a narrow band of flat land to the south. This effectively bisected the flat area of the town. A chain of hills rose steeply to the west.

Aided by his assistant surveyors, Robert Park and William Davison, Kettle prepared a plan in late 1846 that showed a named street layout with almost 2,300 sections superimposed upon the shaded topography (Fig. 9.1).[13] Although the rugged terrain was obviously dissimilar to the topography of Edinburgh's New Town, as has been noted, some have suggested that the grid plan of the New Town was the inspiration for Dunedin's design. In order to achieve the requisite number of rectangular quarter-acre town sections, long rectangular blocks were positioned on the flat land in the north-east, which to an extent maintains the regularity that we associate with James Craig's design of the New Town. Where this grid meets the steep western slopes, Kettle projected roads at 45-degree angles. These alignments lessened the street gradients, provided drainage and formed inclined grids with further rectangular blocks and sections on the hillside. Some of these road alignments appear to take advantage of the topographic alignment of the hill spurs and gullies. Nevertheless, significant earthworks would be required to achieve trafficable gradients on parts of these rising angled streets.[14]

Kettle was required to deliver 'streets and roads of sufficient width for both health and ornament', and sites for fortifications, public buildings, baths, wharves and cemeteries, as well as sites for 'open Squares, or Town Belt or Park, and other places for Health and recreation of the inhabitants'.[15] Accordingly, he ran a green belt along the length of the town on the excessively sloped terrain above all of these planned streets. This separated the town from the suburban sections to the west. Kettle would have been aware that town belts were being established in other colonial settlements such as Adelaide and Wellington.[16] In addition, he may have been familiar with John Sinclair's earlier proposal for New Thurso of 1812, which included a rectilinear green belt. In time, the town belt running across Dunedin's city rise became a much-prized feature, which remains to this day. Upon receipt of the 1846 plan, the Principal Agent of the New Zealand Company, William Wakefield, stated that he thought the arrangement of the proposed town belt and reserves was 'judicious'.[17] His remark must be understood in terms of Kettle's instructions and within the context of other colonial settlement plans. By the time they arrived at Otago, Kettle, Park and Davison already had substantial experience surveying rural land and colonial towns in New Zealand. They were familiar with Wellington and Nelson, which were each surrounded by hills and harbour; Park had journeyed from Wellington through the sites of Wanganui to New Plymouth. They knew other colonial settlements through published plans. In part, the Dunedin design must be seen as a response to earlier colonial layouts, although that investigation remains outside the scope of this chapter.

Although Kettle's plan shows a regular grid formation, in the 1850s there was significant discontinuity because of the topography. Princes Street was interrupted by the prominent spur that was later known as Bell Hill. Kettle's vision was only achieved when substantial earthworks finally completed this road in the early 1860s.[18] With knowledge of the formation of the Mound in Edinburgh between 1781 and 1830, he would have understood the scale of works that would be required in Dunedin. To the present day some of the connections shown on the 1846 plan are only achieved via steep foot pathways. Kettle had earlier written of the possibility of harbour reclamation at Dunedin and he clearly envisaged continuing the northern grid alignment to the south.[19]

FIGURE 9.1.
(Overleaf) Plan of the town of Dunedin, Otakou, New Zealand, late 1846. (CO 700 New Zealand 11/15, Kew, National Archives)

HEAD OF THE HARBOUR OF OTAKOU

PLAN
of the Town of
DUNEDIN
OTAKOU

NEW ZEALAND

Scale

Charles H. Kettle

N. Zealand N° 11/15

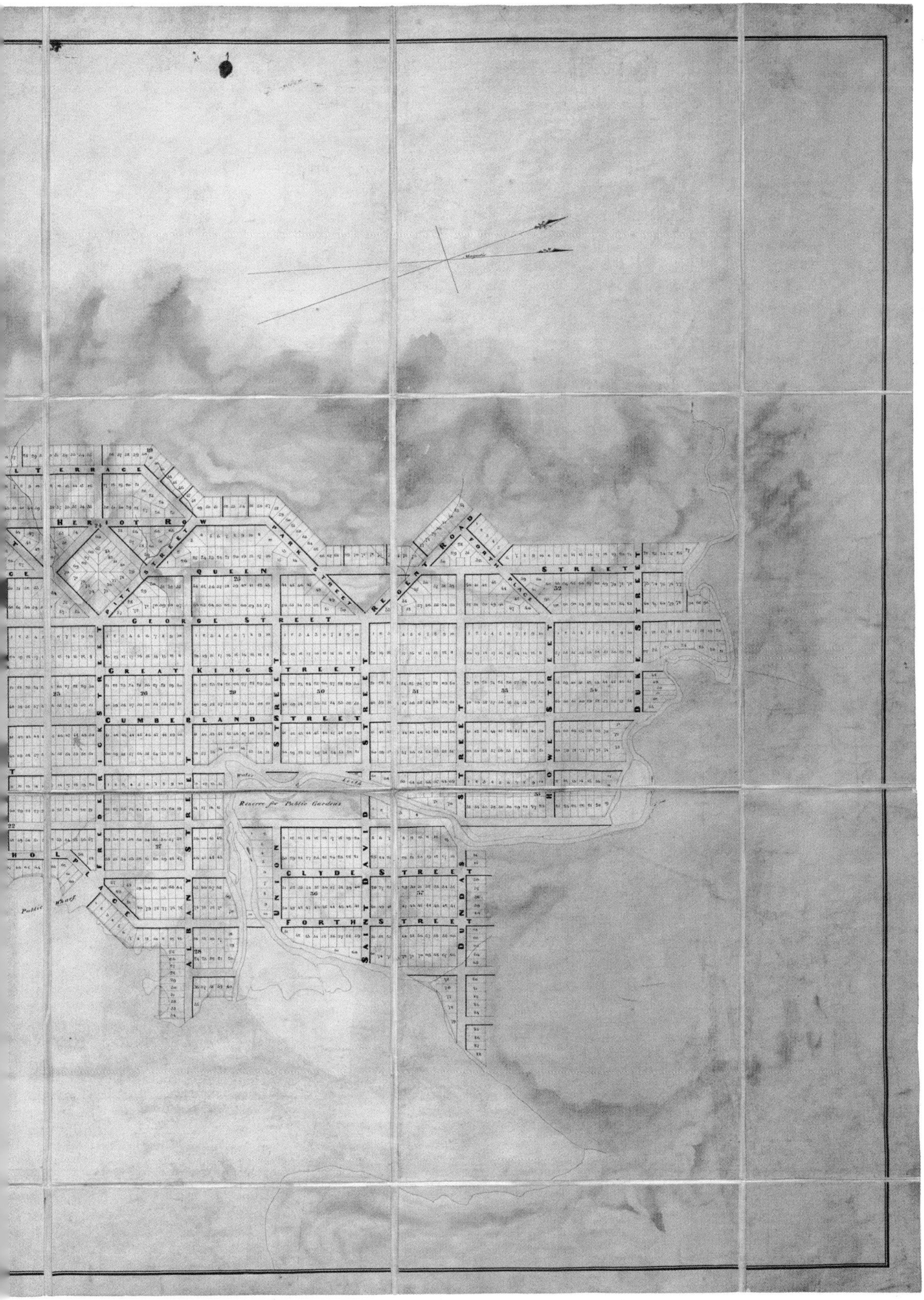

Prior to the Dunedin survey, the harbour settlement of Port Chalmers was planned with a street layout determined by the hilly topography and the size of sections required. For the Dunedin plan the approximate layout of the grid formation was determined before the detailed survey began. Robert Park's survey book indicates that an octagonal circus was envisaged before the line of the long road (Princes Street–George Street) was surveyed.[20] The octagonal form reconciled the 90-degree alignment of the northern orthogonal grid with the inclined alignments of the 45-degree hillside grids, while echoing the circus formations in some British cities. Kettle probably designed his town with an awareness that after Bell Hill was excavated and the southern reclamation was undertaken, this octagonal formation would unify the town design in an elegant, coherent urban arrangement.[21]

Dunedin and the New Town

If Kettle received directions on urban planning or the specific layout, these have not survived. Such matters were usually seen as decisions best left to the colonial surveyor. Kettle's plan makes many nominal connections to the design of Edinburgh. He named Dunedin's principal watercourse 'The Water of Leith' and he labelled fifty street names, most of which recall those of Edinburgh's New Town. The plan shows street names such as Royal Terrace, York Place, Elm Row, St Andrew Street, Hanover Street, Albyn Place and Alva Street. Two streets take names from the Old Town: Canongate and High Street. Possibly mindful of the prominent location of the Canongate in Edinburgh, Kettle gave this name to a street running above a long prominent escarpment in Dunedin. Ten street names recall people from New Zealand or Scotland including Cargill Street, Dowling Street and Park Street. Dionysius Wilfred Dowling was a clerk in the St Andrew Street office of the New Edinburgh Scheme when Kettle was employed there. While many of the street names of Dunedin's northern grid follow those of the first New Town, the ordering and alignment of the streets are dissimilar. Whereas Princes Street and George Street run parallel in Edinburgh's New Town, in Dunedin they are on the same alignment. In a perpendicular orientation to this principal spine there is a progression of random street names taken from the New Town: St Andrew, Hanover, Frederick, Albany, Union, St David, Dundas, Howe and Duke. Appropriating forty street names from Edinburgh suggests that Kettle may have relied on more than his memory of the place, possibly referring to a city map, such as those that were readily available in a *Post Office Directory* or another cheaper publication (Fig. 9.2). If this were the case, it indicates that Kettle may have intended to refer to the Edinburgh design before he designed his colonial town in detail. While he could easily have discussed this prospect with people he met in Britain, there is no record of such communication.

Responding to Edinburgh's topography, the architect James Gillespie Graham had placed the Moray Estate network of Moray Place, Ainslie Place and Randolph Crescent on the falling slope north of the first New Town.[22] With limited space and the requirement for 2,400 sections, Kettle was unable to implement a similar spacious gesture. Nevertheless, the unnamed garden reserve in the centre of the octagon followed a feature of Graham's design and, as stated earlier, it was to provide Dunedin with a central focus and a place to gather – something that the New Town lacks.[23] While Moray Place is a prestigious duodecagonal circus in Edinburgh, on Kettle's map it appears as a large ring road with sections on both sides. A small unnamed eight-sided road and reserve that would eventually become officially known as 'the Octagon' lay at the heart of this formation. Although there were no purely eight-sided street formations in Edinburgh, contemporary plans of St Andrew Square show a central octagonal grassed-space (Fig. 9.2). At about the same dimensions as Dunedin's Octagon, with no through-road and located very near the Edinburgh office where Kettle had been based, this space may have provided an additional prompt for the design of Dunedin's future town centre. Similar shaped grassed spaces were included in the Old Town's George Square and in William Playfair's unbuilt 1819 proposal for Edinburgh's Eastern New Town.[24]

Otago historian Tom Brooking has observed that colonial New Zealanders were very concerned with fairness.[25] In the Dunedin plan we see no evidence of class distinction. Without the alternating hierarchy of major and minor streets that exists between Princes

FIGURE 9.2.
(Overleaf) Detail of Plan of Edinburgh and Leith, by W.H. Lizars, 'From the best Authorities'. Engraved expressly for the *Letter Carriers Directory* (Edinburgh: Ballantyne and Hughes, 1840). This map appeared in the *Post-Office Annual Directory and Calendar for 1841–42*. (Copyright National Library of Scotland)

Canon Mills
Loch
M
6
Deaf & Dumb Institution
Edinburgh Academy
Henderson Row
Claremont St.
Claremont Pl.
Silver Mills
Fettes Row
Royal Crescent
Drummond Place
Cumberland Street
Gt. King Street
Royal Circus
Northumberland Street
Abercromby Place
Jamaica St.
Heriot Row
Queen Street
Gardens
Moray Place
Darnaway St.
Ainslie Place
Albyn Pla.
Young St.
Hill St.
Thistle Street
St. Andrews Ch.
Physicians Hall
St. Colm St.
Charlotte Square
George Street
K
7
Rose Street
Castle Street
Frederick Street
Hanover Street
Princes Street
Club Room
Royal Institution
Earthen Mound
B
Princes Street Gardens
St. John's Chapel
St. Cuthberts Church
Riding Sch.
Diorama
Unitarian Chapel
Hope St.
Charlotte Pl.
Melville Place
Randolph Cres.
Stuart St.
Alva St.
Shandwick Pl.
Maitland St.
Rutland St.
Rutland Square
Atholl Cres.
Dean Street
St. Bernard Crescent
Ann St.
India Place
Stockbridge
Hamilton Pl.
Brunswick St.
Saxe Coburg Place
Brandon St.
Eyre Pl.
Dundas Str.
Pitt Str.
Howe Str.
India Str.
Gloster Pl.
Doune Ter.
Bank of S
Mound Pl.
Lawn-Market
Esplanade
Cleghorn
Nursery
Flower

Broughton Park
Hope Crescent
Annandale St
Haddington Pla.
Leith Walk
Toll
Shrub Pl.
Gayfield Ho.
Gayfield Square
Elm Row
Montgomery St.
Windsor St.
Brunswick St.
Leopold Place
Hillside Crescent
Blenheim Pl.
3
Brunton Pl.
Royal Terrace
Regent Terrace
London Road
Calton Hill
Royal Observatory
National Monument
Nelsons Mont
Bridewell
Jail
Royal High School
Calton Burying Ground
Burns Monument
North Back of Canongate
Canongate
Canongate Church
Gas Work
New Street
Queensberry Ho.
Milton Ho.
Water Gate
Abbey
Palace Yard
Chapel
Back of Canongate
Low Calton
Orphan Hos.
Glenarchys Ch.
College Ch
Trinity Ho.
Physic Gardens
North Bridge
Register Off
Theatre
Stamp Off
Post Off
Waterloo Pl.
Leith St
Greenside St
Union Pl
Picardy Pl.
St Pauls Ch.
Broughton Pl.
Forth Str.
Union St
Barony St.
Albany Str
York Place
St James Square
Market St.
High Street
Tron Ch.
Netherbow
Giles Ch.
Parlt Squ.

and Queen Streets in the New Town, Dunedin's equal-area sections were to be allocated by ballot, so proximity to the commercial centre (then on Princes Street) determined desirability. Pointedly, while Kettle repeated most of the street names of the New Town, he ignored the names of the minor streets where the tradespeople lived. Dunedin has no Rose, Thistle, Young or Hill Streets. Making no attempt to echo the social hierarchy that is fundamental to the layout of the New Town, the Dunedin design makes a significant departure from its supposed model. While this prevented a spacious Edinburgh-type streetscape developing, the lack of major and minor streets ensured that Dunedin would have double-sided shopping streets of an appropriate scale, which is another feature that has been identified as absent in the New Town.[26]

The Site Settled

The majority of settlers on the first two ships, the *Philip Laing* and the *John Wickliffe*, were from villages and farms in the south with many from Midlothian; there were only a few Highlanders.[27] News of their arrival came at very short notice, and hasty arrangements for emigration barracks and baggage storage were attempted. When the first ships moored in March–April 1848, there was no awaiting church, school, public buildings, parkland or jetty. Pegs indicated the unformed street locations.[28] Nevertheless, lots were allocated and makeshift dwellings were erected. Initially the Dunedin site proved difficult, which prompted criticism of the town layout.[29] The streets were rutted and muddy, and streams required culverting[30] (Fig. 9.3). One of Kettle's survey staff, William Davison, criticised his superior for laying out the roads without regard for the topography, a criticism which was restated in subsequent decades.[31] However, such a strategy would have resulted in less regular sections and, consequentially, a more sparsely populated settlement.

In 1863, during the Otago gold rush, a British visitor and campaigner on behalf of women's emigration, Maria S. Rye, complained to *The Times* of London that the Dunedin plan and its street names were prepared in Edinburgh without knowledge of the natural difficulties or capabilities of the country.[32] This was duly reprinted in the colony.³³ Presumably this reflects what she heard in the colony. Kettle was unable to respond as in the previous year – in a town overrun with immigrants drawn by the discovery of gold – he had succumbed to typhoid. However, an anonymous letter writer who had formerly worked under Kettle defended the design.³⁴ It was probably Robert Park who replied that Rye's assertion was absurd, adding 'a comparison of the plans of the two cities shows that in neither the arrangements of the streets, or form of the squares or open places, does Edinburgh and Dunedin correspond in one iota . . .'. While this was not one of Rye's observations, it may be that the writer was attempting to clear a misconception already circulating in the colony. He further stated that in order to best identify the requisite number of town sections Kettle fixed upon the present site '[a]fter repeated and careful examination'. Significantly, he added that the decision to name the streets after those in Edinburgh was an idea of Kettle, rather than the home authorities.

FIGURE 9.3.
Otago Emigration Office letterhead showing Princes Street Dunedin (1859). The view dates from 1858. (AAAC/707/D500/131a – 287, Dunedin, Archives New Zealand)

After Kettle

FIGURE 9.4.
(Opposite) Frank Coxhead, *Princes Street, Dunedin, N.Z*, showing the Cargill Monument (1880s). This is the same streetscape as that shown in Fig. 9.3. (From the album: Australasian Scenery, Reg. O.033275, Wellington, Te Papa Tongarewa)

As the century progressed, the wealth from the gold fields created a streetscape that matched the substance and materiality of an established, old-world town, albeit without the Georgian grandeur of Edinburgh's New Town (Fig. 9.4). By the end of the century, when Dunedin had become industrialised, with significant harbour works and reclamation, the integrity of Kettle's plan was largely maintained, which is testament to the success of his design (Fig. 9.5).

Writers at that time and since have continued to make observations on the design of Dunedin in relation to Edinburgh. In 1898 Dr Thomas Hocken notably claimed that Kettle was instructed to reproduce the *features* of Edinburgh.[35] However, there is no earlier written record indicating that Kettle was directed to do this.[36] More recently, Peter Entwisle fancifully interpreted Kettle's alleged instruction to reproduce the *characteristics* of Edinburgh to amount to 'a specific aesthetic brief' which resulted in the cities sharing a romantic composition juxtaposed with formality in a dramatic setting.[37] Dunedin writer Ian Dougherty has soundly stated that Edinburgh's New Town gave Kettle ideas – but not a blueprint – to the extent that much of the similarity between the two cities is superficial. The sites, he stated, are so dissimilar that Kettle could only make token gestures towards reproducing the special features of Edinburgh.[38] This is an astute verdict which is supported by the findings of this chapter.

These claims for connection between the two city designs provide a valuable prompt for study and reflection. The Dunedin plan had many sources beyond its Scottish namesake. Much of the desire to interpret Dunedin as a New Edinburgh ignores the fact that, before coming to Otago, Kettle, Park and Davison already had substantial experience surveying rural land and colonial towns in New Zealand. Through first-hand experience or by studying plans, they were familiar with other colonial settlements in New Zealand and beyond. While many people have been keen to link Dunedin's design with that of James Craig's New Town, it must be acknowledged that colonial precedents are also likely to have contributed to the town's design. Nevertheless, within the public mind at least, the connection between the designs of the two cities remains strong.

FIGURE 9.5.
(OVERLEAF) *Jubilee of Otago: Dunedin 1898*, J. Wilkie & Co. litho, New Zealand, 1898. (National Library of New Zealand, Wellington, Map Coll. 834.5292ap 1898)

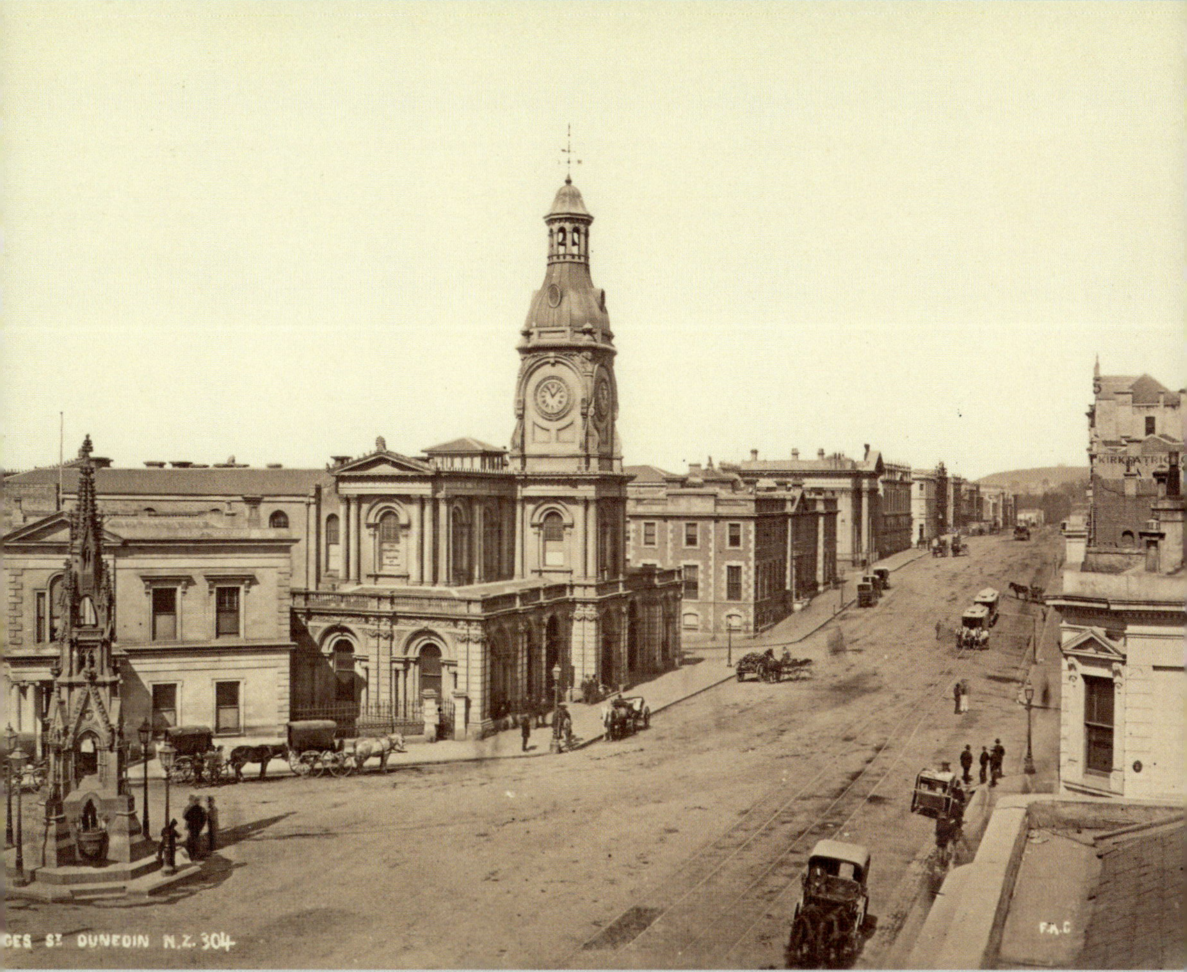
GES St DUNEDIN N.Z. 304
F.A.C

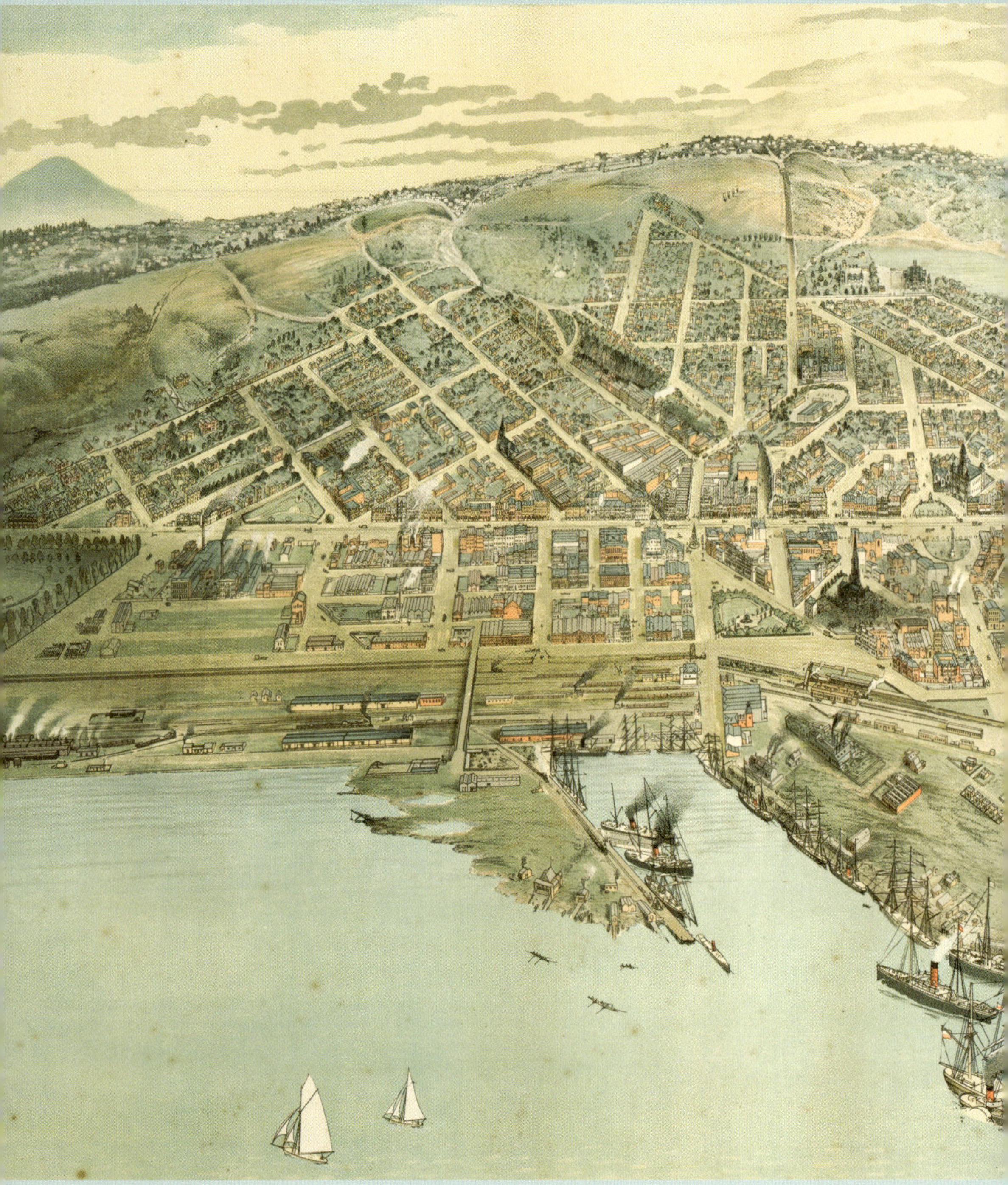

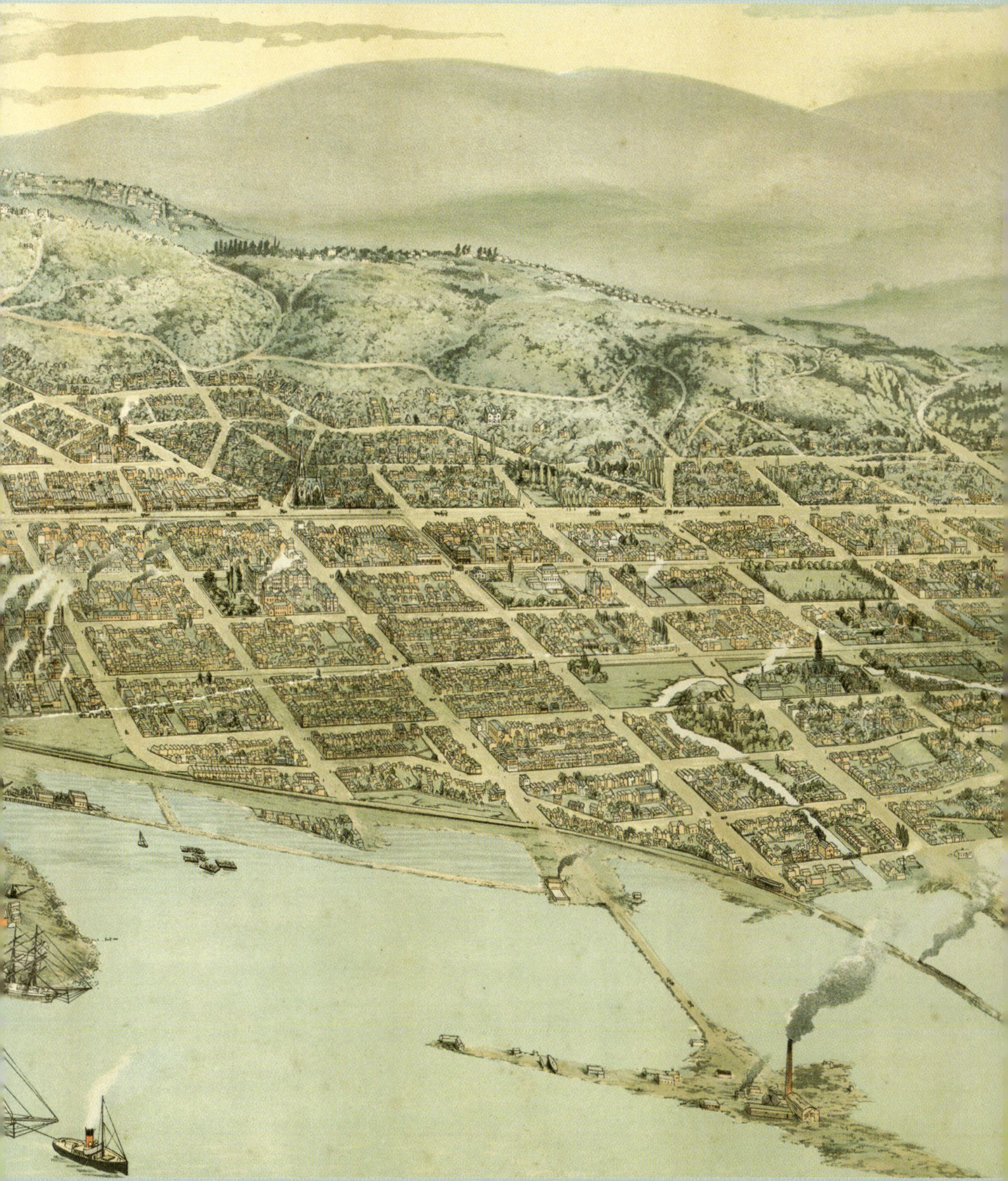

CHAPTER 10

The 'Enlightened' Factory: Textile Industry and the 'Planned Village Movement' in Scotland (1785–1800)

Ophélie Siméon

With the 'planned village movement', the Enlightenment ideals behind the Edinburgh New Town also found a powerful outlet in the Scottish countryside.[1] From the late seventeenth century to the mid nineteenth century, several hundred settlements were either remodelled or built totally anew to develop the economy, notably in the wake of the 1707 Act of Union. While planned farming estates have been extensively studied,[2] it is perhaps less well known that the same will to unite profit and improvement has informed much of Scotland's first generation of industrial concerns. This chapter adopts a comparative approach, analysing a variety of factory villages built in Scotland in the early stages of mass industrialisation (1775–1810), when the textile sector was dominated by rural, water-powered establishments. These industrial settlements were all connected in some way to a small network of industrial improvers. This common trait will help us address the motivation to plan ambitious settlements around industrial sites, and to consider these innovations within the context of Enlightenment-era values. While encouraging Scotland's industrial development was essential after 1707, the importance given to housing quality, rational layout and architectural fashions shows that even on a limited, individual scale, these factory villages were in many ways conscious attempts to better the condition of Scottish workers – thus bringing the ideal of improvement into the industrial age.

Before the 1830s and the dominance of steam-powered urban textile mills, the cotton-spinning industry developed mostly in the

FIGURE 10.1.
British cotton mill villages, 1771–1800.
1 Spinningdale
2 Stanley
3 Deanston
4 Balfron
5 Fintry
6 Faifley
7 Rothesay
8 Johnstone
9 Neilston
10 Barrhead
11 Thornliebank
12 Bridge of Weir
13 Eglinton
14 Blantyre
15 Catrine
16 New Lanark
17 Penicuik
18 Gatehouse of Fleet
19 Backbarrow
20 Styal
21 Cressbrook
22 Darley Abbey
23 Lea Mills
24 Cromford/Masson Mill
25 Belper
26 Linton
27 Fazeley
(Copyright Ophélie Siméon)

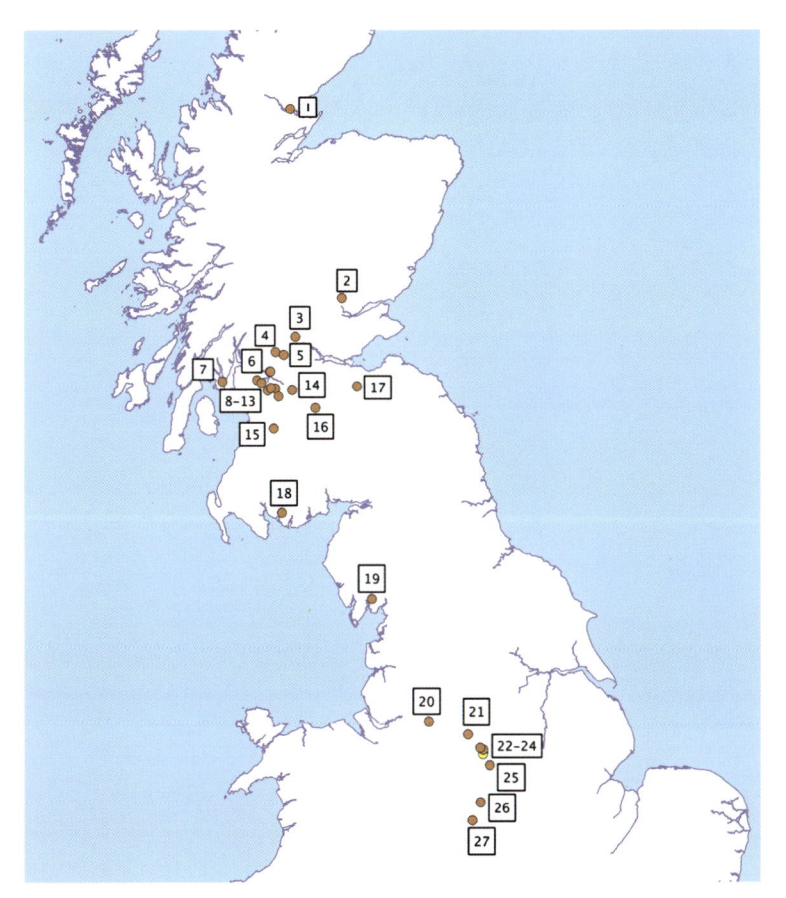

countryside, where strong and reliable water-power sources could be exploited. A majority of cotton factories were equipped with water-frames, a technology developed by Richard Arkwright in the mid 1760s as an improvement upon both the mule and the spinning jenny. In 1771, wishing to put his invention to the test, he established the first cotton mill in history at Cromford, Derbyshire, by the River Derwent. Cromford helped popularise the integrated layout of concentrated labour organisation and fully mechanised production which was to epitomise the factory as opposed to a purely domestic system. With the hope of significant financial returns, would-be industrialists 'all looked up to [Arkwright] and imitated his mode of building'.[3] Between 1771 and the early 1830s, more than seven hundred cotton mills were founded in Britain, 70% of which were water-powered and located in a rural setting (Fig. 10.1).[4] Most of these establishments were repurposed water-mills and textile workshops. In twenty-nine cases only, when the production site was particularly remote, and when the company owner possessed the necessary capital, factories were either extensively remodelled or wholly new-built as planned, self-contained industrial communities. This had been the case at Cromford, which had been previously a nail-making and lead-mining hamlet.[5]

Out of these twenty-seven factory communities, eighteen were founded in Scotland between 1778 and 1810. This was in many ways the result of Richard Arkwright's personal involvement in the development of cotton-spinning north of the border. Around 1784, this Derbyshire cotton lord was keen to expand his activities outside England, where he was facing accusations of plagiarism over his water-frame patents. Scotland seemed like a suitable alternative, possessing ample water resources and a pool of potential business partners equally desirous to challenge England's dominance over the textile industrial sector. By 1785, Arkwright had entered joint ventures with David Dale and others at New Lanark (Lanarkshire), Stanley (Perthshire) and Donside (Aberdeenshire). Patents were also granted at Catrine (Ayrshire) and Deanston (Stirlingshire). In all cases, millwrights and managers received training at Cromford free of charge.

However, the popularity of Arkwright-type mill villages in Scotland also rested on national urbanising traditions. Since the early eighteenth century, widespread planning had been the norm for Scottish estates, with at least 450 settlements established or rehabilitated from 1725 to 1850. As Lorna Philip has argued, this movement was 'inspired by a zeitgeist which combined aesthetic, social and economic aims, in effect a practical implementation of Enlightenment ideals'.[6] Through widespread enclosure, mechanisation and the promotion of state-of-the-art agricultural techniques, local lairds hoped to boost their revenues. Philanthropic concerns were also involved, as many of these planned villages were founded to rehouse and employ displaced crofters in the wake of the Clearances. Lastly, the movement also carried political and patriotic implications, finding a powerful justification in the concept – or national paradigm – of improvement. Village planning was seen as one of the best ways to fuel economic and social progress within the Union.

Often, these endeavours were essentially paternalistic.[7] Change was encouraged as an inescapable aspect of modernity, but many Scottish landowners were ready to balance economic novelty with more traditional relief provisions. Ideally, the promotion of neatly planned communities would 'provide an example and an inspiration to the tenantry without diminishing the landowner's hold over the countryside'.[8]

Factory villages were the direct heirs to such discourses. Indeed, there was traditionally much overlap between agricultural and manufacturing activities on planned Scottish estates. Improvers like George Dempster of Dunnichen, Sir John Sinclair and Robert Rennie argued that only a blend of commercial farming and industry would guarantee economic viability in the Scottish countryside.[9] Consequently, once cotton-spinning established itself as a highly profitable pursuit, many planned agricultural settlements such as Penicuik (Midlothian) and Stanley and Eaglesham (Renfrewshire) transitioned from the plough to the water-frame. Landowners were often personally involved in the promotion of factory villages in Scotland. At Stanley and Catrine, the Duke of Atholl and Claude Alexander of Ballochmyle (respectively) secured feuing and water rights, employed their own factors to design the new mill communities, and recruited managers to run the mills. Significantly, George Dempster, who was also MP for the Perth burghs between 1761 and 1790, had played a key role in the development of cotton-spinning in Scotland. After a visit to Cromford in 1784, he had convinced Richard Arkwright to expand his activities north of the border, and was key in helping him secure business deals with prominent Scottish industrialists, most notably David Dale at New Lanark. Over time, Dempster succeeded in gathering a small, tightly knit network of business partners with an interest in village planning. In addition to being founding partners in the New Lanark Company, he and David Dale had shares at Stanley, and were instrumental in establishing a mill settlement at Spinningdale (Sutherland).

As a cloth merchant, cotton lord and cashier to the Glasgow branch of the Royal Bank of Scotland, Dale was a particularly central figure. As a result of his wide-ranging contacts, he had business interests in at least eight cotton mill villages including Newton Stewart, Blantyre, Balfron, Deanston and Catrine. The last two ventures saw him join forces with two of the most prominent business families in Scotland, the Buchanans and the Finlays, who, in addition to their involvement in cotton-spinning, were Richard Arkwright's commercial agents in Scotland, and the owners of the nation's first brokerage firm, James Finlay & Co., respectively. The Spinningdale partnership was typical of this overlap between agricultural and industrial improvement. In addition to Dale and Dempster, business associates included local lairds, a group of Glasgow tobacco merchants and Highland estate factors. But despite Dempster's claims that 'public spirit' was a prime motive for planning a mill village, more pragmatic incentives were also at play.[10]

Given the existence of 'established kinship groups' among factory village owners, early cotton-spinning communities unsurprisingly bore an air of familiar resemblance.[11] This was first and foremost a necessity informed by shared occupational constraints. Arkwright-type mills had to be spacious enough to accommodate the machinery and water-wheels, while ensuring an adequate distribution of power from the nearby rivers up to the carding and spinning rooms. Following the Cromford model, the first-generation cotton factories were utilitarian, quadrangular buildings, usually between four and seven storeys high. Likewise, the surrounding workers' housing and neighbourhood amenities served pragmatic functions. While spinning offered higher wages than farm work, the harsh, monotonous nature of industrial work and the remoteness of some factory settlements increased the risk of chronic labour shortage. Consequently, providing a full range of amenities to prospective employees became a necessity for any factory owner wishing to attract labourers, reduce turnover and maximise profits. This also offered advantages in terms of discipline and character formation.

Because of their geographical isolation, factory villages 'enabled the entrepreneur to make firm connections between the work, family and social life of the labourer so that the behaviour in one sphere was directly linked to fortunes in another'.[12] Neatly laid-out streets and cottages or tenements were not only designed to attract a prospective labour force. Cotton masters essentially used village planning to assert their authority, as the right to enjoy these facilities was tied to the workers' employment contracts as non-transferable advantages. The conjunction of sanctions on the factory floor and incentives in the form of superior amenities would foster compliance among the workforce. If the factory hands were to understand that the company's interest was also their own, this feeling would hopefully translate into maximum efficiency and harmonious industrial relations.[13] This paternalism was in line with the so-called 'civilising' mission often bestowed upon the earlier generation of planned villages. After Culloden, the Commissioners of the Forfeited Estates considered new settlements as one of the best ways to instil Lowland values of industriousness and respectability (and political acceptance of the new Hanoverian royal dynasty) in 'unruly' Highlanders. Improvers hoped that, thanks to the introduction of rationalised housing and economic pursuits, 'industry cherished by benevolence [would] produce the happy fruits of prosperity and affluence', thus fostering 'mutual confidence betwixt landlord and villagers'.[14]

In England, factory village owners like Arkwright at Cromford or the Strutt family at Belper (Derbyshire) provided housing in the form of terraced cottages. Scottish workers lived in even more modest conditions, frequently in tenement rows. This long-established housing type was popularised at various agricultural planned villages in the Highlands. In all cases, the aim was to provide cheap, sturdy housing to a migrant population of modest origins. At Spinningdale, the workers' barracks were valued at £62 – in comparison, the factory's ten looms were worth £67.[15] At Catrine and most similar settlements, the layout often followed 'a simple ground plan, with two rows of houses facing each other across a wide road or green'.[16]

Yet it seems that the significance of factory villages went beyond mere efficiency to encompass social and patriotic considerations, in line with the earlier planned village movement. At Cromford, Arkwright had favoured paternalistic management practices, and had struck business deals with like-minded partners from the Derwent valley, such as the Strutt and Evans families. His Scottish associates also fitted into the contemporary model of progressive paternalism, with its openness to Enlightenment ideas. Kirkman Finlay, chairman of James Finlay & Co., had ties with the Glasgow Literary and Commercial Society, and was appointed rector of Glasgow University in 1819.

David Dale is another case in point. His business ethos was a mixture of financial shrewdness, religion and philanthropy. A staunch evangelical, he was a founding member and lay pastor of the Old Scotch Independents, a Dissenting Presbyterian group which advocated an active participation in world affairs through pastoral and philanthropic exertion. Given his own modest upbringing – he was born a grocer's son and started out as a linen weaver in Paisley – Dale took great interest in poor relief and public hygiene, which brought him to the attention of English reform circles. In the years 1795–9, New Lanark received six to seven hundred visitors a year on average, a tremendous number for the time considering the village's geographical isolation and the dearth of public transport in the area. In 1796, as part of its inquiries into the possibility of establishing legal safeguards for factory work, the Manchester Board of Health took cues from Dale's management methods and philanthropic provisions, with the obvious intention of using this source material for an upcoming petition to the British Parliament[17] With regard to working hours and educational provision, Dale certainly anticipated some of the rulings of the 1802 Health and Morals of Apprentices Act, which the Board of Health was instrumental in passing. The Act stipulated that children should not work more than twelve hours a day, exclusive of meal breaks; they were also to receive education in the '3Rs' (reading, writing and arithmetic) for a period of four years, and Bible reading on Sundays. In comparison, Dale's operatives at New Lanark and Catrine worked eleven hours a day, including two meal breaks, whereas most cotton-spinners were employed twelve to fourteen hours daily on average.[18] A comprehensive school system was also set up in both factory villages, with infant schools, day and evening classes for older pupils as well as a Sunday school. Educational provision at New Lanark was particularly remarkable for its day. While the curriculum focused on reading, accounting and Bible-reading, children were also given singing, dancing and gymnastics classes.[19]

Dale made no secret that his school system enabled him to fashion his own pool of skilled, polite and compliant workers. Yet he flattered himself that many of his young labourers, including former workhouse children, left his service equipped with sufficient skills and education to guarantee them a good occupation elsewhere, and a stable income. This was at odds with the dominant discourses of the day, which favoured only a minimal training for poor children, based on their supposed low social worth. Dale's wish to improve his workers' individual and collective lot was in any case reminiscent of the social and paternalistic implications at play in the planned village movement.

For Dale, Dempster and the wider community of Scottish improvers, the founding of new factory settlements served as an antidote to the nation's woes: whether these were manifest in the degradation of the urban poor in slums and workhouses, or in the mass emigration of Highlanders to North America, which at that point represented an unwelcomed drain on the nation's human resources. If handled benevolently, according to time-honoured paternal principles and away from urban squalor, the development of industry would become a prime vehicle for social and economic progress from which masters, workers and the whole nation could benefit. In this respect, early mill communities can be seen as an early response to what would become known as the 'social question', even on a limited, individual scale.[20]

In most mill villages, according to the *Old Statistical Account of Scotland*, workers were 'poor people, and reduced families', come to find a better living, sometimes in the wake of the Clearances. Highlanders did form the bulk of the workforce at Deanston, Catrine and New Lanark. In 1791, Dale offered employment to a group of 200 would-be emigrants on their way to the USA whose ship, the *Fortune*, had been wrecked off Greenock.[21] Stanley and Spinningdale were founded to relocate evicted crofters and boost the economy of impoverished Highland areas. For these displaced tenants, cheap, quality housing and other neighbourhood amenities could make a vital difference between destitution and a life of relative ease. Many were therefore ready to accept the intrinsic harshness of factory work, especially as employment was usually given on a family basis.[22]

There is ample physical evidence that most factory owners were keen to offer a pleasant setting to their labour force, although quality varied from place to place. At Spinningdale, financial difficulties hindered planning on a significant scale, and the village offered little more than workers' barracks. At Penicuik, the transition from paper-making to cotton-spinning was marked by a slump in housing standards, as the new proprietors took less interest in welfare provisions than the original planning landowner, Sir James Clerk. In most cases, however, layout and architecture showed a joint concern for functionality, hygiene and aesthetics. At Stanley, the Duke of Atholl's factor, James Stobie, designed the village on an elaborate grid plan.

Mill buildings and tenements were likewise influenced by the artistic fashions of the day. In that respect, they followed a tradition inaugurated by the first large-scale manufactures, such as Boulton and Watt's Soho workshop, and then taken up at Cromford, marked by the joint pursuit of prestige and profit. With their dressed stone buildings, slated roofs, projecting facades and Diocletian windows, Scottish factory villages featured many neo-classical elements, a style associated in Scotland at that time with the brothers John, James and Robert Adam. Picturesque elements were also favoured. At Eaglesham, which was designed following blueprints by the Earl of Eglinton, highlights included 'two rows of elegantly built houses, all of freestone, with a large space between, laid out in fine green fields, interspersed with trees'. At New Lanark, Robert Owen laid out a network of footpaths and walking grounds up to the Falls of Clyde – itself a landmark of picturesque tourism – for the recreational use of guests and workers alike. Bordered with shrubs, flowerbeds and lawns, these arrangements were described by a visitor in 1821 as 'not deficient in variety as to eminence and valley, shade and open ground'. Few factory grounds at that time garnered such aesthetic praise.[23]

Though factory village housing was plain and small, it remained superior to the average working-class dwellings of the day. In addition to back gardens, tenements were usually provided with larders, sculleries and garrets. The village streets were neatly cobbled, with drainage troughs and several outdoor latrines. While there was no piped running water, the inhabitants could draw on supplies from wells, mill lades and nearby rivers. In contrast, Scottish farmers in 'unimproved' estates would usually reside in damp, dark turf cottages, with thatch or heather roofs and dirt floors. In his *Rural Recollections*, agriculturist George Robertson described the housing of late-eighteenth-century Lothian crofters as 'mean hovels', built in a day, with mud-brick walls and no chimney. The urban working-classes mostly lived in overcrowded, unhealthy environments, the result of frequently exploitative landlordism, not of management-driven architectural planning. As industrial archaeologist Michael Nevell argues, 'the valuable commodity [in factory towns] was not the house nor the land but the tenant'.[24]

Like previous improving landowners, David Dale and the other founders of cotton mill communities assumed a socially elevated, paternalistic stance, trading protection for economic efficiency and overall deference. Their paternal management was also representative of the improvement ethos insofar as the desire to maximise profits through close supervision was inseparable from, and indeed complementary to, an interest in their dependants' welfare. As Reinhard Bendix argued, viewing industrial discipline in purely functionalist terms fails to see the management ethos of factory community builders in context. The overlap between philanthropy and profit should not be seen as contradictory, but as creative tension.[25]

There is no evidence – with the notable exception of Robert Owen in the later stage of his business career – that Dale, Kirkman Finlay or Claude Alexander of Ballochmyle ever sought to question fundamentally the existence and nature of the factory system. For instance, the widespread reliance on child labour, undoubtedly one of its most controversial aspects, was never challenged. Bettering the condition of the poor was necessary for the common good, but without bringing them unnecessarily above their station, which would have threatened the status quo.

Yet at a time when welfare policies were either non-existent or in crisis – as with the Old Poor Laws – factory villages offered improved living conditions, especially compared with some industrial towns. Furthermore, the will to put improvement principles into practice was far from typical in the industrial sector. Despite the prestige derived from philanthropic pursuits and refined Enlightenment fashions, only a minority of entrepreneurs possessed both the means and the will to become community builders. The situation had not changed by the 1830s, when the Factory Inquiry Commission reported that among cotton masters, only a 'handful of idealists' were keen on attending to their workers' welfare.[26]

A wholly separate workers' welfare issue was of course slavery – which enabled the inexpensive provision of cotton for businesses such as that of James Finlay & Co., mentioned above.[27] The connection of that topic with the industrialisation processes discussed in this chapter is clearly a distinct area deserving further study, not least due to the impact of its profits on the nature and scale of the planned towns discussed here. The story of the planned towns and villages of the Scottish countryside is, manifestly, a complicated one, but it is hoped, by highlighting the people and locations set out above, that others will take this narrative forward.

CHAPTER 11

Citizenship, Community and the New Towns in Post-War Scotland

Alistair Fair

On 6 May 1947, East Kilbride, to the south-east of Glasgow, was designated a new town, the first in Scotland to be realised as part of an emerging national programme.[1] In 1946, Patrick Abercrombie and Robert Matthew's *Clyde Valley Regional Plan* had identified the village as the potential nucleus of a new town which would relieve some of Glasgow's housing and industrial pressures, along with Cumbernauld, Bishopton and Houston.[2] These proposals were critically received by Glasgow Corporation, which aimed to rehouse its population within the existing city boundary.[3] Nonetheless, East Kilbride was built (as was Cumbernauld from the mid 1950s, and Irvine, replacing Bishopton/Houston, from the late 1960s). The outline town plan for East Kilbride was drawn up by officials in the Department of Health for Scotland (DHS), working under Robert Gardner-Medwin and Frank Connell, with the detailed plans being prepared by East Kilbride Development Corporation's in-house team under Donald P. Reay; landscape design was by Brenda Colvin.[4] Low-density neighbourhoods, largely made up of terraced houses with gardens, were to be arranged around a new town centre, the name of whose original main thoroughfare – Princes Street – recalled its eighteenth-century Edinburgh forebear. By 1958, 5,340 houses had been constructed.[5]

The designation of East Kilbride and the contemporaneous 'first generation' new towns in Britain represented the emergence during the 1940s of an interest on the part of central government in 'planning'. The planned environment formed one element of the nascent

Welfare State, i.e. an expanded state machinery which took greater responsibility for the lives and welfare of its citizens than had hitherto been the case. Planning in general, and the new towns in particular, gave built form to the ambitions of the Welfare State. The interventionist, perhaps paternalist, nature of the new system is evident in the terms in which East Kilbride was conceived. The Department of Health for Scotland was critical of Glasgow's interwar suburbs: 'there grew up in these areas an unco-ordinated mass of peripheral housing development . . ., predominantly of one social class, with no civic identity, practically no independent social facilities and no industry'.[6] In contrast, the new towns would be consciously planned, would integrate housing and places of employment, would house so-called 'balanced communities' of people from different income groups and social classes, and, perhaps most significantly, were intended to have a transformative effect on the lives and outlooks of their residents. In the case of East Kilbride, the DHS suggested that 'the first new town to be established in Scotland should exemplify the best possible standards in such matters as industrial estate layout, the provision of houses at appropriate densities, and planned open space for recreation and amenity and the provision of schools . . ., and of other community facilities'.[7] Such facilities would add to the attractiveness of the town: 'a new town . . . planned on modern lines with the full range of social amenities would have special attractions both for industries wishing to move out from congested premises in Glasgow and other urban areas and for new industries'.[8]

The planning of the new towns has attracted significant attention from historians, while there are also numerous, often celebratory, accounts of their creation by participants.[9] Meanwhile, the experience of new town residents has also begun productively to be discussed.[10] This chapter augments these works by considering the extent to which the new towns were conceived in explicitly 'social' terms, and by proposing that individual and communal 'transformation' was one of the key goals shaping the initial conception of the new towns. In so doing, it builds on previous discussions of community and neighbourhood units in post-war planning,[11] but it develops these arguments by also situating the new towns within an emerging literature concerning the history of civic pride and identity, the notion of citizenship in twentieth-century Britain, and the reforming ambitions of the modernist project as shaped by a range of participants.[12] In so doing, it proposes a lens through which to consider modern architecture and planning in terms which move beyond the purely formal.

The main part of the chapter considers the central place of the ideas of community, citizenship and transformation in the conception of the early post-war new towns, before turning specifically to East Kilbride. The final section considers the fate of these ideas. It accepts that new fashions in planning and the emergence of the affluent 'consumer-citizen' during the 1950s and 1960s increasingly challenged the spatial and social assumptions of the 1940s. Yet, as we shall see, transformative social ambitions remained significant in the conception of the 1960s new towns, the planning of which was not entirely unlike their 1940s predecessors.

The New Towns Act and Transformative Sociability

In 1946, Lewis Silkin, then Minister of Town and Country Planning, told his fellow Members of Parliament of his despair at the standard of pre-war housing in Britain.[13] The suburban estates of the 1920s and 1930s had, he said, 'failed in their purpose of providing a better life'; they offered 'no community life or civic sense'. Silkin made his comments as the Bill enabling the construction of the new towns passed through Parliament. These new towns, he suggested, were 'our last chance'.[14] He saw them as the means by which to effect a transformation in the health, outlook and behaviours of those who moved to them. In the twenty years which followed the New Towns Act of 1946, a sequence of new towns was 'designated', to use the official term for the process by means of which they were conceived and planned. Built on sites across Britain, these towns were only one manifestation of the extent to which notions of 'planning' were from the 1940s increasingly applied to the built environment, the economy and society more generally. In an immediate sense, the new towns were conceived as part of a national programme of urban and industrial decentralisation, and slum clearance. Yet, while the ideas that informed the conception and design of individual towns were often highly specific, Silkin's comments reveal the broader ambitions of the new towns programme. A keynote in the early years was the aim that the built environment should encourage an enhanced communal sociability and, by extension, an active sense of citizenship. In this way, the new towns would be 'transformative' environments. Their conception reflected a deterministic streak shared by many modernist reformers, which affected policy in a range of spheres, from housing to education to the emergence of subsidies for the performing arts.

The construction of new towns after 1945 was hardly a new phenomenon, as other contributors to this volume have shown. However, the post-war new towns represented a significant departure from previous practice. Although local government and private enterprise both had roles at this time in developing peripheral housing estates and extending existing towns, the post-war new towns programme was distinctive in that it was an initiative of central government, which created a powerful Development Corporation for each new town, independent of the local authority. Philosophically, the new towns had their roots in Ebenezer Howard's late-nineteenth-century call for the construction of self-sufficient 'garden cities', distinct from suburban dormitory estates. Howard's ideas led to substantial developments at Letchworth and then Welwyn Garden City, and to further campaigning during the 1920s and 1930s. The Barlow Report of 1940 called for the decentralisation of population and industry, and detailed proposals were put forward in key planning reports such as the *Greater London Plan* (1944) and the *Clyde Valley Regional Plan* (1946). By the time the New Towns Act passed through Parliament in 1946, a comprehensive system of planning had been given form in the creation of the Ministry of Town and Country Planning, and by legislation in 1944 (revised in 1947). Essentially, the pre-war, laissez-faire system, in which controls on development were limited, was replaced by one based on the principle of systematic planning for housing, employment, transport and leisure.

As we have already noted, the new towns were consciously intended as a riposte to inter-war housing estates, whether built by local councils for rent or speculative builders for sale (or, occasionally, for rent).[15] All too often, Silkin suggested, these developments offered little more than housing. Community and other facilities were frequently lacking, while residents had to commute to work. With reference to one of the London County Council's largest interwar estates, Silkin argued that 'a new series of Becontrees would be fatal'.[16] Such comments hide the extent to which the likes of Becontree were not unpopular with their residents,[17] but are revealing of the agenda which shaped the post-war new towns programme, namely that these towns would be 'self-sufficient' by providing employment and leisure opportunities as well as housing. The final report of the government's New Towns Committee – chaired by Lord Reith – elaborated on this idea, proposing settlements of between 30,000 and 50,000 people with housing, industry, shopping and cultural centres.[18] Residents would be diverse in their backgrounds; mention was made of professionals, artists, writers and the retired.[19] In addition, planning would be to the fore. The *Clyde Valley Regional Plan* referred to the potential to avoid 'the nondescript collection of miscellaneous and unrelated buildings that most of the interwar [housing] schemes show'.[20]

The planning of the first generation of new towns was based on the so-called 'neighbourhood unit' (Fig. 11.1).[21] In other words, each town would be built up from a number of distinct residential districts, each with its own schools, local shops and communal facilities.[22] A neighbourhood unit would house between 5,000 and 10,000 people, and would in turn be broken down into smaller groups. Typically, through-traffic would be excluded from the neighbourhood, which was thus conceived as a self-contained physical entity, often with parkland surrounding it. As a form of planning, the neighbourhood unit can be traced back to Howard,[23] but was given definitive form in the United States in the late 1920s by the planner Clarence Perry.[24] Several unbuilt interwar projects in Britain developed the principle, including the MARS Group's late-1930s plans for the reconstruction of London as a sequence of self-contained residential units strung along fast road links like beads on a necklace.[25] The idea was also evident in the conception of such interwar suburban estates as Becontree, or Wythenshawe near Manchester.[26]

By the mid 1940s, the neighbourhood unit had become a central element of national planning policy.[27] Not only did it figure in wartime plans by Abercrombie, but it was also discussed in key

FIGURE 11.1.
Model of East Kilbride new town, showing the distinctive neighbourhood units. (Copyright South Lanarkshire Council)

reports on the form of post-war housing. For example, in 1944 the Westwood Report, which laid out a blueprint for post-war developments in Scotland, called for new housing to be arranged in 'neighbourhood units', set apart from main roads and equipped with open space and community buildings.[28] Similar proposals were made in the Dudley Report (covering housing in England).[29] An exhibition in 1945 predicted that the neighbourhood unit would be the defining feature of post-war planning.[30] By 1956, the term seems to have been sufficiently well-understood to be used without explanation in a booklet intended for visitors to the new towns, which itemised the number of neighbourhood units in each.[31]

In one sense, the neighbourhood unit was a practical device, its size being related to an idea of the number of families required to support local schools and shops. For planners concerned with traffic, meanwhile, it also had practical attractions, with Alker Tripp's influential *Town Planning and Road Traffic* calling in 1942 for the exclusion of through-traffic from residential areas.[32] At the same time, the neighbourhood unit could also be understood in more idealised and nostalgic ways. Comparisons were often made with the village, seen by many proponents of neighbourhood planning as an ideal community made up of people from a range of class backgrounds, and as somewhere with an active social life and a clear identity.[33] The Reith committee framed its ideas in anti-urban terms: 'in great cities and towns the sense of community membership is weak, and this is one of the most serious of modern urban ills'.[34] As the historian James Greenhalgh has argued, 'deep-seated interwar prejudices about suburbia and working-class association were . . . spatialised in plans for neighbourhoods alongside [a] desire to preserve an imagined local community that had been valorised during the war as a deeply desirable and uniquely British quality'.[35] Much was made of the ways in which residents might identify with the neighbourhood; the Reith committee suggested that 'the local or geographic community' was the most important group with which individuals might identify after the family.[36] Though warning that the neighbourhood unit 'should not be thought of as a self-contained community of which the inhabitants are more conscious than they are of the town as a whole',[37] the committee believed – if somewhat imprecisely – that the neighbourhood would offer a useful structure within which to make friends and acquaintances, and that it would encourage a sense of community membership. Particular emphasis was placed on communal leisure activities, and so the Reith committee suggested that a public hall should be provided at an early stage within the neighbourhood centre, with further buildings for leisure following later (Fig. 11.2).[38]

In seeking to promote a neighbourly community and communal outlook, the Reith committee was not alone. In 1935, a Department of Health for Scotland delegation, including the Edinburgh City Architect, Ebenezer Macrae, toured European housing estates. These estates, the delegation felt, demonstrated a greater sense of community than was then evident in Scotland:

> whether this is due to climate, character, or the lack of opportunities for meeting his neighbours under good conditions

FIGURE 11.2.
Woodside neighbourhood centre, Glenrothes new town, with a community hall alongside shops. (Author photograph, 2018)

is difficult to determine. The back green of a Scottish tenement provides little incentive to sociability.[39]

By contrast, in Continental Europe there was

> a real sense of community life. Possibly similar facilities in Scottish tenement schemes might help to woo the Scot from his rather grim community outlook and strengthen those gregarious and sociable instincts which at present his surroundings do little to encourage.[40]

The delegation referred to the way in which continental planners often sited blocks of flats away from the street edge in order to create 'opportunities for creating an atmosphere of community life, for decoration, for planting shrubs and trees'.[41] Nine years later, the Westwood Report similarly argued that 'the planning of new housing is an integral part of planning for community' (Fig. 11.3).[42]

The Reith committee's promotion of 'community' was not solely a means of cultivating local identities or neighbourly friendliness, however, but was also intended to encourage residents to become engaged members of a democratic society. For example, the committee suggested that the 'interests, groupings, and cultural activities of citizens must grow of themselves'.[43] By implication, these activities would be led by the 'citizens' themselves. The choice of the word 'citizens' here is surely significant, implying engagement with wider civic culture. Certainly the committee argued that 'in a true community, everybody feels, directly or through some group, that he has a place and a part, belonging and counting'.[44] Without this feeling, it went on, people 'cannot put down roots nor become conscious of responsibility for a place'.[45] As its use of the word 'responsibility' reveals, the committee's ideal new-town residents would not passively expect things to be done for them. In a literal sense, perhaps, they would feel responsible for maintaining the quality of their immediate environment. At the same time, one might also interpret 'responsibility' in terms of participation in – and leadership of – the voluntary organisations, clubs and societies which would help develop the desired sense of community as well as the quality of new-town life. Potentially, too, 'citizens' would shape the future of the town

FIGURE 11.3.
Housing in the Murray, East Kilbride, winner of a Saltire Society award. Classic mixed development, with flats in blocks of varying height alongside houses, and a grassy area to suggest the idea of community. (Crown copyright HES)

by engaging with the processes and organs of local government, by voting or even standing for election.[46] The stakes were high. In Parliament, Silkin highlighted the extent to which the new towns might be a transformative environment for their residents, suggesting that they could create 'a new type of citizen, a healthy, self-respecting, dignified person with a sense of beauty, structure, and civic pride'.[47] His arguments surely had particular significance at the end of a war against totalitarianism; certainly political passivity was linked by some at this time with the rise of dictatorship.[48]

This link between 'community' and civic engagement was not new; neither was the view that modern architecture and planning could encourage communal tendencies. For example, the 'village colleges' created in interwar Cambridgeshire by the county's Chief Education Officer, Henry Morris, were motivated in part by Morris's desire to create democratically responsible citizens, both children and adults.[49] Education for all ages took place in a single building, participation in the management of the college was encouraged, while activities such as communal lunching for school-age pupils were intended to promote sociability as well as certain behaviours. Meanwhile at Kensal House, the two blocks of flats in west London designed in the mid 1930s by Elizabeth Denby and Maxwell Fry, the intention was similarly to promote certain 'productive' behaviours and a sense of responsibility.[50] In an on-site nursery, children were taught behaviours such as brushing their teeth and serving each other's food at lunchtime, while adults had dedicated space for communal furniture-making and sewing, conceived, in gendered terms, as activities which would serve as useful forms of recreation while empowering the individual and strengthening the family. Residents were also involved in the management of the flats and the adjacent allotments. Finally, during the wartime and post-war years, the National Council for Social Service was a key voice in the drive to construct community centres, the part-financing of which by local authorities was enabled by legislation in 1937 and 1944. Its vision was, like Morris's, a participatory one. In 1945, it suggested that:

> [in] the very life of the [community] centre, in the range of its activities and its method of self government, there is

> encouragement to initiative and to the exercise of freedom (basic qualities of democratic civilisation) combined with the need for reconciling diverse interests and for the bearing of social responsibilities.[51]

This function was, it concluded, explicitly 'political'. In this respect, however, it is significant that the working class was sometimes assumed to be less able to supply the necessary kind of civic initiative and leadership. When it came to the new towns, therefore, the perceived value of the 'balanced' community was in part that it would provide the kind of people who could supply civic leadership. In this respect, the intended contrast between new-town neighbourhoods and the supposedly 'one-class' estates of the interwar period was especially important.

At the same time, the new towns were conceived in other, no less transformative terms. For example, the Reith committee hoped to expand Britons' culinary horizons, seeking to banish traditional teashops and cafés in favour of a new breed of restaurants.[52] It took a cosmopolitan view: what could other countries teach Britain about 'the art of good living' as a way to 'revive' and enrich 'traditional hospitality'? Could restaurants 'of the continental type', perhaps open in the evenings, encourage new standards? Implicit here is a critique of the public house as a venue for sociability; Reith hoped that pubs would increasingly be 'places of social intercourse' and eating, rather than venues for drinking alone.[53] (A system of 'state management' of public houses, originally conceived during the First World War in order to control alcohol consumption in areas with industries essential to the war effort, was introduced in the new towns, and survived into the early 1950s.[54])

The committee also examined leisure activities more generally. It noted 'the growing proportion of people in all classes who are interested in the theatre, music, and other arts', and proposed the construction of cultural buildings in order to shape 'the cultural and social development of the town'.[55] Among them, a 'civic cinema' could show documentary and international films as an antidote to the 'limited cultural range' of commercial cinemas in which 'American productions predominate'.[56] These recommendations – and the committee's interest in the use of leisure time more generally

– reflected a broader debate in which certain kinds of cultural production and leisure activities were deemed during the 1940s, 1950s and 1960s to be of particular value, and so worthy of encouragement. The Arts Council of Great Britain was established in 1945 to provide a small amount of state subsidy for the arts, including theatre, while local authorities were empowered in 1948 routinely to support the performing arts, for example through the creation of civic theatres.[57] In a period of apparently increasing leisure time, the aim was to tempt people away from (American) cinema, bingo, greyhound racing, and the individualistic and materialistic temptations of television, by making what might otherwise seem like elite activities – i.e. theatre, classical music and opera – available to all. New theatres, too, were typically conceived as all-day social meeting places, paralleling the Reith committee's reference to 'cultural and social development'. These attitudes persisted into the late 1960s, when, under Britain's first Minister for the Arts, Jennie Lee, funding for the arts was conceived as an element of the broader Welfare State project, with Lee's intention that Britain become 'gayer and more cultivated' reflecting not only a continuing interest in shaping the tastes of the population in certain ways, but also a view in which modern citizenship was defined in terms of education, an appreciation of culture (if narrowly defined), and a positive attitude to sociability.

How, then, did these ideas of community and transformation play out at East Kilbride? In the next section of this chapter, we look at the town's development after 1947.

East Kilbride

East Kilbride was intended to accommodate overspill population from Glasgow, although in practice this aim rarely meant the rehousing of slum-dwellers; rather, skilled working-class residents were encouraged, with priority for housing being given to those who had secured work in the town.[58] Originally intended for 45,000 people, East Kilbride's population target was raised to 53,000 in 1956 and 70,000 in 1960. The town was presented in optimistic terms by the Secretary of State for Scotland, Arthur Woodburn, who in 1948 referred to 'an example which will carry us through to more hopeful periods, when our towns will be built not merely for the sake of producing industry and wealth, but will have as their foundation the welfare of the people as a whole'.[59] These ambitions informed both the planning of the town and its intended facilities (Fig. 11.4). In terms of its layout, the Development Corporation's architect, D.P. Reay, wrote, perhaps with tongue partly in cheek:

> As a social hypothesis it is assumed that a fruitful and alive social life develops when different people and different groups – different by age, income, occupation, or interest – meet and mix. All social circles should intersect each other. To further this end, it is felt that the bulk of housing should be designed in architectural groups of various sizes – cul de sacs, squares, loops, closes etc., containing anything from ten to one hundred or more houses. When the Housing Department section lets these dwellings an attempt might be made to group people into these dwelling groups. In some cases, a number of professional people may be together, in another a specialised profession such as artists or architects creating its own particular atmosphere. Broadly speaking, in the upper income brackets business and professional people will tend to live together. In the middle income groups occupations may provide the classifying motive and in the lower income groups, hobbies and spare time interests. Keen gardeners, for instance, might like to be near each other, and reasonably well separated from those who go in for training whippets.[60]

The town's projected facilities, meanwhile, embodied the same kind of cultural values as were then shaping the Arts Council's activities. In 1949, one local newspaper reported that East Kilbride might earn the nickname 'highbrow heights' on account of the Development Corporation's plans for 'cinemas showing documentary and international films, two museums set in park-like grounds, houses in unfenced model gardens'.[61] As with the broader national programme, the idea of active, educated citizenship was inscribed in the Development Corporation's plans, both implicitly and explicitly:

A
B
C
D
E
F
8
7
6
5
4
3
2
1
TO CARMUNNOCK
NORTH
CARMUNNOCK ROAD
TO BUSBY PAISLEY GLASGOW
COLLEGE MILTON INDUSTRIAL AREA
CARRUTHERS & CO.
CINCINNATI SHAPER CO.
WATERLOW & SON
EAGLESHAM ROAD
QUEENSWAY
WEST MAINS
KIRKTONHOLME PRIMARY SCHOOL
KIRKTONHOLM PARK
KIRKTONHOLME ROAD
WEST GREENWAY
BALMORAL PLACE
FALKLAND DRIVE
CLOVERHILL PARK
EAST MILTON PRIMARY SCHOOL
DUNCANRIG SECONDARY SCHOOL
WESTWOOD
QUEBEC DRIVE
LE FROY GARDENS
ALBERTA AVENUE
WESTWOOD ROAD
TO EAGLESHAM
HAIRMYRES HOSPITAL
THE MURRAY
LIVINGSTONE DRIVE
HEADHOUSE R.C. PRIMARY SCHOOL
THE MURRAY ROAD
NEWLANDS ROAD
CRAIG HILL
DALE AVENUE
NETHERTON ROAD
TO AULDHOUSE

FIGURE 11.4.
East Kilbride, plan in 1958 showing neighbourhood units (the Murray, Westwood, East Mains, West Mains, and Calderwood), separated by major roads. (Copyright HES, Alexander Buchanan Campbell Collection)

true self-government means that the citizens should help themselves as much as possible. The Development Corporation meet new tenants quarterly to explain the New Town programme and help in the formation of residents' associations for each district. In this way it is hoped to maintain a lively interest among tenants in all the affairs and activities of the town. The aim is to create a high standard of citizenship worthy of a twentieth century community.[62]

Children were reportedly to be educated in 'new town principles' relating to planning and design, while it was hoped that the Community Association would 'foster a communal interest in planning and architecture'.[63]

In practice, however, the provision of community facilities in many of the new towns lagged behind housing.[64] In East Kilbride, the Development Corporation's purchase of the Public Hall was not concluded until 1953–4,[65] and a community hall in the Murray neighbourhood was still incomplete in 1961 (Fig. 11.5).[66] There were attempts to provide community facilities in school buildings, on the lines of Morris's village colleges, but demand for school places was such that these spaces had to be put to educational use.[67] The provision of halls and other community facilities was frequently mired in bureaucracy. In this respect, clause 12 (7) of the 1946 New Towns Act required that proposals for amenities would only be approved by the Minister if they were likely to 'secure for the Corporation . . . a return which is reasonable', a provision usually taken to mean that the rents or fees paid by the users of any amenity should cover both the capital and interest charges.[68] Hire costs were thus likely to be substantial, and beyond the means of community groups. In addition, rising interest rates, increasing construction costs and national restrictions on capital spending during the 1950s impacted on the district council's ability to act. Meanwhile organisations and clubs struggled to raise the funds needed to make effective use of grant-aid schemes.

Amid these faltering attempts at community provision, there was public discussion of 'malaise', and criticism of the lack of facilities.[69] Sir Patrick Dollan, Chairman of the Development Corporation, was unsurprisingly quick to rebut such arguments, pointing out in 1955 that 'East Kilbride is very much alive socially', with more than fifty clubs and societies, events every night in the town's (private) halls, and a higher library membership per head of population than any other town in Britain.[70] In 1961, more than 50% of residents were members of some kind of club or society, although many travelled outwith East Kilbride.[71] Furthermore, while leisure facilities provided by private companies were sometimes seen as undesirably commercial, the provision of the Olympia ballroom and bowling alley in 1961 was welcomed by the Development Corporation: 'this enterprise has done much to provide the kind of up-to-date indoor recreational facilities which the growing youthful town requires'.[72]

Clearly, then, East Kilbride did offer a growing range of leisure opportunities, if in sometimes ad hoc ways; the Development Corporation reported in 1955 that 'improvisation is the keynote'.[73] Nonetheless, historians have also noted the growth of home-based leisure in the new towns,[74] as did contemporary commentators. In 1956, the *Sunday Times* reported:

> Since many men work overtime, evening leisure is not extensive. Both men and women spend their free time watching

FIGURE 11.5. Community centre in the Murray neighbourhood, East Kilbride (demolished before 2003). (Copyright South Lanarkshire Council)

television (sports programmes and plays are the favourites), working in the garden and doing the football pools. Wives nearly all make many of their children's clothes, and knitting machines have become something of a craze. Until it is completed, decoration of the house is a major leisure-time occupation. Both husbands and wives are proving themselves professionally expert at hanging wallpaper and painting woodwork, though schemes of decoration are not always happy.[75]

A 1961 survey similarly recorded that 'in the new town, there is a great emphasis on home life'.[76] For some residents, this emphasis was welcome, with the semi-detached and terraced houses which made up much of the housing in East Kilbride – as in other new towns – allowing a more selective approach to neighbourly contact than was the case for those living in Glaswegian tenement flats, with their shared staircases and, in poorer areas, shared facilities. Furthermore, the forms of new town housing could be understood in aspirational terms. Moving to East Kilbride and to a house allowed residents who had previously lived in flats to reshape their identity in a positive sense, and to project an aspirational sensibility.[77] In 1961, four out of five residents surveyed were glad they had moved, with 'new house' being frequently cited as the reason why this was the case.[78] With an increasing number of new-town women being in employment, and with many men working in skilled occupations, rising wages in real terms meant that new-town residents were especially well placed to profit from the consumer boom and the era of 'never had it so good'. In 1961, a survey noted the higher levels of consumer appliances found in East Kilbride households;[79] in 1970, levels of car ownership were well above the Scottish average.[80]

While East Kilbride (and other new towns) thus allowed residents to reshape their identities through new patterns of consumerism, leisure and domesticity, these developments were not always welcomed by contemporary architectural critics. The low-density urbanism of the first new towns may have been popular with its residents, especially those who may have moved from a crowded flat, but it led to accusations of anti-urban 'prairie planning' by sections of the architectural press and a search for more compact urban forms.[81] Cultural critics were scarcely more positive. The historian Corelli Barnett concluded in 1957 that

> The really awful thing is that the people living in the new towns love them. Nice little gardens to potter in, greens for the children to play on, shelter for the prams and the 8 h.p. cars, schools near home and away from main roads – no wonder they are a smash hit, for they are the exact expression of the lives of the people for whom they were built.[82]

In practice, then, the new towns offered opportunities for transformation which perhaps were rather more individualistic than Reith and others might have hoped for.

Conclusion

The post-war new towns were not simply an opportunity to innovate architecturally, but were also a kind of transformative social experiment.[83] They were to be laboratories in which a new kind of citizen would be created through an engagement first of all with a certain form of spatial planning – the neighbourhood unit – and second through the provision of community facilities. For Reith, they were to be an 'essay in civilisation';[84] looking back, the critic Colin Ward suggested that those who promoted them believed that 'a clean, new, shiny environment would produce new, shiny people'.[85] They thus reveal how the Welfare State can be understood not simply as a framework for housing standards, healthcare, welfare and education, but rather as something which might touch the lives and leisure of the population in broader ways. However, creating the kind of communally minded citizen which Reith, Silkin and others had in mind was difficult in practice. Increasingly affluent, aspirational residents were in many cases more willing to embrace other, more individualistic models of leisure and being.

By the end of the 1950s, new planning and architectural approaches were evident. Cumbernauld, designated in 1955, was conceived as a 'mark 2' new town. The idea of the neighbourhood centre was played down in favour of an emphasis on the town centre, while the residential areas were to be more densely planned than hitherto. Their layout reflected growing unease among some architects and planners with the low densities of the first new towns, as well as an emerging critique by sociologists and others concerning the abstract nature of the neighbourhood idea. Cumbernauld's fast road network responded to the growing importance attached to 'mobility', as post-war affluence led to increasing levels of car ownership, and so challenged the idea that facilities should be provided locally and accessed on foot. Residents could travel further for shopping and leisure activities, and could forge networks beyond their immediate neighbourhood.[86] With the rise of home-centred recreation also countering the communal ideals of the neighbourhood unit, Abercrombie referred to the 'decline' of neighbourhood planning as early as 1956.[87]

Yet the example of East Kilbride reveals that the ideas of sociability and transformation in fact proved somewhat resilient. In one sense, individualism, mobility and community-mindedness need not be mutually exclusive. For example, the *Scotsman* commented of East Kilbride in 1955 that 'television relieves the tedium, and the Community Association and the various tenants' associations are a hatching ground for neighbourliness'.[88] Furthermore, despite the apparent slowness in providing community facilities, the sense of citizenship which such facilities were intended to encourage did seem to be evident in at least some quarters. By 1963, there were 150 clubs, described as having been created by 'the citizens themselves', a telling phrase, as a 'sign of the community spirit that exists in this new town'.[89] That same year, high levels of turnout in the town's first burgh council election suggested that the wish to encourage democratic engagement had succeeded.[90]

In addition, there remained a drive not only to provide community facilities but also to see such facilities as vehicles for transformation, albeit in perhaps more restricted or targeted ways than had been intended in the 1940s. There was, for example, particular concern that young people ought to be provided for. East Kilbride's birth rate was twice the Scottish average; with the town having grown by around 800 houses per year during the 1950s, a 'bulge' in the number of young people was expected during the 1960s.[91] In a context where the 'teenager' was sometimes the subject of suspicion and also occasional panic, Judith Hart, MP for Lanark, argued in Reithian terms that 'the young person needs to establish relationships outside the home within a congenial and good environment', an argument which dovetailed personal development and certain kinds of 'improving' space.[92] It was felt that coffee bars and cafés would suit some, but, perhaps with the post-war increase in secondary education in mind, it was believed that 'the majority are likely to be ready to support something more cultural and more sophisticated, and should be encouraged to do so'.[93] The result was the Key Centre, designed by Alexander Buchanan Campbell on a central site adjacent to the town's Dollan Baths. The centre was conceived as a home for youth organisations in the town as well as somewhere that young people might visit for coffee and dancing; to that end, its design was to be 'gay and welcoming, and sophisticated in the modern idiom'.[94]

In addition, later new towns were discussed and planned in terms which maintained something of the underlying social and transformative intentions of the 1940s, if now filtered through the lens of affluence. For example, Livingston (designated in 1962) was intended 'to give a new opportunity and a new way of life to people from Glasgow'.[95] Although the theory of neighbourhood planning may have lost something of its earlier significance, the self-contained forms of the neighbourhood were maintained in the plan for Livingston. In part, this continuity might be understood as a result of the way in which low-density neighbourhood planning, conceived in part to promote sociability, in reality also successfully accommodated the emergence of home-centred, affluent patterns of living through its exclusion of through traffic, its provision of space for parking and garaging, and its generous provisions of private gardens.

Nonetheless, social ideals remained evident in some of the 1960s new towns. In the case of Runcorn, designated in 1964, the masterplan reported that 'the structure of the town is based on a grouping of communities, each with a local centre'.[96] Livingston substituted the word 'district' for 'neighbourhood', but otherwise was scarcely different, with the planning document suggesting that each district would be 'so planned that it promotes its own identity from within'.[97] Irvine, laid out on the Ayrshire coast at the end of the 1960s by Cumbernauld's planner, Hugh Wilson, was in its final design intended to be a 'comprehensive entity' rather than a 'series of unrelated developments or separate neighbourhoods',[98] but nonetheless was arranged in such a way that the town was broken down into smaller groups: 'the emphasis will be on a subdivision of communities into reasonably sized units'.[99] In addition, the potential for the built environment to structure social relationships was still often stressed. In the case of Livingston, each district shopping centre would be a 'social meeting place', while walkways were framed as an 'extension of the community space' which would play an increasingly important role as car use grew (and, presumably, made roads less pleasant to walk alongside).[100] In Irvine, meanwhile, the arrangement of housing around courtyards was 'intended to increase neighbourliness and avoid the anonymity of the traditional street frontage layout'.[101] One might conclude, then, that the post-war new towns were the antithesis of what Charles McKean perceived in their eighteenth-century Edinburgh predecessor. If Edinburgh's New Town was, in McKean's view, 'one of the most handsome examples of built incivility in Europe' because of its apparent failure to be a 'meeting place',[102] ideas of sociability – built 'civility' – were very much to the fore in the New Town's twentieth-century successors.

PART 4
Age of Conservation

CHAPTER 12

Un idéal médiéval dans l'Athènes du Nord: Patrick Geddes et Édimbourg

Pierre Chabard

Focusing on Patrick Geddes's ideas and work in urban conservation, this chapter investigates the changing relationship between Old and New Towns in the nineteenth century. Although it was seen as the epitome of civilisation in the eighteenth century, the New Town – for Geddes – reflected, rather, a form of political domination from London. Geddes considered that the Athenian identity that the city developed was too artificial, and he therefore concentrated his work on 'conservative surgery' in the Old Town, where the city's origins were truly situated. By reviving parts of the Old Town, Geddes hoped to reconcile the hitherto conflicting identities of the city, and influence a more positive urban change.

Dans l'imaginaire urbain édimbourgeois, les idéaux qui s'incarnent dans les quartiers néoclassiques de New Town, et les valeurs qu'on leur accorde, ont fluctué dans le temps. À la toute fin du dix-neuvième siècle, à une période de crise urbaine majeure, le polygraphe écossais Patrick Geddes (1854–1932), protagoniste important de la réforme urbaine à Édimbourg puis du *Town Planning Movement* britannique, incarne un de ces changements axiologiques.

Édimbourg, qu'il habite de 1870 jusqu'au début des années 1900, constitue le cadre privilégié de son engagement réformateur, à la fois le point de départ et d'arrivée de sa réflexion sur les villes et leurs transformations. C'est en effet à partir de cette matrice urbaine qu'il théorise la Civics, projet d'un nouveau champ scientifique d'inspiration évolutionniste et à visée opératoire, qui convoque l'histoire, la géographie et les sciences sociales pour observer et comprendre le phénomène urbain dans ses multiples dynamiques.[1] Édimbourg, sur laquelle porte son premier *Civic Survey*,[2] lui offre le premier terrain d'application de cette science civique qu'il généralisera par la suite et tentera d'imposer, sans succès, à Londres d'abord comme cadre théorique de la sociologie naissante[3] puis comme socle épistémologique du *town planning*.[4] Édimbourg, enfin, occupe une place centrale dans son ouvrage *Cities in Evolution*,[5] parmi les 139 autres villes évoquées.

Sous-titré *An Introduction to the Town Planning Movement and to the Study of Civics,* l'ouvrage sort en hiver 1915, juste au moment où Patrick Geddes, âgé de 60 ans, quitte la Grande-Bretagne pour l'Inde, où il est appelé auprès du gouverneur de Madras pour travailler sur les villes indiennes. Plutôt une fin qu'un début, *Cities in Evolution* se présente moins comme un ouvrage cohérent, homogène et unitaire, que comme une compilation, plus ou moins organisée, de ses principales contributions au *Town Planning Movement*.[6] C'est donc à la fois une récapitulation de ses diverses activités dans ce champ pendant la décennie 1904–14 et une manière de les valoriser, de les capitaliser en un même objet éditorial, à un tournant de sa carrière.

En frontispice de ce livre composite mais stratégique, c'est justement une photographie de la ville d'Édimbourg qu'il choisit de publier. Montrant Old Town et New Town (respectivement à l'arrière-plan et à l'avant-plan) un peu avant 1910, cette photographie n'a pas été prise ni même commandée par Geddes mais a été sélectionnée par lui dans le fonds d'un jeune photographe professionnel de la ville: Francis Caird Inglis. Installé depuis 1903 au Rock House Studio, ce dernier occupe l'ancien atelier de David Octavius Hill sur Calton Hill. Même s'il n'en est pas l'auteur, Geddes a jugé cette photographie suffisamment démonstrative pour ouvrir son livre majeur, son écrit le plus lu dans les milieux de l'urbanisme.

Prise dans ce contexte éditorial, cette photographie assume un rôle hautement symbolique, d'autant plus important quand on sait le goût de Geddes pour la rhétorique visuelle. Chargée de plusieurs registres de signification, elle illustre non seulement le point de vue général de Geddes sur l'urbain et l'urbanisme mais également sa relation particulière à la ville d'Édimbourg qui assume, pour lui, un rôle de ville-type, à la fois exemplaire et générique.

Intitulée «Édimbourg. Vue depuis Princes Street vers le Château et la Vieille Ville», cette vue de la ville – assez représentative de son iconographie au dix-neuvième siècle – présente son caractère le plus saillant: un paysage aux deux parties bien distinctes voire antithétiques. Perchée sur un éperon rocheux et adossée à l'ancienne forteresse, la ville médiévale est dense, irrégulière et hérissée de clochers. À l'inverse, sur des terrains conquis au dix-huitième siècle par le drainage d'un ancien lac défensif, la ville néo-classique à l'architecture monumentale se déploie le long de larges rues au tracé rectiligne.

Quel est l'usage geddesien de cette image familière, de ce stéréotype? Que fait-il de cette opposition manichéenne qui sert, en général, à mettre en valeur la splendeur architecturale de New Town? Comment en renouvelle-t-il l'interprétation? Comment, en tant que théoricien de l'urbanisme naissant, prend-il position vis-à-vis de ces nouveaux quartiers qui ont justifié que l'on surnomme Édimbourg, l'Athènes du Nord, depuis le milieu du dix-huitième siècle?

Geddes l'athénien

Loin de nier l'analogie entre Athènes et Édimbourg, Geddes se l'approprie en la mettant au travail pour légitimer ses propres idéaux. Adoptant une position personnelle et critique vis-à-vis de l'histoire athénienne d'Édimbourg, il joue des ambigüités d'une analogie qui s'est fondée, selon les époques et leurs enjeux circonstanciels, sur des arguments tantôt culturels, architecturaux ou géographiques.

Penseur à la fois généraliste, encyclopédiste et francophile, Geddes rêve de restaurer l'effervescence intellectuelle, scientifique et éditoriale qui animait Édimbourg au siècle des Lumières écossaises. Au tournant du dix-huitième siècle, si l'analogie avec Athènes était déjà active, elle était surtout culturelle et renvoyait à des référents non pas urbains et architecturaux mais plutôt philosophiques et politiques, soit donc au renouveau de la cité par la mise en place d'académies, d'écoles, de théâtres et de salons. Du point de vue architectural et urbain, les premières visions du New Edinburgh, qui datent des années 1720, ne sont d'ailleurs pas, stylistiquement parlant, néo-grecques, mais s'inspirent plutôt du classicisme louis-quatorzien, et de la ville neuve de Versailles où étaient exilés beaucoup d'aristocrates jacobites.

Cet hellénisme plus culturel qu'architectural permet à Geddes, nationaliste et anti-unioniste, de prendre ses distances vis-à-vis du plan de New Town que James Craig dédicace au roi George III. La régularité hippodamienne de ce plan et le néo-classicisme architectural de ses immeubles désignent certes Édimbourg comme l'Athènes du Nord mais symbolisent surtout, pour Geddes, la domination politique, économique et culturelle de Londres. New Town n'est nouvelle que parce qu'elle s'oppose à l'ancienne, laquelle est trop ancrée dans l'histoire de l'Écosse pour refléter cette nouvelle alliance avec l'Angleterre et trop vétuste pour faire allégeance aux standards culturels londoniens (en terme de confort, de circulation et d'architecture). Par conséquent, aux yeux de Geddes, si New Town renvoie à l'Antiquité, c'est moins à Athènes qu'à Rome, et qu'au «type urbain impérial et césariste»[7] que représente Londres.

Enfin, en tant que savant naturaliste, proche des milieux de la biologie darwinienne et de la géographie humaine, Geddes prend soigneusement position par rapport à la justification géographique de l'Athènes du Nord. Confortée dès les années 1810 par les vues de la ville réalisées par le peintre paysagiste Hugh William Williams, celle-ci se généralise dans la littérature de voyage. Pour Charles Nodier, par exemple, «il semble que le nom d'Athènes du Nord, qui ne lui est pas contesté, soit pour elle un privilège de localité, fondé sur des ressemblances topographiques très sensibles. La ville d'Édimbourg est séparée de la mer par une voie droite de la même figure et de la même longueur que celle qui conduit d'Athènes au Pirée; c'est le faubourg de Leith. Elle embrasse dans son enceinte une montagne surmontée d'une forteresse ou citadelle antique, qui rappelle l'Acropolis. C'est le château d'Édimbourg».[8]

Cependant, dans les développements ultérieurs de New Town, c'est plutôt sur Calton Hill que l'on projette l'Acropole édimbourgeoise. Pas encore urbanisée et située dans l'axe géométrique de George Street, cette colline est disponible pour accueillir les monuments qui font défaut à New Town, et que des architectes tels que

Thomas Hamilton,[9] Charles Robert Cockerell[10] ou William H. Playfair[11] vont dessiner, à partir des années 1820, dans un style néo-grec voire néo-dorique.

En désaccord avec cette option, Geddes la juge incohérente avec la réalité urbaine et géographique d'Édimbourg. Dans le *Survey*, il retrace les étapes du développement de la ville. Son récit des origines tient en trois mots: *hill-fort*, *sea-port* et *agricultural plain*;[12] c'est-à-dire d'une part l'épine rocheuse sur laquelle a été érigée la première place forte au sixième siècle, d'autre part le port de Leith sur l'estuaire du Forth à trois kilomètres de la citadelle, et enfin les plaines fertiles du Lothian qui environnent ces deux éléments. Comme d'autres avant lui, Geddes compare cette situation originelle à celle de la ville d'Athènes: l'Acropole, le Pirée et l'Attique. Cette comparaison est illustrée dans le *Survey* par la juxtaposition de deux gravures anciennes: l'une d'Athènes (probablement prêtée par le Professeur Baldwin Brown, historien, archéologue et proche ami de Geddes)[13] et

FIGURE 12.1.
(Top) View of Edinburgh from the north-west.
(From Patrick Geddes, *Civic Survey of Edinburgh*, 1911)

FIGURE 12.2.
(Above) View of Athens.
(From Patrick Geddes, *Civic Survey of Edinburgh*, 1911)

l'autre d'Édimbourg, inspirée du tableau d'Alexander Nasmyth *View of Edinburgh from Glasgow Road* (1821).

L'analogie entre les deux villes ne tient donc pas, pour Geddes, à une ressemblance de façade mais à une similitude plus profonde de leur substrat géographique. Envisageant le fait urbain à l'aune de l'interaction créatrice entre un milieu régional singulier et les établissements humains qui s'y installent, Geddes estime qu'Athènes et Édimbourg partagent une situation exceptionnellement équilibrée: «Cette coopération ternaire (entre une colline fortifiée, un Port et une Plaine) est propice non seulement à l'efficacité agricole, à l'initiative industrielle et au commerce, mais aussi à la culture civique».[14] Selon Geddes, la comparaison traditionnelle entre Édimbourg et Athènes n'a réellement que peu à voir avec les temples grecs des dix-huitième et dix-neuvième siècles; mais réside plutôt dans les origines géographiques et historiques des deux villes.

Par ces propos, Geddes pointe une anomalie profonde de l'Édimbourg néo-classique. En voulant se doter artificiellement d'une Acropole néo-grecque, elle tourne le dos à sa propre antiquité. En installant arbitrairement son Acropole sur Calton Hill, elle trahit à la fois sa propre géographie et sa propre histoire dont les origines se situent sur Castle Hill, où continuent de subsister les principaux lieux de pouvoir de la ville.

Dans ces conditions, on peut interpréter la publication de la photographie de Francis Caird Inglis, en frontispice de *Cities in Evolution*, comme l'affirmation d'une hiérarchie retrouvée entre l'ancien et le nouveau. Le Château, perché sur son promontoire rocheux, est réinvesti par Geddes de son rôle dominant, symbolique et monumental, au détriment des architectures néo-grecques[15] de New Town, qui se situent clairement à ses pieds sur l'image. Penseur victorien, lecteur de John Ruskin et de William Morris, Geddes considère le noyau médiéval de la ville comme la seule Acropole possible pour l'Athènes du Nord.

Regard stéréoscopique sur la ville-Janus

Au travers la photographie d'Inglis, Geddes resémantise la vieille dualité, le «contraste panoramique entre la vieille et la nouvelle ville»[16] et inverse la hiérarchie entre l'une et l'autre. Mais son propos va bien au-delà. Sa réflexion dépasse l'opposition entre ancien et nouveau, ville médiévale et ville moderne. Elle se déploie sur le plan d'une toute autre dialectique, typiquement réformatrice, entre le normal et le pathologique, entre le sain et le malade au sein du grand organisme urbain métropolitain qu'est devenue la ville d'Édimbourg, parfait reflet de l'âge industriel qu'il appelle «paléotechnique».[17]

Or, dans un célèbre passage de *Cities in Evolution*, Geddes assure que les pathologies sociales et urbaines dont souffre Édimbourg, et qu'il résume par le terme de *slum*, sont également réparties entre Old et New Town. Il parle même à propos de la seconde de «super-slum».[18] En effet, la «spacieuse dignité et le décorum impeccable»[19] des façades des ensembles immobiliers les plus prestigieux construits dans les années 1820, comme Moray Place, dessiné par James Gillespie Graham en 1822, ou de Charlotte Square, par Robert Adam en 1791, ne sont, selon lui, que cache-misères. À l'appui de cet argument, une photographie des arrières de Moray Place décrit «un labyrinthe de mornes courettes pour faire sécher le linge, de méchants murets découpant un réseau de quadrilatères, de triangles disproportionnés et de trapèzes disgracieux».[20]

L'avenir d'Édimbourg ne réside donc, pour Geddes, ni dans New Town, en tant que forme désirable qui se détacherait du fond obscur de Old Town, ni dans une idéalisation pittoresque de la décrépitude de cette dernière. Sa vision d'Édimbourg englobe les deux et polarise l'attention sur un autre contraste, presque photographique, entre le positif et négatif, le sain et le malade: «De même que le zéro et l'infini sont absolument indispensables au mathématicien,» dit-il, «l'enfer et le paradis constituent 'le nécessaire appareil stéréoscopique' du penseur social».[21]

La reconquête symbolique et physique d'Old Town qu'opère Geddes s'appuie sur deux stratégies discursives: d'une part, renverser les valeurs accordées aux deux parties de la ville et, d'autre part, redistribuer à égalité dans les deux les maux pour lesquels, pour mieux justifier la seconde, on stigmatisait la première. Et c'est précisément à James Court, dans le Lawnmarket, qui est alors devenu, comme le reste de la vieille ville, un taudis ouvrier, qu'il s'installe en été 1886 avec sa jeune épouse, volontairement à contre-sens de la migration des élites vers New Town. C'est dans ce quartier qu'il multiplie ses initiatives réformatrices jusqu'au tournant du vingtième siècle dans la perspective d'une régénération à la fois matérielle et culturelle, esthétique et civique de ce quartier.

Un aspect de cette régénération consiste à améliorer les conditions du logement ouvrier, en s'appuyant sur une société philanthropique, l'Edinburgh Social Union, qu'il contribue à fonder en janvier 1885. Cette organisation émane de l'Environment Society, un petit groupe d'intellectuels d'inspiration ruskinienne de l'Université d'Édimbourg (où Patrick Geddes travaille, depuis 1880, comme simple «démonstrateur» en botanique pratique et en histologie végétale). C'est sous l'impulsion d'Anna Morton,[22] belle-sœur d'un des membres du groupe, James Oliphant, et future femme de Geddes,[23] que les activités de l'Environment Society changent progressivement de registre. Très impliquée dans les milieux réformateurs londoniens dès le début des années 1880,[24] Anna incite Geddes à s'intéresser aux travaux d'Octavia Hill dans le quartier de St Marylebone, à Londres. Il organise alors plusieurs voyages d'étude en Angleterre pour observer le travail du Toynbee Hall, de la Nottingham Town and Country Social Guild et de diverses branches de la Kyrle Society. Mais ce sont surtout les méthodes d'Octavia Hill que Geddes et ses confrères décident d'adopter, dans le but de mener une action concrète dans les quartiers insalubres d'Old Town. Fondée à cet effet, l'Edinburgh Social Union sert d'intermédiaire entre les propriétaires et les locataires afin de réguler les loyers, entreprend des travaux d'amélioration, acquiert des immeubles et des parcelles, et finance des œuvres d'art public. Selon Lou Rosenburg, l'Edinburgh Social Union loge, en 1888, environ deux cent familles, réparties sur sept sites: James Court et Whitehorse Close (achetés par des membres), Brown's Close, Gibb's Close, Heron's Court, ainsi que deux autres dans le quartier de St Leonard.[25]

Renouveler le vieil Édimbourg

Le couple Geddes participe, pendant la décennie 1887–96, à de nombreuses opérations d'amélioration de l'habitat populaire dont plusieurs historiens[26] ont tenté de dresser un inventaire détaillé.

Cependant, l'action de Geddes n'est pas aisée à décrire: foisonnante, multiple et tâtonnante, saisissant les opportunités que lui offre un contexte institutionnel lui-même changeant. Sous l'impulsion du Housing for the Working Classes Act, loi votée à Londres en 1890, la municipalité d'Édimbourg, menée par un nouveau *lord provost*, James Alexander Russell (1891–4),[27] relance et réoriente la politique d'éradication du taudis d'Old Town. L'Edinburgh Sanitary Improvement Scheme, que la municipalité adopte en 1893, rompt avec la politique antérieure de démolition massive, prône une politique plus conservatrice en matière d'architecture et s'appuie davantage sur le travail local des organisations privées déjà à l'œuvre: l'Edinburgh Architectural Association (fondée en 1858 et présidée par George Shaw Aitken), la Cockburn Association (fondée en 1875, dont Patrick Geddes est membre entre 1894 et 1914), l'Edinburgh Health Society (fondée en 1880), la Sanitary Society of Edinburgh (fondée en 1884) et l'Edinburgh Social Union (fondée en 1885).

Patrick Geddes tire parti de ces conditions favorables pour s'engager dans une voie plus personnelle, prenant ses distances avec l'Edinburgh Social Union, tout en bénéficiant des avantages financiers qu'apporte cette politique. Il est ainsi nommé coordonnateur officiel de plusieurs opérations publiques dans le quartier de Lawnmarket (la réhabilitation des immeubles de Wardrop's Court et de Riddle's Court).[28] Patrick Geddes, qui «se différencie aussi bien des partisans d'une reconstruction intégrale que de ceux qui opèrent selon les principes de stricte conservation préconisés par la Society for the Protection of Ancient Buildings»[29] (fondée par William Morris en 1877), apparaît alors, dans les rapports officiels, comme directeur des University Halls.

Implantés dans Old Town dès 1887, ces foyers s'inspirent du Toynbee Hall et sont liés au mouvement de l'«extension universitaire».[30] Baptisées University Halls of Residence, ces résidences autogérées d'étudiants sont fondées par Geddes dans l'idée non seulement de restaurer la vocation intellectuelle et universitaire de ce quartier mais aussi de disposer d'une main-d'œuvre jeune, enthousiaste et qualifiée pour l'assister dans ses propres entreprises (plusieurs des disciples de Geddes y résidèrent).[31] Installé dans un appartement situé au n°2 Mound Place, le premier University Hall accueille ses sept premiers habitants co-gestionnaires le 1er mai

1887. Quatre ans plus tard, ils sont quarante, occupant l'ensemble de l'immeuble ainsi qu'une ancienne maison de Riddle's Court. En 1896, ils sont cent vingt, répartis sur plusieurs sites, et notamment à Ramsay Gardens. Cet ensemble résidentiel commandité par Geddes, financé principalement par souscription et par l'héritage paternel de sa femme, est construit à partir de l'ancienne propriété du poète édimbourgeois Allan Ramsay, une demeure acquise par Geddes en 1892. Respectant les plans de l'architecte Stewart Henbest Capper, cet ensemble à l'architecture composite combine styles Arts & Crafts, néo-celtique et Scottish Baronial. Il comprend deux parties, dont l'une (1–12 Ramsay Gardens) englobe l'ancienne demeure de l'écrivain (reconnaissable à son avant-corps octogonal) et un immeuble attenant. Cette partie est inaugurée à l'automne 1893 et est destinée au logement d'étudiants. Dans l'autre partie (13–16 Ramsay Gardens), initiée dès juin 1892 mais achevée en avril 1894, Geddes se réserve un appartement de douze pièces au quatrième étage, où il s'installe avec sa famille à l'automne 1894.

Loin d'être isolé, l'engagement de Geddes en faveur du Vieil Édimbourg reflète une dynamique collective de revalorisation de cette partie de la ville dans les dernières décennies du dix-neuvième siècle. Les nombreuses lithographies de l'artiste et topographe Bruce J. Home, qui sera un des membres fondateurs de l'Old Edinburgh Club en 1908, reflètent cette évolution du regard. À partir des années 1870, ses gravures, qui détaillent les moindres ruelles de la vieille ville, insistent moins sur leur état d'insalubrité et de dégradation que sur leurs qualités pittoresques, leur patine vénérable et leur raffinement architectural.

On trouve, à l'Exposition internationale de 1886, une autre illustration de cette revalorisation de l'Old Edinburgh à la fin du dix-neuvième siècle; l'Old Street of Edinburgh, conçue par l'architecte Sydney Mitchell,[32] en est l'une des attractions les plus populaires. Ce diorama installé dans l'une des travées de la grande halle d'exposition sur les Meadows montrait, dans une mise en scène pittoresque, un ensemble choisi de répliques d'anciens bâtiments de l'Old Town (comme l'Old Tolbooth démoli en 1817). On entrait en passant sous un *facsimile* de l'ancienne Netherbow Port (démolie en 1764) et l'on pouvait déambuler dans la fausse rue pavée et peuplée de figurants en costumes, véritable fiction d'un passé théâtralisé. Pour Geddes, cette attraction qui a été vue par près de trois millions de visiteurs, constitue «probablement la plus admirable reconstruction d'une cité ancienne jamais effectuée et une suggestion de ce qui devrait déjà être mis en œuvre dans certains de nos vieux quartiers, sous une forme permanente».[33]

Les nombreux chantiers que Geddes a initiés autour du Lawnmarket à partir de 1886 et qui sont de plusieurs ordres (démolitions partielles, réalisations nouvelles, reconstructions, rénovations, embellissements, etc.) ne sont pas dénués de cet usage fictionnel de l'architecture. Inspirée de l'action du National Trust for Places of Historic Interest or Natural Beauty, fondé par Octavia Hill, Hardwicke Rawnsley et Robert Hunter en 1895, cette «chirurgie conservatrice» (*conservative surgery*)[34] reconfigure le paysage du Vieil Édimbourg, afin de le rendre à lui-même, de retrouver sous sa décrépitude apparente son prestige passé, et, au-delà, de réconcilier la ville avec son histoire et sa géographie.

Une «eutopie» civique et anti-planificatrice

Mais la finalité de ce projet n'est ni architecturale ni patrimoniale. Il a plutôt une double visée civique et réformatrice, et constitue une réponse à la crise urbaine que connaissent les grandes villes industrielles «paléotechniques» en général et Édimbourg en particulier. Geddes interprète cette crise à l'aune de sa culture de naturaliste évolutionniste, formé aux sciences du vivant dans les années 1870. Si Édimbourg, métropole congestionnée dont la population passe de 160,000 habitants en 1851 à 320,000 en 1911, connaît une phase négative de son évolution c'est, selon lui, parce qu'elle ne permet plus l'interaction créatrice entre l'individu et son milieu géographique, urbain et social. Elle est le lieu d'une rupture entre la cité et la ville. Ses habitants sont plongés dans un univers aliénant qu'ils subissent plus qu'ils ne le façonnent.

Face à ce constat, la solution geddesienne est tout sauf planificatrice. Il est convaincu qu'il est inutile et même contre-productif d'imposer à une ville une forme exogène. La New Town de James Craig constitue d'ailleurs pour lui le paradigme de cet acte planificateur impuissant, qui préfigure les plans d'urbanisme des *town planners* du début du vingtième siècle. À propos du New Edinburgh, il estime que «nous avons là une période de planification urbaine et d'exécution architecturale qui surpasse même la leçon de Londres: bien qu'elle finisse aussi par s'enliser à son tour».[35]

Selon Geddes, on ne peut transformer la ville qu'indirectement, en réformant l'individu, et, à travers lui, le corps social des citoyens, bref, en infléchissant l'humeur civique de la cité. Un citoyen éduqué, conscient du territoire qu'il habite, instruit de son histoire et de sa géographie, retissera un lien créateur avec son milieu urbain et la ville se transformera en conséquence.

Cette réforme civique comporte deux volets. Le premier, épistémologique, consiste à construire une pleine connaissance de la ville, synthèse encyclopédique de tous les savoirs possibles: c'est le rôle de la Civics et de son instrument d'enquête le *Civic Survey*. Le second consiste à partager cette connaissance avec le plus grand nombre. Dans cette perspective éducatrice et pédagogique qui a animé la part la plus foisonnante de son œuvre, Geddes a exploité la plupart des moyens médiatiques de l'époque, et en a testé les formes les plus diverses: expositions, musées, jardins pédagogiques, spectacles théâtraux, mais aussi scénographie du paysage urbain. Sa reconfiguration architecturale du paysage de Old Town tend en effet à transformer la ville en une sorte de musée d'elle-même, où les façades des immeubles racontent sa longue histoire, l'exposent aux yeux de tous.

Mais cette pratique élargie de l'exposition, dans ses registres à la fois textuels, visuels, architecturaux, s'est incarnée avec une grande sophistication dans son entreprise la plus originale au cœur d'Old Town: l'Outlook Tower. Ce musée, laboratoire et observatoire civique est installé dans une bâtisse de sept étages située au sommet de Castlehill Street. Datant pour partie du début du dix-septième siècle, l'édifice a été restauré et surélevé entre 1853 et 1856. Offrant une terrasse panoramique équipée d'une *camera obscura*, il a été utilisé comme attraction populaire pendant plusieurs années.[36] Laissé à l'abandon, il est loué à partir de 1892 puis acheté en 1896 par Geddes pour en faire l'instrument principal de son action réformatrice.[37]

Le visiteur de l'Outlook Tower est censé commencer la visite par le haut. Il peut embrasser la ville d'Édimbourg d'un seul regard circulaire depuis la terrasse panoramique et, à l'intérieur, l'apercevoir grâce à l'écran de la *camera obscura*. Équipée d'instruments d'observation (optiques, astronomiques, météorologiques), la terrasse propose un regard analytique et scientifique sur le paysage Édimbourgeois. Donnant une image picturale de celui-ci, la *camera obscura* convoque quant à elle le regard sensible et synthétique de l'artiste.

La suite du parcours, de la terrasse panoramique jusqu'au rez-de-chaussée, confirme la vocation essentiellement visuelle de l'Outlook Tower. Les cinq niveaux inférieurs sont organisés comme un musée universel, dévoilant aux visiteurs les différentes facettes de la connaissance. À chaque niveau correspond une échelle particulière d'appréhension du Monde, du local au global : Édimbourg et sa région (c'est-à-dire le contenu du *Civic Survey*), l'Écosse, le monde anglophone, l'Europe et la Terre.

Chaque salle est garnie d'un matériel visuel à vocation encyclopédique: cartes, globes, maquettes, peintures, bas-reliefs, vitraux, dioramas, photographies et diagrammes.[38] Le guide de la tour, publié en 1906, assure que l'expérience de l'Outlook Tower ne peut que transformer le visiteur, qu'il soit un simple touriste ou un habitant de la ville: «Il pourrait de plus . . . l'amener, par une conscience plus claire des besoins et des possibilités de la ville, vers une citoyenneté plus énergique et plus effective».[39]

La réforme civique geddesienne est avant tout locale (avant d'être universelle) et individuelle (avant d'être collective); elle engage le sujet comme pivot entre monde intérieur et monde extérieur, entre savoir et action, passé et futur. Apparemment cohérente avec les idéaux réformateurs de son époque, cette approche va en réalité à contre-sens du *Town Planning Movement*. Contrairement à un penseur comme Ebenezer Howard, par exemple, dont la théorie de la cité-jardin s'inscrit explicitement dans la tradition utopienne, Geddes s'oppose radicalement à l'utopie, rejette la brutalité radicale d'une coupure, d'un déni du monde tel qu'il est. L'ère néo-technique ne peut être atteinte, selon lui, en niant le lieu (*ou-topos*) mais en l'améliorant (*eu-topos*), en réalisant ce qu'il contient déjà potentiellement de bon. La formule de la cité néo-technique n'est pas exogène mais doit être déchiffrée dans les conditions spécifiques de sa situation particulière en évolution perpétuelle.

«*Here or nowhere is our Utopia*»,⁴⁰ affirme-t-il, jouant sur les mots du titre du fameux livre de William Morris, *News from Nowhere* (1890). Plutôt qu'une utopie, c'est-à-dire le rêve d'un ailleurs ou d'un autre idéal, Geddes préconise une «eutopie» c'est-à-dire la compréhension et la projection de ce que chaque situation spécifique porte potentiellement de meilleur : «l'Eutopie repose dans la cité qui nous entoure ; et elle doit être planifiée et réalisée, ici ou nulle part, par nous, en tant que citoyens – chacun étant citoyen à la fois de la cité réelle et de la cité idéale, qui, progressivement ne doit faire plus qu'une».⁴¹ Contrairement à la plupart des urbanistes de son temps, Geddes n'adopte d'ailleurs pas une position anti-urbaine. Conscient de la crise qui traverse la Grande Ville, il entend trouver en elle-même la formule de son devenir eutopique et néo-technique.

Ville-Janus

Porteur de cette vision pro-urbaine mais anti-planificatrice de la transformation des villes, Geddes sera un protagoniste important bien que minoritaire du *Town Planning Movement* des années 1900–1910. Sa principale contribution à ce champ réside dans la *Cities and Town Planning Exhibition*, une exposition itinérante dont il est l'initiateur en 1910 et qui sera montée dans plusieurs villes européennes jusqu'en 1914.

Soutenue par le Local Government Board et par son chef, John Burns, l'auteur de la première législation sur l'urbanisme,⁴² cette exposition propose un panorama de l'histoire des villes et une présentation des récentes expériences de l'urbanisme naissant, dont le premier *Town Planning Act* active l'institutionnalisation. Très sophistiquée dans son parcours et dans sa scénographie, l'exposition peut se lire également comme un plaidoyer pour la réforme civique prônée par Geddes.

Édimbourg est l'une des premières villes à accueillir l'exposition, au printemps 1911. Pour des raisons contingentes, la municipalité prête, pour l'occasion, quatre salles en enfilade de la Royal Scottish Academy, l'un des deux musées néo-grecs conçus par William Playfair sur les flancs du Mound, et que l'on aperçoit sur la photographie de Francis Caird Inglis. Geddes n'aurait pas approuvé le choix de ce site mais, fort de son sens de la scénographie, il tire le meilleur parti de la configuration et de la situation de cet édifice inauguré en 1859 et fleuron de la ville néo-classique. Le parcours initiatique mais aussi chronologique de l'exposition suit l'axe longitudinal du bâtiment qui relie, du sud au nord, les deux visages antagonistes d'Édimbourg: New et Old Town. Le bâtiment de la Royal Academy est aussi construit comme un pont au-dessus des voies de chemin de fer. Geddes considère cet écheveau de rails, qui s'est développé de manière anarchique entre les deux parties de la ville, comme une aberration typique de l'ère industrielle. En franchissant ces dizaines de voies ferrées, c'est la condition «paléotechnique» elle-même que l'exposition enjambe, comme pour la dépasser vers un avenir meilleur que Geddes souhaite «néotechnique».

Dans le catalogue de cette exposition, il précise cet argument:

> Cette longue séparation de la ville neuve d'avec l'ancienne a été désastreuse pour les deux; voilà, en fait, la principale explication de ce qu'il y a de pire dans le XIXe siècle à Édimbourg, avec d'un côté le péché et la misère de Old Town, qui brille dans le mal comme la figure de la Méduse et, de l'autre, la respectabilité, la loi, l'ordre de New Town frissonnant dans son isolement minéral – ses rues tracées de la même manière que ses tombes. De même qu'avec le vieil Édimbourg nous avons le type même d'une ville médiévale complète, nous avons, dans les quartiers les plus récents, le type correspondant de la ville moderne . . . – Medusopolis et Gorgonopolis – l'une se tordant dans des maux vivaces, l'autre paralysée dans la pensée et dans les actes.[43]

À l'aune de cette exposition, la photographie de Francis Caird Inglis prend alors tout son sens geddesien. Superposant deux plans dans la profondeur (New Town à l'avant-plan et Old Town à l'arrière-plan), cette image suggère une perspective temporelle qui se perd dans les origines de la ville. Plus précisément, ses deux points de fuite construisent une double perspective. Il s'agit, d'une part, d'une perspective longitudinale (le long de Princes Street). Cette séquence synchronique met en parallèle, juxtapose dans le même présent, les deux parties de la ville. Elle les met ensemble, côte à côte. Elle les renvoie dos à dos dans la même image. La perspective transversale (nord-sud) suggère, quant à elle, une séquence diachronique entre les deux plans, dans le sens à la fois régressif d'un retour aux origines, et progressiste, celui d'une renaissance civique d'Old Town.

En libérant la dynamique vitale de la cité, sa vitalité civique, qui se trouvait paralysée, pétrifiée dans les ordonnancements néo-classiques de New Town, la réforme geddesienne entend au bout du compte réconcilier les deux visages de la ville. C'est en les englobant dans un organisme urbain macroscopique, en interaction avec son milieu géographique élargi, qu'elle peut infléchir positivement le cours de son évolution urbaine.

La photographie de Francis Caird Inglis montre involontairement un Édimbourg très geddesien, reflet de la définition paradoxale de la citoyenneté que le penseur civique envisageait. Celle-ci s'enracine en effet dans deux idéaux différents. Il s'agit d'abord de la République platonicienne, ce qu'il appelle «l'idéal athénien de la citoyenneté»[44] en opposition à la Rome impériale qui renvoie quant à elle au grand Londres colonial. Il s'agit d'autre part de l'idéal civique médiéval, qui se caractérise, selon lui, à la fois par une harmonie entre économie rurale et urbaine mais surtout par un équilibre entre les différents pouvoirs qui la constituent. Ceux-ci se distribuent, eux-mêmes, en deux grandes catégories: le pouvoir temporel (les bourgeois et leur marché, les aristocrates et leur château fortifié) et le pouvoir spirituel (le clergé régulier et ses cloîtres, le clergé séculier et ses églises). Selon Geddes,

> La véritable Cité – petite ou grande, quelque soit son plan ou son style architectural, qu'il s'apparente à Rothenburg ou à Florence – est celle d'un peuple de bourgeois qui se gouverne lui-même depuis son propre hôtel de ville et qui exprime aussi les idéaux spirituels qui gouvernent sa vie, comme dans l'antique Acropole ou, plus tard, dans l'église ou la cathédrale médiévale.[45]

Pré-industriel, démocratique et anti-impérial, cet idéal civique de Geddes était plutôt en phase avec le milieu réformateur et philanthropique où il évoluait à Édimbourg. En revanche, il va le singulariser dans le milieu londonien naissant de l'urbanisme, dominé par les ingénieurs et les architectes; alors que ceux-ci prônent la planification des villes (le *town planning*), Geddes leur oppose la réforme civique (le *city design*). Mais surtout, dans la définition générique que Geddes donne de la citoyenneté, on peut lire en filigrane une vision idéale d'Édimbourg qu'il a sinon réalisée du moins largement propagée.

CHAPTER 13

Edinburgh Old Town and New Town: A Tale of One City?

Ranald MacInnes

I felt that I had seen, not one, but two cities – a city of the past and of the present – set down side by side, as if for the purposes of comparison, with a picturesque valley drawn like a deep score between them, to mark off the line of division.[1]

Hugh Miller, 1824

It (Edinburgh) is certainly one of the most beautiful cities in the world. Imagine a city girded to the north and east by the Firth of Forth, that backs on to a mountain at least eight hundred feet high, whose crest is frequently hidden by clouds, and on whose slopes, extending south and westwards, the city is built.[2]

Gustave d'Eichtal, 1828

It is the dramatic juxtaposition of the Old Town and the New Town for which Edinburgh has become most celebrated, at least since the 1820s when it was at the height of its fame as an 'improved' or 'enlightened' city. However, a visual or conceptual separation was not the intention of the visionary developers of the New Town, which was planned to complement an existing city, and, in fact, to be an 'ornament' to that city like countless 'new town' extensions in contemporary Scottish towns and cities such as Glasgow, Aberdeen and Perth. The aim was to create an Enlightenment City through a process of extension and intervention. The 'juxtaposition' thereby created is both natural and man-made. The cultural distinction between the two 'towns' is also man-made, and Edinburgh decided to play up the separation as it was perceived and reflected back at the city by nineteenth-century visitors such as the Scottish geologist Hugh Miller (1802–1856) or the French sociologist Gustave d'Eichtal (1804–1886) (quoted above). D'Eichtal also noted the – to him – peculiar vehicle for the creation of the New Town, an act of parliament and 'a board to direct operations' which 'called for the leading architects of the time and the numerous plans were publicly discussed, attacked and defended'.[3] By this means, public participation, both in the form of the proposed new town and the idea of its extensions, were enshrined in the civic culture, the idea of Edinburgh New Town.

While the New Town and its high ideals had been perceived from the 1820s in this way as something essentially planned and geometric, in a parallel move the Old Town came to be thought of as somehow ad hoc and 'organic', and this idea connected with a pre-Union improvement narrative based on 'rationalism'. As a result, the idea of two *actual* 'towns' came into being. But this is to confuse the new towns and new settlements of Scotland with these newly laid-out areas within existing Scottish towns, often referred to, confusingly enough, as 'new towns'.[4] The fact that we can celebrate 250 years of the New Town of Edinburgh demonstrates this duality. The Old and New Towns are one entity, closely connected conceptually, historically and developmentally, and the remodelled Old Town is as much a part of the 'masterplanned' city as the New Town. The centrepiece of the Old Town, which was to be a place of commerce, was an Adam-designed classical business 'exchange' and the area continued to be embellished with classical buildings until well into the nineteenth century. In this sense, the 'chronology' of the Old and the New Town hardly applies, except as a cultural concept and, perhaps, as an attempt to limit the city to its 'historical' boundaries, thereby excluding its extensive nineteenth-century industrial suburbs, in line with its carefully projected image, or myth, as a 'professional', non-industrial town.[5] In so doing, as Madgin and Rodger have noted:

> The landscape of the city, mental and physical, has been redefined as a result of planning policies predicated on an

image of the city that differs appreciably from the reality. Place identification with its principal product may trap towns and cities in their historical past, saddling them with myths derived from centuries earlier and conditioning planning and conservation policies according to an embellished, if not fabricated, version of their past.[6]

The Old Town and the New Town of Edinburgh lie almost parallel, separated at first by a newly created park and, latterly, by a deep, 'invisible' railway cutting through Princes Street Gardens in such a way as to preserve the amenity of the New Town and to create an apron of space, a setting, for Edinburgh Castle, which was increasingly viewed as a romantic prospect and was eventually to be intentionally architecturally recast in this mould.[7] The crucial link between the two areas of the city was initially made by the North Bridge, and a further serpentine road connection was made centrally by the 'Mound', a man-made hill graded for wheeled vehicles and made up of excavations produced by the founding and flattening of the site of the New Town. On this ignominious lump were placed two of Europe's great Greek Revival buildings: the Royal Scottish Academy (1822–6 and 1831–6, remodelled 1912) and the National Gallery of Scotland (1850–9), both designed by the romantic genius W.H. Playfair (1790–1857). On the east, the link had earlier been visualised by Robert Adam as massive inhabited bridges – 'megastructures' *avant la lettre* – with their own associated houses and shops, both above and below bridge level, the upper level for the gentle classes. These were the linked developments of the North and South Bridges, the latter linking the Old Town to the southern suburbs. Later, the 'North British' political set-pieces of Regent Bridge and Waterloo Place brutally cut through the Calton Burial Ground to form the eastern entry to Princes Street.

So the intention of the Town Council, who promoted the New Town scheme from the 1720s, was not separation but integration, wholeness and universality: not a new town in the sense of a stand-alone creation but a new extended royalty similar in spirit, if not in execution, to Pombaline Lisbon.[8] It has been convincingly argued[9] that the so-called 'First New Town' as built is an essentially Late Baroque concept overlaid with what has been called the 'Scottish

FIGURE 13.1.
View of the North Bridge and the Old Town, Edinburgh, engraving from Thomas Shepherd, *Modern Athens: Displayed in a Series of Views*, 1829. (Copyright HES)

Historical Landscape',[10] but the scenographic interface or dynamic of old and new was celebrated in a revised, romantic format as early as the 1820s and this has underscored, if not actually created and embellished, the city's celebrated duality. The city entered into a dialectical relationship which shaped the developing form of both the so-called Old Town and the New Town. To put it bluntly, the Old Town was not left to stagnate but was dramatically redesigned to conform to a peculiar strain of superficial nineteenth-century Scottish Romanticism. There was no 'Old Town' until the New Town was built. Efforts over time to engineer connections, entry points, architectural 'gateways' and access corridors intentionally heightened the drama of separation and juxtaposition, but the Old and New Towns are one entity, closely connected conceptually, historically and developmentally.

In broad terms, what is referred to as Edinburgh New Town was developed as an upper-class residential area and this was in line with a late seventeenth- and early eighteenth-century 'zoning' discourse in town planning. The aim of the promoters, responding to a potential loss of the political class to London along with Scotland's parliament, had been to attract 'people of fortune and a certain rank' to the city. It was not intended to empty the Old Town, but perhaps

FIGURE 13.2.
View of North Bridge in the 1930s. (Copyright HES)

to put the merchants in their 'place' in a country still wedded to landed interests and concerned about the moral basis for a commercial polity. In this sense the remodelled Old Town is as much a part of the 'masterplanned' city as the New Town. The new centrepiece of the Old Town was an exchange and the area continued to be embellished with monumental classical buildings. Later interventions, from the 1820s until the present day, sought to reprofile the Old Town as an ancient settlement in an attempt to make the area 'older than it was'.

James Craig's New Town

James Craig's original competition-winning design for Edinburgh New Town was, above all, 'rational' and carried a strong political message of improvement and progress, which would be promoted through continued union with England – an early scheme was in the shape of the new flag of the United Kingdom – but, although 'rational', the new Edinburgh soon began to acquire a deeply romantic image. Its unremitting geometry was to be broken up in the face of a growing desire to expand the town according to the site's topographical contours rather than by flattening the existing. This was a step further than focusing straight streets on existing cultural landscape and built features. At the same time, the idea of massive, closed monumental 'room', as created at Moray Place, underscored the zoning principle, the idea of creating a vast, shared private space within a public realm.

Craig's 1767 scheme consisted of a rectangle on a ridge to the north of the Nor' Loch which he proposed to canalise as an ornamental water feature, but which was later filled in completely. The whole scheme was divided into rectangular street blocks defined by the principal east–west axis of George Street, and the two subordinate east–west axes of Princes Street and Queen Street, both of which were one-sided streets looking out onto gardens. George Street was terminated at each end by a square – St Andrew Square and Charlotte Square – each planned to have an axial public monument as its focus, arguably a kind of 'geometricised' or rationalised version of the Royal Mile. The principal axes and squares comprised terraced houses: the cross streets, although equally classical in manner, mainly consisted of tenements of 'main door', upper and 'double upper' (two-storey) flats.[11] The central plot in each block of the main axis was originally intended for significant public buildings of which only two – St Andrew's Church (relocated in execution from its originally intended St Andrew Square site) and the Assembly Rooms – were built. Minor artisans' streets, Rose Street and Thistle Street, were planned between the principal axes, and mews for coaches and servants in the lanes between them, but in the event only the southern of these minor streets, Rose Street, was wholly built for artisans. Although a major element of formality was achieved at the centre of the east side of St Andrew Square flanking Sir Lawrence Dundas's house, the houses otherwise varied in design within a consistent overall height. Only at Charlotte Square, commissioned by a Town Council concerned about deviation from a masterplan created by Robert Adam in 1791, was a uniform palace-fronted treatment[12] of the houses achieved. Here a new, massive ashlar monumentality set the tone for the next phases of New Town development.

This was the point at which the New Town 'city as monument' ideal became a reality, and the role of the Edinburgh citizen was to worship that monument. Although not completed until twenty-five years later, Charlotte Square survives virtually intact as the New Town's key residential set-piece, and also became the focus of a 'New Town Revival' from the early years of the twentieth century.

This 'revival' was little more than an attempt to roll back the carpet of commercialism and industry which had insinuated itself into the New Town over centuries. As one guide as early as 1849 had put it, the New Town

> omitted from consideration any provision for anything so vulgar as workshops, for any industry whatsoever; and, consequently the formal beauty for which they had laboured was soon broken in upon and at many places destroyed by the necessary and inevitable filling up of any and every vacant space with any and every sort of irregular and utilitarian factory and workshop.[13]

Edinburgh played a key role in developing new town planning techniques in the eighteenth century: the crescent and the circus, along with the arrangement of a row of individual houses into a single, monumental facade, perhaps the key move for the future development of urbanism in Scotland, and its on–off love affair with the tenement. The Scottish tradition of tenement living had created significant possibilities for the monumental development of 'palace fronting' for middle-class housing. Whereas in England rows of 'terraced' housing required to be scaled down to an affordable middle-class level and were latterly given a picturesque treatment, in Edinburgh the form could remain on a 'heroic' scale by creating flatted accommodation. So, as Edinburgh New Town changed and expanded to house the middle classes, a culture of respectable apartment dwelling emerged. More than half of New Town residences are in flats, sometimes, paradoxically perhaps, laid out over two floors: 'main door' with basement or upper floor, or 'double upper' entered from a common staircase or 'close' with an internal private staircase to the upper floor. The architectural roots of this cultural tendency lay in the Old Town but were transposed to the New Town. By the late seventeenth century, future patterns of urban development were already being worked out: the dense tenement block and the row house, or 'terrace'.[14]

Urban housing layouts in the Old Town were distinctive in that they abandoned the long narrow medieval plot in favour of street block development. This was difficult to achieve because of pre-existing tenure, but once it had been demonstrated to be commercially successful the process was carried through in a number of projects which continue to dominate the upper part of the Royal Mile. A monumental type of purpose-built collective dwelling-block, prompted by the capital's burgeoning economy, began to emerge. The first of these was Mylne's Land, Leith (1678), a four-storey block with attic and basement, but later developments were concentrated on the Old Town such as Mylne Square (1684–8), the first to break out of the medieval layout by building across several closes (entries between individual blocks) in a unified design. These houses, intended exclusively for the rich but 'made down' in the nineteenth century, attempted to compress elements of a great apartment into a tight plan. By the end of the eighteenth century much of the High Street had been transformed into a succession of similar ashlar tenements of a type later to be developed in the New Town, some of great height on a continuous wall plane. The building of individual dwellings in rows was very rarely contemplated at this time.[15]

Unusually, the layout and the elevations of all later New Town schemes were established at the feuing stage, that is, when the building land was sold off in plots. Developers now had to buy in to pre-designed schemes, such as James Craig's plan for the east end of Princes Street. This further reinforced the idea of comprehensive design and it was only in the twentieth century that the power of the feudal superior[16] began to wane. Municipal Edinburgh harnessed private and trust fund resources in a civic enterprise with a national focus as capital city. James Brown's St James Square (1773, demolished in 1965) was an early palace-fronted tenement, and the South Bridge scheme to link the southern suburbs took this idea further with four great blocks conceived as 'palaces' within a grand scheme. Non-commercial public buildings were incorporated within the overall residential layout of the New Town: churches were to terminate either end of the main east–west axis. Other public buildings were added in Craig's later versions, and by a combination of design and historical accident Edinburgh New Town took on a highly original form.

Robert Adam's Register House (1774–6) occupied a key position on the edge of the first New Town framing a vista across the North Bridge, and thereby visually closing the gap by means of a long square of classical development. As is often said, there were no buildings of state in the original plan: the scheme, as described in the 1720s by the Earl of Mar, was based on recapturing the prestige of the existing city by creating an attractive suburb. As a result, there was little hierarchy in the positioning of buildings (i.e. building plots had broadly equal status with one another), although the attempt to put a church at the 'head' of the scheme failed.[17] Lacking a fixed hierarchy to refer to, a more 'democratic' design was possible and Edinburgh became a self-regarding 'people's city'. What was just as remarkable as the formal force of this grand plan for a new 'city as monument', was the consistency with which it was carried out over the following decades, through increasingly restrictive development controls by the Town Council and the private landowners and trusts concerned. In the later twentieth century, it was the City Council and the state who took over the role of protector of Edinburgh's amenity through national planning legislation but also through an act of parliament designed, among other things, to 'protect' Edinburgh's unique environment.[18]

Although in form the buildings were urban and of a fairly consistent scale, in function all were originally planned as suburban residential dwellings, at first for the aristocracy and later for the professional and merchant classes. However, from the early years of the nineteenth century the first New Town gradually became the city's main business district with some surviving residences. The social situation was changing rapidly and a new class of urban bourgeoisie was demanding prestigious accommodation, especially with the developing association of the Old Town with poor living conditions. Although a few aristocrats had their townhouses built in the New Town, merchants and professionals were by far the dominant groups and they tended to demand spatial (i.e. an entire house on one house plot) as opposed to the horizontal zonal separation of the tenement. The New Town was by no means a commercial failure. Its proposed development was based on an old hierarchy that was being undermined and its houses became one of the key areas for the cultural expression of the new middle class, many of whom continued to work in the Old Town's hospitals, courts and newspaper offices. The 'shared palaces' of residential development also had their shared parks. The interests of landscaping were served by the creation of a network of pleasure grounds, especially after 1800; the first enclosure of a garden, in St Andrew Square, took place in 1770.

The development of the Mound complex to link further the Old and New Towns in the late 1840s–50s further bridged the valley between the Old and New Towns, but this was hardly a designed solution. An estimated 2 million cartloads of 'builder's rubbish' – the result, as we saw, of flattening the natural contours of the site of the first New Town – had simply been dumped in the gap while an appropriate solution was argued over. The eventual set-piece composed by the National Galleries is one of the most stunning in this last phase of Romantic Classicism. Set against the backdrop of the Castle Rock, the Galleries complex has come to represent the dramatic interface of the Old Town and the New.

By 1820, Edinburgh had created a role for itself as city of 'narrative', an unfolding historical drama. The city's reputation had been founded on philosophy, particularly the work of David Hume and Adam Smith. Now it was time for this 'first historical nation'[19] to conceptualise its past through the historical scene-setting of the novel. Here, of course, Walter Scott was pre-eminent. 'It is singular', as Scott put it, 'to walk close beneath the grim old Castle and think what scenes it must have seen.'[20] The idea of historic buildings 'witnessing' events and therefore somehow containing a cultural narrative was important to Scott's art, and in time became part of the scientific rhetoric of antiquarianism and archaeology: buildings as 'documents'. Architecture as scene-setting was also important for Scott – as we can see in his organisation of the visit of King George IV to Edinburgh in 1822 – when the city was itself laid out as a theatrical arena of living 'history'. Denis Dighton, the king's official painter, depicted the king's arrival through the new entry to the town over the bridge of Waterloo Place. Scott's presentation was as a city of history: its architecture expressing its development over time. Scott's attitude to the New Town was expressed only in terms of amenity.[21] It was only a matter of time, however, before the New Town would become conscious of *itself* as a narrative. This is important to an understanding of the development of the Old/New duality, the beginning of 'Old Town' romanticism and perhaps also of decay, seen, at first, from a distance on the eastern approach but soon to be penetrated and framed by 'improvements'. The antiquities of the Old Town were to be identified and 'protected', as in the case of the Mercat Cross or Weigh House preservation campaigns. Already we can see Edinburgh continued to hold a mirror up to itself, reflecting its romantic image as it had since the late seventeenth century in looking out from itself to terminating landmarks.

The framework had been laid for an eclectic, set-piece city. It was now up to architects to subscribe to the developing idea of the entire city, not merely the New Town, as a monument. The best example of the tendency is a group of buildings created over a period of thirty years: the spired Tolbooth St John's Church of 1839 was placed by James Gillespie Graham at the head of the vista on the Mound, within the Old Town, but operated visually from the New Town. Then, in 1843 the rival Free Church of Scotland sited their New College at the top of the Mound, directly in front of the Tolbooth Church. However, the architect W.H. Playfair, aware of the scenographic possibilities of the two compositions, did not block the view of the church, but instead 'captured' its steeple in the frame of the New College's towers. To complete the grouping on the Mound, Playfair was asked in 1849 by the Board of Manufactures to prepare designs for the twin National Gallery and Royal Scottish Academy. In response to criticisms that no building should be erected on this 'sensitive' ('separating') location, Playfair described it as 'being like the hub of a wheel, the centre-point of the great cyclorama of North Edinburgh'.[22] From this time onwards, no Modern Athenian building was designed in isolation; an unscripted, unspoken 'context' had been created. The first major Gothic intervention actually located in the New Town was the 61-metre-high Sir Walter Scott Monument (1837–46). Following on from this set-piece interface of the Classical with the Gothic within the New Town itself, Sir George Gilbert Scott made a decisive later contribution. St Mary's Cathedral in the western New Town was begun in 1874 as a centralised design in heavy rubble masonry with a single spire, but two western spires were added later (completed 1917), creating the fantastic, Schinkel-like vista with Scottish medieval details along neo-classical Melville Street, reaching above Princes Street in some views, and also framed in views from within New Town houses.

Edinburgh World Heritage Site and the Rise of Conservation Planning

In 1995, after much international deliberation and debate, the 'Old and New Towns' of Edinburgh became a UNESCO World Heritage Site. To a great extent, the creation of a vast new heritage zone based on existing character-based individual conservation areas, unified and internationalised a very strong conservationist tendency which had developed from the early years of the nineteenth century. A crucial phrase in the site's inscription as a World Heritage Site refers to the importance of the city's 'planned alignments'[23] – Edinburgh was now officially recognised as a city of views. Old Town interventions had, from the 1820s, sought to re-profile the area as an ancient settlement. However, this project only ossified the existing social relationship of the Old Town to the New Town as characterised by Robert Louis Stevenson, a middle-class explorer in this decaying 'inner city'. He noted, in the 1870s, that 'Even in the chief thoroughfares Irish washings flutter at the windows, and the pavements are encumbered with loiterers . . . To look over the South Bridge and see the Cowgate below full of crying hawkers, is to view one rank of society from another in the twinkling of an eye.'[24]

In this sense at least, Robert Adam's earlier vision of stratified, horizontal zoning of the classes had actually happened. While earlier UK spatial planning schemes such as John Gwynn's *London and Westminster Improved* (1766) had proposed a lateral segregation of functions, Adam had created a multi-level 'zoning' scheme. Stevenson also noted that it had become fashionable to decry the 'revolutionary improvements of Mr Chambers',[25] which had led on from the remarkable scheme for an entire Scotch Baronial-style shopping area in the Old Town at the newly created Cockburn Street in the 1850s.[26] However, the context in which Cockburn Street was created is, in fact, broadly hard-edged and classical, 'rational'. So the 'historic' context was as much an imposition as a reality. An earlier improvement scheme at Victoria Street, which had also incorporated shops, had been carried out under the 1827 Improvement Act and was designed in what was referred to as the 'Old Scots or Flemish style'. A theme of conservation in Edinburgh had been set and this was to create and reinforce a historic new duality. During the initial period of construction the 'dialogue' between the Old Town and the New Town was all-important. Princes Street, for example, was a one-sided panorama terrace but this idea was turned on its head later at Jeffrey Street in the Old Town when the Cockburn Association objected to a two-sided improvement street which displayed its rear to the New Town. Later, in the 1930s, the massive intervention of St Andrew's House on Regent Road at the east end of the New Town dealt with the two sides of Edinburgh by responding with a planar stripped Classicism on the New Town side and a powerful Romantic Classicism of composed masses on the south side as seen from the Old Town.

Modern Athens had two personalities, but they were, and are, locked in an intense historical embrace. The stateliness, dignity and history of Edinburgh were challenged by shopping and its close cousin 'heritage' tourism which were both the drivers of change and, later for the conservationists, the enemy of post-Second World War conservation in Edinburgh. Shopping, having been celebrated in the late nineteenth and early twentieth centuries, was now regarded as having 'cheapened' Princes Street with competing architecture and garish advertising. Both shopping and tourism were thought of by many as antithetical to the dignity of the capital while contributing hugely to its growth and development. The newly commercialised Princes Street had become first the focus of pride as an ultra-modern shopping street, but then the focus of concern. The desire for richness in architecture had grown in Edinburgh, as elsewhere, towards the end of the nineteenth century, within the bounds of traditional Classicism with Renaissance proportions; but in Princes Street the requirement for large-scale shops and hotels, competing with each other for attention, created a situation which many found tasteless.

A conscious revival of 'stately', monumental Classicism took place in the late nineteenth century inspired by the 'rediscovered' work of Robert Adam. The natural home of this wider 'Adam Revival' was, of course, Edinburgh New Town. The beginnings of the revival were first seen mainly in interior decoration, part of a rejection of late nineteenth-century 'dark' and 'cluttered' interiors the alternative to which was an austere 'whiteness'. However, it was extended into the revival of the New Town *itself* in 1904, when the

4th Marquess of Bute transformed and refurbished in Adam style No. 5 Charlotte Square, Adam's urban masterpiece. Traces of the building's natural evolution, including expensive plate glass windows, were expunged in favour a more 'authentic' appearance, part of a trend that grew steadily throughout the twentieth century and culminated in an extreme phase of restoration.

The trend continued even into the 1930s as a 'national' alternative to Modernism. T.P. Marwick's department store on Princes Street for Jay's (1938–9, demolished in 2002) is an example. Again a past style had been re-visited and fed back into a new movement in architecture. 'Neo-New Town' appeared as late as 1954–5 at Sir William Kininmonth's stone monumental Adam House in Chambers Street, a university examination hall. The cubic modernity of the 1960s reconstruction of the Victorian architecture of Princes Street – the 'Princes Street Panel' – related also to the 'simple grandeur' of the New Town. Just as the work in the Old Town had reinvested the area with security, safety and dignity, so the restoration of the New Town would re-establish its social and architectural place. The Princes Street Panel wished to created cubic, Modernist blocks in keeping with the New Town's satisfying geometric rigour. In this sense, Modernism meshed with conservation. Neo-classical architecture was seen by many as presaging Modernism in some quarters. Modernism was a 'return' to reason from Romanticism. Emil Kaufmann's *Von Ledoux bis Le Corbusier* (1933)[27] illustrates the point, as does Louis Kahn's championing of simple ante-bellum architecture in the US. In Scotland, Reiach and Hurd's *Building Scotland* (1941)[28] presented international modern and seventeenth-century Scottish architecture as models to follow. Internationally, a backwards leap over the historicist nineteenth century was paradoxically being made by progressive architects. Hurd went on to reconstruct, repair and even recreate eighteenth-century architecture in the Old Town.

The Adam Revival/neo-New Town movement meshed with the aims of the Edinburgh New Town Conservation Committee (ENTCC) from the 1970s. This movement sought to 'restore' the New Town but in its zeal much that was ad hoc, never completed or 'jarring' was removed, to the extent that the developmental history of the site was compromised. Building on what had been achieved in the Royal Mile improvements, the New Town improvers carried their message over to the New Town by means of a highly successful international conference in 1970. The conference drew an immediate commitment from Edinburgh City Council and from central government to begin an ambitious and very expensive New Town repair scheme which was the envy of Glasgow and has continued to the present day under a World Heritage Site banner which overarches the merged bodies of the ENTCC and the Edinburgh Old Town Committee for Conservation and Renewal (notice the difference in concept). The aim was to make grants available to owners' groups rather than target specific areas as had happened elsewhere, notably the Marais district in Paris. Crucially, there was a wish to complete the job of creating the New Town. One influential speaker at the conference, Patrick Nuttgens, said that 'conservation implies the completion of an area . . . the completion of potential patterns'.[29] No value was to be placed on work that had 'disrupted' the New Town ideal and so we see the New Town today as it was never experienced, with the loss of almost everything regarded as second rate or out of keeping. The thinking was applied at one extreme to large areas or individual city blocks, and also, at the other extreme, to the minutiae of fanlights, railings, roof coverings, bootscrapers, windows and lanterns. Here we witnessed a need not to value change but to wipe out traces of the New Town's historical life.

From the 1980s a new eclecticism permitted a reassessment of style in architecture, including 'national' styles. However, 'national' no longer necessarily meant Baronial, and here the Baronial or the Old Town style was not widely revived except in Ian Begg's controversial and powerful 'neo-Baronial' design for the Scandic Crown Hotel (1988–9), which was also, in its way, a continuation of traditional contextual 'infill' of the Old Town. For some Modernists and conservationists, Begg, who had worked for Robert Hurd on the earlier stripped phase of conservationist Old Town infill, had crossed a historicist line by copying historical details and attaching rough-hewn stone to a steel-framed building. Again, committed Modernists and conservationists found themselves allied to a pre-Postmodern cause related to 'honesty' and a Ruskinian 'truth to materials' and construction.

Meanwhile, there was also a brief return to a form of monumental Classicism. Campbell and Arnott's Saltire Court (1989–91), which sat in a key geographical position between the Old and New Towns, was a huge, mixed-use block that seemed almost to reflect the agglomerated palace-fronting of the Edinburgh Golden Age. As connected as it seems to be with the Edinburgh narrative, Postmodern Classicism as a style had a short life in the city, as elsewhere. However, the tendency within Postmodern Classicism towards 'completion' and replication was exceptionally strong in Edinburgh. Afterwards, a much less rhetorical, but somehow regular and classical, stone style came through, exemplified in the work of Reiach and Hall at 10 George Street (1987), where the architects demolished an 'intrusive' 1960s office building and, with their new design, sought to 'engage the Georgian condition' with a gridded stone block. During the early 1990s, 'infill' buildings in the New Town, from Victorian churches to high-quality 1960s commercial buildings, were demolished in favour of sympathetic new designs.

FIGURE 13.3.
Dublin Street Church in the New Town, before it was demolished and replaced by a replica tenement in the 1990s. (Copyright HES)

Since the late 1990s we have seen a change in attitudes to 'conserving' Edinburgh New Town: a move away from a rigorous approach of 'restoration' towards a looser 'controlled diversity' in conservation and new build. The work of two practices, Richard Murphy Architects and Malcolm Fraser Architects, has exemplified a trend towards sympathetic contemporary 'infill' in both the New Town and the Old Town. However, both practices have continued to reflect the ongoing planning duality of the two locations.

There is another, highly controversial, area, that of 'setting', which has impacted on World Heritage Sites in recent years at

Vienna, London, Liverpool, Cologne and elsewhere. In Edinburgh there have been several development issues at Caltongate, Haymarket, the St James Centre, the Royal High School and elsewhere, where the physical impacts proposed for historic buildings constitute a lesser issue than a potentially more damaging impact on their setting. To a large extent, this is merely the extension of a local debate to an international stage. As we have seen, the idea of a 'city of views' was well established by the middle of the nineteenth century, and from then on there were various campaigns to preserve the setting of the city's heritage and amenity, including the historical appearance of Cockburn Street, the removal of an entire block of proposed housing at Jeffrey Street, the work of Patrick Geddes in preserving and regenerating the Old Town and the elaborate pre-construction mock-up in the early 1920s of Lorimer's Scottish National War Museum at Edinburgh Castle.

There is clear evidence in the buildings that Edinburgh, as an idea and as an architectural narrative, has been continually referred to since the sixteenth century. The New Town and the Old Town have continued to inform and inspire contemporary architecture. From the mid 1990s, there were to be small-scale interventions in the Old Town, following patterns established by existing old buildings and referring back to the work of earlier restorers. In recent years, Edinburgh has specialised in small contemporary interventions both in the Old Town and the New Town. In very recent years, the strictures of the conservation movement of the 1970s have loosened to some extent and we have seen new development, beginning in the late 1990s at Dublin Street Lane, which recognised and interpreted a surviving historic 'village' within the overlaid New Town.

Finally, as one authority has noted: 'Perhaps the last new town is not to the North of the city but to the South in Marchmont and Warrender where picturesquely sinuous streets and baronial architecture, built on a flat site Craig would have envied, mark a final rewriting of the dormitory suburb in a style which at once rejected the Classicism and the ashlar of the northern New Towns while wholeheartedly embracing their scenographic conventions. Spottiswood Street frames the castle as surely as Castle Street.'[30] In the end, it seems that the most powerful idea behind the development of Edinburgh has been Edinburgh itself.

Part 5

The New Town Celebrations

CHAPTER 14

Commemorating the Founding of the New Town of Edinburgh in 1967 and 2017

Clarisse Godard Desmarest

The Modernist ideal of progress, through mass provision of new buildings, triumphed in the post-war period with architects like Le Corbusier. In Edinburgh, which was not bombed, the Modern Movement can be charted in the succession of University schemes for the rebuilding of eighteenth-century George Square and surrounding area: the first University development plan (1945), the Abercrombie Plan (1949) and the proposed redevelopments by Basil Spence, Robert Matthew and Percy Johnson-Marshall in the 1950s–60s. The Arts Tower (David Hume Tower), built in 1963 to Sir Robert Matthew's designs, is an example of significant intervention in the 'cultural quarter' of Scotland's capital.

In 1967, the 'Princes Street Panel', which had been set up in 1954, proposed a comprehensive redevelopment of Princes Street, a major axis in James Craig's eighteenth-century New Town. By then, the heterogeneous, nineteenth-century appearance of the street was considered a problem, and several Victorian and Edwardian buildings had been demolished, including William Burn and David Bryce's New Club (1834 and 1859; demolished 1967) and David Rhind's Life Association block (1855; demolished 1968). With the aim of overcoming the lack of integration of the street (a consistent theme since the Abercrombie Plan), the Panel proposed that all new developments should incorporate a continuous elevated walkway. The British Home Stores, by Kenneth Graham of Robert Matthew, Johnson Marshall & Partners (1965), was the first of the redevelopments that followed the Princes Street guidelines. Such a formula was repeated in Alan Reiach's buildings on 84–87 Princes Street (1966).[1] A contemporary megastructure was realised at the east end of Princes Street: Ian Burke & Martin's monumental St James Centre (1964–70). This controversial complex, which contained a car park, a hotel, a shopping centre and offices, replaced an elegant Georgian Square originally laid out by James Craig in the late eighteenth century (mostly demolished in 1966).

For a long time, old buildings and preservation had remained a peripheral consideration but, with the part-demolition of George Square in the 1950s and further demolitions in Princes Street in the 1960s, many of Edinburgh's citizens grew concerned about their architecture. In response to the knocking-down of historic buildings and to large-scale developments, several conservation bodies were formed which complemented the action of the historic Cockburn Association, an institution formed in 1875. The creation of the Scottish Georgian Society in 1956 was prompted by the George Square redevelopment plans. The Scottish Civic Trust (an offshoot of the Civic Trust, in London) was established in 1967, with Maurice Lindsay as its chair and Sir Robert Matthew one of its key trustees. The late 1960s therefore saw a move away from an ethos of redevelopment to a more conservation-based philosophy, and the most successful campaign of the Trust was the safeguarding of the New Town of Edinburgh.[2]

This chapter aims to demonstrate that the 1967 celebrations of the bicentenary of the founding of the New Town formed part of a growing concern over the condition of the New Town which, arguably, led to the eventual ascendency of conservation within Scotland. The Civic Amenities Act of 1967 enabled the designation of Conservation Areas. It was, ironically, at the instigation of Robert Matthew, architect of the George Square redevelopment, that an international conference on 'The Conservation of Georgian Edinburgh' was held in Edinburgh in 1970 and a government-supported body, the Edinburgh New Town Conservation Committee, was set up to safeguard this unique piece of urban architecture. The 1967 commemorative events in Edinburgh took place five years after the Loi Malraux legislation, allowing for the protection of historic districts, was passed in France and three years after the Marais in

Paris became the first *secteur sauvegardé*. The scope of the 1970 conference organised by the Scottish Civic Trust was deliberately international. In a comparative presentation relating the New Town to the Marais, François Sorlin, chief inspector of the Centre des Monuments Historiques, argued that Edinburgh could learn from Paris the need for a strategic plan to avoid decay, problems of traffic, and to prepare for the growth of commercialisation.[3] To discuss the bicentenary commemorations in Edinburgh, this present analysis relies on contemporary press articles as well as minutes of the Town Council, the Edinburgh Festival Society, the Edinburgh Architectural Association (EAA) and the Old Edinburgh Club.

The Social and Cultural Background of Edinburgh in 1967

The year 1967 marked the bicentenary of the New Town and the twenty-first anniversary of the Edinburgh International Festival of Music and Drama. Because the celebrations of the New Town anniversary formed part of the 1967 Festival, it is necessary to provide the context to that year's Festival. Since the inaugural event of August 1947, the Festival had transformed Edinburgh, a city not previously renowned for its encouragement of the arts, into a world stage for culture. The Festival aimed to offer the very best in music and drama, and Festival posters were designed by the multi-faceted French artist and director Jean Cocteau in the early 1960s.[4] By then, commercial art galleries had opened in the city, boutiques had been burgeoning along Rose Street, discotheques sprang up and folk singers poured in. The role of culture was reappraised and there was a renewed commitment by the British state to a patronage of the arts.[5] Festivals flourished in Britain, and Edinburgh's reputation as Festival City was established in 1967, when the Festival had come of age.

Simultaneously, the kind of elite culture presented by the Festival and supported by the Arts Council of Great Britain was increasingly challenged by left-wing theatre groups, the Labour movement, Scottish folk singers and Scottish nationalists.[6] The social and cultural shifts of the 1960s were apparent, as a new 'liberal' and youth culture exploded; the optimistic and colourful 'Summer of Love' kicked off in July 1967 and the Beatles' No. 1 single 'All You Need is Love' was its anthem. The ABC Regal cinema on Lothian Road played host to Cliff Richard and the Beatles in 1964,[7] Bob Dylan and the Hawks in 1966, and the Beach Boys and Helen Shapiro in 1967. The Rolling Stones performed in the Usher Hall in September 1964. In sport, the summer of 1967 was marked by a sense of renewed confidence in Scotland. In football, Scotland humiliated England 3–2 at Wembley in April, and in the following month Celtic won the European Cup Final.[8] Politician Winnie Ewing won the Hamilton by-election for the Scottish National Party in November 1967. This unexpected victory in a Labour stronghold marked a turning point in Scotland, as a sense of national identity increased from the late 1960s. This was still the time of the peaceful 'love' revolution, before the 1968 watershed when movements of protest and violence erupted in Europe.[9]

This new 'liberal' culture was represented in the Festival City. Although still a minority pursuit in the 1960s, experimental theatre was one of the many expressions of the arrival of counter-culture. The older culture was put under pressure from the art and experiment of the *avant-garde*. During this period, the Festival's Fringe, organised in a loose kind of way (1947), was growing in both physical size and visibility but was not recognised by the local authority, Edinburgh Corporation,[10] which only sponsored the official Festival.[11] Sparks of vitality, although present in the official Festival programme, were missing from the atmosphere in the city itself in 1967.[12] Peter Diamand, the Dutch director of the Festival (1966–72), complained about 'a streak of Puritanism' and the Corporation's reluctance to increase the Festival grant. There was a tendency in the Corporation to consider festivals wasteful when public funding could be allocated towards civic amenities.[13] In September 1967, Scottish writer Tom Nairn penned a bitter essay, 'The Festival of the Dead', published in the *New Statesman*. He condemned the 'tartanry' that characterised Scotland and the stifling weight of Presbyterianism:

> The three-week Festival is exactly like an interminable church fete in atmosphere . . . Edinburgh's soul is Bible-black, pickled in boredom by centuries of sermons, swaddled in the shabby gentility of the Kirk.[14]

For Nairn, the 1960s was a period of stasis, a 'cultural desert'.[15] Although the Scottish capital styled itself the Athens of the North, playwright Tom Stoppard suggested it was rather the Reykjavik of the South.[16] The conservative Progressive Party was indeed the majority party in Edinburgh Corporation throughout the period 1945–70, and the links between local government and the Church of Scotland were very strong.[17] The sensitivity and moral conservatism of some councillors was well known, and there had been much controversy over a girl who appeared nude in a drama performance during the 1963 Festival. This performance, held in the McEwan Hall (owned by the University of Edinburgh), was frowned upon by ministers of the Church of Scotland, which testifies to the moral conflict within Edinburgh in the high sixties. Censorship and traditional values were still very much alive, and it was only slowly that Scotland cast off the shadow of John Knox and gained new cultural confidence. One may therefore ask who steered the 1967 New Town celebrations in the city, and whether this commemoration was part of a conservative agenda.

The New Town Bicentenary Celebrations in Edinburgh

Although the 250th anniversary of the founding of the New Town passed relatively unnoticed in Edinburgh in 2017, many events were happening in the city fifty years earlier, in 1967. Scottish architect, historian and conservationist Ian G. Lindsay (1906–1966) had been one of the first to suggest that steps be taken to mark the bicentenary.[18] In the course of a lecture to the New Club on 16 December 1965, he pointed out that the New Town would be 200 years old in October 1967.[19] In the spring of 1966, exactly 200 years after the architectural competition for the New Town was announced in April 1766, the Corporation accepted the principle that the bicentenary should be fittingly recognised and agreed to sponsor the arrangements. A coordinated approach was made by three bodies: the Edinburgh Festival Society (Alexander Schouvaloff), the Old Edinburgh Club (David Simpson and Catherine Cruft) and the Edinburgh Architectural Association (Alan Reiach, Eric

Hall and James Dunbar-Nasmith). This project followed an earlier unfruitful attempt to organise an exhibition on town planning as part of the 1966 Festival.[20]

A sub-committee was formed to coordinate the 1967 celebrations, which were to commemorate the foundation stone of the New Town two centuries earlier. The committee was chaired by James McKay, treasurer to the Corporation, and was composed of four city councillors along with one representative of the Festival Society and three representatives of the Old Edinburgh Club, the Edinburgh Architectural Association and other organisations with a special interest in the history and development of the New Town.[21] The newly formed Regent, Royal and Carlton Terraces Association, with Sir Robert Matthew as Chairman, and the Saltire Society also expressed their willingness to cooperate in the celebrations.[22] The sub-committee subscribed three guineas towards A.J. Youngson's *The Making of Classical Edinburgh*, a book which was published by Edinburgh University Press in the autumn of 1966 to coincide with the bicentenary of the New Town.[23] In place of Ian Lindsay, who died in August 1966, Youngson, Professor of Economics at the University of Edinburgh, was appointed a representative of the Edinburgh Architectural Association on the sub-committee. The book, for which publicity appeared during the 1967 summer celebrations, brought the New Town into the wider public consciousness.[24]

The Corporation agreed that an exhibition should be held in the Waverley Market during the Festival period. In consultation with Dennis Brown, Deputy City Architect, a scenario was prepared by Alexander Schouvaloff, the artistic assistant and Deputy Director of the International Festival. He insisted that this exhibition was to be 'as theatrical as possible in order to make the exhibition primarily an entertainment'.[25] In preparation for the 1967 Festival, Schouvaloff had explored experimental productions in Off-Broadway theatres in New York and in Montparnasse in Paris and, as noted below, the Edinburgh show was influenced by *avant-garde* theatre. Waverley Market was a large space next to the North British Hotel, which was used for fairs, dog shows and flower shows before its demolition in 1972 (Fig. 14.1). Since a decision (by arbitration) was made in 1771 that the land from the North Bridge to Hanover Street should be laid out as a pleasure garden, building had not

FIGURE 14.1.
Edinburgh, view looking east from the Scott Monument, inscribed 'Edinburgh, Calton Hill and Waverley Market from Scott Monument M&Co', Scottish Colorfoto, c. 1880. (Copyright HES: https://canmore.org.uk/collection/1201796)

been permitted on the south side of Princes Street, and Waverley Market therefore sat below the level of Princes Street.

John L. Paterson[26] and Peter Daniel, lecturers in architecture and town planning at the Edinburgh College of Art, respectively, as well as practising architects, were chosen by the special subcommittee for the bicentenary celebrations as designers for the exhibition, on condition that they should supervise all stages of its construction in cooperation with the City Architect and under his general direction.[27] The total budget for the exhibition was fixed at £35,000, and the overall responsibility for the project was to rest with the Corporation.[28] The exhibition overall stayed within budget, with an additional net cost of £535, and the service rendered by Paterson in designing and supervising the exhibition was eventually fully appreciated by the city.[29] (The Sir Walter Scott Bicentenary Celebration, 'Writer to the Nation', which was held in Waverley

Market in the summer 1971, was also designed by Paterson.) Apart from some marginal damage to the roof glazing in the Waverley Market, the 1967 exhibition was a successful enterprise, and there was discussion subsequently about re-erecting part of the exhibition in Nice.[30] In Edinburgh, several requests were made to the Corporation for borrowing part of the display material.

The 1967 anniversary was marked in many ways in the city, and a programme of events ranging over a period of months began in June 1967. A civic procession attended by the Lord Provost and Council was organised from the Assembly Rooms to St Andrew's and St George's Church, on George Street, where a special bicentenary service was held on Sunday 11 June 1967. Classified advertisements were placed at frequent intervals in newspapers, including the *Scotsman* and *Evening News*.[31] To inform the public, the BBC and STV made films on the bicentenary of the New Town.[32] In addition to a large-scale exhibition in Waverley Market, more specialised exhibitions were on view. 'Edinburgh New Town Bi-centenary Stands' – twelve information boards sponsored by Edinburgh Corporation and designed by Paterson for the Edinburgh Architectural Association presided over by James Dunbar-Nasmith – were erected in the New Town during the festival period.[33] Colin McWilliam, an architectural historian with a specialised knowledge of Georgian Edinburgh, undertook research and prepared the narrative for the boards, which Youngson was invited to review.[34] The information board 'James Craig and the New Town' was arranged by Huntly House Museum, Canongate, 'Origin of the New Town' by Edinburgh Central Public Library, George IV Bridge, and 'Auld Reekie and New Town' by Register House, Princes Street. The Scottish National Museum of Antiquities on Queen Street, the National Gallery on the Mound, the Scottish National Portrait Gallery on Queen Street, the Royal Scottish Museums on Chambers Street, were all contacted by the Corporation about the possibility of displaying a special exhibition for the bicentenary.[35]

A fireworks display in Princes Street Gardens, with Princes Street closed to traffic for the occasion, was organised in August 1967. Nine monuments and buildings in the city were floodlit during a ceremony held on 15 August.[36] Commemorative covers in the form of envelopes and date stamps with the city coat of arms were issued by the Postmaster General after successful lobbying from the Lord Provost H.A. Brechin and Deputy Town Clerk E.F. Catford.[37] These were to commemorate the New Town bicentenary and the Festival's twenty-first anniversary. As regards publicity material, a colour film of the history of the New Town was produced by the Scottish Committee of the Arts Council and the Films of Scotland Committee, with a £3,000 sponsorship from the Corporation.[38] Colin McWilliam and David Bruce prepared the commentary of this 20–25 minute film. In addition, photographs of the exhibition were commissioned and purchased by the Corporation for its records.[39]

School children were engaged in New Town project work and, during 1967, as many as thirty-three large groups visited the Edinburgh Room to use material or to hear talks on the work and resources of the department.[40] Organised parties of children were taken to visit temporary displays, such as the exhibitions at the Waverley Market and Huntly House Museum. Coach tours of the New Town were scheduled during the summer of 1967, with recorded commentaries prepared by Youngson.[41] The Corporation considered naming one of the new streets in the St James Square redevelopment area as 'James Craig Street'.[42] The bicentenary of the New Town was the subject of some lectures at the second International Congress on the Enlightenment, which met in St Andrews in August 1967, and Jean-Paul Sartre featured among the provisional list of speakers.[43]

The Exhibition Arrangement and its Significance

The 'Two Hundred Summers in a City' exhibition took place in Waverley Market, 16 August to 16 September 1967.[44] The exhibition belongs to a series of historic-city exhibitions organised in Scotland (and indeed elsewhere in Europe) from the late nineteenth century, when this new type of attraction was becoming popular – a reconstruction of Old London was first shown at the International Health Exhibition in the summer of 1884 and its immediate successor was Old Edinburgh in 1886, followed among others by Old Manchester in 1887, *Oud Antwerpen* in 1895, *Alt Berlin* in 1896, *Gamla Stockholm* in 1897 and *Vieux Paris* at the Paris Exposition of 1900. Both the

1886 and 1967 Edinburgh exhibitions coincided with an assertion of national and cultural 'difference' from England, which means that the shows must be read within both a social and a political context. The 1886 exhibition was replete with Scottish symbolism, but the concerns from civil society reflected unionist nationalism, not political separation.[45] Late Victorian Scots were in fact mostly loyal to the Union and the Empire. In 1967, by contrast, the Union relationship was put under pressure by economic crisis and the first signs of deindustrialisation. The post-war democratic consensus which the Scots consistently voted for began to unravel with Prime Minister Harold Wilson's devaluation of the pound in 1967 and a Scottish nationalist MP being returned to Westminster. The 1886 exhibition was also part of a context of continuing rivalry in Scotland between Edinburgh, the capital, and Glasgow, the heart of Scottish industries; the two international fairs held in Glasgow in 1888 and 1901 were a direct response to the Edinburgh ones. In the 1960s, Scottish civic pride and nationalism was expressed politically, and was increasingly directed at England. It is therefore possible to read the 1967 exhibition as the manifestation of an increased cultural energy in Scotland – an energy that burgeoned further in the 1980s and 1990s in reaction to the extended Tory political hegemony in Westminster.

Paterson designed the exhibition to entertain and stimulate the public to an awareness of the architectural heritage of the city. The show was a popular triumph: it dominated Edinburgh's social life that summer and attracted flocks of visitors including many families – significantly, the 1886 exhibition had also been a major success.[46] The aim of Paterson was not to recreate realistically what had already been built but to suggest, in a series of stylised designs based on fact, the atmosphere and period of the city during the previous 200 years. In his notes, he remarked:

> Designing a visual celebration about a city I found both a fascinating and a difficult problem. Fascinating because I had to find a visual equivalent for the two hundred years of a city's history. Difficult because the physical reality of that city was immediately adjacent to the entrance of the exhibition hall that was used for the presentation.[47]

The New Town effectively sat across Princes Street from Waverley Market. In an attempt to evoke the poetry of the Athens of the North, Paterson selected elements of the history of Edinburgh and hoped to involve spectators in some kind of 'environmental theatre':

> This poetry I hoped to contain within a general framework of what I call environmental theatre. That is, spectators and scenery are not separated as in normal theatrical presentations; they are involved within the scene. The spectators as well as being onlookers, also become the actors on the stage of a city.[48]

The principle that performers and audience shared the same environment, a fundamental principle of environmental theatre, was formulated by Richard Schechner, a professor at New York University's School of the Arts, in an article entitled '6 Axioms of Environmental Theatre' (1968). This performance theory was experimented with by the Performance Group formed in New York by Schechner in 1967. The exhibition in Edinburgh was therefore relying on new ideas developed in cultural production.[49] For Paterson, the display was a visual celebration, with light and colour, and also sound, as if the aim was to recreate some kind of indoor performance.

In his presentation of 'New Environment', an exhibition he curated for the Scottish Arts Council (September 1968), Paterson wrote about the constant state of transition of cities which he described as 'living organisms'.[50] This must be read in the Edinburgh context, as Patrick Geddes's biological approach and civic experiments were immensely influential – and the Outlook Tower in the heart of the Old Town was an obvious example of this. Geddes's *Cities in Evolution* (1915), which draws heavily on Darwin's theories of evolution, was familiar to contemporaries. The Souvenir Programme for the bicentenary exhibition, compiled by Peter Daniel, a landscape architect, raises the question: 'What does this New Town contribute to the image of Edinburgh today?' Daniel insisted that if the New Town was to survive as a place where people lived, it needed absolute protection from passing road traffic and commuter parking, as well as from commercial colonisation and inferior redevelopment. As a member of the Geddes Society, Daniel was heavily influenced by this great nineteenth-century Scottish thinker. Daniel quoted the words Geddes pronounced from the Outlook Tower in the Old Town in 1910, when he explained his Edinburgh Town Planning Exhibition:

> The essential purpose of this exhibit is to show the necessity ... and the fruitfulness of studying the geography and history of your town before trying to make plans either for future growth or to correct past mistakes. For natural environment cannot be neglected by either architect, engineer, or politician without long enduring penalties.[51]

Daniel and Paterson shared, with Geddes, this post-Darwinian idea of looking at the history of a city before moving on, hence the need for surveys.[52] Forty years after the 1910 exhibition, Geddes's beliefs helped form the great Civic Survey and Plan made for Edinburgh by Sir Patrick Abercrombie. The Royal Commission on the Ancient and Historical Monuments of Scotland (RCAHMS) also carried out a condition survey of the houses in the New Town in the late 1960s. In this tradition, one of the aims of the 1967 exhibition, as formulated by Daniel, was to push spectators into thinking about a new, better plan for the city.

The 1967 historic-city exhibition was divided into six units, as was explained in the exhibition catalogue.[53] Unit One, 'The heart of Midlothian', invited one to step into a scene of the Old Town set in a toy theatre inspired by R.L. Stevenson's essay 'A penny plain and two-pence coloured' in which the author recalled seeing, as a boy, a toy theatre in a Leith Walk window. Unit Two, 'Gallery of maps and pictorial views', focused on the Old Town and shed light on the reasons for the expansion of Edinburgh across the North Loch. This section contained seven maps or views of Edinburgh from the late sixteenth to the nineteenth centuries. Unit Three of the exhibition was based on a reconstruction of a street recognisable as George Street by around 1830 (Fig. 14.2). Such a reconstruction of the city's past is reminiscent of the 'Old Edinburgh Street' which occupied a central position in the exhibition building at the International Exhibition of Industry, Science and Art held in Edinburgh

FIGURE 14.2.
'Two Hundred Summers in a City' exhibition, Edinburgh, view along George Street to Charlotte Square, design dated 1967. (John L. Paterson Collection, copyright HES: https://canmore.org.uk/collection/1150302#attribution)

in 1886. For that exhibition, located in the Meadows, an attempt had been made by designer Sydney Mitchell (1856–1930) to recreate demolished buildings which had stood in the Royal Mile, including the Netherbow gateway, in order to represent ancient street patterns. Patrick Geddes, a great admirer of the exhibition, displayed photographs of 'Old Edinburgh' in the Outlook Tower exhibition twenty-five years later.[54] But, in contrast to the Old Town street recreated in 1886, the New Town street scene in the Waverley Market conveyed the impression of Arcadia: the idealised image of classical architecture set in pastoral surroundings, which was so important to the Augustan world. The New Town of Edinburgh fulfilled this ideal to a certain extent by creating squares, terraces and crescents adjacent to landscaped gardens so that one is always aware of nature.

In this reconstruction of 'George Street', life-size pictures of nineteenth-century characters taken from Benjamin W. Crombie's *Men of Modern Athens: Being Portraits of Eminent Personages, Existing or Supposed to Exist in the Metropolis of Scotland* (Edinburgh, 1839) and John Kay's *Original Portraits and Caricature Etchings* (Edinburgh, 1837) went on display, with the striking effect of challenging the barrier between art and life – perhaps another influence of American and European experimental theatre. Nineteenth-century judges, advocates, ministers, merchants or gentlemen sketched by the two famous caricaturists were shown in what was the grandest street in the first New Town development.[55] The house facades in this scenographic space lit up to reveal period interiors, with furniture showing the elegance of Regency and Georgian interiors. The *Scotsman*, in August 1967, showed photographs of the exhibition inauguration, with the Lord Provost featured in a mock Charlotte Square (Fig. 14.3). *Edinburgh Tatler* (October 1967) presented photographs of visitors standing alongside cut-out figures and enjoying the immersive nature of the exhibition. A particular story of Edinburgh was being told, though, and the display appears to have been mediated by a rather socially conservative agenda. The Corporation and the various patrons of the exhibition were guided by a positive view of the 'olden times', when Edinburgh was forward-looking and established itself as a centre for culture.

Unit Four was composed of two sections: 'The Georgian Rooms' and the 'Victorian Room'. The former contained oils, watercolours, aquatints, mezzotints and engravings by nineteenth-century artists including Samuel Dukinfield Swarbreck, Thomas H. Shepherd, John Wilson Ewbank and Alexander Kay. The pictures were lent by public and private organisations and individuals – including the New Club, Huntly House Museum, the Bank of Scotland and John Nelson. They showed significant views of the city, including the North Bridge, Calton Hill, Edinburgh Academy, the University of Edinburgh, the Royal Institution, as well as several panoramas. Perspectives of the city had already been on display in the Outlook

FIGURE 14.3.
'Two Hundred Summers in a City' exhibition showing officials, including the Lord Provost, in a mock Charlotte Square. *Scotsman*, 15 August 1967. (Copyright HES: https://www.scran.ac.uk/)

Tower, and such 360-degree views corresponded to the images shown at world fairs in the nineteenth century. The 'Victorian Room', which recorded the nineteenth-century changes in the city, showed a gallery of photographs, or calotypes, by early Scottish photographers David Octavius Hill, Thomas Keith and Robert Adamson. A photograph of the construction of the Scott Monument was included, as well as nineteenth-century scenes in the city. Although the late Victorian decay of the old historic centre was shown, it was mainly a sleek vision of the historic city that was presented to visitors.

Unit Five, 'Edinburgh 1967', was an attempt to recreate the complex nature of urban life as illustrated by statistics. Projected sequences of Edinburgh and its citizens on screens around a circular area created a constantly moving kaleidoscope (Fig. 14.4). We may consider this scene as an adaptation, with modern resources, of Robert Barker's 1787 panorama 'View of Edinburgh'. A 'permanent' panorama was situated on the Mound in the early nineteenth century.[56] The sphere, which was often used by thinkers and architects as denoting utopia, echoes Étienne-Louis Boullée's proposed cenotaph for Isaac Newton (1784). The scientist was the embodiment

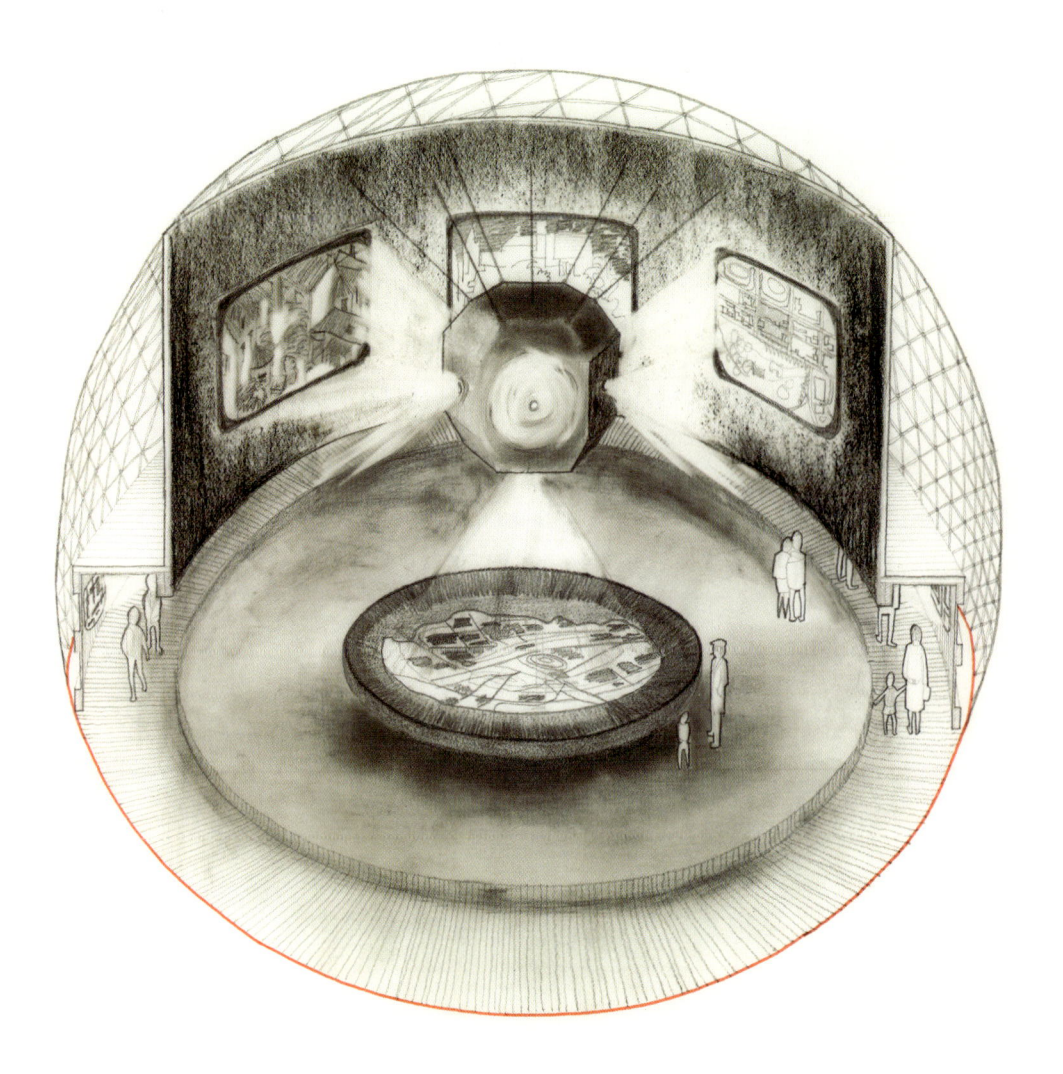

FIGURE 14.4.
'Two Hundred Summers in a City' exhibition, interior perspective elevations for unit 5, 1967. (John L. Paterson Collection, copyright HES: https://canmore.org.uk/collection/1150261)

of Enlightenment ideas, and such a reference would have been in line with Edinburgh's claim to be the cultural capital of the United Kingdom in the late eighteenth century. Closer to us, this projection recalls too the geographer Élisée Reclus's proposal for a grand globe to be built at the 1900 World Exhibition in Paris, a project which inspired Geddes's Outlook Tower. With moving dioramas, the visitors had access to a better understanding of the reality they lived in, and such a didactic dimension to the exhibitions was essential to both Geddes and Reclus, and indeed also to Paterson and Daniel.

Unit Six, 'City-Scope', created an enclosure and was designed to stimulate (through form, space, light, colour and sound) the imagination of the spectator into an awareness of the possible nature of future cities (Fig. 14.5). As appears on the design, a ramp for visitors surrounds a central steel framework, and horizontal and vertical cylinders interpenetrate the whole structure. The pattern of the maze seems to have inspired this unit, and the labyrinth was deliberately used again by Paterson in his 1968 exhibition to present a synthetic image of the town. The central globe in the 'City-Scope' may well therefore embody the search, in mythology, for the secret centre of the world. The kinetic effect of light was important to Paterson, who considered the hypnotic effect of lights reflecting on polished and faceted surfaces, theatrical spectacles, stained glass and neon signs in twentieth-century cities.[57] Paterson was also interested in the symbolism of ornaments and buildings, including obelisks, columns and towers, as disguised elements to earlier culture. The towers in the 'City-Scope' may well suggest humanity's quest for a higher truth and for a sense of self-awareness. Both Units Five and Six reflect environmental art and the work of artists such as Kusama, Samaras, Christo, Boriani, Spindel and others who sought to enclose the spectator within the artefacts they created.

The sound used in the Waverley Market exhibition was arranged by A. Brown with the cooperation of BBC Scotland and the School of Scottish Studies at the University of Edinburgh. Modern pop and electronic music was played in Units Five and Six of the exhibition. Background music commissioned by Paterson was composed and arranged by Fritz Spiegl and Hans Wild from an original street song 'The wind, the wind, the wind blows high . . . she is the girl from the golden city'.[58] The chorus was a clear allusion to Edinburgh's golden age.

To conclude, the Waverley Market exhibition was one of many shows that took place around the city in 1967.[59] There was an exhibition on French artist André Derain at the Royal Scottish Academy, 'Treasures from Scottish Houses' at the Royal Scottish Museum (on Chambers Street),[60] Nicolas de Staël at the Gallery of Modern Art (Royal Botanic Garden), 'Open 100' in the David Hume Tower

Figure 14.5.
'Two Hundred Summers in a City' exhibition, interior perspective elevations for unit 6, 1967. (John L. Paterson Collection, copyright HES: https://canmore.org.uk/collection/924820)

(George Square).[61] There was also a smaller exhibition of Scottish church metalwork in the National Museum of Antiquities, and an exhibition on the works of Charles Cameron, official architect of Catherine the Great of Russia, at the English-Speaking Union (Atholl Crescent). This artistic agenda shows an outward-looking Scotland.

The New Town bicentenary coincided with the coming of age of the Edinburgh International Festival. By the 1960s, the Festival was well known and was a source of national pride. By that time, contemporaries were also conscious of their architectural heritage, and of the singularity of this great ensemble formed by the New Town. This was fully acknowledged by François Sorlin, writing in 1970, 'the New Town of Edinburgh [had] no equivalent in the world'.[62] By offering the public a 'restored' version of the city, the 1967 exhibition achieved its main aim: to raise people's awareness about the national and, indeed, international quality of their architecture. Paterson warned that, unless the New Town was protected, the alternative was the prospect of a visual celebration in 2067 entitled 'One Hundred Winters in a Wasteland'. The 1967 commemoration gave a boost to taking action about the New Town. At the first meeting of the Scottish Civic Trust, Robert Matthew urged that something had to be done about this urban heritage, and he thereafter persuaded the Edinburgh Architectural Association to carry out a condition survey of the entire area.[63] This social–architectural survey addressed the growing sense that the New Town existed as a 'milieu' which needed a detailed assessment. The costed findings and recommendations made by the Edinburgh Architectural Association were presented at the international conference held in the Assembly Rooms, on George Street, in June 1970. Action was soon taken to restore buildings, and grants were provided towards the cost of preserving buildings of merit. By December of that year the Edinburgh New Town Conservation Committee (ENTCC) was set up, jointly financed by the government and Edinburgh Corporation, and run by eighteen members representing the Corporation, the Historic Buildings Council and amenity societies.[64]

The celebrations of the New Town bicentenary and the concern for national heritage which came to prevail in the 1970s were contemporary with a revival of Scottish nationalism. Edinburgh was central to this sense of identity as the stateless nation's capital and the seat of defining, historic institutions: the Courts, the Church and the University. By contrast, this unique urban landscape, now part of a world heritage site, was largely ignored in 2017, and the City Council in Edinburgh scheduled no major display on the New Town.

Notes

Abbreviations: ECA Edinburgh City Archives, NLS National Library of Scotland, NRS National Records Office

Introduction

1. To be included on the World Heritage List, sites must be of outstanding universal value and meet at least one out of ten selection criteria. Edinburgh's inscription is for the 'Old and New Towns of Edinburgh'. See: http://whc.unesco.org/en/list/728
2. Dunedin represents the Gaelic name for Edinburgh.
3. Originally Midlothian County Buildings.
4. National Library of Scotland (NLS), RY.IV.e4 (22).
5. John Campbell of the Royal Bank to George Innes, 19 August 1749. National Records of Scotland (NRS), GD113/3/306, f. 9.
6. Soane Museum, Adam volume 9/45, 9/56 and 9/58–61.
7. Soane Museum, Adam volume 1/60 and Adam volume 32/3–7.
8. Batty Langley's 'English order' preceded James Adam's British order, and appears as plates 309 and 310 in *Ancient Masonry, Both in Theory and Practice . . .* (London, 1734–36). There were other parallels at this time: the frontispiece to the 1761 edition of Kirby's *Perspective of Architecture*, which was designed by Hogarth, shows a column making use of the Garter star and the Prince of Wales's feathers, and in 1781 one of George III's favourite architects, Henry Emlyn, came up with a design for 'The Britannic Order', which he published in his *A Proposition for a New Order in Architecture, with Rules for Drawing the Several Parts.*

Chapter 1 Edinburgh: Smart City of 1700

1. Murray Pittock, *Enlightenment in a Smart City: Edinburgh's Civic Development, 1660–1750* (Edinburgh: Edinburgh University Press, 2018).

NOTES TO CHAPTER 1

2 Jane Jacobs, *The Economy of Cities* (London: Jonathan Cape, 1970 [1969]), 88, 100; Edmund Phelps, *Mass Flourishing* (Princeton, NJ: Princeton University Press, 2013), 105.

3 American Institute of Architects, *Cities as a Lab: Designing the Innovation Economy*, 6 (2013) (http://cityminded.org/cities-lab-designing-innovation-economy-9757#).

4 Phelps, *Mass Flourishing*, 82; *The Times*, 21 June 2017, 33.

5 David McCrone and Angela Morris, 'Lords and Heritages: The Transformation of the Great Lairds of Scotland', in T.M. Devine, ed., *Scottish Elites* (Edinburgh: John Donald, 1994), 170–86; NRS GD 18/4362. For wage history, see A.J.S. Gibson and T.C. Smout, *Prices, Food and Wages in Scotland* (Cambridge: Cambridge University Press, 1995), 275–7.

6 Marguerite Wood, 'Survey of the Development of Edinburgh', *Book of the Old Edinburgh Club*, vol. 34 (1974), 23–56 (32); Laura A.M. Stewart, *Urban Politics and the British Civil Wars* (Leiden: Brill, 2006), 137.

7 Joan Dejean, *How Paris Became Paris* (New York: Bloomsbury, 2014), 132–35; Jerry White, *London in the Eighteenth Century* (London: The Bodley Head, 2012), 10; Bob Harris, *A Tale of Three Cities* (Edinburgh: John Donald, 2015), 40–2; Charles McKean, *Edinburgh: Portrait of a City* (London: Century, 1991), 6, 19; *Caledonian Mercury*, 7 January 1740; *Extracts from the Records of the Burgh of Edinburgh 1689–1701*, ed. Helen Armet (Edinburgh: Oliver and Boyd, 1962), 293; *Extracts from the Records of the Burgh of Edinburgh 1701–1718*, ed. Helen Armet (Edinburgh: Oliver and Boyd, 1967), 24, 30; NLS MS 17602 f. 25; James Ray, *A Journey Through Part of England and Scotland Along with the Army Under the Command of his Royal Highness the Duke of Cumberland* (London: Osborne, 1747), 94; Hugo Arnot, *The History of Edinburgh* (Edinburgh: West Port Books, 1998 [1779]), 194; R.A. Houston, *Social Change in the Age of Enlightenment: Edinburgh, 1660–1760* (Oxford: Clarendon Press, 1994), 169; Hamish Coghill, *Lost Edinburgh* (Edinburgh: Birlinn, 2014), 233, 30; Christopher J. Berry, *The Idea of Commercial Society in the Scottish Enlightenment* (Edinburgh: Edinburgh University Press, 2015), 2, 14; Jeremy Black, *Eighteenth-Century Britain 1688–1783* (Basingstoke: Palgrave Macmillan, 2008 [2001]), 17; R.A. Houston, 'Fire and Filth: Edinburgh's Environment, 1660–1760', *Book of the Old Edinburgh Club*, n.s. 3 (1994), 25–36 (26, 27, 33); Helen Armet, 'Notes on Rebuilding Edinburgh in the Last Quarter of the Seventeenth Century', *Book of the Old Edinburgh Club*, vol. 29 (1956), 111–42 (111); NLS MS 17602 f. 25 and Thomas Ferguson, *The Dawn of Scottish Social Welfare* (London: Nelson, 1998), 138–39, for street cleaning; Mary Cosh, *Edinburgh: The Golden Age* (Edinburgh: John Donald, 2003), 2, for a dismissive attitude to the city in the first half of the eighteenth century; Wood, 'Survey', 33; D. Bell, *Edinburgh Old Town* (Edinburgh: Tholis, 2008), 20.

8 Bob Harris and Charles McKean, *The Scottish Town in the Age of Enlightenment 1740–1820* (Edinburgh: Edinburgh University Press, 2014), 493.

9 Coghill, *Lost Edinburgh*, 53, 61; Houston, *Social Change*, 76, 107, 112; Harris and McKean, *The Scottish Town*, 59; Robert Miller, *The Municipal Buildings of Edinburgh* (Edinburgh: Printed by Order of the Town Council, 1895), 112; Armet, 'Notes on Rebuilding Edinburgh', 112–14; *Burgh Records*

1689–1701, 285–6, 293; Christopher A. Whatley and Derek Patrick, *The Scots and the Union* (Edinburgh: Edinburgh University Press, 2006), 192; Bell, *Edinburgh Old Town*, 21, 141–42; *Ancient Law and Customs of the Burghs of Scotland,* vol.2 AD 1424–1707 (Edinburgh: Scottish Burghs Record Society, 1910), 157; Edinburgh City Archives Moses Bundle VI: 162/6285, 164/6348.

10 *Proposals for Carrying on Certain Public Works in the City of Edinburgh* (NLS MS 19979), 7; A.J. Youngson, *The Making of Classical Edinburgh* (Edinburgh: Edinburgh University Press, 1988 [1966]), 1, 3, 5, 10; Edward Glaeser, *Triumph of the City* (London: Pan, 2012), 64; Peter Burke, *A Social History of Knowledge* (Cambridge: Polity, 2008 [2000]), 28.

11 Harris and McKean, *The Scottish Town*, 28, 56, 105; I.D. Whyte, 'Scottish and Irish urbanization in the seventeenth and eighteenth centuries: a comparative perspective', in S.J. Connolly, R.A. Houston and R.J. Morris, eds, *Conflict, Identity and Economic Development: Ireland and Scotland, 1600–1939* (Preston: Carnegie, 1995), 14–28 (24); Manuel de Landa, *A Thousand Years of Nonlinear History* (New York: Swerve, 1997), 19, 28; Brian Boydell, *A Dublin Musical Calendar 1700–1760* (Dublin: Irish Academic Press, 1988), 24; Bruno Latour, *Reassembling the Social: An Introduction to Actor-Network-Theory* (Oxford: Oxford University Press, 2005), 1, 30; Lindy Moore, 'Urban schooling in seventeenth and eighteenth-century Scotland', in Robert Anderson, Mark Freeman and Lindsay Paterson, eds, *The Edinburgh History of Education in Scotland* (Edinburgh: Edinburgh University Press, 2015), 79–96 (80); Phelps, *Mass Flourishing*, viii, 105.

12 McKean, *Edinburgh*, 17; Bell, *Edinburgh Old Town*, 12, 14, 16–17, 101–2; Richard Rodger, *The Transformation of Edinburgh: Land, Property and Trust in the Nineteenth Century* (Cambridge: Cambridge University Press, 2001), 14. A Scots mile was 1814 metres, about 1.125 English miles.

13 William Maitland, *History of Edinburgh* (Edinburgh, 1753), 216–17; Ray, *Journey*, 84.

14 R.A. Houston, 'The Economy of Edinburgh 1694–1763: the Evidence of the Common Good', in Connolly et al., *Conflict, Identity and Economic Development*, 54; Robert D. Anderson, Michael Lynch and Nicholas Phillipson, *The University of Edinburgh: An Illustrated History* (Edinburgh: Edinburgh University Press, 2003), 64.

15 McKean, *Edinburgh*, 15.

16 Maitland, *History of Edinburgh*, dedication; Bell, *Edinburgh Old Town*, 12, 14, 16–17; Lisa Kahler, 'Freemasonry in Edinburgh, 1721–1746: Institutions and Context', unpublished PhD thesis (University of St Andrews, 1998), 19.

17 T.C. Smout, *Scottish Trade on the Eve of Union 1660–1707* (Edinburgh: Oliver & Boyd, 1963), 132, 188; Murray Pittock, 'John Law's Theory of Money and its Roots in Scottish Culture', *Proceedings of the Society of Antiquaries of Scotland*, 133 (2003), 391–403 (396–98).

18 Thomas Piketty, *Capital*, trans. Arthur Goldhammer (Cambridge, MA: Belknap Press/Harvard University Press, 2014), 251; Berry, *Commercial Society*, 73; L.M. Cullen, 'The Scottish Exchange on London, 1673–1778', in Connolly et al., *Conflict, Identity and Economic Development*, 29, 33; Leah Leneman and Rosalind Mitchison, *Sin in the City: Sexuality and Social Control*

NOTES TO CHAPTER 1

      in Urban Scotland 1660–1780 (Edinburgh: Scottish Cultural Press, 1998), 9; S.G. Checkland, *Scottish Banking: A History, 1695–1973* (Glasgow and London: Collins, 1975), 76.

19 Edinburgh City Archives Moses Bundles VII 181/10, 12; McKean, *Edinburgh*, 99.

20 Helen Dingwall, *Late Seventeenth-Century Edinburgh: A Demographic Study* (Aldershot: Scolar Press, 1994), 9, 10, 20, 64, 71, 121, 142–3, 175, 279; H. Dingwall, *Physicians, Surgeons and Apothecaries: Medicine in Seventeenth-Century Edinburgh* (East Linton: Tuckwell Press, 1995), 20; Houston, *Social Change*, 105; Peter G. Vasey, 'The Canonmills Gunpowder Manufactory and a Newly Discovered Plan by John Adair', *Book of the Old Edinburgh Club*, ns vol. 4 (1997), 103–6 (103); Richard Leppert, *Music and Image* (Cambridge: Cambridge University Press, 1988), 9; Mark Greengrass, *Christendom Destroyed* (London: Penguin, 2015 [2014]), 136; T.M. Devine, 'The Merchant Class of the Larger Scottish Towns in the Seventeenth and Early Eighteenth Centuries', in George Gordon and Brian Dicks, eds, *Scottish Urban History* (Aberdeen: Aberdeen University Press, 1983), 92–111 (93, 96–8, 107); T.M. Devine, *Scotland's Empire 1600–1815* (London: Allen Lane, 2003), 8, 31; Helen Smailes, 'David Le Marchand's Scottish Patrons', unpublished paper (1996), 2; Richard Savile, *Bank of Scotland: A History 1695–1995* (Edinburgh: Edinburgh University Press, 1996), 11; Houston, 'Economy of Edinburgh', 48; *Edinburgh Gazette*, 6–9 November 1699; James Campbell Irons, *Leith and its Antiquities*, vol. 2 (Edinburgh: Morrison & Gibb for the subscribers, 1897), 143; White, *London*, 3.

21 Arnot, *History of Edinburgh*, 135; Ray, *Journey*, 94; Boydell, *Dublin Musical Calendar*, 24; Coghill, *Lost Edinburgh*, 16, 94, 106; Harris and McKean, *The Scottish Town*, 28, 56; Kahler, 'Freemasonry', 14, 16; Jerry Brannigan and John McShane, *Robert Burns in Edinburgh* (Glasgow: Waverley Books, 2015), 127; Houston, *Social Change*, 6; Dejean, *Paris*, 3, 4, 12; Bell, *Edinburgh Old Town*, 113.

22 Clare Jackson, *Restoration Scotland, 1660–1690* (Woodbridge: the Boydell Press, 2003), 31.

23 Aonghus MacKechnie, 'The Earl of Perth's Chapel of 1688 at Drummond Castle and the Roman Catholic Architecture of James VII', *Architectural Heritage*, 25 (2014), 107–31 (115, 127n); Coghill, *Lost Edinburgh*, 80, 118; Houston, *Social Change*, 51–2, 205; *Book of the Old Edinburgh Club*, vol. 11 (Edinburgh: T & A Constable, 1922), 140; Jackson, *Restoration Scotland, 1660–1690*, 21; Greengrass, *Christendom Destroyed*, 245; Dejean, *Paris*, 123–4; Checkland, *Scottish Banking*, 28, 69; Douglas Watt, *The Price of Scotland: Darien, Union and the Wealth of Nations* (Edinburgh: Luath Press, 2007), 13, 83, 211.

24 Daniel Defoe, *A Tour Through the Whole Island of Great Britain*, ed. Pat Rogers (Harmondsworth: Penguin, 1971 [1724–26]), 575, 578, 581; Arnot, *History of Edinburgh*, 318–19. For the effect of the disappearance of the Scottish burgh mercat cross as a sign of authority and contested authority, see Harris and McKean, *The Scottish Town*, 105; Ray, *Journey*, 82.

25 See James Wilson's *The Last Speech and Dying Words of the Cross of Edinburgh*, NLS APS 4.83.4; Bob Harris, 'Landowners and Urban Society in Eighteenth-Century Scotland', *Scottish Historical Review*, 92:2 (2013), 231–54 (237).

26 Alastair Mann, *James VII: Duke and King of Scots, 1633–1701* (Edinburgh: John Donald, 2014), 127–9; Allan I. Macinnes, 'William of Orange- "Disaster for Scotland?"', in Esther Mijers and David Onnekirk, eds., *Redefining William III: The Impact of the King-Stadtholder in International Context* (Aldershot: Ashgate, 2007), 201–23 (205–6); Watt, *Darien*, 13, 17.

27 Savile, *Bank of Scotland*, 11.

28 Mann, *James VII*, 122, 129, 137, 138, 139, 163, 164; David Allan, 'The Universities and the Scottish Enlightenment', in Anderson et al., *Education in Scotland*, 101; Stuart Harris, 'New Light on the First New Town', *Book of the Old Edinburgh Club* ns 2 (1992), 1–13 (1); Wood, 'Survey', 33.

29 Greengrass, *Christendom Destroyed*, 187; Archibald Pitcairne, *The Phanaticks*, ed. John MacQueen (Edinburgh: Scottish Text Society, 2012), 158.

30 *The Autobiography of Sir Robert Sibbald* (Edinburgh, 1833), 13, 41; Royal College of Physicians of Edinburgh, *The Sir Robert Sibbald Physic Garden* (Edinburgh: Stationery Office, 1997), 3–4; A.D.C. Simpson, 'Sir Robert Sibbald: The Founder of the College', *Proceedings of the Royal College of Physicians of Edinburgh Tercentenary Congress 1981* (Edinburgh: Royal College of Physicians of Edinburgh, 1982), 61–3; Morrice McCrae, *Physicians and Society* (Edinburgh: John Donald, 2007), 7–10; Helen Dingwall et al., *Scottish Medicine: An Illustrated History* (Edinburgh: Birlinn, 2011), 53; *Burgh Records 1689–1701*, 118; Priscilla Minay, 'Eighteenth and Early Nineteenth Century Edinburgh Seedsmen and Nurserymen', *Book of the Old Edinburgh Club* ns 1 (1991), 7–27 (7); E. Patricia Dennison, *Holyrood and Canongate: A Thousand Years of History* (Edinburgh: Birlinn, 2005), 99; Douglas Duncan, *Thomas Ruddiman* (Edinburgh and London: Oliver & Boyd, 1965), 24.

31 *The Edinburgh Courant*, 25–28 July 1707; *Burgh Records 1681–1689*, liii; Maitland, *History of Edinburgh*, 336–9; Stephen W. Brown, 'Newspapers and Magazines' in Stephen W. Brown and Warren MacDougall, eds, *The History of the Book in Scotland*, vol. 2 (Edinburgh: Edinburgh University Press, 2012), 354; Arnot, *History of Edinburgh*, 317; John H. Jamieson, 'The Sedan Chair in Edinburgh', *Book of the Old Edinburgh Club*, vol. 9 (1916), 177–234; Vanessa Brett, *Bertrand's Toyshop in Bath Luxury Retailing 1685–1765* (Wetherby: Oblong, 2014), 111; T.C. Smout, *Scottish Trade on the Eve of Union 1600–1707* (Edinburgh and London: Oliver & Boyd, 1963), 10; Dejean, *Paris*, 125–6; White, *London*, 10; Edinburgh City Archives Moses Bundle VI: 164/6324, 6347.

32 Edinburgh City Archives SL 225/3/1; SL 225/3/2/1/1–50; SL 3/2/2; SL 225.

33 J. Gilhooley, *A Directory of Edinburgh in 1752* (Edinburgh: Edinburgh University Press, 1988), 58, 65–9, 71, 75, 77, 80; Stana Nenadic, 'Necessities: Food and Clothing in the Long Eighteenth Century', in Elizabeth Foyster and Christopher A. Whatley, eds, *A History of Everyday Life in Scotland, 1600–1800* (Edinburgh: Edinburgh University Press, 2010), 137–63 (148); Brannigan and McShane, *Robert Burns*, 84–5; *Book of the Old Edinburgh Club*, vol. 11, 78–9; Alexander Law, *Education in Edinburgh in the Eighteenth Century* (London: University of London Press, 1965), 11, 59; Elizabeth Einberg, *William Hogarth: A Complete Catalogue of the Paintings* (New Haven, CT: Yale University Press, 2016), 19.

34 Roger L. Emerson, *Academic Patronage in the Scottish Enlightenment* (Edinburgh: Edinburgh University Press, 2008), 3.
35 Clé Lesger, *The Rise of the Amsterdam Market and Information Exchange*, trans. J.C. Grayson (Aldershot: Ashgate, 2006), 139n, 140, 246–8.
36 NLS MS 2233 f. 28; Youngson, *Classical Edinburgh*, 4, 10.

Chapter 2 Scotland's Planned Towns and Villages

1 J.M. Houston, 'Village Planning in Scotland, 1745–1845', *Advancement of Science*, 5 (1948), 129–32; Douglas Lockhart, ed., *Scottish Planned Villages*, Scottish History Society, 5th series, vol. 16 (Edinburgh: Scottish History Society, 2012).
2 Although the 'authority value' of some Roman sites was retained; for instance at Cramond, where the church occupies a location within the Roman fort. Scotland witnessed three Roman invasions: c.70–88, 140–65 and 208–11.
3 John Gifford, *The Buildings of Scotland: Fife* (New Haven, CT: Yale University Press, 1988), 357.
4 Ian Campbell, 'Planning for Pilgrims: St Andrews as the Second Rome', *Innes Review*, 64:1 (2013), 1–22.
5 N.M. McQ Holmes, 'The Evidence of Finds for the Circulation and Use of Coins in Medieval Scotland', *Proceedings of the Society of Antiquaries of Scotland*, 134 (2004), 242–3.
6 Richard Oram, *David I: The King who made Scotland* (Stroud: Tempest, 2004).
7 P.J. Dixon et al., *The Origins of the Settlements at Kelso and Peebles, Scottish Borders*, Scottish Archaeological Internet Report, 2 (2003), 50.
8 Formalised town plans required standard land allotments, or 'lots' (cf. French *parcelle*), per house – for which see Tait's work, referenced below.
9 Recording a property sale to Bishop Archibald of Moray (1253–98), proclaimed at Berwick's tolbooth: see *Registrum Episcopatus Moraviensis* [etc.] (Edinburgh: Bannatyne Club, 1837), 143.
10 David Laing, 'A Contemporary Account of the Earl of Hertford's Second Expedition to Scotland [etc.]', *Proceedings of the Society of Antiquaries of Scotland*, 1, part 3 (1855), 273–4.
11 Colin Martin and Richard Oram, 'Medieval Roxburgh: A Preliminary Assessment of the Burgh and its Locality', *Proceedings of the Society of Antiquaries of Scotland*, 137 (2007), 357–404.
12 John Marquess of Bute et al., *The Arms of the Baronial and Police Burghs of Scotland* (Edinburgh: William Blackwood, 1903), plate facing p. 278. David relocated to Kelso his 15-year-old religious establishment from Selkirk, which he had founded c.1113.
13 Wendy B. Stevenson, 'The Monastic Presence: Berwick in the Twelfth and Thirteenth Centuries', in *The Scottish Medieval Town*, ed. M. Lynch et al. (Edinburgh: John Donald, 1988), 99; Northumberland County Council and English Heritage, *Northumberland Extensive Burgh Survey: Berwick-upon-Tweed* (Morpeth, 2009); Eric Cambridge et al., 'Berwick and Beyond: Medieval Religious Establishments [etc.]', *Archaeologia Aeliana*, series 5, 29 (2011), 33–93.

14 Joseph Bain, ed., *Calendar of Documents Relating to Scotland Preserved in Her Majesty's Public Record Office, London*, vol. 2 (Edinburgh: Register House, 1881), 332–3. Spade's Mire is discussed in K.G. White, 'The Spades Mire, Berwick-upon-Tweed', *Proceedings of the Society of Antiquaries of Scotland*, 96 (1962), 355–60.

15 https://flemish.wp.st-andrews.ac.uk/2014/01/25/berwick-upon-tweed-and-the-torching-of-the-red-hall/ (accessed 15 May 2018).

16 David P. Bowler et al., *Perth: The Archaeology and Development of a Scottish Burgh* (Perth: Tayside and Fife Archaeological Committee, 2004).

17 Robin Tait, 'Configuration and Dimensions of Burgage Plots in the Burgh of Edinburgh', *Proceedings of the Society of Antiquaries of Scotland*, 136 (2006), 297–310.

18 Francis M. Cowe, 'The Street Names of Medieval Berwick', *Berwick Bulletin*, 25 June, 1980.

19 Frederick Sheldon, *History of Berwick-Upon-Tweed* (Edinburgh: Adam and Charles Black, 1849), 44. https://books.google.co.uk/books?id=oQwNAAAAYAAJ&printsec=frontcover&source=gbs_ge_summary_r&hl=en#v=onepage&q=circular&f=false (accessed May 2018).

20 Cowe, 'Street Names of Medieval Berwick'.

21 The continuation of Wallace Green beyond the wall, at Low Greens, is shown on John Wood's map of 1822: https://maps.nls.uk/view/74400014 (accessed May 2018).

22 Bain, *Calendar of Documents*, 310.

23 A wall evidently existed by 1296 (see Sheldon, *History of Berwick-upon-Tweed*); and if Barbour is to be believed, it was serviceable, though evidence for this is conflicting. The defences were rebuilt or strengthened directly afterwards by the English. John Barbour, *The Bruce*, ed. A.A.M. Duncan (Edinburgh: Canongate, 1997), 620, 636.

24 Cowe, 'Street Names of Medieval Berwick'.

25 The first bridge was swept away in 1199, but quickly replaced. Whether the initial intention was to connect Scotland to England, or to a temporarily extended Scotland (David had annexed northern England, from Newcastle to Clitheroe), is unclear.

26 Rev. Joseph Stevenson, ed., *Documents Illustrative of the History of Scotland* [etc.], 2 vols (Edinburgh: Register House, 1870), vol. 2, 153. A semi-circular layout exists at Palace Green, but it seems too simplistic to suggest this is a boundary relict of 'la Roundele'.

27 Joseph Stephenson (trans.), *Mediaeval Chronicles of Scotland: Chronicle of Melrose; Chronicle of Holyrood* (Dyfed: Llanerch Enterprises, 1988), 122.

28 Northumberland County Council and English Heritage, *Northumberland Extensive Burgh Survey: Berwick-upon-Tweed* (Morpeth, 2009), 5.

29 http://www.bl.uk/onlinegallery/onlineex/mapsviews/mapgb; http://maps.nls.uk/scotland/rec/127 (accessed December 2017).

30 Its construction was to be overseen by former Bordeaux mayor Sir Richard le Waleys. It might have been gridded on the bastide model both knew from France and introduced by Edward to conquered Wales (e.g. at Flint).

31 Joe Donnelly, 'An Open Economy: The Berwick Shipping Trade, 1311–1373', *Scottish Historical Review* 96:1 (2017), 1–31 (3).

NOTES TO CHAPTER 2

32 Marcus Merriman, *The Rough Wooings: Mary Queen of Scots 1542–1551* (East Linton: Tuckwell Press, 2000), 23.
33 Perhaps the same process occurred at similarly crown-less St Mary's, Dundee, the burgh having been twice devastated by English soldiers ('Dresden-ed', according to Merriman, *The Rough Wooings*, 361), in the 1540s and 1650s.
34 Anne Turner Simpson and Sylvia Stevenson, *Duns: The Archaeological Implications of Development* (Scottish Burgh Survey, 1981), 1.
35 Laing, 'A Contemporary Account', 278–9.
36 NRS, RHP85686.
37 John Gifford, *The Buildings of Scotland: Highland and Islands* (New Haven, CT: Yale University Press, 2002 [1992]), 368.
38 NLS. Acc9769, personal papers, 4/1p.
39 K. Cruft et al., *The Buildings of Scotland: Borders* (New Haven, CT: Yale University Press, 2006), 613, 621.
40 Similarly strategic urban developments or pairings took place elsewhere. For instance, Bo'ness was developed in the seventeenth century as Hamilton's east-facing commercial port.
41 Edinburgh City Archives, Charter no.104.
42 John Hill Burton et al., eds, *The Register of the Privy Council of Scotland*, 37 vols (Edinburgh: Register House, 1877–1970) 3rd series, vol. 14, 22, 86–7.
43 Hon. William H.L. Melville, ed., *Leven and Melville Papers* [etc.] (Edinburgh: Bannatyne Club, 1843), 626.
44 NLS ms 7014, f. 13.
45 Aonghus MacKechnie, 'A King, Catholics and Canongate Kirk', *History Scotland*, 7:6 (2007), 22–8.
46 John Mason, 'The Weavers of Picardy', *Book of the Old Edinburgh Club*, vol. 25 (1945), 1–33. The block was rebuilt to Robert Burn's similar design in the 1800s following John Baxter's unsuccessful bid for the opportunity.
47 John Gifford, *The Buildings of Scotland: Edinburgh* (New Haven, CT: Yale University Press, 1984), 172–5, 233–5.
48 Ibid., 394.

CHAPTER 3 THE DESIGNS OF THE 6TH EARL OF MAR

1 [John Erskine, 6th and 11th earl of Mar], 'The Legacy of the 6th Earl of Mar', transcript in the Mar and Kellie Collection, Alloa, Scotland, 37: includes the description of Edinburgh; [John Erskine, 6th and 11th earl of Mar], '*Projets d'un palais pour les roys de France pres de L'Etoile*', MS 728.82 (acc. no. 496/1), unpaginated, Westminster Public Library, England: includes the description of Paris.
2 Margaret Stewart, *The Architectural, Landscape and Constitutional Plans of the Earl of Mar, 1700–32* (Dublin: Four Courts Press, 2016), 292–6, 299–304.
3 [Mar], '*Projets*'.
4 Thierry Mariage, *The World of André Le Nôtre*, trans. Graham Larkin (Philadelphia, PA: , 1998), 86–7.
5 [Mar], 'Legacy', 9.

6 'Examen et comparaison de la grandeur de Paris, de Londres, et de quelques autres Villes du Mondes . . . Par M. Delisle l'Aine', in *Histoire de l'Académie royale des sciences, avec les mémoires de mathématique et de physique* (Paris: Martin, Coignard, Guerin, 1725), 48–57: www.biodiversitylibrary. org/page/27658255#page/218/mode/1up [accessed 5 February 2018]

7 'Remarques sur un Ecrit de M. Davall, qui se trouve dans les Transactions Philosophiques de la Societé Royale de Londres, n°402, an. 1728, touchant le comparison qu'a fait M. Delisle, de la grandeur de Paris avec celle de Londres . . . 1725, p. 48, Par M. De Mairan', in *Histoire de l'Académie royale des sciences, année 1730* (Paris: Imprimerie Royale, 1732), 573: /www. biodiversitylibrary.org/item/22523#page/729/mode/1up.

8 Ibid., 573.

9 Mariage, *The World of André Le Nôtre*, ix, 8.

10 Andrew Fletcher of Saltoun, 'Second Discourse' (1698) and *An Account of a Conversation Concerning a Right Regulation of Governments for the Common Good of Mankind . . .* (1703), in *Fletcher of Saltoun: Selected Political Writings and Speeches of Andrew Fletcher of Saltoun*, ed. David Daiches (Edinburgh: Scottish Academic Press, 1979), 27–66, 104–35.

11 Stewart, *Earl of Mar*, 160–1.

12 [Mar], '*Projets*'.

13 W. Forbes Gray, 'The Royal Exchange and Other City Improvements', *Book of the Old Edinburgh Club*, 1938, 170–2.

14 [Mar], 'Legacy', 26.

15 J. Reid, *New Lights on Old Edinburgh* (Edinburgh, 1894), 20–1.

16 Ibid., 20–1.

17 A.J. Youngson, *The Making of Classical Edinburgh 1750–1840* (Edinburgh: Edinburgh University Press, 2002 [1966]), 4–12.

18 Ibid., 11.

19 Stewart, *Earl of Mar*, 48–9, 298–9.

Chapter 4 Georgian New Towns of Glasgow and Edinburgh

1 Daniel Defoe, *A Tour Through the Whole Island of Great Britain* (London and New Haven, CT: Yale University Press, 1991 [1724–6]), 331–1.

2 National Records of Scotland (NRS), CS232/P/3/18 – George Paterson v John Douglas, 1762.

3 NRS, GD220/5/831, Duke of Montrose, 6 February 1720.

4 Robert Renwick, ed., *Extracts from Burgh Records of Glasgow, 1708–1738* (Glasgow: Corporation of Glasgow, 1909), 130–2.

5 Ibid., 482.

6 Ibid., 414.

7 Edinburgh City Archives, Town Council Minutes, 2 November 1720.

8 Edinburgh City Archives, Mary Chapel Minutes, 1755–71, 4 August 1759.

9 NLS, MS16680, f.186.

10 Kitty Cruft and Anthony Lewis, 'James Craig: A Biographical Sketch', in Kitty Cruft and Andrew Fraser, eds, *James Craig, The Ingenious Architect of the New Town of Edinburgh* (Edinburgh: Mercat Press, 1995), 1–12.

NOTES TO CHAPTER 4

11 Edinburgh City Archives, SL34/4/1, Mary's Chapel, *Book of Apprentices 1706–1774*: 'James Craig a boy in Geo Watsons' hospital was on 7th May 1755 bound app: to D. Patrick Jameson mason for 6 years after said date: app fee £20 star from & c as usual from such Indentures – the Indenture being this 16th June 1759 presented to a General Meeting It is by order thereof entered but with condition that the 6 years for the purpose of being free of this incorporation shall only commence from this date (16 June 1758)'.
12 Edinburgh City Archives, James Craig, South Canongate Road, 1765, Middle District Road Committee Minutes, Trunk.
13 Edinburgh City Archives, Sederunt Book of the Committee appointed by the Town Council of Edinburgh for Forwarding the Scheme of a Communication with the Fields on the North of the City by a Bridge over the Nor' Loch, 7 November 1764 to 31st January 1770, 10 December 1766.
14 Writers to the Signet Library, *Information for John Deas v Lord Provost, Hume, Young, Trotter*, 4 March 1773.
15 Writers to the Signet Library, *Duplies for Lord Provost to Replies for Feuars*, 30 April 1774.
16 *Caledonian Mercury*, 20 June 1767.
17 Edinburgh City Archives, Sederunt Book of the Committee appointed by the Town Council of Edinburgh for Forwarding the Scheme of a Communication with the Fields on the North of the City by a Bridge over the Nor' Loch, 7 November 1764 to 31 January 1770, 10 December 1766.
18 Edinburgh City Archives, McLeod Bundle, Miscellaneous Petitions to Edinburgh Town Council, 1 April 1654–31 December 1839, C3, Miscellaneous Council Papers 1765–9.
19 Anthony Lewis and John Lowrey, 'James Craig: Architect of the First New Town of Edinburgh', *Architectural Heritage*, 5:1 (1994), 39–49.
20 Yale University Library, Beinecke Library, Sir John Pringle, 11 January 1771, L391.
21 Advocates Library, Arniston, vol. 111, f. 25: *Information for George Heriot's Hospital, Pursuers against John Cleland, later Gardener to Old Life's Yard, now residing in Linlithgow and Walter Ferguson, writer in Edinburgh, Defenders*, 16 April 1773, 4.
22 It is not clear why Shooter's Hill was chosen, but presumably the ground was available for development and the landowners wanted to see the proposed New Town.
23 *Bath Chronicle*, 6 November 1766.
24 *Derby Mercury*, 16 January 1767.
25 *Derby Mercury*, 27 March 1767.
26 *London Evening Post*, 28 March 1767.
27 T. Mowl and B. Earnshaw, *John Wood, Architect of Obsession* (Bath: Millstream Books, 1988), 165–70.
28 Anthony Lewis, 'Archival Sources for the Builders of the Library and Hall of the Royal College of Physicians of Edinburgh, 1776–1782', *Scottish Archives*, 14 (2008).
29 *Caledonian Mercury*, 14 April 1781, 28 April 1781.

30 Edinburgh City Archives, Register of Plans of the City, 1784–1785, Plan 10, New town with a circus by James Craig, Plan 14, Another plan of the extended royalty with a circus – with sections and elevations, 006B.
31 *Caledonian Mercury*, 20 June 1781.
32 Iain Gordon Brown and Anthony Lewis, 'David Allan's Portrait of James Craig and its Documentary Significance', in Cruft and Fraser, *James Craig, The Ingenious Architect of the New Town of Edinburgh*, 66–77.
33 D. Lieberman, 'Legal Needs of a Commercial Society: the jurisprudence of Lord Kames', in I. Hont and M. Ignatieff, eds, *Wealth and Virtue: The Shaping of Political Economy in the Scottish Enlightenment* (Cambridge: Cambridge University Press, 1983).
34 T.C. Smout, 'The Landowner and the Planned Village in Scotland, 1730–1830', in N.T. Phillipson and R. Mitchison, eds, *Scotland in the Age of Improvement* (Edinburgh: Edinburgh University Press, 1970), 93–4.

Chapter 5 Royal Welcomes in Edinburgh New Town

1 The royal Palace of Holyroodhouse was too much in disrepair to allow for an overnight stay.
2 An overview of Scottish triumphal entries can be found in Douglas Gray, 'The Royal Entry in Sixteenth-Century Scotland', in Sally Mapstone and Juliette Wood, eds, *The Rose and the Thistle. Essays on the Culture of Late Medieval and Renaissance Scotland* (East Linton: Tuckwell Press, 1998), 10–37; Giovanna Guidicini, 'Scottishness on Stage: Creating and Performing Scotland's National Identity During Triumphal Entries in the 16th and 17th Centuries', in Jodi A. Campbell, Elizabeth Ewan and Heather Parker, eds, *The Shaping of Scottish Identities: Family, Nation, and the World Beyond* (Guelph: Centre for Scottish Studies, 2011), 113–27. The entry organised in 1536 for Madeleine of Valois had to be cancelled when the young queen died prematurely; see Robert Lindsay, *The Chronicles of Scotland*, ed. John Graham Dalyell, vol. 1 (Edinburgh: George Ramsay, 1814), 108–11. Also, on the civic festivity organised in 1558 in Edinburgh for Mary Queen of Scots' French wedding, see Sarah Carpenter and Graham A. Runnals, 'The Entertainments at the Marriage of Mary Queen of Scots and the French Dauphin François, 1558: Paris and Edinburgh', *Medieval English Theatre*, 22 (2000), 145–61.
3 On Roman triumphs, see Mary Beard, *The Roman Triumph* (Cambridge, MA: Harvard University Press, 2007), 42–106, 219–56; on their medieval and early modern counterparts, see Michael McCormick, *Eternal Victory: Triumphal Rulership in Late Antiquity, Byzantium, and the Early Medieval West* (Cambridge, MA: Cambridge University Press, 1990), 131; Gordon Kipling, *Enter the King: Theatre, Liturgy, and Ritual in the Medieval Civic Triumph* (Oxford: Clarendon Press, 1998), 6–48.
4 Patricia E. Dennison and Michael Lynch, 'Crown, Capital, and Metropolis. Edinburgh and Canongate: The Rise of a Capital and an Urban Court', *Journal of Urban History*, 32 (2005), 22–4.
5 Guidicini, 'Scottishness on Stage', 113–19.

NOTES TO CHAPTER 5

6   David Calderwood, *The History of the Kirk of Scotland*, vol. 7 (Edinburgh: Wodrow Society, 1845), 245.
7   Alex Tyrrell, 'The Queen's "Little Trip": The Royal Visit to Scotland in 1842', *Scottish Historical Review* 82:213 (2003), 48–9.
8   Thomas D. Lauder, *Memorial of the Royal Progress in Scotland* (Edinburgh: Adam and Charles Black, 1843), 92, 10; John Plunkett, *Queen Victoria: First Media Monarch* (Oxford: Oxford University Press, 2003), 40–1.
9   Robert Mudie, *A Historical Account of His Majesty's Visit to Scotland* (Edinburgh: Oliver & Boyd, 1822), 196.
10 See, for example, Thomas Morer's 'Short Account of Scotland' (1715) in P. Hume Brown, ed., *Early Travellers in Scotland* (Edinburgh: David Douglas, 1891), 266–90.
11 Lindsay, *Chronicles of Scotland*, vol. 2, 377.
12 John Prebble, *The King's Jaunt: George IV in Scotland* (London: Harper Collins, 1988), 44–6.
13 Mudie, *His Majesty's Visit to Scotland*, 109.
14 Appearing, for example, during the celebrations for James VI and I's arrival in 1617. 'Excerpts from MS. Master of Works Accounts at Register House. Vol. 15, 1616–9, Edinburgh Castle, etc.' as mentioned in Anna J. Mill, *Mediaeval Plays in Scotland* (London: Benjamin Blom, 1924), 345.
15 Andrew Lincoln, *Walter Scott and Modernity* (Edinburgh: Edinburgh University Press, 2007), 1–9; Steven Parissien, *George IV, The Great Entertainment* (London: John Murray, 2001), 321–5. The tartan as a politically meaningful attire is also analysed in Prebble, *The King's Jaunt*, 73–4 and 268–9; and in Kenneth McNeil, *Scotland, Britain, Empire: Writing the Highlands, 1760–1860* (Columbus, OH: Ohio State University Press, 2007), 80–1.
16 This printed pamphlet was nominally anonymous, but Sir Walter Scott is its acknowledged author. Walter Scott, *Hints Addressed to the Inhabitants of Edinburgh and Others, in Prospect of His Majesty's Visit, by an Old Citizen* (Edinburgh: William Blackwood, Waugh and Innes, and John Robertson, 1822), 6–7.
17 On the social, cultural and political reasons behind the construction of the New Town, see A.J. Youngson, *The Making of Classical Edinburgh 1750–1840* (Edinburgh: Edinburgh University Press, 1966), 1–17; and Ian H. Adams, *The Making of Urban Scotland* (Montreal: Croom Helm, 1978), 73–7. On the decline of the Old Town, see Ian Campbell and Margaret Stewart, 'The Evolution of the Medieval and Renaissance City', in Brian Edwards and Paul Jenkins, eds, *Edinburgh: the Making of a Capital City* (Edinburgh: Edinburgh University Press, 2005), 33–5.
18 Mark Dorrian, 'The King and the City: On the Iconology of George IV in Edinburgh', *Edinburgh Architecture Research*, 30 (2006), 32.
19 Charles McKean, 'Twinning Cities: Modernisation versus Improvement in the Two Towns of Edinburgh', in Edwards and Jenkins, *Edinburgh: the Making of a Capital City*, 57–9.
20 Dorothy Bell, *Edinburgh Old Town: the Forgotten Nature of an Urban Form* (Edinburgh: Tholis, 2008), 91–5, 111–22; Lincoln, *Walter Scott and Modernity*, 11–14.

21. James Buist, *National Record of the Visit of Queen Victoria to Scotland* (Perth: Perth Printing Company, 1842), 52.
22. Mudie, *His Majesty's Visit to Scotland*, 106.
23. Ibid., 107.
24. Lauder, *Memorial of the Royal Progress in Scotland*, 97–8.
25. Ibid., 99.
26. Queen Victoria, *Leaves from the Journal of our Lives in the Highlands, 1848–61* (Edinburgh, 1868), reprint ed. Arthur Helps (New York: Cambridge University Press, 2010), 4.
27. Youngson, *The Making of Classical Edinburgh*, 4–12. For a discussion of the Anglophile agenda of the Edinburgh New Town design and organisation, see McKean, 'Twinning Cities', 46–7. Urban improvements as metaphors for social modernisation in Scottish New Towns are also discussed in Bob Harris and Charles McKean, *The Scottish Town in the Age of the Enlightenment, 1740–1820* (Edinburgh: Edinburgh University Press, 2014), 78–84.
28. Mudie, *His Majesty's Visit to Scotland*, 125–6.
29. Ibid., 34.
30. Ibid., 104.
31. Lauder, *Memorial of the Royal Progress in Scotland*, i–v.
32. Alasdair R. MacDonald, 'The Triumph of Protestantism: The Burgh Council of Edinburgh and the Entry of Mary Queen of Scots, 2 September 1561', *Innes Review*, 48:1 (1977), 75–6.
33. Mudie, *His Majesty's Visit to Scotland*, 18–19.
34. Prebble, *The King's Jaunt*, 188–9.
35. John G. Lockhart, *Memoirs of the Life of Sir Walter Scott* (Edinburgh: Adam and Charles Black, 1852), 481.
36. Lauder, *Memorial of the Royal Progress in Scotland*, 101. On Peel's reasons to sabotage the organisation of the welcome, see Tyrrell, 'The Queen's "Little Trip"', 53–5.
37. Lauder, *Memorial of the Royal Progress in Scotland*, 102.
38. Mudie, *His Majesty's Visit to Scotland*, 107.
39. Queen Victoria, *Leaves from the Journal of our Lives in the Highlands*, 8.
40. Lauder, *Memorial of the Royal Progress in Scotland*, 142.
41. Mudie, *His Majesty's Visit to Scotland*, 22.
42. Lauder, *Memorial of the Royal Progress in Scotland*, 130.
43. On entertainment trumping historical accuracy, see Parissien, *George IV, The Great Entertainment*, 326.
44. Lincoln, *Walter Scott and Modernity*, 82–6.
45. Giovanna Guidicini, 'Municipal Perspective, Royal Expectations, and the Use of Public Space: The Case of the West Port, Edinburgh 1503–1633', *Architectural Heritage*, 22 (2011), 44.
46. The position of the enlarged civic border is visible in *The Great Reform Act Plans and Reports* (London: House of Commons, 1832).
47. Mudie, *His Majesty's Visit to Scotland*, 105.
48. Lauder, *Memorial of the Royal Progress in Scotland*, 121–2.

Chapter 6 Craft Businesses in Edinburgh New Town

1. 'An Account of a Scheme for Enlarging and Improving the City of Edinburgh and for Adorning it With Certain Public Buildings and other Useful Works', *Scots Magazine*, August 1752, 369–79 (375).
2. A.J. Youngson, *The Making of Classical Edinburgh 1750–1840* (Edinburgh: Edinburgh University Press, 1966) provides details.
3. David Scott Mitchell, 'The Development of the Architectural Iron Founding Industry in Scotland', PhD Thesis (University of Edinburgh, 2013).
4. Edinburgh Dean of Guild Court, Box 1782/24 (ECA).
5. Edinburgh Dean of Guild Court, Box 1809/11.
6. Edinburgh Dean of Guild Court, Box 1770/12, 1777/10, 1787/22, 1792/2.
7. Alyssa Jean Popiel, *A Capital View: The Art of Edinburgh* (Edinburgh: Birlinn, 2014), 43.
8. *Scotsman*, 11 December 1824.
9. *Aberdeen Journal*, 21 May 1806; *Caledonian Mercury*, 2 August 1806. Joe Rock, 'John Steell, father and son, sculptors'. Online at: https://sites.google.com/site/joerocksresearchpages/john-steell-father-and-son-sculptors.
10. National Archives of Scotland, CS96/415/1, sequestration of John Steele, gilder and dealer in prints, Edinburgh. Sederunt books 1819–25.
11. *Caledonian Mercury*, 8 October 1838.
12. R.E. Graves, revised by Robin L. Woodward, 'Steell, Sir John Robert (1804–1891)', *Oxford Dictionary of National Biography* (2004).
13. *Scotsman*, 20 January 1827.
14. Ibid., 13 May 1826.
15. *Edinburgh Post Office Directory*, 1833–4.
16. *Scotsman*, 17 April 1833.
17. Edinburgh Dean of Guild Court, Box 1807/26.
18. Edinburgh Dean of Guild Court, Box 1817/111, 9 October 1817.
19. Edinburgh Dean of Guild Court, Box 1824/144, 11 November 1824.
20. *Scotsman*, 21 August 1824.
21. Ibid., 16 April 1823.
22. Ibid., 14 April 1827.
23. National Portrait Gallery, British Artists' Suppliers, 1650–1950, online resource: 'John Taylor (1802–1853)'; *Scotsman*, 20 August 1851.
24. 'Extensive Robbery', *Scotsman*, 20 January 1830; Death Notice and 'Sale of Gold and Silver Watches, Silver Plate and Jewellery at no. 11 George Street', *Scotsman*, 18 March 1846.
25. Stephen Jackson, 'William Trotter, Cabinetmaker, Entrepreneur and Lord Provost, 1772–1833', *Book of the Old Edinburgh Club*, vol. 6 (2005), 73–90.
26. London Metropolitan Archives, Sun Alliance Insurance Records, 1792, vol. 345, policy 572037.
27. Francis Bamford, 'A Dictionary of Edinburgh Wrights and Furniture Makers, 1660–1840', *Furniture History*, 19 (1983), 1–137 (115–16).
28. Edinburgh Dean of Guild Court, Box 1824/61, 22 April 1824.
29. *Scotsman*, 12 December 1857, obituary; National Library of Scotland, MS Acc.7603, records of Dowell's Ltd, Auctioneers, Edinburgh, introduction.

30. *Scotsman*, 3 January 1824, lists the 'joiners shop', then occupied by Dowell, for sale. It is described as a coach-house and stable with a 40-foot frontage.
31. NRS CS96/452, Sequestration of James Dowell, Cabinetmaker and Upholsterer, Edinburgh, 1829–31.
32. *Scotsman*, 24 May 1828.
33. *Scotsman*, 12 December 1857.
34. See, for example, advertised sale, *Scotsman*, 30 May 1832.
35. NRS CS96/204, James Watson, Cabinetmaker in Edinburgh, Wages Book 1844–52.
36. *Scotsman*, 2 July 1851.
37. *Post Office Directory* entries show his business at 89 George Street for a few years, then 145 George Street, finally settling at 121 George Street.
38. Despite the sequestration, the business was run as a going concern and sold on that basis by the Trustees. After Watson & Co. ceased trading, the premises at 121 George Street were occupied by another cabinetmaking firm called R. Simpson. *Edinburgh Post Office Directory*, 1853–4.
39. NRS CS96/204, 64, James Watson, Cabinetmaker in Edinburgh, Wages Book 1844–52.
40. Ibid., 91.
41. Edinburgh Dean of Guild Court, Box 1800/1*.
42. *Edinburgh and Leith Directory to July 1800*.
43. On these later suburban developments, see Richard Rodger, *The Transformation of Edinburgh: Land, Property and Trust in the Nineteenth Century* (Cambridge: Cambridge University Press, 2001).
44. For more information on Hamilton & Inches and their craftsmen and women today, see 'Craft conversations' in the project website for the 2013–16 Leverhulme-funded project 'Artisans and the Craft Economy in Scotland c.1780–1914', which has informed the writing of this chapter: www.artisansinscotland.wordpress.com.

Chaper 7 Edinburgh as a Communications Hub

1. *Statistical Account of Scotland*, 1799. See https://stataccscot.edina.ac.uk/static/statacc/dist/viewer/osa-vol6-Parish_record_for_Edinburgh_in_the_county_of_Edinburgh_in_volume_6_of_account_1/?search=Edinburgh.
2. *Edinburgh and Leith Directory, 1799*, 6–15. October, November and June were the most popular months for fairs. See https://digitial.nls.uk/directories/browse/archive/83157225. Subsequent references to 1799–1800 relate to this volume. Elsewhere, subsequent consultation of Edinburgh and Leith Directories is based on digital copies in the National Library of Scotland, and volumes held in Edinburgh Central Library and University of Edinburgh Centre for Research Collections. I am indebted to the staff in each for their assistance in making volumes available.
3. *Williamson's Directory for the City of Edinburgh, Canongate, Leith and Suburbs 1773–74*, online at: http://digital.nls.uk/directories/browse/archive/83036363.
4. A full price day return currently costs £24.70 (2019).

NOTES TO CHAPTER 7

5   *Williamson's Directory 1773–74*, 111–13; *Edinburgh and Leith Directory to July 1800*, 50–4.
6   The cost of a ticket was £1 to Berwick, £3.77 to York and £7.88 to London (equivalent to £940 in 2019 prices!).
7   *Old Statistical Account* and the *New Statistical Account of Scotland* both make reference to turnpikes and the nature of road transport in a number of parishes.
8   E.P. Thompson, 'Time, work-discipline, and industrial capitalism', *Past & Present*, 38 (1967), 56–97.
9   F.M.L. Thompson 'Nineteenth century horse sense', *Economic History Review*, 29 (1976), 60–81.
10 Paul Laxton and Richard Rodger, *Insanitary City: Henry Littlejohn and the Condition of Edinburgh* (Lancaster: Carnegie Publishing, 2013), fig. 3.4.
11 The west-coast route was marginally longer: 391 miles. The Edinburgh–Aberdeen route of 109 miles took twenty-one hours leaving Edinburgh at 6pm and arriving at Aberdeen post office at 3pm the following day.
12 *Edinburgh Post Office Directory*, 1825.
13 All distances are one way. Where a ferry was involved this is noted.
14 45 Geo.3, cap. xxi. An Act for Regulating the Police of the City of Edinburgh, and Adjoining Districts (1805).
15 Laxton and Rodger, *Insanitary City*, 45–58.
16 52 Geo.3 cap. 172, section 64. An Act for Regulating the Police of the City of Edinburgh and the Adjoining Districts (1812).
17 See David G. Barrie, *Police in the Age of Improvement: Police Development and the Civic Tradition in Scotland 1775–1865* (Cullompton: Willan, 2008), 33–7. See also D.G. Barrie and S. Broomhall, 'Public men, private interests: the origins, structure and practice of police courts in Scotland c.1800–1833', *Continuity and Change*, 27:1 (2012), 83–123.
18 7–8 Geo.4, cap. lxxvi. An Act for carrying into effect certain Improvements within the City of Edinburgh (1827).
19 There were eleven Improvement Acts between 1805 and 1830 drawn up by the City of Edinburgh and passed by parliament. Mostly these were concerned with street cleaning, watching, and the provision of amenities and control of behaviour in public places.
20 Malcolm Noble, 'Common Good and the reform of local government, Edinburgh 1820–56', unpublished PhD thesis (University of Edinburgh, 2016), Ch. 7.
21 Richard Rodger, *The Transformation of Edinburgh: Land, Property and Trust in the Nineteenth Century* (Cambridge: Cambridge University Press, 2001), 59–68.
22 There were a further 70 lodgings in Leith which, before it gained 'independence' and separate burgh status in 1833 was part of the administrative jurisdiction of Edinburgh.
23 Edinburgh became an important staging post to and from the Highlands. A romance with the Scottish Highlands fuelled by Walter Scott's novels, Queen Victoria's personal obsession, and the development of sporting estates in place of the crofting economy, all facilitated by railway companies' belated reach into remote areas, contributed to the demand for the hotel trade in Edinburgh. However, the importance of visiting national and international

trade delegations, learned societies and the burgeoning power of Edinburgh's financial sector was probably more significant in the development of capacity in the hotel sector after 1850. See Alastair J. Durie, *Scotland for the Holidays: Tourism in Scotland c.1780–1939* (East Linton: Tuckwell Press, 2004); R. Rodger, 'The "Common Good" and civic promotion: Edinburgh 1860–1914', in Robert Colls and Richard Rodger, eds., *Cities of Ideas: Civil Society and Urban Governance in Britain 1800–2000* (Aldershot: Ashgate, 2004), 144–77.

Chapter 8 Edinburgh New Town in the Early twentieth Century

1. James Grant, *Cassell's Old and New Edinburgh: Its History, its People and its Places*, vol. 3 (Edinburgh: Cassell, 1880), 119.
2. NLS: https://maps.nls.uk/towns/rec/418.
3. A.J. Youngson, *The Making of Classical Edinburgh* (Edinburgh: Edinburgh University Press, 1988 [1966]), 80–2.
4. Grant, *Cassell's Old and New Edinburgh*, vol. 3, 121–3.
5. NRS GD152/53/2/Bundle8/8-9. Petition of William Forbes Esq, to the Lord Dean of Guild, 29 September 1836.
6. NRS GD152/204/1/5/1-3. James Hill, Mound, Edinburgh, 1 July 1844.
7. ECA Box: 1823/55. Petition of T. Arrol, 92 Princes Street, 1 May 1823.
8. ECA Box: 1823/35. Petition of T. Arrol and M. Fowler, 91 Princes Street, 10 April 1823.
9. ECA Box: 1823/90. Petition of T. Arrol and M. Fowler, 91 Princes Street, 19 June 1823.
10. ECA Box: 1824/13. Petition of M. Fowler, 91 Princes Street, 12 February 1824.
11. NRS GD152/217/5/Bundle2/14.
12. Patrick Neill, *Considerations regarding the Edinburgh, Leith and Newhaven Railway: addressed to the Commissioners of Improvements; the inhabitants of the eastern divisions of Princes Street and of the streets under which the tunnel is proposed to be carried; and to the shareholders of the railway company* (Edinburgh: Bell & Bradfute; John Anderson Jun.; John Lindsay & Co., 1837).
13. NLS APS.2.91.101. Robert Grieve, *Prize Essay on Princes Street* (Leith: Printed by J.D. Suthren, 1878), 6–7.
14. Ibid., 3.
15. NLS: https://maps.nls.uk/view/74414124.
16. Grieve, *Prize Essay*, 7.
17. Alan Reiach and Robert Hurd, *Building Scotland: A Cautionary Guide* (Edinburgh: Saltire Society, 1941), n.p.
18. Patrick Abercrombie and Derek Plumstead, *A Civic Survey and Plan for the City & Royal Burgh of Edinburgh* (Edinburgh & London, 1949).
19. The title is a deliberate and appropriate evocation of the Geddesian past. Patrick Geddes, the inventor of the Civic Survey, may still have some relevance to the debates taking place in Edinburgh in the late 1940s.
20. Abercrombie and Plumstead, *A Civic Survey and Plan*, plate 1.

NOTES TO CHAPTER 9

21 Reiach and Hurd, *Building Scotland*.
22 John Lowrey, 'Ebenezer Macrae and the Abercrombie Plan for Edinburgh', in David Jones and Sam McKinstry, eds, *Essays in Scots and English Architectural History: A Festschrift for John Frew* (Donington: Shaun Tyas, 2009), 151–76.

CHAPTER 9 THE EDINBURGH OF THE SOUTH: SEEKING THE NEW TOWN

1   R.A. Lawson, 'Dunedin Harbour and Church Hill', *Otago Daily Times*, 26 September 1862, 5. See also, J.G.S. Grant, letter, *Otago Witness*, 12 April 1856, 2.
2   William Ferguson, *The Identity of the Scottish Nation: An Historic Quest* (Edinburgh: Edinburgh University Press, 1998), 302. The spelling 'Dun-Eidin' also appears.
3   K.C. McDonald, *City of Dunedin: A Century of Civic Enterprise* (Dunedin: Dunedin City Corporation, 1965), 3; Peter Entwisle, *Behold the Moon: The European Occupation of the Dunedin District 1770–1848* (Dunedin: Port Daniel Press, 2010), 159; Peter Entwisle, 'Saving the Romantic City: Charles Kettle's Plan for Old Dunedin: Identifying and Preserving its Values' (2005), Misc-MS-1930, Hocken Library, University of Otago, Dunedin; Ian Dougherty, *Dunedin: Founding a New World City* (Dunedin: Saddle Hill Press, 2017), 23.
4   Tom Brooking, *And Captain of their Souls: An Interpretative Essay on the Life and Times of Captain William Cargill* (Dunedin: Otago Heritage Books, 1984), 29.
5   *Seventeenth Report of the Directors of the New Zealand Company* (London: Stewart and Murray, 1845), 131.
6   'Settlement of Otago', *New Zealand Journal*, 6 (17 January 1846), 15–17 (15).
7   For example, Scott's 'Marmion' and 'The Lay of the Last Minstrel', James Hogg's 'At the Close of the Year 1812' and David Macbeth Moir's 'Mary's Mount'.
8   Thornton and Collie of Edinburgh published these titles in the 1840s.
9   'A New Feature in Scotch Banking: The Dunedin Bank', *Bankers' Magazine*, 1 (1844), 241, 333, 395.
10 D.W. Dowling, 'Journal kept at Edinburgh, 1843–1844', Kew, National Archives, CO 208/295; Marguerite Martin, 'The Life and Work of Charles Henry Kettle' (unpublished MA thesis, University of Otago, Dunedin, 1934), 27–9.
11 Dowling, 'Journal kept at Edinburgh'.
12 Martin, 'Life and Work of Charles Henry Kettle', 40–1.
13 Based upon the plan's accession date within the New Zealand Company's London files, it seems likely that the plan was included in Kettle's dispatch of 7 November 1846. Charles Kettle to William Wakefield, Wellington, 7 November 1846, 'Correspondence from Otago, 1844–47', Kew, National Archives, CO 208/96.
14 'Dunedin: Then and Now', *Otago Witness*, 27 May 1897, 9.
15 T.C. Harington to William Wakefield (14 August 1845), 'Correspondence to Otago, 1843–52', Kew, National Archives, CO 208/165.
16 'Municipal Council', *New Zealand Colonist and Port Nicholson Advertiser*, 2 June 1843, 2.

17 William Wakefield to Charles Kettle (30 November 1846), 'Correspondence from Otago, 1844–47', Kew, National Archives, CO 208/96.
18 Arthur Salmond, *First Church of Otago and How It Got There* (Dunedin: Otago Heritage Books, 1983), 30–1.
19 Charles Kettle to William Wakefield (10 August 1846), 'Correspondence from Otago, 1844–47', Kew, National Archives, CO 208/96.
20 Norman Ledgerwood, *The Heart of the City: The Story of Dunedin's Octagon* (Dunedin: Norman Ledgerwood, 2008), 6; Nola Easdale, *Mungo Park's Trunk* (Christchurch: Te Waihora Press, 2009), 60. Park's handwritten survey book records the name 'Octagon' for the small central formation although this name does not appear on Kettle's 1846 plan.
21 Ben Schrader, *The Big Smoke: New Zealand Cities 1840–1920* (Wellington: Bridget Williams Books, 2016), 69.
22 John Stuart-Murray, 'Landscape, Topography and Hydrology', in Brian Edwards and Paul Jenkins, eds, *Edinburgh: the Making of a Capital City* (Edinburgh: Edinburgh University Press, 2005), 64–80 (66).
23 Charles McKean, 'James Craig and Edinburgh's New Town', in Kitty Cruft and Andrew Fraser, eds, *James Craig 1744–1795* (Edinburgh: Mercat Press, 1995), 48–56 (55).
24 W.H. Lizars, 'This is the plan referred to and approved of at a meeting of the joint committees for laying out the grounds to the east of the Calton Hill' (Edinburgh: s.n., 1819): https://maps.nls.uk/view/102190426.
25 Tom Brooking, 'The Great Escape: Wakefield and the Scottish Settlement of Otago', in *Edward Gibbon Wakefield and the Colonial Dream: A Reconsideration* (Wellington: GP Publications, 1997), 123–32, 127.
26 McKean, 'James Craig and Edinburgh's New Town', 127.
27 Erik Olssen, *A History of Otago* (Dunedin: John McIndoe, 1984), 33.
28 A.H. McLintock, *The History of Otago: The Origins and Growth of a Wakefield Class Settlement* (Dunedin: Otago Centennial Historical Publications, 1949), 147.
29 McDonald, *City of Dunedin*, 5.
30 Olssen, *A History of Otago*, 35.
31 Nola Easdale, *Kairuri: the Measurer of the Land* (Petone: Highgate, 1988), 107; untitled leading article, *Otago Witness*, 25 August 1860, 5.
32 Maria S. Rye, 'Miss Rye's Emigrants', *The Times*, 29 May 1863, 5.
33 'Miss Rye's Letter to *The Times*', *Otago Daily Times*, 31 August 1863, 5; 'Original Correspondence', *Otago Daily Times*, 14 September 1863, 5.
34 Honor to whom Honor is Due [nom de plume of Robert Park?], 'Original Correspondence: Miss Rye's Letter to The Times', *Otago Daily Times*, 14 September 1863, 5.
35 T.M. Hocken, *Contributions to the Early History of New Zealand* (London: Sampson Low, Marston and Co., 1898), 81–2.
36 W.J. Watt, *Dunedin's Historical Background* (Dunedin: Dunedin Planning Department, 1972), 5.
37 Entwisle, 'Saving the Romantic City', 2.
38 Dougherty, *Dunedin: Founding a New World City*, 23.

Chapter 10 The 'Planned Village Movement' in Scotland

1. Douglas Lockhart, ed., *Scottish Planned Villages*, Scottish History Society, 5th series, vol. 16 (Edinburgh, 2012).
2. Susanna Wade Martins and Miles Glendinning, *Buildings of the Land: Scotland's Farms 1750–2000* (Edinburgh: RCAHMS, 2009).
3. Sir Robert Peel, *Evidence to the Select Committee on the State of Children Employed in Manufactories* (London: House of Commons Parliamentary Papers, 1816), 132 – hereafter PP 1816 (397).
4. Ophélie Siméon, *Robert Owen's Experiment at New Lanark: From Paternalism to Socialism* (London: Palgrave Macmillan, 2017), 39.
5. R.S. Fitton and A.P. Wadsworth, *The Strutts and the Arkwrights 1758–1830: A Study of the Early Factory System* (Manchester: Manchester University Press, 1968), 104.
6. Lorna J. Philip, 'The creation of settlements in rural Scotland: planned villages in Dumfries and Galloway', *Scottish Geographical Journal*, 2 (2003), 77–102 (100).
7. Jean Dunlop, *The British Fisheries Society, 1768–1893* (Edinburgh: John Donald, 1978).
8. T.C. Smout, 'The landowner and the planned village', in Rosalind Mitchison and Nicholas Phillipson, eds, *Scotland in the Age of Improvement* (Edinburgh: Edinburgh University Press, 1970), 73–106 (75); Siméon, *Robert Owen's Experiment at New Lanark*, 31.
9. George Dempster, 'Plan for improving the estates of Skibo and Polrossie', in Sir John Sinclair, ed., *Old Statistical Account of Scotland*, 7 (1791), 362–83; Robert Rennie, 'Plan of an inland village', *Prize Essays and Transactions of the Highland Society*, 2 (1803), 261–3; Sir John Sinclair, *Analysis of the Statistical Account of Scotland* (London, 1826), 5–8; Anthony Cooke, 'Cotton and the Scottish Highland Clearances – the development of Spinningdale 1791–1806', *Textile History*, 26 (1995), 89–94 (89).
10. George Stewart, *Curiosities of the Glasgow Citizenship: Short Biographical Notices of the Principal Merchants, Manufacturers, etc. of Glasgow in 1783* (Glasgow: Chamber of Commerce and Manufacture, 1881), 50; Dempster, 'Plan for improving . . . Skibo and Polrossie', 383; Cooke, 'Development of Spinningdale', 91.
11. T.M. Devine, *The Tobacco Lords: A Study of the Tobacco Merchants of Glasgow and their Trading Activities c.1740–1790* (Edinburgh: Edinburgh University Press, 1975), 45.
12. George Edwin Revill, 'Paternalism, community and corporate culture: a study of the Derby headquarters of the Midland Railway Company and its workforce, 1840–1900', unpublished PhD thesis (Loughborough University, 1989), 34.
13. Mary B. Rose, *The Gregs of Quarry Bank Mill: The Rise and Decline of a Family Firm, 1750–1914* (Cambridge: Cambridge University Press, 1986), 102; Siméon, *Robert Owen's Experiment at New Lanark*, 55.
14. James Robertson, *General View of the Agriculture in the Southern Districts of the County of Perth* (London, 1794), 61–2, quoted in Smout, 'The landowner and the planned village', 79.

15 Ospidale MSS, Account of Balnoe Co., 1 November 1794, quoted in Cooke, 'Development of Spinningdale', 92.
16 Smout, 'The landowner and the planned village', 86–7.
17 Ian Donnachie, 'Historic tourism to New Lanark and the falls of Clyde 1795–1830: The evidence of contemporary visiting books and related sources', *Journal of Tourism and Cultural Change*, 2 (2005), 145–62 (147); David Dale, 'Copy of a letter from Mr. David Dale to T.B. Bayley, Esq., Glasgow, Feb 23, 1796', *Proceedings of the Board of Health in Manchester* (Manchester: S. Russell, 1805), 54–64; Siméon, *Robert Owen's Experiment at New Lanark*, 16.
18 Parliamentary Papers 1816 (397); Siméon, *Robert Owen's Experiment at New Lanark*, 35.
19 Dale, 'Copy of a letter', 56; *Courier and Evening Gazette*, 10 November 1794, quoted in Siméon, *Robert Owen's Experiment at New Lanark*, 37.
20 David Dale to Alexander Campbell of Barcaldine, 18 August 1791, Campbell Family of Barcaldine Papers, National Records of Scotland, GD170/1743; Sinclair, *Analysis of the Statistical Account*, vol. 1, 172–7; Smout, 'The landowner and the planned village', 79; Siméon, *Robert Owen's Experiment at New Lanark*, 32, 37.
21 Sinclair, *Old Statistical Account of Scotland*, vol. 13, 332–3; vol. 15, 40.
22 Maxine Berg, 'Women's work, mechanisation and the early phases of industrialisation in England', in Patrick Joyce, ed., *The Historical Meaning of Work* (Cambridge: Cambridge University Press, 1987), 64–98; Siméon, *Robert Owen's Experiment at New Lanark*, 28.
23 David J. McLaren, *David Dale of New Lanark: A Bright Luminary to Scotland* (Milngavie: Heatherbank Press, 1999), 46; *New Statistical Account of Scotland*, vol. 7 (1845), 402, quoted in Smout, 'The landowner and the planned village', 95; Thomas Hogkin Jr, 'Robert Owen the socialist: a visit to New Lanark in 1821', *Friends' Quarterly Examiner* 46 (1812), 160, quoted in Siméon, *Robert Owen's Experiment at New Lanark*, 56.
24 Smout, 'The landowner and the planned village', 73; George Robertson, *Rural Recollections* (Edinburgh: Cunninghame Press, 1829), 78, quoted in Rosalind Mitchison, 'Scotland 1750–1850', in F.M.L. Thompson, ed., *The Cambridge Social History of Britain*, vol. 1 (Cambridge: Cambridge University Press, 1990), 155–208 (158); Michael Nevell, 'Living in the industrial city: housing quality, land ownership and the archaeological evidence from industrial Manchester, 1740–1850', *Journal for Historical Archaeology*, 15 (2011), 594–606 (600), quoted in Siméon, *Robert Owen's Experiment at New Lanark*, 34.
25 Reinhard Bendix, *Work and Authority in Industry: Managerial Ideologues in the Course of Industrialisation*, ed. Mauro F. Guillén (New Brunswick: Transaction Books, 2001 [1956]), 16; Siméon, *Robert Owen's Experiment at New Lanark*, 38.
26 Stanley D. Chapman, 'Workers' housing in the cotton factory colonies, 1770–1850', *Textile History*, 7 (1976), 112–39 (130), quoted in Clive Leivers, 'The provision of allotments in Derbyshire industrial communities', *Family and Community History*, 12 (2009), 51–64 (62). See also Siméon, *Robert Owen's Experiment at New Lanark*, 38.
27 See https://glasgowmuseumsslavery.co.uk/2018/08/14/slave-cotton-in-glasgow/

Chapter 11 The New Towns in Post-War Scotland

1. Rob Close, John Gifford and Frank Arneil Walker, *Buildings of Scotland: Lanarkshire and Renfrewshire* (New Haven and London: Yale University Press, 2016), 277.
2. Patrick Abercrombie and Robert Matthew, *The Clyde Valley Regional Plan 1946* (Edinburgh: HMSO, 1949), 7.
3. For more on the debates about decentralisation and reconstruction in Glasgow, see Florian Urban, 'Modernising Glasgow – tower blocks, motorways and new towns 1940–2010', *Journal of Architecture*, 23:2 (2018), 265–309.
4. Close et al., *Lanarkshire and Renfrewshire*, 279; 'New Town Project: Chief Architect and Planning Officer', *Scotsman*, 20 July 1948.
5. Close et al., *Lanarkshire and Renfrewshire*, 278.
6. Department of Health for Scotland, *New Town at East Kilbride* (Edinburgh: HMSO, 1947), 2.
7. Ibid., 12.
8. Ibid., 12.
9. For historical accounts, see John R. Gold, *The Experience of Modernism: Modern Architects and the Future City, 1928–1953* (London: Spon, 1997), 194–200; John R. Gold, *The Practice of Modernism: Modern Architects and Urban Transformation, 1954–1972* (Abingdon: Routledge, 2007), 146–64; Elain Harwood, *Space, Hope and Brutalism: English Architecture, 1945–1975* (New Haven and London: Yale University Press, 2015), 1–47; Guy Ortolano, *Thatcher's Progress: From Social Democracy to Market Liberalism through an English New Town* (Cambridge: Cambridge University Press, 2019). For participants' accounts see Frank Schaffer, *The New Town Story* (London: Paladin, 1970).
10. Lynn Abrams, Barry Hazley, Valerie Wright and Ade Kearns, 'Aspiration, agency, and the production of new selves in a Scottish new town, c.1947–c.2016', *Twentieth Century British History*, 29:4 (2018), 576–604.
11. Andrew Homer, 'Creating new communities: the role of the neighbourhood unit in post-war British planning', *Contemporary British History*, 14:1 (2000), 63–80; James Greenhalgh, *Reconstructing Modernity: Space, Power and Governance in Mid-Twentieth Century British Cities* (Manchester: Manchester University Press, 2017), 121–56.
12. Alistair Kefford, 'Constructing the affluent citizen: state, space and the individual in post-war Britain, 1945–79', PhD thesis (University of Manchester, 2015); Peter Shapely, 'Civic pride and redevelopment in the post-war British city', *Urban History* 39:2 (2012), 310–28; Elizabeth Darling, *Re-Forming Britain: Narratives of Modernity Before Reconstruction* (Abingdon: Routledge, 2007).
13. Hansard, House of Commons Debates, 8 May 1946, vol. 422 cols 1072–184 (col 1076).
14. Ibid., col. 1076.
15. Ibid.
16. Ibid, col. 1088.
17. 'Municipal Dreams: The Becontree Estate', online at: https://municipaldreams.wordpress.com/2013/01/08/the-becontree-estate-built-in-england-

where-the-most-revolutionary-social-changes-can-take-place-and-people-in-general-do-not-realise-that-they-have-occurred/ [accessed 20 July 2018].

18 New Towns Committee, *Final Report of the New Towns Committee*, Cmnd. 6876 (London: HMSO, 1946), 64–5.
19 Ibid., 10.
20 Abercrombie and Matthew, *Clyde Valley Regional Plan*, 303.
21 Homer, 'Creating new communities', 63–80.
22 New Towns Committee, *Final Report*, 16.
23 Schaffer, *New Town Story*, 71.
24 Homer, 'Creating new communities', 65.
25 Gold, *Experience of Modernism*, 145–51.
26 Greenhalgh, *Reconstructing Modernity*, 132.
27 Ibid., 121–2, 132.
28 Scottish Housing Advisory Committee, *Planning our New Homes* (Edinburgh: HMSO, 1944), 87.
29 Sub-committee of the Central Housing Advisory Committee, *Design of Dwellings* (London: HMSO, 1944), 58–63.
30 'Up Your Street Exhibition', *Architects' Journal*, 102 (9 August 1945), 97.
31 'The New Towns Grow: what to see, how to get there' [pamphlet, c. 1956].
32 H. Alker Tripp, *Town Planning and Road Traffic* (London: Edward Arnold, 1942), 89.
33 Greenhalgh, *Reconstructing Modernity*, 132–37.
34 New Towns Committee, *Final Report*, 42.
35 James Greenhalgh, 'Consuming communities: the neighbourhood unit and the role of retail spaces on British housing estates, 1944–1958', *Urban History*, 43:1 (2016), 158–74.
36 New Towns Committee, *Final Report*, 42.
37 Ibid., 16.
38 Ibid., 16, 43–5.
39 Department of Health for Scotland, *Working Class Housing on the Continent* (Edinburgh: HMSO, 1935), 9.
40 Ibid., 10.
41 Ibid., 18.
42 Scottish Housing Advisory Committee, *Planning Our New Homes*, 87.
43 New Towns Committee, *Final Report*, 43.
44 Ibid., 42.
45 Ibid.
46 The 1944 Dudley Report suggested that neighbourhood units might form the basis of town ward boundaries. See Sub-committee of the Central Housing Advisory Committee, *Design of Dwellings*, 59.
47 Hansard, House of Commons Debates, 8 May 1946, vol. 422 col. 1091.
48 L.E. White, *Community or Chaos? Housing Estates and their Social Problems* (London: NCSS, 1950), 22.
49 David Holbrook, 'Henry Morris and the village college idea', *Culture, Education and Society*, 39:4 (1985), 328–34 (329): 'training ground of a rural democracy realising its social and political duties'.
50 Darling, *Re-Forming Britain*, 157–67.

NOTES TO CHAPTER 11

51 [National Council of Social Service], *Community Centres – Living Communities* [1945], 7.
52 New Towns Committee, *Final Report*, 46.
53 Ibid., 46–7.
54 NRS, SEP15/47, State Management in the New Towns.
55 New Towns Committee, *Final Report*, 43–4.
56 Ibid., 45.
57 For more on theatre, see Alistair Fair, *Modern Playhouses: An Architectural History of Britain's New Theatres* (Oxford: Oxford University Press, 2018), chapters 1 and 2.
58 Urban, 'Modernising Glasgow', 302.
59 South Lanarkshire Archives (hereafter SLA), EK 9/1/2, clippings, 'Mr Woodburn opens New Town Exhibition', *Hamilton Advertiser*, 19 June 1948.
60 NRS, SEP15/196/1, Notes for Meeting on Social Development – 7 January 1949.
61 SLA, EK 9/1/2, clippings, 'New Town aims high for culture', *Glasgow Bulletin*, 26 July 1949.
62 SLA, EK 1/5/7, East Kilbride Development Corporation (hereafter EKDC) Annual Report, 31 March 1955.
63 'Public demand for new town', *The Times*, 22 January 1951.
64 Norman Mackenzie, *The New Towns: The Success of Social Planning* (London: Fabian Society, 1955), 14–15.
65 SLA, EK 1/5/6, EKDC Annual Report, 31 March 1954.
66 SLA, EK 1/5/13, EKDC Annual Report, 31 March 1961.
67 NRS, SEP15/193/59, memo by J.J. Farrell, 10 April 1963.
68 Mackenzie, *The New Towns*, 14.
69 NRS, SEP15/264, 'Notes of Meeting held on December 4th' [1959].
70 'East Kilbride amenities', *Scotsman*, 11 May 1955.
71 NRS, ED27/515, 'Social characteristics of a new town'.
72 SLA, EK 1/5/13, EKDC Annual Report, 31 March 1961.
73 SLA, EK 1/5/7, EKDC Annual Report, 31 March 1955.
74 Abrams et al., 'Aspiration', 580; Greenhalgh, 'Consuming communities'.
75 'The new society – II', *Sunday Times*, 24 June 1956.
76 NRS, ED27/515, 'Social characteristics of a new town'.
77 Abrams et al., 'Aspiration', 585.
78 NRS, ED27/515, 'Social characteristics of a new town'.
79 Ibid.
80 NRS, SEP15/193, J.M. Livingstone and A.J.M. Sykes, 'East Kilbride 70: An economic and social survey', 15.
81 Harwood, *Space, Hope and Brutalism*, 33.
82 'The New Towns', *Time and Tide London*, 13 July 1957.
83 Peter Self, 'Introduction: new towns in the modern world', in Hazel Evans, ed., *New Towns: the British Experience* (New York: Wiley, 1972), 1–10 (1).
84 Gilbert McAllister, 'Planning new towns', *Spectator*, 5 April 1946, 8–9 (8), citing the Interim Report.
85 Colin Ward, *New Town, Home Town: the Lessons of Experience* (London: Gulbenkian Foundation, 1993), 10.
86 Greenhalgh, *Reconstructing Modernity*, 139, 146–7.
87 Homer, 'Creating new communities', 70.

88 SLA, EK 9/1/5, clippings, 'New town types: Social groupings emerge at East Kilbride', *Scotsman*, 10 May 1955.
89 NRS, SEP15/193, 'East Kilbride' [colour booklet].
90 Ibid.
91 NRS, SEP15/264, 'Youth problems in East Kilbride'.
92 Ibid.
93 NRS, SEP15/264, Ministry of Housing and Local Government, 'Social provision in new towns', 7–9.
94 NRS, ED27/515, 'Draft Brief to Architect'.
95 *Livingston Master Plan Report* (Edinburgh: Livingston Development Corporation, 1963), 28.
96 *Runcorn New Town Masterplan* (Runcorn: Runcorn Development Corporation, 1967), 45.
97 *Livingston Master Plan Report*, 35.
98 *Irvine New Town Plan* (Irvine: Irvine Development Corporation, 1971), 10.
99 Ibid., 120.
100 *Livingston Master Plan Report*, 43, 56–7.
101 *Irvine New Town Plan*, 120.
102 Charles McKean, 'The incivility of Edinburgh's New Town', in W.A. Brogden, ed., *The Neo-Classical Town: Scottish Contributions to Urban Design since 1750* (Edinburgh: Rutland Press, 1996), 37–45 (45).

CHAPTER 12 PATRICK GEDDES ET ÉDIMBOURG

1 Patrick Geddes a détaillé la *Civics* dans ses trois conférences à la Sociological Society de Londres, les 18 juillet 1904, 23 janvier 1905 et 19 mars 1906: 'Civics: as applied sociology. part I', in *Sociological Papers 1904*, vol. 1 (London and New York: Macmillan, 1905), 103–18; 'Civics: as concrete and applied sociology, part II', in *Sociological Papers 1905*, vol. 2 (London and New York: Macmillan, 1906), 57–119; 'A suggested plan for a civic museum and its associated studies', in *Sociological Papers*, vol. 3 (London and New York: Macmillan, 1907) 197–237.
2 Patrick Geddes, *The Civic Survey of Edinburgh* (Edinburgh: Outlook Tower, 1911).
3 John Scott and Ray Bromley, *Envisioning Sociology: Victor Branford, Patrick Geddes, and the Quest for Social Reconstruction* (Albany, NY: State of New York University Press, 2013).
4 Pierre Chabard, *Exposer la ville: Patrick Geddes et le Town Planning Movement*, unpublished PhD thesis (Université Paris VIII, 2008).
5 Patrick Geddes, *Cities in Evolution: An Introduction to the Town Planning Movement and to the Study of Civics* (London: Williams and Norgate, 1915).
6 Pierre Chabard, 'Comment un livre change: *Cities in Evolution* et les usages de Patrick Geddes (1912–1972)', *Genèses: Sciences Sociales et histoire*, 60 (2005), 76–97.
7 Geddes, *Cities in Evolution*, 254.
8 Charles Nodier, *Promenades de Dieppe aux montagnes d'Écosse* (Paris: J.-N. Barba, 1821), 125–6.

NOTES TO CHAPTER 12

9   La Royal High School (1826–9) est inspirée des Propylées.
10 Le National Monument (1824–9), dessiné avec William H. Playfair, constitue une réplique inachevée du Parthénon.
11 Le Dugald Stewart Monument (1832) est inspiré du monument de Lysicrate à Athènes.
12 Geddes, *Civic Survey of Edinburgh*, 542.
13 University of Strathclyde, Patrick Geddes Papers, TGED-1-6-7 [Marcel Hardy], 'Edinburgh Survey', [c.1910].
14 Geddes, *Civic Survey of Edinburgh*, 542.
15 En l'occurrence les deux édifices que William H. Playfair dessine dans les années 1850 au Mound: Royal Academy et National Gallery of Scotland.
16 Geddes, *Civic Survey of Edinburgh*, 539.
17 Geddes développe l'opposition entre ères 'paléotechnique' et 'néotechnique' dans 'The twofold aspect of the industrial age: Paleotechnic and Neotechnic', *Town Planning Review*, 3:3 (1912), 176–87 (texte intégralement repris dans le chapitre 4 de *Cities in Evolution*, 60–83).
18 Geddes, *Cities in Evolution*, 120.
19 Ibid., 119.
20 Ibid., 122.
21 Ibid., 87.
22 Helen Elizabeth Meller, *Patrick Geddes: Social Evolutionist and City Planner* (London and New York: Routledge, 1990), 74. Fille d'un marchand écossais de Liverpool, Anna Morton (1857–1917), excellente musicienne, s'est impliquée très tôt dans le monde de la Réforme sociale.
23 Ils se rencontrent en hiver 1883 et se marient le 17 avril 1886, juste avant d'emménager dans un appartement situé dans un *tenement* du début du dix-huitième siècle, à James' Court, Lawnmarket.
24 National Library of Scotland, MS.10545 f. 143. Kate Crooke à Patrick Geddes (essai de biographie d'Anna Morton), Liverpool, 29 juillet 1917.
25 Lou Rosenburg and Jim Johnson, *Renewing Old Edinburgh: The Enduring Legacy of Patrick Geddes* (Edinburgh: Scottish Centre for Conservation Studies, Edinburgh College of Art, 2010).
26 Volker M. Welter, 'The return of the muses: Edinburgh as a museion', in M. Giebelhausen, ed., *The Architecture of the Museum, Manchester* (Manchester: Manchester University Press, 2003), 144–159; Lou Rosenburg and Jim Johnson, '"Conservative surgery" in Old Edinburgh', in B. Edwards and P. Jenkins, eds, *Edinburgh: The Making of a Capital City* (Edinburgh: Edinburgh University Press, 2005), 134–41.
27 Diplômé en santé publique à l'Université d'Édimbourg, James Alexander Russell (1846–1918) est *lord provost* de 1891 à 1894. Actif dans le milieu réformateur, il est membre de la Social and Sanitary Society of Edinburgh et fera partie des membres fondateurs de la Town and Gown Association Ltd en 1896.
28 Welter, 'Return of the muses', 151.
29 Rosenburg and Johnson, '"Conservative surgery" in Old Edinburgh', 135.
30 Initié à l'Université de Cambridge en 1867, l'*University Extension* consiste à proposer hors-les-murs des programmes de cours pour adultes, destinés aux ouvriers. Patrick Geddes fut l'un des pionniers de ce mouvement en Écosse

dans les années 1880. Philip Mairet, *Pionneer of Sociology: The Life and Letters of Patrick Geddes* (London: Lund Humphries, 1957), 58.

31 Parmi les premiers résidents de ces University Halls, on compte notamment Victor Branford, John Arthur Thompson, John Ross, Andrew Herbertson, William Speirs Bruce, John Duncan, Robert Smith, Edward McGegan, Thomas R. Marr et Riccardo Stephens.

32 Volker Welter, '"Slum, semi-slum, super-slum": Some reflections by Patrick Geddes on Edinburgh's New Town', *Architectural Heritage*, 10 (1999), 66–73.

33 Geddes, *Civic Survey of Edinburgh*, 565.

34 Emprunté à la médecine, ce concept de *conservative surgery* appartient plus au vocabulaire oral qu'écrit de Geddes. Absent de *Cities in Evolution*, il apparaît dans ses rapports indiens, notamment celui de Madras. T.G. MacGee, 'Planning the Asian city: the relevance of "conservative surgery" and the concept of dualism', in J.V. Ferreira and S.S. Jha, eds, *The Outlook Tower: Essays on Urbanization in Memory of Patrick Geddes* (Bombay: Popular Prakashan Private, 1976), 266.

35 'Here, then, we have a period of town planning and of architectural execution surpassing even the lesson of London; yet breaking down, also, in its turn': Geddes, *Civic Survey of Edinburgh*, 556.

36 Nikolaus Pevsner, *The Buildings of Scotland* (Harmondsworth: Penguin, 1984 [1978]), 192.

37 Pierre Chabard, 'L'Outlook Tower, anamorphose du monde', *Le Visiteur*, 7 (2001), 64–89.

38 Pierre Chabard, 'Architects of knowledge', in Simon Schaffer, John Tresch and Pasquale Gagliardi, eds, *Aesthetics of Universal Knowledge* (London: Palgrave McMillan, 2017), 53–76.

39 [Anna Geddes], *A First Visit to the Outlook Tower* (Edinburgh: P.G. and Colleagues, 1906), 19.

40 Geddes, *Cities in Evolution*, 87.

41 Ibid., vii.

42 Le Housing, Town Planning Act 1909 constitue un tournant en matière de gestion de l'urbanisme.

43 Patrick Geddes and Frank C. Mears, *Explanatory Guide Book and Outline Catalogue, Cities and Town Planning Exhibition* (Edinburgh: A.T. Hutchinson, 1911), 66.

44 Geddes, *Cities in Evolution*, 373.

45 Ibid., 254.

Chapter 13 Edinburgh Old and New Towns: A Tale of One City?

1 Hugh Miller, *My Schools and Schoolmasters: Or, The Story of my Education* (Edinburgh: W.P. Nimmo, 1873 [1824]), 309.

2 Barrie M. Ratcliffe and W. Chaloner, *A French Sociologist Looks at Britain: Gustave d'Eichtal and British Society in 1828* (Manchester: Manchester University Press, 1986), 74.

3 Ibid., 75.

NOTES TO CHAPTER 13

4. The phrase 'new town' in Scotland was originally applied to extensions or developments within existing settlements or new estate and industrial developments. It was only in the twentieth century that the term was exclusively applied to entirely new, self-contained settlements.
5. R. Madgin and R. Rodger, 'Inspiring capital? Deconstructing myths and reconstructing urban environments, Edinburgh, 1860–2010', *Urban History*, 40:3 (2013), 507–29.
6. Ibid.
7. R.J. Morris, 'The capitalist, the professor and the soldier: the re-making of Edinburgh Castle, 1850–1900', *Planning Perspectives*, 22 (2007), 55–78.
8. Helena Murteira, 'Place for Lisbon in eighteenth century Europe: Lisbon, London and Edinburgh, a town-planning comparative study', PhD thesis (University of Edinburgh, 2006).
9. Margaret Stewart, *The Architectural Landscape and Constitutional Plans of the Earl of Mar, 1700–32* (Dublin: Four Courts Press, 2016).
10. Ibid.
11. The majority of the accommodation in the New Town as developed was flatted. The Town Council had attempted to stop the provision of flats in Charlotte Square but the developer adopted a clever variation of shared, tenemental accommodation in the end blocks of a type that progressed to the 'main door' and 'double upper' solutions which offered accommodation on two floors within a tenement. Sir Walter Scott's 'house' in Castle Street, for example, was a double upper flat.
12. A palace-front is a classical symmetrical main elevation of a large building or, as in the case of the New Town, an architectural design where several houses appear to be one palatial composition with emphasis given to the centre and ends by means of engaged porticoes, temple-fronts and end-pavilions.
13. T. and W. McDowall, *New Guide to Edinburgh* (Edinburgh, 1849), 10.
14. The term 'terrace' to describe a connected row of dwellings is derived from the Adam brothers' later Adelphi Terrace in London. Ironically, the Adelphi scheme also introduced Edinburgh-style purpose-built flats to the London market.
15. The first such developments were planned in squares, influenced by contemporary London; early examples included Argyle Square (completed c.1742) and Brown and Adam Square (both of the 1750s), all now demolished.
16. The feudal system applied in Scots law on land ownership, and meant that a landowner as a vassal had obligations to a feudal superior including the payment of a feu duty.
17. The planned church was replaced to the dismay of the Town Council by the mansion of Sir Lawrence Dundas, designed by Sir William Chambers (1774).
18. City of Edinburgh District Council Order Confirmation Act 1991.
19. David Hume, in his own day more famous as a historian than as a philosopher, stated: 'I believe this is the historical age and this the historical nation': *The Letters of David Hume*, ed. J.Y.T. Greig (Oxford: Oxford University Press, 1932), vol. 2, 230.
20. Walter Scott, *The Journal of Sir Walter Scott*, ed. W.E.K. Anderson (Edinburgh: Canongate Classic, 1987), 79.

21 For example, Scott worried that development north of Queen Street, which took place during his residency of a double upper flat on [North] Castle Street, would block his light.
22 Andrew Fraser, *The Building of Old College* (Edinburgh: Edinburgh University Press, 1989); I. Gow, 'Playfair: a northern Athenian', *RIBA Journal*, 97 (May 1990), 36–9.
23 'The dramatic topography of the Old Town combined with the planned alignments of key buildings in both the Old and the New Town, results in spectacular views and panoramas and an iconic skyline.' Excerpt from 'Brief Synthesis': http://whc.unesco.org/en/list/728.
24 Robert Louis Stevenson, *Edinburgh: Picturesque Notes* (London: Seeley, 1889 [1878]), 33, 39. The 'Irish washings' reference is typical of the casual racism of the day.
25 William Chambers was Lord Provost of Edinburgh (1865–9), and was responsible for major 'improvement' projects under the terms of the City Improvement Act (1866), including the restoration of and the building of Jeffrey Street, St Mary's Street and Blackfriars Street. See also Aileen Fyfe, *Steam-Powered Knowledge: William Chambers and the Business of Publishing, 1820–1860* (Chicago, IL: University of Chicago Press, 2012).
26 James Grant, *Cassell's Old And New Edinburgh: Its History, its People and its Places*, vol. 3 (Edinburgh: Cassell, 1880), 283–6; *The Builder*, 2 August 1851 and 29 September 1860; John Gifford, Colin McWilliam and David Walker, *The Buildings of Scotland: Edinburgh* (London: Penguin, 1984), 223–4.
27 Emil Kaufmann, *Von Ledoux bis Le Corbusier* (Vienna and Leipzig, 1933).
28 Alan Reiach and Robert Hurd, *Building Scotland: A Cautionary Guide* (Edinburgh: Saltire Society, 1941).
29 *The Conservation of Georgian Edinburgh: The Proceedings and Outcome of a Conference Organized by the Scottish Civic Trust in Association with the Edinburgh Architectural Association and in Conjunction with the Civic Trust, London* (Edinburgh: Edinburgh University Press, 1972), 76.
30 Richard Emerson, quoted from an email conversation of 19 May 2016.

Chapter 14 Commemorating the Founding of the New Town

1 The walkway proposal was abandoned in 1975.
2 The Council's proposal for an inner ring road was cancelled before it had even been started.
3 Scottish Civic Trust, *The Conservation of Georgian Edinburgh: The Proceedings and Outcome of a Conference Organized by the Scottish Civic Trust in Association with the Edinburgh Architectural Association and in Conjunction with the Civic Trust, London* (Edinburgh: Edinburgh University Press, 1972), 85–96.
4 The 1967 Festival Poster was designed by Hans Schleger and Associates.
5 The Labour government's White Paper *A Policy for the Arts: the First Steps* (1965) was the first major reappraisal of the role of culture since the Arts Council had been set up in 1946. It demonstrated the government's attempts to develop a clear policy for the arts. In the run-up to its

NOTES TO CHAPTER 14

publication, between 1960 and 1964, the Arts Council's funding more than doubled: Angela Bartie, *The Edinburgh Festivals: Culture and Society in Post-War Britain* (Edinburgh: Edinburgh University Press, 2013), 152.

6 The Scottish Committee of the Arts Council was renamed the Scottish Arts Council in 1967.

7 The band, which was received with popular enthusiasm in the city, performed twice in April and October 1964. Davie Jones, later achieving fame as David Bowie, and the Manish Boys were also on stage in 1964.

8 BBC Scotland launched regular colour transmissions in July 1967.

9 The principal Festival exhibition in 1968 was of the work of Charles Rennie Mackintosh. Martin Luther King and Robert Kennedy were assassinated in 1968, and Enoch Powell made his famous 'Rivers of Blood' speech in April that year.

10 Prior to the local government reorganisation in 1974–5 the terms 'Edinburgh Corporation' and 'Edinburgh City Council' were basically interchangeable.

11 The movement of experimental theatre permeated the Fringe and the Official Festival alike in the high sixties. The transfer of ideas between the two festivals increased and intellectual vitality affected both.

12 For a discussion of the 1967 Festival Programme, see Eileen Miller, *The Edinburgh International Festival 1947–1996* (Brookfield: Scolar Press, 1996), 68–70.

13 Clear priority was given towards developing infrastructure in the lead-up to the Commonwealth Games which took place in Edinburgh in 1970.

14 Tom Nairn, 'The Festival of the Dead', *New Statesman*, 276–7.

15 Tom Nairn, *The Break-up of Britain: Crisis and Neo-Nationalism* (Edinburgh: Big Thinking, 2003), 106.

16 Tom Stoppard, *Jumpers* (1972).

17 Many members of municipal government were also Kirk elders. The Church of Scotland, as represented by the General Assembly, remained a conservative body (see the Proceedings of the 1967 General Assembly). Frequent scandals occurred on the stages of the Festival, the Fringe and the Traverse Theatre.

18 Ian Lindsay carried out conservation schemes in burghs such as Culross, Dunkeld and Inveraray. He made a great impact, between 1945 and 1966, in the field of government listing. The preservationists became an avant-garde of the modern heritage movement, opposing, from within government, the general enthusiasm for reconstruction: M. Glendinning, R. MacInnes and A. MacKechnie, *A History of Scottish Architecture* (Edinburgh, Edinburgh University Press, 1996), 421–6; D. Watters and M. Glendinning, *Little Houses: The National Trust for Scotland's Improvement Scheme for Small Historic Homes* (Edinburgh, RCAHMS, 2006), 12–62.

19 The approaching bicentenary was the theme of the Annual General Meeting of the Old Edinburgh Club held on 4 March 1966: *Edinburgh Corporation Committee Minutes*, 13 April 1966, 474.

20 Edinburgh City Archives [ECA], EFS/1, Edinburgh Festival Society to E.F. Catford, 29 March 1966. The Cockburn Association proposed that New Town proprietors be encouraged to improve their properties for the

occasion: ECA, LP/10/7, Cockburn Association to the Lord Provost, 8 November 1966.
21. ECA, LP/10/7, Eric Hall to E.F. Catford, 13 May 1966.
22. The Regent, Royal and Carlton Terraces Association came into being on 12 January 1966 for the purpose of preserving and improving the general amenity of the properties situated in those areas and of safeguarding the architectural attractions of the neighbourhood and its surroundings: ECA, LP/10/7, Regent, Royal and Carlton Terraces Association to the Town Clerk, 5 March 1966, and Saltire Society to the Lord Provost, Sir Duncan Weatherstone, 21 April 1966.
23. ECA, LP/10/7, *Edinburgh Corporation Committee Minutes*, 10 August 1966, 133, and Edinburgh University Press to Town Clerk, July 1966.
24. ECA, LP/10/7, Edinburgh University Press to the Corporation, 14 June 1967, and E.F. Catford to Edinburgh University Press, 10 July 1967.
25. Edinburgh Festival Society to Town Clerk, 29 March 1966.
26. After qualifying at Edinburgh College of Art in 1957, Paterson worked in the office of Sir Robert Matthew for part of the redevelopment of the Gorbals area of Glasgow, 1959–63. He designed exhibitions and also made several documentary films.
27. Paterson accepted a fee of 9 per cent of the relevant cost of the exhibition with a maximum fee of £2,100, exclusive of the additional payable expenses in connection with visits to suppliers and contractors: *Edinburgh Corporation Committee Minutes*, 21 December 1966, 297. Peter Daniel acted as Paterson's assistant. City Display Ltd, London, was granted the contract for the construction of the exhibition: *Edinburgh Corporation Committee Minutes*, 12 April 1967, 422.
28. ECA, LP/10/7, conditions of let of the Waverley Market. Part of the exhibition in the Waverley Market was purchased by the Scottish Arts Council and other sections were placed in permanent storage: *Edinburgh Corporation Committee Minutes*, Minutes of Meeting of 16 October 1967, 169. An advance payment of £10,000 was made available in November 1966: *Edinburgh Corporation Committee Minutes*, Minutes of Meeting of 17 November 1966, 253.
29. *Edinburgh Corporation Committee Minutes*, 24 January 1968, 265–6.
30. ECA, LP/10/7, Paterson to Publicity Office (Edinburgh Corporation), 25 September 1967.
31. ECA, LP/10/7, Publicity Officer to Catford, 5 July 1967.
32. '200 Years Now' was shown on BBC1 on Sunday 17 December 1967.
33. ECA, LP/10/7, Paterson to Hewitson, Town Planning Officer, 19 May 1967.
34. ECA, LP/10/7, Youngson to Catford, 30 May 1967. For writing the text, McWilliam was paid £50. McWilliam directed the architectural history and conservation courses at Edinburgh College of Art, and later Heriot-Watt University. In 1968, architect Guy Oddie replaced Matthew as head of the Department of Architecture at Edinburgh University; the next post-holder of the Forbes Chair of Architecture following Matthew's death in 1975 was Isi Metzstein (from 1985). See M. Glendinning, *Modern Architect: the Life and Times of Robert Matthew* (London: RIBA, 2008), 307.

NOTES TO CHAPTER 14

35 ECA, LP/10/7, E.F. Catford to R.B.K. Stevenson, 11 January 1967. Museums agreed to pinpoint items in their collections which had a bearing on the New Town's development or were related to the period when the New Town was new.
36 ECA, LP/10/7, Lighting engineer to publicity officer (Edinburgh Corporation), 22 June 1967.
37 ECA, LP/10/7, *Edinburgh Corporation Committee Minutes*, Minutes of Meeting of 24 May 1967, 29, Catford to the Lord Lyon, 29 May 1967, and Lord Lyon to Catford, 30 May 1967. For an example of the action undertaken at an earlier stage, see for example E.F. Catford to T. Oswald, 3 January 1967 (ECA, LP/10/7). The Earl of Dalkeith, MP, agreed to contact the Postmaster General on behalf of the Lord Provost: Earl of Dalkeith to Mr McNicoll, 4 January 1967 (ECA, LP/10/7). The Postmaster General refused, however, to issue special postage stamps for fear that further demands might arise from other parts of the country.
38 ECA, LP/10/7, H. Forsyth Hardy (Films of Scotland) to E.F. Catford, 13 January 1967.
39 Three bound volumes of photographs of the exhibition were purchased, one for placing in the City Archives, one for the Central Library, and one for retention by the Lord Provost as a memento of the event. *Edinburgh Corporation Committee Minutes*, Minutes of Meeting of 16 October 1967, 170.
40 'Annual Progress Report by the Libraries and Museums Committee for the year to 30th September 1967', in *Council Records, 1967–68*.
41 ECA, LP/10/7, Transport manager to publicity manager, 8 June 1967.
42 ECA, LP/10/7, Catford to Park, 7 February 1967, and Youngson to Catford, 9 March 1967. Youngson favoured naming a street after Craig in the St James Square redevelopment. As part of the bicentenary activities the tombstone of Lord Provost George Drummond in the Canongate Churchyard was restored. The burial place of James Craig in Greyfriars Churchyard was identified by a plaque: *Edinburgh Corporation Committee Minutes*, Minutes of Meeting of 13 March 1967, 398–9; ECA, LP/10/7, 'Account for supplying and laying a plaque at the burial place of James Craig 11 August 1967 (£188, 15 sh.)'.
43 ECA, LP/10/7, New Town Bicentenary, note by Catford dated 14 October 1966.
44 Opening hours were 11am to 9pm on weekdays and 2pm to 6pm on Sundays.
45 Graeme Morton, *Unionist Nationalism: Governing Urban Scotland 1830–1860* (East Linton: Tuckwell Press, 1999), 22–48, 189–200.
46 A four-minute silent film of the Festival exhibition shows that the exhibition was a family experience. 'Edinburgh Festival Exhibition', dir. M. Latyszewski, September 1967: National Library of Scotland, Moving Image Archive.
47 Edinburgh Central Library, Edinburgh Room, DA2222. Edinburgh Corporation, Publicity Department, Notes on 'Two Hundred Summers in a City', 1.
48 Ibid., 2.
49 The Traverse Theatre, founded by Richard Demarco, and the La MaMa were leading experimental theatres. With their liberal approach, they offered challenges to ethical and moral conservatism.

50 John L. Paterson, *New Environment: A Scottish Arts Council Exhibition* (Edinburgh: Scottish Arts Council, 1968), unpaginated.
51 Peter Daniel, *Two Hundred Summers in a City: Edinburgh 1767–1967: Souvenir Programme* (Edinburgh: R. and R. Clark Limited, 1967), unpaginated.
52 The aim of Geddes's survey was to disclose the 'lines of development and deterioration' of the city so that 'the task of practical civics [grew] correspondingly clear, both for municipal statesmanship and for individual and associated effort': P. Geddes, *The Civic Survey of Edinburgh* (Edinburgh: Civics Department, 1911), 538.
53 For Daniel's detailed script, see Paterson to Catford, 14 February 1967 (ECA, LP/10/7). Minute attention was paid to detail, and special ties were made for attendants at the exhibition. They were also available in the best shops in the city: Maddocks & Dick Ltd to Catford, 31 July 1967 (ECA, LP/10/7).
54 Geddes, *Civic Survey of Edinburgh*, 540.
55 It was George Street, not Princes Street, which was planned as the principal thoroughfare.
56 Charles Halkerston, *Princes Street from the Mound, Edinburgh*, oil on panel, 1843, City Art Centre, Museums and Galleries Edinburgh.
57 Paterson, *New Environment*.
58 ECA, LP/10/7, Publicity Officer to Catford, 18 July 1967.
59 They are listed in *The Tablet*, 2 September 1967, and the *Scotsman*, 19 August 1967.
60 In his introduction to the exhibition catalogue *Treasures from Scottish Houses*, Ian Finlay, the Scottish Museum director, stressed the links between Scotland, France, the Low Countries and Italy, and added that the scope of the exhibition held at the Museum was international, showing the decorative arts of Europe. Because of this show, Finlay had to decline the Corporation's suggestion for a special display in the Museum: Ian Finlay to Catford, 12 January 1967 (ECA, LP/10/7).
61 'Open 100' was a contemporary art exhibition organised by Richard Demarco and sponsored by the Festival Society and Edinburgh University.
62 Scottish Civic Trust, *Conservation of Georgian Edinburgh*, 5.
63 In October 1966, Matthew had presented the Corporation with a research project, 'Present Condition and Prospects of Preservation, Repair and Improvement of the New Town of Edinburgh', to be carried out in the Department of Architecture at the University of Edinburgh: Town Planning Officer to the Town Clerk, 5 October 1966 (ECA, LP/10/7).
64 Matthew was a member in his capacity as Secretary of State's conservation adviser. The ENTCC's first director, from 1972, was Desmond Hodges: Glendinning et al., *History of Scottish Architecture*, 477.

Select Bibliography

Abercrombie, Patrick and Robert Matthew. *The Clyde Valley Regional Plan 1946* (Edinburgh: HMSO, 1949).
Adams, Ian H. *The Making of Urban Scotland* (Montreal: Croom Helm, 1978).
Anderson, Robert D., Michael Lynch and Nicholas Phillipson. *The University of Edinburgh: An Illustrated History* (Edinburgh: Edinburgh University Press, 2003).
Anderson, Robert, Mark Freeman and Lindsay Paterson, eds. *The Edinburgh History of Education in Scotland* (Edinburgh: Edinburgh University Press, 2015).
Armet, Helen. 'Notes on rebuilding Edinburgh in the last quarter of the seventeenth century', *Book of the Old Edinburgh Club*, vol. 29 (1956), 111–42.
Arnot, Hugo. *The History of Edinburgh* (1779; Edinburgh: West Port Books, 1998).
Bartie, Angela. *The Edinburgh Festivals: Culture and Society in Post-War Britain* (Edinburgh: Edinburgh University Press, 2013).
Beard, Mary. *The Roman Triumph* (Cambridge, MA.: Harvard University Press, 2007).
Bell, Dorothy. *Edinburgh Old Town: The Forgotten Nature of an Urban Form* (Edinburgh: Tholis, 2008).
Berg, Maxine. 'Women's work, mechanisation and the early phases of industrialisation in England', in Patrick Joyce (ed.), *The Historical Meaning of Work* (Cambridge: Cambridge University Press, 1987), 64–98.
Berry, Christopher. *The Idea of Commercial Society in the Scottish Enlightenment* (Edinburgh: Edinburgh University Press, 2015).
Black, Jeremy. *Eighteenth-Century Britain 1688–1783*, 2nd edn (Basingstoke: Palgrave Macmillan, 2008 [2001]).
Brooking, Tom. *And Captain of their Souls: an Interpretative Essay on the Life and Times of Captain William Cargill* (Dunedin: Otago Heritage Books, 1984).
Brown, Stephen W. and Warren MacDougall, eds. *The History of the Book in Scotland*, vol. 2 (Edinburgh: Edinburgh University Press, 2012).
Buist, James. *National Record of the visit of Queen Victoria to Scotland* (Perth: Perth Printing Company, 1842).
Calderwood, David. *The History of the Kirk of Scotland*, 8 vols (Edinburgh: The Wodrow Society, 1842–49), vol.7 (1845).

Checkland, S.G. *Scottish Banking: A History, 1695–1973* (Glasgow and London: Collins, 1975).

Close, Rob, John Gifford and Frank Arneil Walker. *The Buildings of Scotland: Lanarkshire and Renfrewshire* (New Haven, CT: Yale University Press, 2016).

Coghill, Hamish. *Lost Edinburgh* (Edinburgh: Birlinn, 2014).

Colls, Robert and Richard Rodger, eds. *Cities of Ideas: Civil Society and Urban Governance in Britain 1800–2000* (Aldershot: Ashgate, 2004).

Cooke, Anthony. 'Richard Arkwright and the Scottish cotton industry', *Textile History*, 10 (1979), 196–202.

Cooke, Anthony. 'Cotton and the Scottish Highland Clearances – the development of Spinningdale 1791–1806', *Textile History*, 26 (1995), 89–94.

Cooke, Anthony. *Stanley. From Arkwright Village to Commuter Suburb: 1784–2003* (Perth: Perth and Kinross Libraries, 2003).

Cooke, Anthony. 'The Scottish cotton masters, 1780–1914', *Textile History*, 40 (2009), 29–50.

Cosh, Mary. *Edinburgh: The Golden Age* (Edinburgh: John Donald, 2003).

Cruft, Kitty and Andrew Fraser. *James Craig, The Ingenious Architect of the New Town of Edinburgh* (Edinburgh: Mercat Press, 1995).

Cruft, Kitty, John Dunbar and Richard Fawcett. *The Buildings of Scotland: Borders* (New Haven, CT: Yale University Press, 2006).

Daiches, David, ed. *Selected Political Writings and Speeches of Andrew Fletcher of Saltoun* (Edinburgh: Scottish Academic Press, 1979).

Darling, Elizabeth. *Re-Forming Britain: Narratives of Modernity Before Reconstruction* (Abingdon: Routledge, 2007).

Defoe, Daniel. *A Tour Through the Whole Island of Great Britain* (London and New Haven, CT: Yale University Press, 1991 [1724–6]).

Dennison, E. Patricia. *Holyrood and Canongate: A Thousand Years of History* (Edinburgh: Birlinn, 2005).

Dennison, E. Patricia and Michael Lynch. 'Crown, capital, and metropolis, Edinburgh and Canongate: the rise of a capital and an urban court', *Journal of Urban History*, 32 (2005), 22–43.

Department of Health for Scotland. *Working Class Housing on the Continent* (Edinburgh: HMSO, 1935).

Devine, T.M. *The Tobacco Lords: A Study of the Tobacco Merchants of Glasgow and their Trading Activities c. 1740–1790* (Edinburgh: Edinburgh University Press, 1975).

Devine, T.M., ed. *Scottish Elites* (Edinburgh: John Donald, 1994).

Devine, T.M. *Scotland's Empire 1600–1815* (London: Allen Lane, 2003).

Dingwall, Helen. *Late Seventeenth-Century Edinburgh: A Demographic Study* (Aldershot: Scolar Press, 1994).

Dingwall, Helen. *Physicians, Surgeons and Apothecaries: Medicine in Seventeenth-Century Edinburgh* (East Linton: Tuckwell Press, 1995).

Donnachie, Ian. 'Historic tourism to New Lanark and the falls of Clyde 1795–1830. The evidence of contemporary visiting books and related sources', *Journal of Tourism and Cultural Change*, 2 (2005), 145–62.

Donnachie, Ian, and George Hewitt. *Historic New Lanark. The Dale and Owen Industrial Community since 1785* (Edinburgh: Edinburgh University Press, 1993).

SELECT BIBLIOGRAPHY

Dorrian, Mark. 'The king and the city: on the iconology of George IV in Edinburgh', *Edinburgh Architecture Research*, 30 (2006), 32–36.
Dougherty, Ian. *Dunedin: Founding a New World City* (Dunedin: Saddle Hill Press, 2017).
Dunlop, Jean. *The British Fisheries Society, 1768–1893* (Edinburgh: John Donald, 1978).
Durie, Alastair J. *Scotland for the Holidays: Tourism in Scotland c.1780–1939* (East Linton: Tuckwell Press, 2004).
Edwards, Brian and Paul Jenkins, eds. *Edinburgh, the Making of a Capital City* (Edinburgh: Edinburgh University Press, 2005).
Emerson, Roger L. *Academic Patronage in the Scottish Enlightenment* (Edinburgh: Edinburgh University Press, 2008).
Entwisle, Peter. *Behold the Moon: The European Occupation of the Dunedin District 1770–1848* (Dunedin: Port Daniel Press, 2010).
Evans, Hazel, ed. *New Towns: the British Experience* (New York, 1972).
Extracts from the Records of the Burgh of Edinburgh 1689–1701, ed. Helen Armet (Edinburgh: Oliver and Boyd, 1962).
Extracts from the Records of the Burgh of Edinburgh 1701–1718, ed. Helen Armet (Edinburgh: Oliver and Boyd, 1967).
Fair, Alistair. *Modern Playhouses: an Architectural History of Britain's New Theatres* (Oxford: Oxford University Press, 2018).
Ferguson, Thomas. *The Dawn of Scottish Social Welfare* (London and Edinburgh: Nelson, 1998).
Ferguson, William. *The Identity of the Scottish Nation: an Historic Quest* (Edinburgh: Edinburgh University Press, 1998).
Fitton, R.S. and A.P. Wadsworth. *The Strutts and the Arkwrights 1758–1830: A Study of the Early Factory System* (Manchester: Manchester University Press, 1968).
Foyster, Elizabeth and Christopher A. Whatley, eds. *A History of Everyday Life in Scotland, 1600–1800* (Edinburgh: Edinburgh University Press, 2010).
Geddes, Patrick. *The Civic Survey of Edinburgh* (Edinburgh, Outlook Tower, 1911).
Gifford, John. *The Buildings of Scotland: Edinburgh* (New Haven, CT: Yale University Press, 1984).
Gifford, John. *The Buildings of Scotland: Fife* (New Haven, CT: Yale University Press, 1988).
Gifford, John. *The Buildings of Scotland: Highland and Islands* (New Haven, CT: Yale University Press, 1992).
Glaeser, Edward. *Triumph of the City* (London: Pan, 2012).
Glendinning, Miles. *Modern Architect: the Life and Times of Robert Matthew* (London: RIBA, 2008).
Glendinning, Miles, Ranald MacInnes and Aonghus MacKechnie. *A History of Scottish Architecture* (Edinburgh, Edinburgh University Press, 1996).
Gold, John R. *The Experience of Modernism: Modern Architects and the Future City, 1928–1953* (London: Spon, 1997).
Gold, John R. *The Practice of Modernism: Modern Architects and Urban Transformation, 1954–1972* (Abingdon: Routledge, 2007).
Gordon, George and Brian Dicks, eds. *Scottish Urban History* (Aberdeen: Aberdeen University Press, 1983).

Grant, James. *Cassell's Old and New Edinburgh: Its History, Its People, and Its Places. Illustrated . . .* (London, 1885).

Gray, W. Forbes. 'The Royal Exchange and other city improvements', *Book of the Old Edinburgh Club*, vol.22, 1938.

Greenhalgh, James. *Reconstructing Modernity: Space, Power and Governance in Mid-Twentieth Century British Cities* (Manchester: Manchester University Press, 2017).

Harris, Bob. 'Landowners and urban society in eighteenth-century Scotland', *Scottish Historical Review*, 92:2 (2013), 231–54.

Harris, Bob. *A Tale of Three Cities* (Edinburgh: John Donald, 2015).

Harris, Bob and Charles McKean. *The Scottish Town in the Age of the Enlightenment, 1740–1820* (Edinburgh: Edinburgh University Press, 2014).

Harwood, Elain. *Space, Hope and Brutalism: English Architecture, 1945–1975* (New Haven, CT: Yale University Press, 2015).

Hocken, T.M. *Contributions to the Early History of New Zealand* (London: Sampson Low, Marston and Co., 1898).

Houston, R.A. *Social Change in the Age of Enlightenment: Edinburgh, 1660–1760* (Oxford: Clarendon Press, 1994).

Houston, R.A. 'Fire and faith: Edinburgh's environment, 1660–1760', *Book of the Old Edinburgh Club*, 3 (1994), 25–36.

Houston, R.A. 'The economy of Edinburgh 1694–1763: the evidence of the Common Good', in S.J. Connolly, R.A. Houston and R.J. Morris (eds), *Conflict, Identity and Economic Development: Ireland and Scotland, 1600–1939* (Preston: Carnegie Publishing, 1995), 45–63.

Hume Brown, Peter, ed. *Early Travellers in Scotland* (Edinburgh: David Douglas, 1891).

Jackson, Clare. *Restoration Scotland, 1660–1690* (Woodbridge: Boydell Press, 2003).

Jacobs, Jane. *The Economy of Cities* (1969; London: Jonathan Cape, 1970).

Kipling, Gordon. *Enter the King: Theatre, Liturgy, and Ritual in the Medieval Civic Triumph* (Oxford: Clarendon Press, 1998).

Knox, W.W. *Hanging by a Thread: The Scottish Cotton Industry, c.1850–1914* (Preston: Carnegie Publishing, 1995).

Lauder, Thomas Dick. *Memorial of the Royal Progress in Scotland* (Edinburgh: Adam and Charles Black, 1843).

Law, Alexander. *Education in Edinburgh in the Eighteenth Century* (London: University of London Press, 1965).

Laxton, Paul and Richard Rodger. *Insanitary City: Henry Littlejohn and the Condition of Edinburgh* (Lancaster: Carnegie Publishing, 2013).

Ledgerwood, Norman. *The Heart of the City: The Story of Dunedin's Octagon* (Dunedin: Norman Ledgerwood 2008).

Leneman, Leah and Rosalind Mitchison. *Sin in the City: Sexuality and Social Control in Urban Scotland 1660–1780* (Edinburgh: Scottish Cultural Press, 1998).

Lincoln, Andrew. *Walter Scott and Modernity* (Edinburgh: Edinburgh University Press, 2007).

Lindsay, Robert. *The Chronicles of Scotland*, ed. John Graham Dalyell, 2 vols (Edinburgh: George Ramsay, 1814).

Lockhart, D.G, 'The planned village', in M.L. Parry and T.R. Slater (eds), *The Making of the Scottish Countryside* (London: Taylor and Francis, 1980), 249–70.

SELECT BIBLIOGRAPHY

Lockhart, D.G. ed. *Scottish Planned Villages*, Scottish History Society, 5th series, vol. 16 (Edinburgh, 2012).
Lockhart, John G. *Memoirs of the Life of Sir Walter Scott* (Edinburgh: Adam and Charles Black, 1852).
Lowrey, John. 'From Caesarea to Athens, Greek Revival Edinburgh and the question of Scottish identity within the unionist state', *Journal of the Society of Architectural Historians*, 60:2 (2001), 136–57.
Maitland, William. *History of Edinburgh* (Edinburgh, 1753).
Martin, Marguerite. 'The life and work of Charles Henry Kettle', unpublished MA thesis (University of Otago, Dunedin, 1934).
McCormick, Michael. *Eternal Victory, Triumphal Rulership in Late Antiquity, Byzantium, and the Early Medieval West* (Cambridge, MA.: Cambridge University Press, 1990).
McDonald, K.C. *City of Dunedin: A Century of Civic Enterprise* (Dunedin: Dunedin City Corporation, 1965).
McKean, Charles. *Edinburgh: Portrait of a City* (London: Century, 1991).
McLaren, David J. *David Dale of New Lanark: A Bright Luminary to Scotland* (Milngavie: Heatherbank Press, 1999).
McLintock, A.H. *The History of Otago: The Origins and Growth of a Wakefield Class Settlement* (Dunedin: Otago Centennial Historical Publications, 1949).
McNeil, Kenneth. *Scotland, Britain, Empire: Writing the Highlands, 1760–1860* (Columbus, OH: Ohio State University Press, 2007).
Meller, Helen Elizabeth. *Patrick Geddes: Social Evolutionist and City Planner* (Abingdon: Routledge, 1990).
Mijers, Esther and David Onnekirk, eds. *Redefining William III: The Impact of the King-Stadtholder in International Context* (Aldershot: Ashgate, 2007).
Miller, Robert. *The Municipal Buildings of Edinburgh* (Edinburgh: Printed by Order of the Town Council, 1895).
Mitchison, Rosalind. 'Scotland 1750–1850' in F.M.L. Simpson (ed.), *The Cambridge Social History of Britain*, vol. 1 (Cambridge: Cambridge University Press, 1990), 155–208.
Morton, Graeme. *Unionist Nationalism: Governing Urban Scotland 1830–1860* (East Linton: Tuckwell Press, 1999).
Mudie, Robert. *A Historical Account of His Majesty's Visit to Scotland* (Edinburgh: Oliver and Boyd, 1822).
Nevell, Michael. 'Living in the industrial city: housing quality, land ownership and the archaeological evidence from industrial Manchester, 1740–1850', *Journal for Historical Archaeology*, 15 (2011), 594–606.
Nisbet, Stuart M. 'The making of Scotland's first industrial region: the early cotton industry in Renfrewshire', *Journal of Scottish Historical Studies*, 29 (2009), 1–28.
Olssen, Erik. *A History of Otago* (Dunedin: John McIndoe, 1984).
Parissien, Steven. *George IV: The Great Entertainment* (London: John Murray, 2001).
Phelps, Edmund. *Mass Flourishing* (Princeton, NJ: Princeton University Press, 2013).
Philip, Lorna J. 'The creation of settlements in rural Scotland: planned villages in Dumfries and Galloway', *Scottish Geographical Journal*, 2 (2003), 77–102.

Pittock, Murray. *Enlightenment in a Smart City: Edinburgh's Civic Development, 1660–1750* (Edinburgh, Edinburgh University Press, 2018).

Plunkett, John. *Queen Victoria: First Media Monarch* (Oxford: Oxford University Press, 2003).

Pollard, Sidney. 'The factory village in the industrial revolution', *The English Historical Review*, 79 (1964), 513–31.

Prebble, John. *The King's Jaunt: George IV in Scotland* (London: Harper Collins Publishers, 1988).

Proposals for Carrying on Certain Public Works in the City of Edinburgh (NLS MS 19979).

Ray, James. *A Journey Through Part of England and Scotland Along with the Army Under the Command of his Royal Highness the Duke of Cumberland* (London: Osborne, 1747).

Reiach, Alan and Robert Hurd. *Building Scotland: A Cautionary Guide by Alan Reiach and Robert Hurd* (Edinburgh: C. J. Cousland and Sons for the Saltire Society, 1941).

Rodger, Richard. *The Transformation of Edinburgh: Land, Property and Trust in the Nineteenth Century* (Cambridge: Cambridge University Press, 2001).

Salmond, Arthur. *First Church of Otago and How It Got There* (Dunedin: Otago Heritage Books, 1983).

Savile, Richard. *Bank of Scotland: A History 1695–1995* (Edinburgh: Edinburgh University Press, 1996).

Schaffer, Frank. *The New Town Story* (London: Paladin, 1970).

Schrader, Ben. *The Big Smoke: New Zealand Cities 1840–1920* (Wellington: Bridget Williams Books, 2016).

Scott, Walter. *Hints Addressed to the Inhabitants of Edinburgh, and Others, in Prospect of His Majesty's Visit* (Edinburgh: William Blackwood, 1822).

Scottish Civic Trust. *The Conservation of Georgian Edinburgh: The Proceedings and Outcome of a Conference Organized by the Scottish Civic Trust in Association with the Edinburgh Architectural Association and in Conjunction with the Civic Trust, London* (Edinburgh: Edinburgh University Press, 1972).

Scottish Housing Advisory Committee. *Planning our New Homes* (Edinburgh: HMSO, 1944).

Siméon, Ophélie. *Robert Owen's Experiment at New Lanark: From Paternalism to Socialism* (London: Palgrave Macmillan, 2017).

Smout, T.C. 'The landowner and the planned village', in Rosalind Mitchison and Nicholas Phillipson (eds), *Scotland in the Age of Improvement* (Edinburgh: Edinburgh University Press, 1970), 73–106.

Smout, T.C. *Scottish Trade on the Eve of Union 1600–1707* (Edinburgh and London: Oliver and Boyd, 1963).

Stevenson, Robert Louis. *Edinburgh: Picturesque Notes* (1878; London: Seeley, 1889).

Stewart, Laura A.M. *Urban Politics and the British Civil Wars* (Leiden and Boston, MA: Brill, 2006).

Stewart, Margaret. *The Architectural Landscape and Constitutional Plans of the Earl of Mar, 1700–32* (Dublin: Four Courts Press, 2016).

Tripp, H. Alker. *Town Planning and Road Traffic* (London: Edward Arnold, 1942).

SELECT BIBLIOGRAPHY

Urban, Florian. 'Modernising Glasgow – tower blocks, motorways and new towns 1940–2010', *Journal of Architecture*, 23:2 (2018), 265–309.

Wade Martins, Susanna and Miles Glendinning. *Buildings of the Land: Scotland's Farms 1750–2000* (Edinburgh: RCAHMS, 2009).

Ward, Colin. *New Town, Home Town: The Lessons of Experience* (London: Gulbenkian Foundation, 1993).

Watt, Douglas. *The Price of Scotland: Darien, Union and the Wealth of Nations* (Edinburgh: Luath Press, 2007).

Watt, W.J. *Dunedin's Historical Background* (Dunedin: Dunedin Planning Department, 1972).

Whatley, Christopher A. and Derek Patrick. *The Scots and the Union* (Edinburgh: Edinburgh University Press, 2006).

White, Jerry. *London in the Eighteenth Century* (London: The Bodley Head, 2012).

White, L.E. *Community or Chaos? Housing Estates and their Social Problems* (London: NCSS, 1950).

Wood, Marguerite. 'Survey of the development of Edinburgh', *Book of the Old Edinburgh Club*, 34 (1974), 23–56.

Youngson, A.J. *The Making of Classical Edinburgh 1750–1840* (Edinburgh: Edinburgh University Press, 1966).

Index

Page references in *italic* refer to illustrations. Page references with the suffix 'n' are within the endnotes.

Streets and buildings listed are in Edinburgh unless otherwise stated.

Abercrombie, Patrick 159, 162, 193, 197, 212, 264
Abercrombie Report 159, 162, 253
Aberdeen 80, 116, 129, 136, 234
Aberdour 136
Aberdour Castle 32
Abernethy 136
Académie Royale des Sciences 69, 70
Academy of St Luke 37
accommodation
    in the New Town 140, 141–6
    provision of 134, 141–6, 150
    rapid rise in 144, 145
Adair's Temperance Hotel 145
Adam, James 5, 6, 190
Adam, John 84–7, 95, 190
Adam, Robert 3, 95, 190, 223, 236, 241, 245–7
    plans for Lisbon 3, 6
    plans for New Town 4, 5, *8, 10–11*, 239
Adam, William 80, 82, 107
Adam House 247
Adamson, Robert 267
Addison, Joseph 95
Adelaide 169
Adelphi Terrace, London 299n
Advocates' Library 31

Ainslie Place 173
Aitken, George Shaw 225
Aitken's Temperance Hotel 145
Albany, Duke (James) of 31
Albert, Prince 14, 99, 100, 110, 113
Alemore, Lord 86
Alexander II, King of Scotland 43
Alexander III, King of Scotland 50
Alexander, Claude 185, 191
Allan, Alasdair 2
Allan, David 92
Alloa 70, 137
Amsterdam
    herb garden 32
    street lighting in 22
Anderson, Robert Rowand 61
Anne of Denmark, Queen (of James VI and I) 100, 111
Argyll, 3rd Duke of 56
Argyll, Marquis of 29
Arkwright, Richard 183–7
Arnott, Ian Emslie 248
Arrol, Thomas 151, 152
Arthur's Seat 72
artisans, provision for 114, 117, 121, 127, 239
Arts Council of Great Britain 204, 255, 300n

INDEX

Arts Tower 253
Assaville, Nicolas d' 59
Assembly Rooms 239, 260
Athelstaneford 136
Athens 221, 246
Atholl, Duke of 185, 190
Auchtermuchty 136
Avenue des Champs-Élysées, Paris 70
Ayr Bank 87

bakers 118
Balcarres, Countess of 28
Balfour, Dr Andrew 32
Balfron 183, 185
Bank of Scotland 27, 30, 108, 266
Barker, Robert 267
Barlow Report (1940) 196
Barnett, Corelli 211
Barrhead 183
Bath (city) 89
Beach Boys, The 256
Beatles, The 256
Becontree 197
Begg, Ian 248
Bell Hill, Dunedin, NZ 169, 172
Bellhouse Brae 21
Belper 187
Beltane, Feast of 30
Bendix, Reinhard 191
Berlin 76
Bernard Street 108
Berwick-upon-Tweed 46, *48*, 57, 62, 63
  annexation of 50, 63
  Castle 44, 49
  leading burgh 44
  street plan 47
Bishopton 193
Black Friars Wynd 32
Blairadam 82
Blantyre 183, 185
Blythswood, Colonel 94
Boak, Ann 124
Bois de Boulogne, Paris 70
Bonar, John 126
Bo'ness 278n

bookselling and printing 34, 36, 119
Boswell, James 95
botanic gardens 35
Boullée, Étienne-Louis 267
Boulton & Watt Ltd 190
Bowmore, Islay 57
Brandon Street 112
brass founders 117, 118
Brechin, H.A. 261
Bridge Committee 84, 86
Bridge of Weir 183
Bristo Street 131, 136
British Home Stores 253
Brochs 41
Brooking, Tom 173
Broomielaw, Glasgow 80, 81
Broughton Street 120, 127, 141
Brown, A. 269
Brown, Professor Baldwin 221
Brown, Dennis 258
Brown, James 241
Brown, John 125
Bruce, David 261
Bruce, Sir William 57
Bryce, David 253
Bryden, Robert & Sons 119
Buchanan, Andrew 258
Buchanan, George 82
Buchanan's Temperance Hotel 145
Building Acts 148, 151
Bunnahabhain Distillery, Islay 57
Burden's Temperance Hotel 145
burghs, creation of 41, 42
Burke, Ian 254
Burke, Peter 24
Burn, William 253
Burnett, J.J. 149
Burns, John 230
Bute, 4th Marquess of 247

cabinet makers 121–5
Caledonian Mercury 35
Calton Hill 72, 107, 127, 220
Cambuskenneth Abbey 46
Cameron, Charles 270, 290
Cameron, John (hotelier) 142

Cameron's (coaches and hauliers) 131, 136
Campbell, Alexander Buchanan 213
Campbell, Colen 79
Campbell, Daniel 78, 79
Campbell, Margaret 126
Campbell's 'Thane of Fife' coaches 134
Campbeltown 55, 56
Candlemaker Row 31
Canongate, Dunedin 172
Canongate, Edinburgh 26, 29, 33, 34, 44, 85, 102, 109, 260
Canongate Kirk 30, 58
Capper, Stewart Henbest 226
Cargill, Capt William 166
Cargill Monument, Dunedin *179*
Carron Iron Works, Falkirk 115
Castle Street 141, 250
Castle Wynd 21
Catford, E.F. 261
Catherine the Great 270
Catrine 183–5, 187–9
Celtic FC 256
Chambers, Sir William 95, 245, 299n
charity concerts 36
Charles I, King 100, 111
Charles II, King 30, 59
Charlotte Square 5, *8*, *10*, 106, 223, 239, 247
Cheisly, Sir Robert 34
children, working conditions of 188–90
Church of Scotland 94, 166
Cities and Towns Planning Exhibition (1910) 230
Civic Amenities Act (1967) 254
Cleansing Committee (1678) 21
Clearances 184, 189
Clerk, Sir James 86, 190
Clyde Report (1943) 162
Clyde Valley Regional Plan (1946) 193, 196, 197
coach services 130–5, 140
Cocher, Emmanuel 2
Cochrane, Lt Col John 126

313

Cockburn, Lord Henry (judge) 126
Cockburn, William (cabinet maker) 122
Cockburn Association 157, 225, 246, 254
Cockburn Street 140, 245, 250
Cockerell, Charles Robert 221
Cocteau, Jean 255
Colvin, Brenda 193
Commissioners of the Forfeited Estates 187
Committee for Trade 31
Committee of Princes Street Proprietors 155
Company of Scotland 30, 31
Connell, Frank 193
Conservation Areas 254
Constable, Archibald 150
Constitution Street 108
Cooper, Richard 37
Coopers 117
Corbusier, Le (Charles Édouard Jeanneret) 253
cotton mill villages 183–5
Coutts, John 30
Cowdenknowes 51
Cowgate 26, 72, 131, 140, 245
Craig, James 78, 84, 93, 95, 96, 113, 220, 260, 280n
   awarded freedom of Edinburgh 87
   plans for New Town 3, 9, 72, 85–7, 88–9, 90–6, 147, 157, 227, 239, 241, 253
   royal approval 88, 89
Craig, Sir James Gibson 151
Craig, John Sr (carpenter) 79–82
Craig, John Jr 82
Craig, Robert (grandfather of James) 84
Craig, William (father of James) 84
Cramond 276n
Crombie, Benjamin W. 266
Cromford 183–7, 190
Cruft, Catherine 257
Cumbernauld 62, 193, 211
Cunzie House: *see* Scottish Mint

Dale, David 184–9, 191
Dalkeith, Palace of 99
Daniel, Peter 259, 263, 264, 269
Darien 57
David I, King of Scotland 2, 41, 42, 45, 47, 62, 63
David Hume Tower 253, 269
Davison, William 168, 169, 174, 178
Dean Village 59
Deanston 183–5, 189
Defoe, Daniel 78, 79
Delisle, Guillaume 69, 70
delivery of the keys 100, 111–13
Demarco, Richard 303n
Dempster, George 185, 186, 189
Denby, Elizabeth 202
Derain, André 269
Development Corporations (New Towns) 196, 205, 208, 209
Diamand, Peter 256
Dibdin, Thomas 122
Dighton, Denis 243
Disruption of the Church (1843) 166
Dollan, Sir Patrick 208
Dollan Baths, East Kilbride 213
Donside 184
Dougherty, Ian 178
Douglas, Alexander 151
Douglas, John 79, 82
Dowell, James 122, 123
Dowling, Dionysus Wilfred 172
Dreghorn, Allan 11, 78, 80–4, 96
Dreghorn, Robert Sr 81
Dreghorn, Robert Jr 81
droving 21
Drummond, Sir George 9, 38, 72, 73, 84
Dryburgh Abbey 46
Drysdale's Turf coffee house 131
Dublin Street Church 249
Dudley Report 198
Dumbarton 43
Dumbreck, William 144
Dunbar (town) 43
Dunbar-Nasmith, James 258, 260
Dundas, Alexander 122
Dundas, Sir Lawrence 239, 299n

Dundee Town House 80
Dunedin, NZ 2, 57, *170–1*, *180–1*
   design of 15, 18, 168, 169
   Edinburgh of the South 165
   familiarity of name 167
   first settlers 174, 175
   street names 169, 172
Dunedin Bank 167
Dunfermline 42
   Palace and Abbey 51
Dunkeld 58
Dunlop, Colin and Robert 82
Duns 50, 52–5
Duns Law 52
dyers 118
Dylan, Bob 256

Eaglesham 185, 190
East India Company 30
East Kilbride 193–5, *198*, 201, 204–11
   built to high standards 194, 210
   focus on community 201, 205, 208
   high birth rate 212
   high levels of car ownership 210
   leisure opportunities 199, 209
   neighbourhood units 198
   population 204, 212
   proposed facilities 205, 206
East Kilbride Development Corporation 205, 208, 209
Edinburgh
   accommodation for visitors 134, 140
   as Athens of the North 42, 107, 222, 257, 263
   as Auld Reekie 3, 260
   challenges of mass tourism 246
   changing identity 99
   charter for expansion 106
   coach services 130–5, 140
   cosmopolitan nature of 29, 238
   cultural metropolis 38, 113
   encouraging civility 107, 112, 113

INDEX

forward-thinking 105, 106, 111
as picturesque 73, 110
as Reykjavik of the South 257
romantic image 238
sanitary system 225
scientific reputation 105
self-regarding 'people's city' 241
as a theatrical arena 243
transport network 134, 137
urban management 137
wealth of 27
Edinburgh and Glasgow Railway Company 144, 152
Edinburgh Architectural Association 225, 255, 257, 258, 271
Edinburgh Castle 25, 110, 222, 236
Edinburgh City Council 109, 248
Edinburgh Courant 35
Edinburgh Evening Courant 35
Edinburgh Festival Fringe 256
Edinburgh Festival Society 255, 257, 258
Edinburgh Gazette 35
Edinburgh Health Society
Edinburgh Improvement Act (1827) 139
Edinburgh International Festival 255, 256, 258, 270
Edinburgh Merchant Company 31
Edinburgh New Town Conservation Committee 247, 248, 254, 271
Edinburgh Old Town Committee for Conservation and Renewal 248
Edinburgh Social Union 224, 225
Edinburgh Town Council 3, 23, 85, 86, 88, 91, 137, 255
Edinburgh University 36, 224
Edward I, King of England 50
Edzell, proposals for 55, 56
Eglinton (mill village) 183
Eglinton, Earl of 190
Eichtal, Gustave d' 234, 235
Elgin 43, 44
Elliot, Archibald 155
Elliot, Sir Gilbert 9, 31, 37, 38, 107

English-Speaking Union 270
engravers 116
Enlightenment, The 19
Entwistle, Peter 178
Environment Society 224
Erskine, John *see* Mar, 6th Earl of
Erskine, Rev Dr John 85, 86
Evelyn, John 65
Ewbank, John Wilson 266
Ewing, Winnie 256
Expositions: (1886) 226; Paris (1900) 261, 268

Factory Enquiry Commission 191
factory villages 183–91
children's working hours 188, 189
educational provision 188, 190
paternalistic employers 186, 187, 189–91
Faculty of Advocates 36, 37
Falls of Clyde 190
Fergus, Peter 84
Ferguson, Walter 90
Ferrier, Louis Henry 119
Films of Scotland Committee 261
Findlay, John Ritchie 59, 60
Finlay, Ian 304n
Finlay, James & Co 186, 187, 192
Finlay, Kirkman 187, 191
Fintry 183
fire regulations (1701) 23
fleshers 120
Fletcher, Andrew of Saltoun 70, 73
Flodden Wall 24
Forbes, William 150
Forres 44
Forsyth, Alexander 33
Forsyth, R.W. (department store) 149, 162
Fort William 58
Fowler, Margaret 151, 155
Fraser, Malcolm 249
Frederick Street 141, 149, 158
Free Church of Scotland 166, 244
French Consulate 2

Fry, Maxwell 158, 202
Gallery of Modern Art, Edinburgh 269
garden cities 57, 196
Gardner-Medwin, Robert 193
Gatehouse of Fleet 183
Gaulle, Charles de 2
Geddes, Patrick 18, 217–33, 263, 268, 269
as an Athenian 219
close identity with Edinburgh 217
in India 218
Geddes Society 264
General Assembly Building 106
General Register House 107, 241, 260
Geographer-Royal for Scotland 31
George I, King 72
George III, King 88, 220
George IV, King 99–101, 104, 105, 107–10, 113, 144, 243
images of Scottishness 104, 105
George IV Bridge 139
George Inn Coaches 131
George Square, Edinburgh 173, 252, 253, 269
George Street, Dunedin 172
George Street, Edinburgh 83, 91, 107, 121–27, 138, 141, 155, 162, 220, 239, 260
George Watson's College 84
Gerard, Alexander 94
Gibb, Robert 32, 33
Gibbs, James 76, 79, 82
Glaeser, Edward 24
Glasgow
beautification of 78, 79
development of 78–85
Duke of Montrose's house 78, 79
and New Towns 193, 194, 204, 213
railway development 144, 155
Shawfield 79
street plan 79, 83

Town Council 79, 81, 82, 96
Trongate 79
Glasgow Cathedral 78, 82
Glasgow Green 82
Glasgow University 21, 187
Glass Development Committee 158
Gleave, J.L. 162
Glencoe, Massacre of 58
Glenrothes 200
goldsmiths 27, 28
Graham, James Gillespie 173, 223, 223, 244
Graham, Kenneth 253
Grand Tour 29
Grant, James 148
Grant & Moire, printers 115
Grassmarket 25, 130, 140
Greater London Plan (1944) 196
green belts 169
Greenhalgh, James 199
Gregory, David 94
Gretna 57
Grieve, Robert 156
Guise, Mary of 29
Gwynn, John 91, 245

hackney carriages 32, 138
Haddington 44, 51
Haig, Alexander 125
Halkerston's Wynd 32
Hall, Eric 257
Hamilton, Thomas 8, 9, 221
design for National Gallery and RSA 9, *12–13*
Hamilton & Inches 127
Hanover, House of 7, 104
Hanover Street 122, 141
Hare, L.B. 125
Hargreaves (hauliers) 136
Hart, Judith MP 213
hauliers 136, 137
Hawksmoor, Nicholas 65
Hay, Alexander 33
Health and Morals of Apprentices Act (1802) 188
Henderson, David 87
Herriott, Alexander 34
High Street, Dunedin 172

High Street, Edinburgh 23, 25, 26, 84, 109
Hill, David Octavius 15–17, 218, 267
Hill, Col John 58
Hill, Octavia 224, 227
Historiographer-Royal 31
Hocken, Thomas 178
Hodges, David (jeweller) 121
Hogg, James 167
Hogganfield, Glasgow 82
Holyrood Palace 26, 31, 32, 61, 70–2, 100, 110, 281n
Holyrood Park 72
Home, Bruce J. 226
Hope, Robert 94
Hortus Medicus garden 32
hotels, provision of 14, 141, 144–6, 150, 246
Housing for the Working Classes Act (1890) 225
Houston (town) 193
Houston, Alexander 82
Houston, Sir Robert 41
Howard, Ebenezer 196, 197, 229
Howe Street 141
Howey & Co. (hauliers) 136
Hudson's Bay Company 31
Hume, David 243
Hunter, Robert 227
Hunter Square 59
Huntly House Museum 260, 261, 266
Hurd, Robert 158, 159, 247, 248

Île-de-France, Paris 69, 70
Improvement Act (1827) 245
Inglis, Francis Caird 218, 222, 230, 232
International Congress on the Enlightenment (1967) 261
International Exhibition of Industry, Science and Art (Edinburgh, 1886) 264
International Health Exhibition (1884) 261
Inveraray 62
Inveraray Castle 56

Inverness 58
Inverurie 44
Irvine 193, 213, 214

Jacobite Risings 7, 56, 73, 102
Jacobs, Jane 19
Jamaica Street 120, 127, 141
James IV, King of Scotland 100
James V, King of Scotland 104
James, VI and I, King 55, 100, 101, 111
James VII and II, King 9, 30, 58, 71
James VIII and III, King 65, 66
James Court 223, 224
James Street 141
Jamieson, Patrick 84, 85, 280n
Jedburgh Abbey 46, 49
Jeffrey Street 246
Jenners Stores 162
Jerusalem 50
jewellers 117
Johnson-Marshall, Percy 253
Johnstone 183
Jordan, Robert Furneaux 158–61
Juvarra, Filippo 76

Kahn, Louis 247
Kames, Lord 86, 94
Kaufmann, Emil 247
Kay, John 266
Keith, Thomas 267
Kelso 44, 45
Kensal House 202
Kettle, Charles 15, 167–9, 173, 174, 177, 178
Key Centre, East Kilbride 213
Kilpatrick, John 120
Kininmonth, Sir William 162, 247
Kirkwood, James & Sons (printers) 115, 116
Kirkwood, Robert 148, 159
Knox, John 257
Kyrle Society 224

Lammermuir Hills 51
Lamotte, Charles 92

INDEX

Landa, Manuel de 25
'lands', character of 26
Laurie, Gilbert 87
Laurie, John 86, 113
Law, John 28
Lawnmarket 29, 223, 225
Lawson, Gavin 79
Lee, Jennie 204
leisure facilities in new towns 199–204
Leith 27, 32, 57, 95, 99, 109, 116, 131, 140, 141, 144, 146, 220, 221
Leith Walk 112
Letchworth 196
Libberton's Wynd 29
libraries 36
Lindsay, Sir David 55
Lindsay, Ian G. 257, 258, 301n
Lindsay, Maurice 254
Lisbon 236
    earthquake (1755) 3
    proposals by Robert Adam 3, 6
Livingston 213, 214
Lizars, W.H. 173
lodging houses 120, 131, 141, 144
Loi Malraux legislation 254
London County Council 197
London Evening Post 91
Lorimer, Robert 250
Louis XIV, King of France 68, 70
Luckenbooths 25, 28, 37
Luke, Robert 81

mail coaches 128–30
Mainard the Fleming 45, 47, 48
Malt Tax riots (1725) 79, 80
Manchester Board of Health 188
Mar, 6th Earl of (John Erskine)
    constitutional plan 64
    plans for Edinburgh 9, 72–7
    plans for London 65, *66–7*
    plans for Paris 65, *68–69*
Margaret, Queen
    (of Alexander III) 50
Margaret Tudor, Queen
    (of James IV) 100

MARS Group 197
Martin, Alexander 115
Marwick, T.P. 247
Mary of Guise, Queen
    (of James V) 29, 100, 104
Mary, Queen of Scots 100, 109
Matthew, Sir Robert 193, 253, 254, 258, 271
May's Temperance Hotel 145
McCallam, James 124
McFarlane, Miss J. 126
McGibbon, David 152, 155
McGibbon, Matthew 35
McGill, Alexander 59, 79
McGill, John and Thomas 120
McGrath, Raymond 158
McKay, James 258
McKean, Charles 214
McKean, John 151
McLaurin, Colin 94
Macrae, Ebenezer 92, 162, 199
Macreadie, Alex 151
McWilliam, Colin 260, 261
Meadows, The 265
Melrose 49
Melrose Abbey 46, 49, 51
Melville Monument 107
Mercat cross, removal of 30
Merchants' Exchange 84
Miller, Hugh 234, 235
Milne's Square 30
Ministry of Town and Country Planning 196
Mitchell, A.G. Sydney 59, 226, 265
Moir, David Macbeth 167
Modernism. 158, 247
Moray Estate 173
Moray Place, Dunedin 173
Moray Place, Edinburgh 173, 223
Morow, John 51
Morris, Henry 202
Morris, Robert 94
Morris, William 222, 225
Morton, Anna 224
Morton, Earl of 32
Mound, The 8, 155, 230, 243, 244, 267

muckmen 21
Muir's Coaches 131
Murdoch, John 83
Murphy, Richard 249
Mylne, Robert 85
Mylne, William 85–87
    plan for New Town 86, 87
Mylne Square 241
Mylne's Land, Leith 241

Nairn, Tom 256, 257
Nasmyth, Alexander 150
National Council for Social Service 202
National Monument of Scotland 106
National Museum of Antiquities 270
National Portrait Gallery 63
National Trust, foundation of 227
neighbourhood units, concept of 197, 198, 211, 213
Neilston 183
Nelson, John 266
Nelson, NZ 166, 169
neo-classical design 59, 190, 247
Nesbitt, James 81
Netherbow 25, 29, 111, 226, 265
Nevell, Michael 191
New Club 159, 253, 257, 266
New Edinburgh Scheme, NZ 166, 167
New Lanark 183–85, 188–90
New Plymouth, NZ 166, 169
New Thurso 169
New Town, Edinburgh
    1970 Conference 248, 254
    accommodation for visitors 140, 141
    Bicentenary celebrations 257–71
    as a business district 84, 150, 242
    centrality of 113
    as a cultural metropolis 38, 113, 235
    designed to stimulate prosperity 114

early proposals for 84
harmonisation 94, 157
juxtaposition with Old Town 234
as a monument 239
as a narrative 243
one entity with Old Town 235
provision for artisans 117
post-war modernisation 157, 159, 162
repair scheme 248
second New Town (1802) 127
without commerce 147, 240
New Town Planning Committee 85
new towns in Scotland 1, 2, 193–212
communities, emphasis on 199, 200, 202, 203
definition of term 196
leisure facilities 199, 204, 209
principles behind 196, 202, 203, 298n
social experiment 202, 211, 212
see also Cumbernauld, East Kilbride, Glenrothes, Irvine, Livingston
New Towns Act (1946) 195, 196, 208
New York, University of 263
New Zealand Company 166, 167, 169
Newhaven 110
Newton Stewart 185
Nicolson Square 108
nobility
classes of 20, 21
large numbers in Edinburgh 21, 33, 34
Nodier, Charles 220
Nor' Loch 21, 25, 31, 72, 84, 85, 239
draining of 73, 168
North Bridge 85, 127, 131, 138, 140, 155, 236, 237–38, 241, 258, 266
collapse of 87
North Frederick Street 119
North St David Street 117

Nôtre, André le 68, 69
Nottingham Town & Country Social Guild 224
Nuttgens, Patrick 248

Octagon, Dunedin 173
Old Assembly Close, fire in 115
Old Bank Close 30
Old Edinburgh Club 226, 255, 257
Old Melrose 42
Old Poor Laws 191
Old Scotch Independents 188
Old Statistical Account 189
Old Town, Edinburgh 61
cosmopolitan character
one entity with New Town 24, 234, 235
redesigned 237
stablers 140
as a vertical environment 28
Oliphant, James 224
Oliphant, Laurence 37
Otago, NZ 167, 174, 178
Outlook Tower 228, 229, 263, 265, 268
Owen, Robert 190, 191

painters and decorators 118, 126
palace-front buildings 240, 299n
Paris 29, 71, 96, 159, 261, 268
Exposition (1900) 261, 268
plans for redevelopment 68–9
street lighting in 22
Paris Gazette 35
Paris, Matthew 50
Park, Robert 168, 172, 177, 178
Parliament Close 21, 28, 30, 34, 59
Parliament House 29
Parliament Square 2, 26, 28, 30
Paterson, John L. 259, 260, 263, 269, 270
Paterson's Court 115
Patrick Geddes Centre 1, 2
Peddie, John Dick 155
Peebles 43
Peel, Sir Robert 109
Penicuik 183, 185, 189

Perry, Clarence 197
Phelps, Edmund 20
Philip, Lorna 184
Phillipson, Nicholas 34
physic gardens 32
Physicians' Hall 9, 95
Picardy Place 59
Picturesque 73, 76, 190
Pilkington Glass Company 158
Pinkerton Estate 82
planned towns and villages 41, 182–91
plasterers 115
Playfair, William H. 155, 156, 173, 221, 230
design for National Gallery and RSA 8, *14–15*, 236, 244
Plumstead, Derek 159
Pombal, Marquês de 6
Pool, Matthew (hotelier) 144
Poole's Hotel 150
Porcacchi, Thomaso 50
Port Chalmers, NZ 172
Port Glasgow 78, 80
Porte Saint-Honoré, Paris 29
Post Office 30
postal service, development of 30, 128–30
Princes Street, Dunedin 172, 177, *179*
Princes Street, Edinburgh 7–9, 79, 85, 121, 122, 138–41, 146, 147, 150, 154–58, 162, 219, 221, 236, 239, 241, 246, 262
conversion into flats 151
harmonious appearance 156
monotony of design 148, 149
plans for redesign 158–9, *160–1*, 162
triple-deck roadway proposal 162
ultra-modern shopping 246
Princes Street Gardens 155, 236, 260
Princes Street Panel 162, 247, 253

INDEX

Pringle, Sir John 88
printers 115
Privy Council 20, 23, 31
Progressive Party 257
public houses, state management of 203
Pugin, A.W.N. 159

Queen Street 9, 83, 119, 144, 155, 239
Queensferry Road 110

railways, development of 128, 144, 155, 156, 236
Ramsay, Allan 36–8, 226
Ramsay Gardens 226
Randolph Crescent 2, 173
Rawnsley, Canon Hardwicke 227
Reay, Donald P. 193, 205
Reclus, Élisée 268
Regent Bridge 139, 236
Regent Road 100, 246
Regen Terrace 2, 258
Regent, Royal and Carlton Terraces Association 258
Reiach, Alan 158, 159, 162, 247, 254
Reid, Robert 5
Reith, Lord John 197, 211
Rennie, George 166, 172
Rennie, Robert 185
Restoration, The 29
Rhind, David 155, 253
Ritchie, David (hauliers) 136
River Clutha, NZ 167
River Derwent, Derbyshire 183
River Kelvin 81
River Seine, Paris 70, 71
River Teviot 46
River Tweed 46, 49
Robert I, King of Scotland 51, 60
Robertson, George 190
Robertson, Howard 158
Robertson, James 126
Robinson, Robert 84
Rodger, Richard 26
Romanticism 167, 237, 247

Rose Street 117–20, 122, 131, 141, 239, 255
  businesses in 117, 118
  designed for artisans 117
Roseburn 127
Rosenburg, Lou 224
Ross, Lady 126
Rothesay 183
Rough Wooings 51
Roundele, la 49
Roxburgh 45, 46, 50, 51, 63
Royal African Company 31
Royal Bank of Scotland 27, 185
Royal College of Physicians 31, 32, 37, 91, 92
Royal Commission on the Ancient and Historical Monuments of Scotland (RCAHMS) 264
Royal Mile 2, 21, 26, 265
Royal Scottish Academy 8, *11, 14*, 155, *156*, 230, 231, 236, 244, 269
Royal Scottish Museum 269
Royal Society of Scotland 35
Ruchill House, Glasgow 82
Rue de Rivoli, Paris 159
Runcorn 213
Ruskin, John 222
Russell, James Alexander 225
Rye, Maria S. 174, 175

Saint-Germain-en-Laye 68
Saint-Quentin, France 59
St Andrew Square 107, 173, 243
St Andrew Street 141, 149
St Andrews, Fife 42, 45
St Andrews Cathedral 62
St Andrew's Church, Edinburgh 107, 239
St Andrew's House, Edinburgh 246
St Andrew's in the Square, Glasgow 82, 83
St David Street 141
St George's Church 5, *10*, 107
St Giles' Cathedral 2, 51
St James Centre 254
St James Square 90, 241

St John's Church 244
St Mary's Cathedral 244
Saltire Court 248
Saltire Society 201, 256
Sanitary Society of Edinburgh 225
Sartre, Jean-Paul
Scandic Crown Hotel 248
Schouvaloff, Alexander 257, 258
Scots Magazine 85
Scots Postman 35
Scotsman building 61, 108
Scott, J. & Co. (coaches) 1131
Scott, Mr (banker) 126
Scott, Sir George Gilbert 244
Scott, Sir Walter 63, 104, 107, 109, 111–13, 243, 287n
  Bicentenary celebrations 259
Scott Monument 117, 244
Scottish Arts Council 263
Scottish Civic Trust 271
Scottish Enlightenment 32, 35
Scottish Exchange 27, 108
Scottish Georgian Society 254
Scottish Hub 2
Scottish Mint (Cunzie House) 29
Scottish National Gallery 8, *12–14*, 155, 236, 243, 244, 260
Scottish National Party 256
Scottish National War Museum 250
Scottish Parliament 23
Selkirk 43
Senckenburg, Johann Christian 32
Shakespeare Square 116, 141
Shapiro, Helen 256
Shawfield, Glasgow 78, 79, 83
Shepherd, Thomas H. 266
shoemakers 117
Shooters' Hill New Town 90, 91
Sibbald, Sir Robert 32, 35
Silkin, Lewis 195, 211
Simon of Senlis 50
Simpson, David 257
Sinclair, George 21
Sinclair, Sir John of Thurso 169, 185

319

Skara Brae 41
slavery 78, 191
Smith, Adam 26, 243
Smith, James 30, 57, 79
Society for the Protection of Ancient Buildings 225
Sorlin, François 9
South Bridge 33, 59, 73, 138, 236, 241, 245
South St Andrew Street 116, 145
South St David Street 126, 145
Spence, Basil 253
Spiegl, Fritz 269
Spinningdale 183, 185–87, 189
stablers 140
Staël, Nicolas de 269
Stanley, Perthshire 183–85, 189, 190
Steell, John (carver and gilder) 116, 117
Steell, Sir John (artist, son of above) 116, 117
Steen, William 34
Steuart, David 91, 92
Stevenson, Robert Louis 245, 264
Stirling 43, 49
Stobie, James 190
Stockbridge 127
Stoppard, Tom 257
Stornoway 55, 57
Stranraer
street cleaning, initiation of 21, 22
street lighting 22
Stromness, Orkney 55
Strutt family 187
Sturgeon, Nicola 2
'Summer of Love' (1967) 255
Sun Alliance Co 122
Sunday Times, 209
Sutherland, James 32
Swarbreck, Samuel Dukinfield 266

Talman, William 65
Taylor, John & Co. (cabinet makers) 120
temperance hotels 145
Temple of Science 32

tenement living, tradition of 240
terraced houses 59, 58, 299n
Thirty Years' War 31
Thistle Street 117, 119–23, 141, 239
  craft businesses in 119, 122
Thomson, Charles (engraver) 116
Thomson, James (poet) 84, 92, 95, 157
Thomson, Mary 84
Thornliebank 183
Times, The 176
tinsmiths 117
Toddie's Well 21
Tolbooth 226
Top Shop (Princes Street) 149
Tripp, Alker 198
Tron Kirk 138
Trotter, Sir Alexander 155, 156
Trotter, William (cabinet maker) 122
True Britain Coaches 130
Tuckett, Frederick 166, 168
Tuileries Palace, Paris 68
Turin 76
'Two Hundred Summers' exhibition 261, 268, 270

Union Canal, opening of 139
Union of the Parliaments (1707) 7, 30, 64, 70, 73, 113, 182
Unwin, Raymond 57
urbanism, rise of 70, 73, 76, 227, 229, 230, 240
Usher Hall 256

Versailles, Palace of 69
Victoria, Queen 14, 99–104, 107, 109–13, 287n
Victoria Hall 106
Victoria Street 139, 245
village colleges 202
Virginia Mansion, Glasgow 82

Wakefield, Edward Gibbon 165, 166
Wakefield, William 169
Waldie's Coaches 131, 134

Waleys, Sir Richard le 278n
Walker, Alexander (hotelier) 144
Walker's Hotel 150
Wallace, William 60, 61
wallpaper printers 115, 126
Wanganui, NZ 166
Ward, Colin 211
Wars of the Three Kingdoms 31
Water of Leith, Dunedin 172
Waterloo Place 236
Watson, James (cabinetmaker) 124
Watson & Co. 124, 125
Waverley Market 259, 265, 269
weavers 59, 114, 188
Webster, Dr Alexander 86
Weir's Museum 150
Well Court 59
Wellington, NZ 166
Welwyn Garden City 196
West Port 25, 111
Westwood Report (1944) 198, 200
Wet, Jacob de 31
Wild, Hans 269
Wilkie, David 105
Wilkinson's Coaches 131
Williams, Hugh William 220
Wilson, Harold 262
Wilson, Hugh 213
Wishart, D.S. 162
Wood, John the Elder 91, 94
Woodburn, Arthur 204
World Exhibition (Paris 1900) 261, 268
World Heritage Site status 1, 245, 248, 249
World War 1 41
Wornum, G. Grey 158
Wren, Christopher 65
Writers to the Signet 36
Wythenshawe 197

Yair, John 36
Yorke, F.R.S. 158
Young, Trotter & Hamilton (cabinetmakers) 122
Youngson, A.J. 9, 25, 258

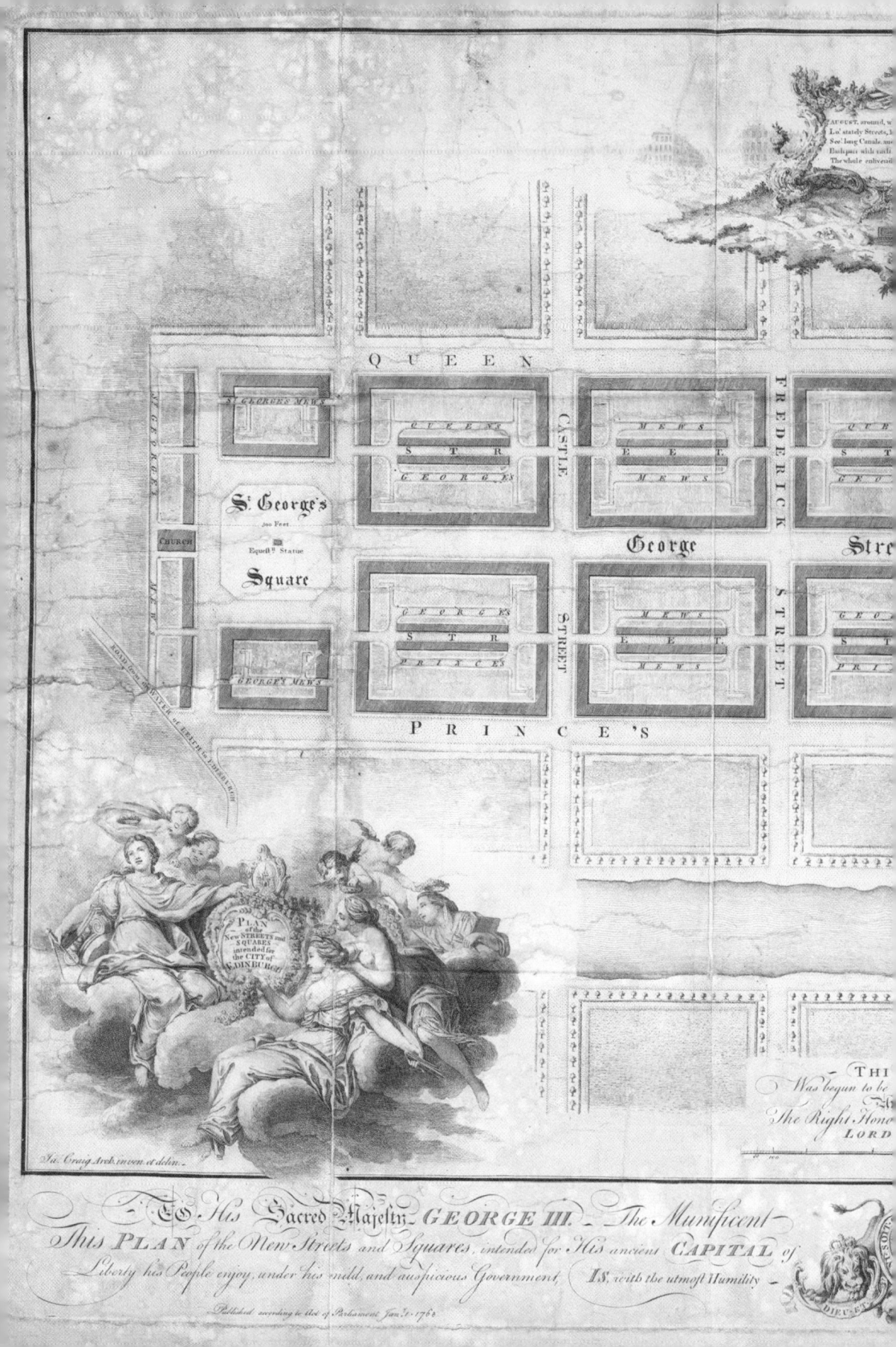

PLAN of the New Streets and SQUARES intended for the CITY of EDINBURGH

QUEEN STREET

ST GEORGE'S MEWS

St George's
300 Feet
Equest.ᵈ Statue
Square

CHURCH
MEWS

GEORGE'S MEWS

QUEEN STREET
GEORGE STREET

MEWS
MEWS

CASTLE STREET

GEORGE STREET

FREDERICK STREET

QUEEN ST
GEORGE

GEORGE'S STREET
PRINCE'S

MEWS
MEWS

GEORGE ST
PRINCE

ROAD FROM QUEENSFERRY TO EDINBURGH

PRINCE'S STREET

Ja. Craig Arch. inven. et delin.

THIS
Was begun to be
The Right Hono.
LORD

TO His Sacred Majesty GEORGE III. The Munificent
This PLAN of the New Streets and Squares, intended for His ancient CAPITAL of
Liberty his People enjoy, under his mild, and auspicious Government, IS, with the utmost Humility

Published according to Act of Parliament Jan.ʳ 1. 1768.